THE
POLITICS
OF
RELIGION
IN
RUSSIA
AND THE
NEW STATES
OF EURASIA

THE INTERNATIONAL POLITICS OF EURASIA

Editors:
Karen Dawisha and Bruce Parrott

This ambitious ten-volume series develops a comprehensive analysis of the evolving world role of the post-Soviet successor states. Each volume considers a different factor influencing the relationship between internal politics and international relations in Russia and in the western and southern tiers of newly independent states. The contributors were chosen not only for their recognized expertise but also to ensure a stimulating diversity of perspectives and a dynamic mix of approaches.

Volume 1
The Legacy of History in Russia and the New States of Eurasia
Edited by S. Frederick Starr

Volume 2
National Identity and Ethnicity in Russia and the New States of Eurasia
Edited by Roman Szporluk

Volume 3
The Politics of Religion in Russia and the New States of Eurasia
Edited by Michael Bourdeaux

Volume 4
The Making of Foreign Policy in Russia and the New States of Eurasia
Edited by Adeed Dawisha and Karen Dawisha

Volume 5
State-Building and Military Power in Russia and the New States of Eurasia
Edited by Bruce Parrott

Volume 6
The Nuclear Challenge in Russia and the New States of Eurasia
Edited by George Quester

Volume 7
Political Culture and Civil Society in Russia and the New States of Eurasia
Edited by Vladimir Tismaneanu

THE INTERNATIONAL POLITICS OF EURASIA

Volume 3

THE
POLITICS
OF
RELIGION
IN
RUSSIA
AND THE
NEW STATES
OF EURASIA

Editor:
Michael Bourdeaux

M.E. Sharpe
Armonk, New York
London, England

Library of Congress Cataloging-in-Publication Data

The politics of religion in Russia and the new states of Eurasia /
[edited by] Michael Bourdeaux.
p. cm. — (International politics of Eurasia ; v. 3)
Includes bibliographical references and index.
ISBN 1–56324–356–3 (alk. paper).
ISBN 1–56324–357–1 (pbk. : alk. paper)
1. Religion and state—Russia (Federation)
2. Russia (Federation)—Religion—20th century.
3. Religion and state—Former Soviet republics.
4. Former Soviet republics—Religion—20th century.
I. Bourdeaux, Michael. II. Series
BL980.S65P65 1995
322'.1'0947—dc20   94–40242
CIP

Printed in the United States of America

The paper used in this publication meets the minimum requirements of
American National Standard for Information Sciences—
Permanence of Paper for Printed Library Materials,
ANSI Z 39.48-1984.

BM (c)   10   9   8   7   6   5   4   3   2   1
BM (p)   10   9   8   7   6   5   4   3   2   1

Contents

About the Editors and Contributors

Michael Bourdeaux is the founder and director of the Keston Institute at Oxford, formerly the Centre for the Study of Religion and Communism. He was ordained into the Anglican Church in 1960 and was recently installed as an Honorary Canon in the Diocese of Rochester. His most recent publications include *The Gospel's Triumph Over Communism* (1991) and *The Role of Religion in the Fall of Soviet Communism* (1992).

Karen Dawisha is a professor of government at the University of Maryland, College Park. She graduated in Russian and Politics from the University of Lancaster in England and received her Ph.D. from the London School of Economics. She has served as an advisor to the British House of Commons Foreign Affairs Committee and as a member of the Policy Planning Staff of the U.S. State Department. She has received fellowships from the Rockefeller Foundation, the Council on Foreign Relations, and the MacArthur Foundation. She is a member of the Royal Institute of International Affairs and the Council on Foreign Relations. Her publications include *Russia and the New States of Eurasia: The Politics of Upheaval* (coauthored with Bruce Parrott, 1994), *Eastern Europe, Gorbachev, and Reform: The Great Challenge* (2nd ed. 1990), *The Kremlin and the Prague Spring* (1984), *The Soviet Union in the Middle East: Politics and Perspectives* (1982), *Soviet-East European Dilemmas: Coercion, Competition and Consent* (1981), and *Soviet Policy Toward Egypt* (1979).

Bruce Parrott is a professor and director of Russian Area and East European Studies at the Johns Hopkins University School of Advanced International Studies, where he has taught for twenty years. He received his B.A. in Religious Studies from Pomona College in 1966, and his Ph.D. in Political Science in 1976 from Columbia University, where he was assistant director of the Russian Institute. His publications include *Russia and the New States of Eurasia: The Politics of Upheaval* (coauthored with Karen Dawisha, 1994), *The Dynamics of*

Soviet Defense Policy (1990), *The Soviet Union and Ballistic Missile Defense* (1987), *Trade Technology and Soviet-American Relations* (1985), and *Politics and Technology in the Soviet Union* (1983).

Abdujabar Abduvakhitov is the director of the Meros Academy in Tashkent and previously taught at the Oriental Institute of Tashkent. He has written widely on Islam in the Middle East, including articles on the Muslim Brotherhood in Syria and Egypt and the Suni and Shi'a relationship in the Middle East. Currently he is writing on Islam in Central Asia.

Muriel Atkin is a professor in the History Department at George Washington University in Washington, D.C. Some of her recent publications include *The Subtlest Battle: Islam in Soviet Tajikistan* (1989), "The Islamic Revolution That Overthrew the Soviet State" (1993), and "The Politics of Polarization in Tajikistan" (1994).

Serhiy Bilokin is a researcher at the Institute of History, Ukrainian Academy of Sciences. He previously worked on the preservation of the Kiev-Pichersk Monastery. He has written on relations of the Ukrainian Orthodox Church and the state and on the Ukrainian government's policy toward the church.

Bohdan Bociurkiw is currently a professor of political science at Carleton University. He has written extensively on the role of religion in Ukraine. His publications include *The Ukrainian Greek-Catholic Church and the Soviet State, 1939–46, Ukrainian Churches Under the Soviet Rule: Two Case Studies* (1984), and *The Politics of Religion in Ukraine: The Orthodox Church and the Ukrainian Revolution, 1917–1919* (1985).

Vsevolod Chaplin is the director of public relations, Department for External Church Relations, Moscow Patriarchate. He graduated from the Moscow Theological Seminary in 1988 and from the Moscow Theological Academy in 1994, with a degree of Candidate of Theology.

John B. Dunlop is a senior fellow at the Hoover Institution researching the fields of contemporary history, nationalism, cultural politics, and the politics of religion as they pertain to the Russian Federation. He most recently authored the book *The Rise of Russia and the Fall of the Soviet Union* (1993).

Robert F. Goeckel is an associate professor of political science at the State University of New York at Geneseo. He has published widely on church-state relations in Eastern Europe and the former USSR, in particular on the former East Germany (*The Lutheran Church and the East German State*, 1990). He is currently writing a history of Soviet policy toward the Baltic Lutheran churches from 1940 to 1991.

Erjan Rafik-Ogly Kurbanov is presently a doctoral student in the Sociology Department at the University of Maryland at College Park. He has coauthored the articles "Changing Perception of Societal Problems Among Soviet Youth" (1992) and "Ethnonationalist and Political Attitudes Among Post-Soviet Youth: The Case of Russia and Ukraine" (1993).

Rafik Osman-Ogly Kurbanov is a senior researcher at the Institute of Philosophy in Moscow. He has written more than 200 papers on various topics, including the philosophical problems of modern science, Islam in political and cultural life, and the influence of Western culture on the life of Muslims in the former Soviet Union.

Vasyl Markus is the editor in chief of the Encyclopedia of the Ukrainian Diaspora. He is a senior professor of political science at Loyola University of Chicago. Among his most recent publications is *Incorporation of Carpatho-Ukraine to Soviet Ukraine in 1944–45* (Kiev, 1993).

Dimitry V. Pospielovsky is a professor of Russian and European history at the University of Western Ontario. Since 1990 he has been an annual visiting professor on Russian church history at numerous Orthodox seminaries, universities, and other educational establishments in Russia. His publications include *The Russian Church Under the Soviet Regime, 1917–1982* (1984) and *A History of Soviet Atheism in Theory and Practice, and the Believer* (1987).

M. Nazif Shahrani is a professor of anthropology and Central Asian studies, and the director of Middle Eastern Studies at Indiana University, Bloomington, Indiana. He is currently doing research in the newly independent nations of Muslim Central Asia. He has published *The Kirghiz and Wakhi of Afghanistan: Adaptation to Closed Frontiers* (1979); and is coeditor of *Revolutions and Rebellions in Afghanistan: Anthropological Perspectives* (1984).

Mikhail Sivertsev is senior researcher at the Institute of USA and Canada Studies, Russian Academy of Sciences. He has written extensively on the phenomenology of religion, ancient and nontraditional forms of religion, and most recently, on religious movements and parties in Russia and the NIS.

Preface

This book is the third in a projected series of ten volumes produced by the Russian Littoral Project, sponsored jointly by the University of Maryland at College Park and the Paul H. Nitze School of Advanced International Studies of the Johns Hopkins University. As directors of the project, we share the conviction that the transformation of the former Soviet republics into independent states demands systematic analysis of the determinants of the domestic and foreign policies of the new countries. The series is intended to provide a basis for comprehensive scholarly study of these issues.

We would like to thank the contributors to this volume for their help in making the first phase of the Russian Littoral Project a success and for revising their papers in a timely fashion. We are especially grateful to Canon Michael Bourdeaux of Keston Research Institute, Oxford, for acting as such an excellent editor. No one else could have brought his depth of experience in studying religion in communist and former communist lands, and we are grateful for his help in shaping the intellectual agenda for the conference. In addition to the academic papers presented during the regular sessions of the conference, several speeches were delivered by activists who contributed to our knowledge of the real situation for believers and religious institutions in the former Soviet Union. Some of the information presented is reflected in this volume, although the contributions themselves could not be reprinted here. For their part, we would like to thank Fr. Gleb Yakunin, Bishop Basil Rodzianko, Evgen Sverstiuk, Dadahan Hasanov, and Abdoumannob Poulatov. In addition, we are grateful to Janine Ludlam, the executive director of the project, for her skillful handling of the complex logistics of the workshops on which the book is based and for her unstinting labor in preparing the final manuscript. Thanks also go to Florence Rotz for her assistance in typing and editing the contributions by the scholars from the newly independent states and to Michael Turner for help in page proofing.

Russian Littoral Project

The objective of the Russian Littoral Project is to foster an exchange of research and information in fields of study pertaining to the international politics of Eurasia. The interaction between the internal affairs and foreign policies of the new states is being studied in a series of workshops taking place in Washington, D.C., London, Central Asia, and other locations between 1993 and 1995. Scholars are invited from the new states, North America, and Europe to present papers at the workshops.

In preparing for this series of workshops, we formulated several questions that were given to the authors in the hopes that they would form a basis for our workshop discussions and their papers. The following represents a partial listing of those questions and should provide the reader with an idea of the core issues addressed in this volume: How will the postcommunist revival of religion affect the new states' internal politics and relations with one another? Will the revival of Russian Orthodoxy, Ukrainian Catholicism, Ukrainian Orthodoxy, and Islam fuel instability in the region? Have political leaders in the new states sought to appeal to religious sentiments among their citizens? Have the spokesmen of organized religion become involved in each country's domestic politics and foreign-policy debates, or have they eschewed political entanglements? Judging by opinion surveys, how reliable is religious affiliation as a predictor of political and foreign-policy attitudes among the citizens of the new states? To the degree that religious denominations become actively involved in politics, how much political cohesion will they be able to muster? Given Tsarist Russia's historic identity as a Christian country and a foe of Islam, will postcommunist Russia accept the possibility that new Islamic states on its border may be moderate, or will it equate Islam with fundamentalism? Will Christian religious leaders, particularly in Russia, tacitly encourage or actively oppose anti-Semitism, and what, if any, role will anti-Semitism play in Russia's relations with the Middle East and Central Asia?

Focusing on the interaction between the internal affairs and the foreign relations of the new states, the project workshops examine the impact of the following factors: history; national identity and ethnicity; religion; political culture and civil society; economics; foreign policy priorities and decision making; military issues; and the nuclear question. Each of these topics is examined in a set of three workshops, first with respect to Russia, then with respect to the western belt of new states extending from Estonia to Ukraine, and finally with respect to the southern tier of new states extending from Georgia to Kyrgyzstan. The Russian Littoral Project is also planning a conference on the comparative collapse of empires and the reconstitution of multinational states.

The Russian Littoral Project could not have been launched without the generous and timely contributions of the project's Coordinating Committee. We wish to thank the committee members for providing invaluable advice and expertise concerning the organization and intellectual substance of the project. The members of the Coordinating Committee are: Dr. Adeed Dawisha (George Mason University); Dr. Bartek Kaminski (University of Maryland and The World Bank); Dr. Catherine Kelleher (The Brookings Institution); Ms. Judith Kipper (The Brookings Institution); Dr. Nancy Lubin (Carnegie Mellon University); Dr. Michael Mandelbaum (The School of Advanced International Studies); Dr. James Millar (The George Washington University); Dr. Peter Murrell (University of Maryland); Dr. Martha Brill Olcott (Colgate University); Dr. Ilya Prizel (The School of Advanced International Studies); Dr. George Quester (University of Maryland); Dr. Alvin Z. Rubinstein (University of Pennsylvania); Dr. Blair Ruble (The Kennan Institute); Dr. S. Frederick Starr (Oberlin College); Dr. Roman Szporluk (Harvard University); and Dr. Vladimir Tismaneanu (University of Maryland).

We are grateful to the Pew Charitable Trusts for funding the workshops from which this book is derived; we are especially grateful to Kevin Quigley, Peter Benda, Joel Carpenter, and Christopher Smith for their support of the project. For funding the workshops on which several future volumes will be based, we express our thanks to the MacArthur Foundation (in particular Kennette Benedict and Andrew Kuchins), the National Endowment for the Humanities, and the Ford Foundation (in particular Geoffrey Wiseman).

We also wish to thank President William Kirwan of the University of Maryland at College Park and President William C. Richardson of The Johns Hopkins University, who both have given indispensable support to the project. Thanks are also due to: Dean Irwin Goldstein, Associate Dean Stewart Edelstein, Director Marcus Franda of the Office of International Affairs, and Department of Government and Politics Chair Jonathan Wilkenfeld at the University of Maryland at College Park; Provost Joseph Cooper and Vice-Provost for Academic Planning and Budget Stephen M. McClain at The Johns Hopkins University; Professor George Packard, who helped launch the project during his final year as dean of the School of Advanced International Studies (SAIS), SAIS Dean Paul D. Wolfowitz, and to SAIS Associate Dean Stephen Szabo.

Finally, we are grateful for the guidance and encouragement given by Patricia Kolb at M.E. Sharpe, Inc. Her confidence in the success of the project and the series is deeply appreciated.

Karen Dawisha
Department of Government and Politics
University of Maryland at College Park

Bruce Parrott
The Johns Hopkins University
School of Advanced International Studies

THE
POLITICS
OF
RELIGION
IN
RUSSIA
AND THE
NEW STATES
OF EURASIA

1

Introduction

Michael Bourdeaux

Before considering the fall of a modern empire, an event still too close at hand for us to be able to see the collapse of communism in any true perspective, it may be instructive for a moment to reflect on the fall of two ancient civilizations.

> I met a traveller from an antique land,
> Who said—"Two vast and trunkless legs of stone
> Stand in the desert. . . . Near them, on the sand,
> Half sunk a shattered visage lies, whose frown,
> And wrinkled lip, and sneer of cold command,
> Tell that its sculptor well those passions read
> Which yet survive, stamped on these lifeless things,
> The hand that mocked them, and the heart that fed;
> And on the pedestal, these words appear:
> My name is Ozymandias, King of Kings,
> Look on my Works, ye Mighty, and despair!
> Nothing beside remains. Round the decay
> Of that colossal Wreck, boundless and bare
> The lone and level sands stretch far away."

Shelley's reflections on a shattered empire are intensely evocative for our generation. Stalin, less than forty years after his death, has gone the way of Ozymandias; the "colossal wreck" of communist ideology is as complete as the poet's vision of a long-forgotten world. The difference is, of course, that in our time the world remains intensely aware of the disease and pollution haunting the ruins, the consequences of which will confront the world for generations to come.

Moving in from an ancient desert to one of humankind's oldest cities, we call to mind the image of the walls of Jericho. The massed cohorts of believers in the Soviet Union did not surround the citadel of atheism, blow upon their trumpets, and see the Kremlin walls fall down. Yet what happened in Moscow between 1989 and 1991 was scarcely less dramatic than the fall of Jericho described in the Book of Judges. No purely human forces undermined the walls of the ancient city; it is equally hard to argue that human agency alone secured the collapse of the old system across the millions of square miles of the world's largest empire with scarcely a shot fired. It was not even an implosion: the skeleton could no longer support the massive weight of the body, and it keeled over and died.

Purveyors of conventional wisdom have analyzed the collapse of communism from many points of view: economic, political, ideological, structural, military. Not even the downward thrust of this huge inertia, armed head to foot against external forces but defenseless, as it turned out, against internal ones, is susceptible to analysis in purely materialistic terms.

Nevertheless, the attempt has been made. The respected American journal *The National Interest* devoted a special issue to "the strange death of Soviet Communism." Its 144 pages contained many helpful insights and useful analyses, but only half a sentence on religion, and that in the framework of an—albeit inspired—forecast of the collapse of communism by the British columnist Bernard Levin, not in an analytical article.[1]

But in the period of first stocktaking there were other insights, also. Could there be elements, perhaps even at the heart of events, that defied conventional analysis? The Oxford scholar Timothy Garton Ash was the first fully to investigate the unique and charismatic role of the Polish pope, Karol Wojtyla (John Paul II), in destabilizing the Polish communist system and leading the way to a decisive rejection by the people of Marxist dogma.[2]

A passionate book by the American scholar George Weigel seized upon this theme more emphatically: the Roman Catholic Church was the catalyst for the dramatic overturning of the system.[3] Yet all this referred to the external empire, not primarily to the Soviet Union itself. Were any comparable forces at work there? Elsewhere I have argued in the affirmative.[4] There were even isolated voices in the early 1980s, perhaps little regarded at the time, that pinpointed religion, allied to nationalism, as the Achilles' heel of the Soviet system:

> When I look at the complex ethnic map of the Soviet Union I see Lithuanians, I see Jews, I see Ukrainians and Armenians, yes, I see a myriad of Muslims and of Russians. I don't see "Soviets,". . . I see an empire in the process of decay, because there's no binding loyalty which will keep it together. The Red Army, not Marxism-Leninism, provides its cement. Sixty years, many purges and a world war on from the death of Lenin, the subject peoples retain their individuality, they retain their hopes. . . . Religion strikes the deepest chord of all in the hearts of people who will never accept Moscow along with enforced atheism.[5]

However, that the system should collapse so utterly, with scarcely even a death throe and with no passionate call to arms to defend it, is assuredly one of the most astonishing events in human history.

The present volume is relevant to that theme. It perforce has to take much for granted: a knowledge of the rejection of religion by the Bolsheviks even well before the Revolution of 1917; the violent persecution of the church, which began not under Stalin, but Lenin (and how the system excoriated Aleksandr Solzhenitsyn for saying just this); the nationwide revival of church life, both permitted and unofficial, during World War II; renewed persecution under Khrushchev, leading to the astonishing fact that there were three times as many Orthodox churches open in the USSR on the day Stalin died than on the day Gorbachev came to power; and the gray Brezhnev years, with their insidious attempt to undermine church life by promoting church leaders who, with much success, proclaimed to the world that there was no persecution.

The general background to this book, then, is the unrelenting communist attempt to combat religion, either by direct physical attack, by reeducation of the masses, or by undermining its integrity through subversion of its leadership.

There was, nevertheless, a more settled period for the Russian Orthodox Church after World War II, when the country was more concerned with rebuilding its life and shattered economy than with continuing the task of combating the church, which had helped win the war by adding its weight to the patriotic cause. Even during this period, the Ukrainian Catholic Church was liquidated because of its identification with the nationalist (anti-Soviet) cause.

This status quo was shattered by Khrushchev's antireligion campaign of 1959–64. Believers had, in the postwar period, come to think that they could be accepted, albeit only in the lower echelons of society, as both Christians and loyal Soviet citizens. The seismic shattering of this illusion in 1959 inaugurated what was to be the penultimate phase of the conflict between religion and state atheism.

I lived in this atmosphere, arriving in the Soviet Union as a member of the first British-Russian student exchange precisely as the first issue of *Nauka i religiia* (Science and Religion) hit the bookstalls in September 1959. This journal became the flagship of the new campaign, launched to attack Judaism, Islam, and religious survivals in general, not just Christianity.

The next five years saw the mass closure of churches and mosques (there were very few synagogues open to begin with), the imposition of a more complacent leadership on the churches, a sharp reduction in the numbers training for the priesthood (eight theological schools had been permitted to reopen after the war following their total closure in the prewar period), and the virtual annihilation of monastic life. The press published constant virulent attacks against individual believers, accusing them of every conceivable crime in the name of religion, from murder and rape to embezzlement. There was no right of reply. The prison camps, which had seen a fall in the number of inmates following Khrushchev's "secret speech" attacking Stalin in 1956, began to be repopulated with thousands of believers.

Nevertheless, by discontinuing the campaign in that form after the fall of

Khrushchev in 1964, the regime tacitly admitted that its campaign had been counterproductive. Dissident voices representing eventually every religion and Christian denomination became gradually more insistent and coordinated during the Brezhnev period of "stagnation," as Gorbachev was to call it. Despite every attempt by the Soviet propaganda machine to discredit it, the human rights movement in the USSR, with its strong religious element, became a factor of real significance on the domestic and, eventually, the international scene.

It was the Israeli victory in the Six-Day War with the Arabs in 1967 that finally emboldened Soviet Jews to voice their demands for emigration. The attempted repression of this movement awoke world opinion, eventually on a massive scale, to the issue of justice in Soviet society.

The more immediate background to this book is the transformation of religious life under Gorbachev. Some Western journalists have given credence to the popular notion that Mikhail Sergeevich Gorbachev was in some way "responsible" for this renewal. This is a misapprehension. For years, for decades even, fresh water had been flowing from hidden wellsprings, invisible to all but the most intent foreign observer. Religion flourished even in the most abject conditions. On a visit to Israel, I asked a former victim of Stalin's camps who was once a communist and later a committed Jewish believer how he had preserved his faith under conditions of the most severe hardship. His reply was, "I did not preserve my faith; it preserved me." Testimonies to Christian conversion abound from the 1930s to the 1980s.[6]

Unquestionably this refusal of the human spirit to be dominated by a materialistic ideology was a contributory factor to the collapse of communism. Equally certain, it is impossible to quantify and define the precise way in which it did this. The answer lies in the depths of human nature rather than on the front line of conflict.

Marxist ideology never understood the true nature of religion, analyzing it by materialistic and worldly criteria: a tool of privilege or class dominance, due to collapse as the ideal society emerged. Neither did Marxism ever understand human nature. Building an ideal society, it was claimed, would provide the crucible in which the new Soviet man (*Homo sovieticus*) would be created. At the end of empire, so history judged, the Christian doctrine of original sin corresponded more to the reality than the communist goal of an attainable millennium. The utter moral ruin left behind by the old system was more absolute than even its most passionate opponents imagined.

Yet somehow, in some places, in some hearts, Christian values survived among Slavic and Baltic peoples; Muslim ethics were not entirely obliterated by the massive transformation imposed on Central Asian society.

Curiously, it was the Christian "millennium"—not the illusory communist one—the celebration of a thousand years since the conversion of the Eastern Slavs in 988, that brought into the open the issues discussed above. It was one of the coincidences of history that the commemoration of this thousand years should fall precisely during the heyday of Gorbachev. Had the anniversary occurred ten, or even five, years before 1988 the state would have prevented major celebrations, or more likely controlled them as a propaganda exercise glorifying the liberalism of Soviet religious policy (something very similar did happen during the East German "Luther" celebrations of 1983).

As it was, demands for justice for believers had been growing for years. Some voices had even, at great peril, called for a repeal of the old Stalinist laws on religion. Human rights activists had emerged within every single branch of the religious community: from Catholics and Lutherans in the Baltic states to Buddhists and Muslims in the East. It could not be said, in truth, that the Russian Orthodox Church had been in the forefront of these demands; yet isolated individuals who exposed the persecution and called for justice were gaining a greater hearing, not least before the court of world public opinion. International agreements were beginning to highlight not only respect for human rights in general but also mentioned religious liberty as a specific issue. The Helsinki Accords of 1975, published in full in the press of signatory nations (the United States, Canada, and every country of Europe except Albania), proclaimed independent monitoring of human rights as an essential adjunct of improved performance. This stimulated relevant groups throughout the Soviet republics to make their claim in a more coordinated way. There was now a legal context, and "Helsinki monitors" emerged in almost every one of the republics, usually with strong religious representation.

It was, however, only in 1986, a year after Gorbachev's accession, that the first signs of a positive government response to the human rights and religious liberty issues emerged.[7] Gorbachev began to make his peace with the campaigners. If the release from labor camp and emigration of Anatolii Shcharanskii, the highest-profile victim of the anti-Jewish campaign, in February 1986 had been an obvious sop to world opinion, the summons back to Moscow from illegal exile of the nuclear scientist and intellectual leader of the human rights campaign, Andrei Sakharov, at the end of the year signaled a rewriting of the agenda for Soviet society; so was the release from labor camp and permission to emigrate granted to the best known of the Christian prisoners, the young poet Irina Ratushinskaia.

Gorbachev was manifestly fazed by the inability of Soviet society to undertake planned reforms. His views at this time were fashioned not only by the perilous state of the Soviet economy but also by the Chernobyl explosion (April 1986), which in a way symbolized the submergence of the rights of individuals beneath the demands of "improving" society as a whole.

In 1987 almost all those imprisoned for religious, nationalist, or human rights offenses were released. Gorbachev"s intimation of a new deal was taking on the face of reality. It was in this atmosphere that the millennium year of 1988 dawned for the Orthodox Church. This would have been an auspicious time for Soviet believers even without an anniversary to celebrate. Manifestly, the

Gorbachev regime prepared to make a deal with the believers, whatever was due to happen within the sphere of church life itself.

Since the end of World War II, the governments control of religious institutions, such as they were, had been mediated through two "councils," one covering the Orthodox Church, the other all other religious manifestations, from Islam and Buddhism to Adventists and Baptists. Khrushchev's policy logically welded them into a single organization in 1961, the Council for Religious Affairs. The head of this body was a KGB appointee, and his role was to coordinate all police and legal activity against believers over the huge territory of the USSR. His position was remote yet threatening, and in his employ were tens of thousands of identified and paid activists who themselves collaborated with even greater numbers of unidentified "spies" at various levels in the churches.

Konstantin Chernenko's regime appointed a more visible and, as it turned out, mercurial personality to the office of chairman of the Council for Religious Affairs, Konstantin Kharchev.[8] Starting as a hard-liner, he rapidly changed tack to adapt to Gorbachev's perestroika. Gorbachev, I have argued elsewhere,[9] confronted with the deadweight of Soviet conservatism, saw believers as a potential dynamic force at the lowest level of the plowed field and the workbench, people who might be more ready to change than the ideologues who controlled the structures above them.

Gorbachev's last gasp as a proponent of atheism was directed, as it happened, against Islam, in a speech he made in Tashkent en route to India in November 1986.[10] In the event, this did not conceal any serious substance and, as M. Nazif Shahrani points out in this volume, perestroika in the Islamic republics was far from being in the forefront of Gorbachev's program, in that Soviet policy in Central Asia seemed to have been the USSR's most successful colonial enterprise.

In 1988, for the first time in Soviet history, the spotlight illuminated for a few spectacular weeks the Russian Orthodox Church.[11] It was as if "Holy Russia," long concealed—many thought suffocated—under the official ideology, dramatically reemerged virtually without the sounding of an introductory "*Gospodi, pomilui,*" which reverberates so insistently at the beginning of the Slavonic liturgy.

The flood of light caught first of all Gorbachev, summoning the leaders of the church (or as they unconvincingly claimed, meeting them at their own request) to the Kremlin on 29 April 1988 to hear his historic pronouncement:

> Believers are Soviet people, workers, patriots, and they have the full right to express their convictions with dignity. . . . This is especially true of ethics and morals, a domain where universal norms and customs are so helpful in our common cause.[12]

For the first time a communist leader in power was calling for full cooperation with believers. Following Gorbachev's record of the previous two years, there was no reason to believe the appeal was not genuine.

The scene soon shifted a short distance down the road from the Kremlin to the Danilov Monastery. This fortress like complex had been confiscated soon after the Revolution and had subsequently become a secure prison for juvenile offenders. Curiously, the Andropov regime had returned it to the church in 1983, thus permitting a monastery to function in Moscow for the first time since the Revolution. A long and expensive restoration had begun and now, in time for the millennium celebrations, it was ready for reopening. Just at this time, 30 May 1988, President Reagan was in Moscow for a summit meeting with Gorbachev. His program included a visit to the Danilov Monastery, and the television cameras of the world recorded the splendor of its magnificent restoration.

This led immediately into the millennium celebrations themselves the next week (5–12 June in Moscow, followed by regional events the week after). During their climax every Soviet newspaper, national radio, and both television channels recorded events and echoed to the sound of Orthodox chant. Solemn voices proclaimed the continuity of Russian history from its beginning to the present day. As an eyewitness to these events, I described the climax of the celebrations in the Bolshoi Theater in these terms:

> The day ended with a jubilee concert in the presence of dignitaries representing both church and state (Raisa Gorbachev and President Gromyko were the most notable secular figures present). . . . No fewer than seven choirs, six orchestras and some of the stars of Soviet screen and concert platform combined in a joint celebration of the millennium by church and state. . . . As the final cries of *slava* ("praise") [of Glinka's opera, *A Life for the Tsar*] resounded throughout the theatre, the blue sky above the stage set opened to reveal a carillon of real church bells which engulfed the Bolshoi in a peal of thunder. Before any audience this would have been a coup de theatre. In a country where the ringing of church bells had been outlawed for decades, this was more than symbolism: it was a pledge of a new beginning.[13]

Gorbachev kept the promise of a new deal for religion that he made at the Kremlin reception. The Stalinist laws de facto no longer operated from that moment. New liberal statutes guaranteeing true freedom of religion would come into being in 1990.

This, then, is the multicolored backdrop against which the authors in this book describe different facets of the present: facets that, it must be said, in no way form a homogeneous polyptych. Until five years ago the subject of religion could be neatly framed by the parameters of Soviet policy and ideology, however diversified the picture within.

Now no definitions are possible. Religion, often allied with nationalism, played a role in the destabilization process preceding the collapse of the Soviet system. But that by no means signifies that it was prepared for the debacle of communism. Only Poland, throughout the whole Soviet empire, was an exception, and the Catholic Church even there, having planned the undermining of communism in a systematic way, did not find it easy to adapt to a society that inevitably began to manifest the influence of encroaching secularism as soon as the ruling power folded.

In the Soviet Union the scene was chaotic. The Orthodox Church claimed the allegiance of millions of Slavs spread unevenly throughout the fifteen republics. It saw itself, in a sense, as a protector of Russian rights against the rising tide of other forms of nationalism. What was its new role to be in the Russian heartland? This book presents three views.

In broad generalization, Dimitry Pospielovsky and John Dunlop both see the renewal of the life of the Orthodox Church as a massive gain for Russia and for the world. However, while the former feels confident in the leadership of the Moscow Patriarchate, the latter has grave reservations that its excessive allegiance to Russian nationalism carries with it the danger of claiming more than its territory. Father Vsevolod Chaplin presents a view from inside the patriarchate itself.

In chapter 6 I write of current attempts to bring in new legislation, raising the question as to whether the Orthodox Church is seeking special privileges. Fierce argument rages as to what formulations are fair to all in a society that has only just rejected the totality of its practice of seventy years. Even if just laws exist, what is the guarantee that they can be enforced in an area where some subtlety and experience would seem to be a prerequisite? Mikhail Sivertsev provides a different perspective by looking at the role of religion in the evolution of a multiparty system.

The concatenation of religion and nationalism in the late Soviet period emerged most forcibly in the Catholic areas of western Ukraine and Lithuania. The rise of Ukrainian nationalism, fueled by passionate demands for the reestablishment of the Ukrainian Catholic Church, which had been illegally suppressed for forty years, became one of the truly destabilizing factors of the Soviet empire in the late 1980s. Its reestablishment in 1989 was an event of major importance, affecting political events well beyond the purely ecclesiastical sphere. A question on the agenda of the late 1990s is whether Ukraine can hold together as a unitary state. The Catholic Church in L'viv and surrounding territories is a more cohesive element than anything in the east of the country. It is a guardian of language, culture, and a sense of historical destiny, that are largely absent from the industrial heartland east of Kiev, where attachment to Russia (and the Orthodox Church) is much stronger. Thus this volume devotes three chapters to various aspects of the Ukrainian question.

One could hardly maintain that such a small territory as Lithuania played a role comparable to Ukraine in destabilizing the old system, yet its influence was out of all proportion to its size. Lithuania, along with the other Baltic states, had strong grounds for disputing the legitimacy of Soviet power in international forums. Perestroika, for so many in the region, meant the right to self-determination, and it was democratically elected President Vytautas Landsbergis who first claimed Lithuanian independence from the USSR in March 1990. The end of this story was the shooting of Lithuanians on the streets of Vilnius in January 1991, an event that horrified people both in the Soviet Union and worldwide and was a key factor in the final domestic discrediting of Gorbachev's leadership. Robert Goeckel's chapter covers the whole area of religion and politics in the Baltic states.

No area of the former Soviet Union has been a greater loser in the collapse of Soviet power than the Caucasus. More ethnically diverse than any other part of the former Soviet Union, the threat to stability was correspondingly great. The chapter by Rafik Osman-Ogly Kurbanov and Erjan Rafik-Ogly Kurbanov emphasizes the almost tribal patchwork underlying the religious picture of an area that has been seriously underreported in the Western press yet is destined to play a strategic role in the future, straddling, as it does, the border between Europe and Asia.

Conventional wisdom among academics used to declare that if the Soviet Union were ever to unravel it would be initiated by events inexorably but slowly developing in Soviet Central Asia. Not so much the rise of Islam (which was considered dead and buried), but the greater population increase among Oriental peoples and the declining birthrate in Europe would be the determining factors. In the event, Central Asia played virtually no role in the collapse of the empire, and it was left even less prepared for these events than Russia itself.

The three chapters on this area put firmly in their place those in the West who speculate that the whole region is now prey to the rage of Islamic fundamentalism. Nevertheless, the religious element is a vital spoke, perhaps even the hub, of a revolving wheel that might roll in any direction in this vast territory with a future even less clear than that of Siberia and the former Soviet Union in Europe.

This volume covers a huge swath of the world's largest landmass, and its subject matter is correspondingly complex. Even so, there is so much left out that a further volume would be necessary to encompass the omissions.

The Jewish religion has numerically few adherents; most of the key activists having emigrated to Israel. Nevertheless, there are those who do believe that Jewish culture has some future in European Russia and is not to be entirely transferred to Israel.

Buddhists form the majority in the former Buriat-Mongol Autonomous Republic around Ulan-Ude. Here cross-border ties with the larger number of Buddhists in Mongolia itself, always a satellite of Moscow but now fully independent, are a strong factor.

The diverse tribes of Siberia, not unlike American Indians and Australian aborigines, are claiming ancient territorial rights over lands from which the old system expropriated them. Their ancient tribal faith is resurfacing in some places as a focal point for self-identification.

Even the European areas of Moldova and Belarus do not feature in this volume. In both, the Orthodox Church is strong despite decades of persecution. In the former, Russian and Moldovan influences vie with each other; in the latter, Catholicism is also influential in many areas.

Indeed, the conflict between Catholicism and Russian Orthodoxy on Russian soil, following the reestablishment by the Vatican of Russian Catholic bishoprics, is a controversial subject that might have had its own chapter.

Perhaps the gap most to be regretted is the lack of a study of Protestantism in Russia and Ukraine. Although widely scattered and relatively few in number, Protestants formed a notable minority just about everywhere in the Soviet period. Officialdom reflected this in its continued frustrated attempts to suppress the voice of independence that Baptists, Pentecostals, and Adventists represented. Decades of protest have been followed by the present period of consolidation, where existing links with fellow believers in America, Scandinavia, and Germany have become even more important than during the time of persecution. For those who wish to read about this, there is a recommended recent book, *Protestantism and Politics in Eastern Europe and Russia*.[14]

Out of the chaos of toppled walls and the remains of colossal statues in the desert, new human systems for the governing of society have to emerge. Events of the last decade prove that the systematic attempt to deprive human nature of its inclination to the divine failed abjectly. Religion is destined to be an important factor in the new societies that are emerging. This book is the product of an interim period during which many questions are being asked but few answers have been found. Religion, at this time, faces the challenge of either contributing to the process of destabilization or of fulfilling its potential as an agent of reconciliation. Meanwhile, the well-being of hundreds of millions of people hangs in the balance.

Notes

1. *The National Interest*, no. 31 (Washington, D.C., 1993).
2. Timothy Garton Ash, *We the People: The Revolution of '89* (Cambridge: Granta, 1990).
3. George Weigel, *The Final Revolution: The Resistance Church and the Collapse of Communism* (New York: Oxford University Press, 1992).
4. Michael Bourdeaux, *The Role of Religion in the Fall of Soviet Communism* (London: Centre for Policy Studies, 1992).
5. Michael Bourdeaux, Templeton Prize Speech, Grand Cayman, British West Indies, 1984.
6. See Michael Bourdeaux, *Risen Indeed: Lessons in Faith from the USSR* (London: Darton, Longman and Todd, 1983).
7. The overall picture is described in Michael Bourdeaux, *The Gospel's Triumph Over Communism* (Minneapolis: Bethany House, 1991); originally published under the title *Gorbachev, Glasnost and the Gospel* (London: Hodder and Stoughton, 1990).
8. For further information, see Bourdeaux, *Gospel's Triumph*, pp. 74–86.
9. Ibid., pp. 39–41.
10. Ibid., p. 37.
11. For a full account, see ibid., pp. 42–64.
12. Ibid., p. 44.
13. Bourdeaux, *Gospel's Triumph*, pp. 61–63.
14. Ed. Sabrina Petra Ramet (Durham, NC: Duke University Press, 1992).

I

Russia

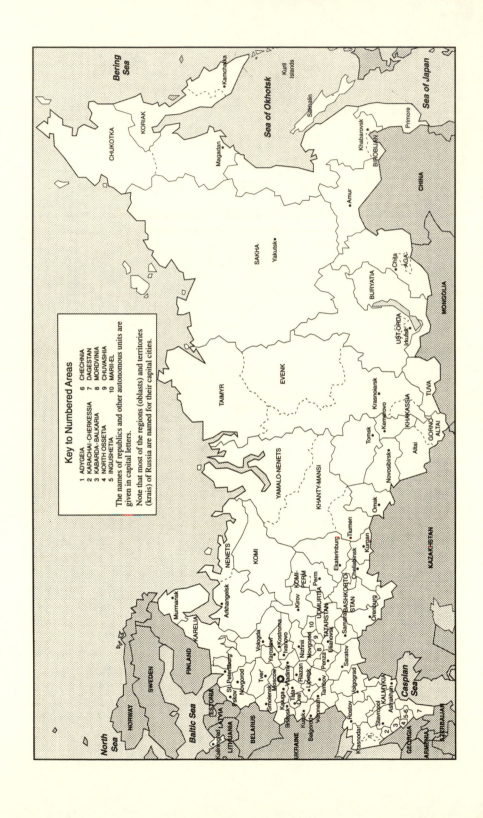

Key to Numbered Areas

1 ADYGEIA
2 KARACHAI-CHERKESSIA
3 KABARDA-BALKARIA
4 NORTH OSSETIA
5 INGUSHETIA
6 CHECHNIA
7 DAGESTAN
8 MORDVINIA
9 CHUVASHIA
10 MARII-EL

The names of republics and other autonomous units are given in capital letters.

Note that most of the regions (oblasts) and territories (krais) of Russia are named for their capital cities.

2

The Russian Orthodox Church as an "Empire-Saving" Institution

John B. Dunlop

On 26–28 May 1993, the first All-World Russian Assembly (*Vsemirnyi russkii sobor*) was held with pomp and elaborate fanfare in Moscow. Observers of the political scene in Russia were familiar with the Russian Assembly, a right-wing "empire-saving" organization whose most notable leader was former KGB Major General Aleksandr Sterligov.[1] What was striking about the May 1993 event, however, was the dominant role played by the leadership of the Moscow Patriarchate.

The conference took place at the Danilov Monastery, headquarters of the Russian Orthodox Church, and was addressed and given a blessing by Patriarch Aleksii II, the church's first-hierarch. Metropolitan Kirill of Smolensk and Kaliningrad, chairman of the patriarchate's Department of External Ecclesiastical Relations, led the church's representation to the Assembly and delivered the keynote address. Academician Igor' Shafarevich, a leader of the right-wing National Salvation Front who spoke at the Assembly, stressed in his comments that "for the first time such an undertaking is taking place under the auspices of the Moscow Patriarchate."[2] In a similar vein, a journalist writing for the hardline daily *Sovetskaia Rossiia* observed that the Assembly "was not only sanctified by the presence of the patriarch of all Russia, Aleksii II, but it conducted its work under the protection of the church."[3]

Queried about such comments, Metropolitan Kirill of Smolensk chose to describe the church's role somewhat differently. "The Assembly," he stipulated, "did not take place under the auspices of the Russian Church but with its spiritual participation. . . . If the Assembly had been conceived as a political event, then the Russian church would never have taken part in it."[4] Contrary to the metropolitan's assertion, it seems clear that the All-World Russian Assembly did indeed constitute a political event.

Despite differences of opinion, participants in the Assembly were able to agree on a number of key political formulations. First, they were able to concur on the apparently burning question of who is an ethnic Russian (*russkii*) and who is not. According to the agreed-upon definition, "the term Russian is a generic, collective concept that includes Great Russians, Little Russians, and Belarusians."[5] In other words, the Assembly resolved that all Ukrainians and Belarusians were in fact ethnic Russians. This meant by extension, presumably, that the existence of Ukraine and Belarus as sovereign states was due to some kind of a misunderstanding.

The term "Russian," the Assembly decided further, could also be extended to all "aliens" (*inorodtsy*) who had accepted the Orthodox faith. A Jew or a Tatar, thus, could become an ethnic Russian through the baptismal font; a Ukrainian or Belarusian, by contrast, was already ipso facto a Russian, whether or not he or she had been baptized.

The participants in the Assembly also appealed for a reconstituting of the former Soviet Union. One speaker, Valentin Kovalev, summarized what had been agreed on during the Assembly: "Millions of our compatriots, Russian people, in one hour became citizens of foreign states and lost a governmental tie to Russia. We do not have the right to remain indifferent to the tragedy of our compatriots. In this regard, we propose that Russians be declared a divided nation, and that the right of the Russian people to unite be solemnly proclaimed."[6] The fate of Russians in a divided nation was compared to that of Germans prior to 1989.

While some, Kovalev noted, might object that the 1975 Helsinki Accords mandated the "inviolability of borders in Europe," the responsibility for future infringements of this act would, he warned, lie not with Russia but with the former republics of the Soviet Union, "which despite these [Helsinki] accords provoked the destruction of the USSR and the establishment of new borders on the Eurasian continent."[7]

In addition to calling for a re-creation of the USSR, the Assembly's participants agreed that the democratic concept of "the separation of powers" was a Western invention unsuitable for Russia. "The idea of the separation of powers," the Assembly decided, "will never take hold on Russian Orthodox soil, because as the Lord said, 'Every kingdom divided against itself is brought to desolation . . . ' (Matthew 12:25)." Only the "power of the Soviets"—and especially of the Russian Supreme Soviet, then headed by rightist chairman Ruslan Khasbulatov—needed to be preserved. The Russian presidency, the courts, and all "mayoralities, municipalities, and prefectures" should be abolished, albeit "in a constitutional manner."[8] In the struggle between Boris Yeltsin and the "democrats," on the one hand, and their rightist opponents, on the other, the Assembly sided unequivocally with conservatives who advocated "All power to the Soviets!"

The Assembly also spoke out against "the discrediting of the Russian army and its martial traditions" and called for "a struggle with crime and corruption."[9] These were frequently voiced concerns of the Russian right.

From "Empire Saving" to "Empire Expanding"

At the May 1993 Russian Assembly, the leadership of the Moscow Patriarchate sided decisively with "empire savers" who wanted to re-create the USSR. It soon emerged that the Holy Synod of the Russian Orthodox Church was entertaining even grander visions. In August 1993, the newspaper *Nezavisimaia gazeta* published an article by Vladlen Sirotkin, an expert for the Committee on Freedom of Conscience of the Russian Supreme Soviet, that summarized the views of that committee's chairman, Archpriest Viacheslav Polosin, on the establishment of a "Eurasian Orthodox-Muslim Union," which might with time supersede the present Russian Federation.[10] According to Sirotkin, the plan enjoyed the strong support of the Holy Synod of the Moscow Patriarchate.

The ambitious plan outlined by Sirotkin built upon the writings of the interwar émigré "Eurasians," who argued that the name "Russia" was a misnomer for the geopolitical space occupied by the Russian Empire. Rather than being called Russia, they believed, that space should be termed Eurasia (*Evraziia*), because it belonged to a separate cultural world and had strong links to the so-called Turanian (Turkic and Iranian) East, as well as to other Slavs.[11]

The émigré founders of the Eurasian movement had believed that a Eurasian political party must eventually come to the fore and supplant the Communist Party as the ruling political force in Eurasia. They strongly opposed Western-style democracy, favoring instead an authoritarian form of rule that would consult, but not necessarily heed, the vox populi.

For the interwar Eurasians, the West represented a voracious opponent that sought to turn Russia into a colonial appendage of itself. The Eurasians believed that Russians were constitutionally incapable of participating in Western culture. Above all else, the interwar Eurasians should be viewed as empire savers. As Nicholas Riasanovsky of Berkeley has noted, "Eurasianism can be considered a determined defense of Russia, one and indivisible, in an age when empires crumbled. And, indeed, if the Russian empire were a symphonic unity of peoples—more than that, if there were no Russian empire at all but only one organic Eurasia—the issue of separation lost its meaning."[12]

Fr. Georgii Florovskii, arguably the leading Orthodox theologian of the twentieth century and formerly a professor at Harvard and Princeton, was one of the founders of the Eurasian movement, but he broke sharply with its adherents in 1923. His probing essay, "The Eurasian Temptation," published in the émigré journal *Sovremennye zapiski* in 1928, remains in many ways relevant today.[13]

In his essay, Florovskii suggested that the original Eurasians should be termed "red-blacks," because they combined elements of both communism and fascism. Indeed the Eurasians themselves, as Florovskii noted, considered themselves a "third maximalism," along with the maximalisms of communism and fascism.

The resurrection of a formerly obscure émigré ideology in the 1990s should, upon reflection, cause little surprise. With the effective demise of

Marxism-Leninism as a "glue" holding the Soviet Union together, empire savers have been required to cast about for substitutes. Eurasianism, like Marxism-Leninism, offers a meta-ethnic schema for continuing to yoke the various former Soviet republics together. The proto-fascist weekly *Den'* (recently renamed *Zavtra*) has been promoting the serviceability of Eurasianism as a useful empire-saving ideology, but so, too, have authoritarian "centrists" like former presidential adviser Sergei Stankevich.[14]

The schema advocated by Archpriest Viacheslav Polosin of the former Russian parliament and endorsed by the Holy Synod of the Moscow Patriarchate would extend the outreach of Eurasianism well beyond the boundaries of the former Soviet Union. In their hands, Eurasianism would become an empire-expanding as well as an empire-saving mechanism. What they seek, breathtakingly, is to reconstitute the *Byzantine* as well as the prerevolutionary Russian and Soviet empires.

As Vladlen Sirotkin has outlined the plan, the hierarchy of the Russian Orthodox Church, the Muslim clergy on the territory of the former Soviet Union, and "the authentically patriotic strata of the population of Russia" would join to initiate a "gathering of the lands" around Moscow and "the reconstitution of a great state." "If anyone is still respected," Sirotkin insists, "it is the church clergy. . . . And, after all, the hierarchs of the Russian Orthodox Church have had the political experience—both positive and negative—of direct participation in mass socioreligious movements." The vast undertaking being contemplated, Sirotkin notes, would "change the geopolitical map not only of Europe but also of Asia."

The geopolitical sprawl resulting from a successful implementation of this plan would include an "Eastern Christian Spiritual Union consisting of the peoples of Russia, Ukraine, Belarus, Georgia, and Armenia, "in cooperation with the Muslims of Kazakhstan, Central Asia, the North Caucasus and the Caucasus." With the apparent exception of the Baltic states, this proposed "union" would effectively reconstitute the Soviet Union.

The Moscow Patriarchate's plan, it emerged, envisioned even more ambitious goals than simply re-creating the Soviet Union (minus the Baltic states). Added to the proposed Eastern Christian Spiritual Union would be "the seven million Copts of Egypt," "the approximately two million Orthodox of Lebanon and Syria," and "the peoples of Greece, Cyprus, United Yugoslavia (Serbia and Montenegro) [and] Bulgaria." Such a colossal new entity would indeed "change the geopolitical map" of Europe and Asia![15]

Writing in the pro-democracy weekly *Obshchaia gazeta,* Marina Pavlova-Sil'vanskaia has discussed such recent empire-expanding efforts at considerable length.[16] While political elements in Serbia, Greece, and Armenia have been supportive of these initiatives, she notes, Georgians, Ukrainians, Belarusians, Moldovans, and Romanians have been generally cool to the plans. Moscow Patriarchate clergy named by her as participating in the initiatives are Patriarch Aleksii II, Archpriest Polosin, Fr. Vsevolod Chaplin, and Archimandrite Ashurkov.

These ambitious empire-saving schemes would appear also to have had the support of Ruslan Khasbulatov, the thrustful leader of the former Russian parliament. In early September 1993, Khasbulatov told the hardline weekly *Den'* that "he expects the resurrection of a new kind of Soviet empire," and he called for "the development of a new common state ideology based on Russian traditions."[17] Eurasianism would seem to have answered the needs of Khasbulatov, a Muslim by background, who, by his own testimony, performed the hajj to Mecca in 1992 at the invitation of the king of Saudi Arabia.[18] Speaking at a scientific center of the Russian Academy of Sciences in September 1993, Khasbulatov "proposed joint elections by CIS member-states to the CIS Inter-parliamentary Assembly," adding that "the joint parliament could form a common CIS government."[19]

Recent Moscow Patriarchate Empire-Saving Activities

In coming out unambiguously on behalf of empire saving (and empire expanding), the Moscow Patriarchate leadership had been merely continuing a recent trend.[20] With the marked decline in the appeal and prestige of Marxist-Leninist ideology during the Gorbachev period, Russian rightists found themselves increasingly looking to the Russian Orthodox Church as an institution that might potentially play a role in propping up the threatened unity of the Soviet state. Thus, in mid-1990, Russian Communist Party leader Ivan Polozkov termed the church "a natural ally of the Communist Party in the struggle for moral values and against interethnic conflicts."[21] At an April 1991 conference of the hardline "Soiuz" parliamentary faction, the Russian clergy was, along with the army, singled out as one of two "eternal institutions of [Russian] statehood."[22]

In May 1990, the aging and infirm Patriarch Pimen died and was replaced the following month by the current first-hierarch, Aleksii II (Ridiger), born in 1929. Aleksii's accession coincided with the rise of Soiuz and other rightist elements not prepared to countenance the secession of the minority union republics. As one of the leading lights of the Brezhnevite ecclesiastical nomenklatura—Aleksii had served as chancellor of the Moscow Patriarchate from 1964 through 1988—the new patriarch had fully assimilated the philosophy known as *sergianstvo*, named after Metropolitan and Patriarch Sergii (d. 1944), who had proclaimed in 1927 that the "joys and sorrows of the [communist] Motherland" were those of the Russian church.[23]

Once he had been named patriarch in mid-1990, Aleksii set about firming up the threatened unity of both the Russian church and the "inner" Soviet empire, the USSR proper. For Aleksii, it became clear that the vital interests of the church and the Soviet state fully coincided.

The growth of secessionist sentiment in the minority union republics, and especially in the key republic of Ukraine, with its large Orthodox populace, required that Aleksii take action to preserve the endangered unity of the Russian church. In a late 1990 interview with *Literaturnaia gazeta*, he assailed "the so-called [Ukrainian] autocephalists—those who want to see in Christ not their Lord and judge, but an ally in a political struggle."[24]

Aleksii's empire-saving activities became especially noteworthy in December 1990, when he appended his signature to the "Letter of the Fifty-Three," which was published on the pages of *Sovetskaia Rossiia*.[25] (A photograph of the fifty-three signatures was appended next to the published text of the letter.) The signatories of this hardline appeal to "Comrade M.S. Gorbachev" included three activists who would later be arrested as leaders of the August 1991 putsch—Oleg Baklanov, Aleksandr Tiziakov, and General Valentin Varennikov, commander of army ground troops—as well as such conservative luminaries as General Mikhail Moiseev, chief of the Military General Staff, General Iurii Shatalin, commander of the ground troops of the USSR Ministry of Internal Affairs, and writers Iurii Bondarev, Stanislav Kuniaev, and Aleksandr Prokhanov.

The authors of the "Letter of the Fifty-Three" proposed to Gorbachev that "immediate measures be carried out to counter separatism, subversive anti-state activity, incitement, and inter-ethnic discord, employing for this purpose the law and the powers granted to you." Should these measures prove inadequate, the authors recommended "the introduction of emergency rule and presidential rule in zones of major conflicts." Among the forces that Gorbachev could rely on in reestablishing order, the authors observed, were "the church" and "the Party of Communists, which is the in process of renewing itself."

Aleksii's signature to this brutal "empire-saving" document, which was widely viewed by Russian "democrats" as having helped prepare the January 1991 attempted putsch in the Baltic, became a scandal among Orthodox believers and Russian intellectuals. Badly embarrassed by the episode, Aleksii acted more circumspectly at the time of "Bloody Sunday" in Vilnius, Lithuania, in mid-January 1991. In his statement on that occasion, Aleksii assigned blame for the bloodletting both to the Lithuanians and to the Soviet "center," though the Lithuanians appeared, in his eyes, to be more at fault than the USSR authorities.[26]

During this charged period extending from the end of 1990 through August 1991, Aleksii's opinion tended closely to mirror that of Soviet president Mikhail Gorbachev. In March 1991, Aleksii invited representatives from churches and religious organizations based in the Soviet Union to a conference held at the Danilov Monastery in Moscow at which the participants spoke out in favor of "preserving the community" of the Soviet Union, thereby effectively endorsing the Gorbachev-sponsored 17 March referendum on the future of the USSR.[27]

During the period preceding the August putsch, Aleksii repeatedly underlined his firm solidarity with the twenty-five million Russians living in the non-Russian periphery. "We cannot but be agitated," he stated in one interview, "by the fate of Russian people [*russkie*] who live beyond the borders of Russia. . . .

When our compatriots are called 'migrants' or 'occupiers,' I consider this a direct violation of human rights."[28]

The August 1991 attempted coup represented an empire-saving initiative par excellence. The putsch was launched on 19 August because a new union treaty that was to be signed the following day would have devolved major powers to Russia and other union republics. As they struggled against massive odds to preserve Russian "sovereignty," President Yeltsin and the other Russian leaders sought to marshal support abroad—especially from U.S. President Bush—and from leading figures in Russia.

At the top of the list of key domestic figures stood the name of Patriarch Aleksii. At considerable personal risk, Vice President Aleksandr Rutskoi traveled to the patriarch's residence on the morning of the 19 August to hand-deliver a personal appeal from Yeltsin. Rutskoi was told that the patriarch was ill and could not see him. On the following day, however, the patriarch issued a statement in support of USSR President Gorbachev—but not of Yeltsin—that objectively served to help the cause of the Russian government. The patriarch also appealed to the Soviet armed forces to remain calm and "not to permit fraternal blood to be shed."[29] Once the coup had failed, Aleksii abandoned such measured steps, vigorously anathematizing the coup perpetrators, who, as dedicated communists, were presumably indifferent to the patriarch's opinion.

Other leading Moscow Patriarchate hierarchs performed with notably less dignity than did the patriarch. According to one account, Metropolitans Kirill of Smolensk, Iuvenalii of Krutitsy, and Filaret of Kiev—all permanent members of the ruling Holy Synod—declined to affix their signatures to the patriarch's statement issued on 20 August. On the previous day, 19 August, at a meeting of the Congress of Compatriots, which had brought eight hundred émigrés to Moscow, Metropolitans Kirill, Iuvenalii, and Pitirim of Volokolamsk sat "as if nailed to their seats" while many émigrés stood in a gesture of support for Gorbachev and Yeltsin.[30]

The failure of the August putsch led directly to the breakup of the USSR in December 1991 and to the blitz-formation of the new Commonwealth of Independent States. Those developments, in turn, imparted new energy to empire savers of all persuasions, including the permanent members of the Moscow Holy Synod. "The canonical territory of the Moscow Patriarchate," Patriarch Aleksii underlined in mid-1992, "includes not only Russia, but Ukraine, Belarus, Moldova, the countries of the Baltic, Azerbaijan, Kazakhstan, and Central Asia."[31] "It would be wrong," Aleksii insisted in early 1993, "automatically to transfer the causes for the division of the USSR to the church sphere. One cannot form fifteen local Orthodox churches in a country that has been divided into fifteen sovereign states."[32] If the Russian church could maintain a grip on the Orthodox churches in the other union republics, then that success would objectively assist efforts by Russian empire savers to reassemble the Soviet Union.

Ukraine

For Russian empire savers of all stripes, Ukraine represents the indispensable key and cornerstone to reconstituting the Soviet empire. At the May 1993 All-World Russian Assembly, as we have seen, Ukrainians were adjudged to be ethnic Russians *tout court*. For Russia to "lose" Ukraine, therefore, would be to acquiesce to the loss of a part of itself. In the eyes of the Moscow Patriarchate leadership, the threatened departure of thousands of Ukrainian parishes was a debacle to be averted at all costs.

An estimated thirty million of Ukraine's fifty-two million citizens identify themselves as Orthodox Christians. In a recent survey of 2,051 residents of five urban areas located in central, eastern, and southern Ukraine, researchers at the Kiev International Institute of Sociology found that more than 50 percent of the respondents identified themselves as Orthodox, while a mere 1 percent considered themselves Uniate or Roman Catholic, and another 2 percent professed to be Protestants, Baptists, Jews, or Muslims.[33] Only in western Ukraine, where there are an estimated five million Uniate Catholics, does another denomination provide serious competition for the Orthodox Church.

The upsurge of separatist sentiment in Ukraine during 1989 began greatly to concern the leadership of the Moscow Patriarchate, as did the legalization of the Uniate Church by Gorbachev in December of that year. The Uniates began seizing parishes from the patriarchate in western Ukraine, and this caused then-Patriarch Pimen to appeal to Gorbachev, the secretary general of the United Nations, and the pope for help in halting the forced takeover of churches.[34]

Not only was the Moscow Holy Synod suddenly faced with vigorous competition from Uniates in western Ukraine, it also confronted the specter of the reemergence of a Ukrainian Autocephalous Orthodox Church. Bishop Ioann (Bodnarchuk) of Zhytomyr, a Moscow-ordained hierarch, had assumed the leadership of the renewed autocephaly effort; for this, he was summarily defrocked by a November 1989 decision of the Moscow Holy Synod. This punitive action, however, did nothing to deter Ukrainian autocephaly sentiment; on 5–6 June 1990, seven Orthodox bishops, more than two hundred priests, and five hundred laymen held a council in Kiev during which they elected Mstyslav (Skrypnyk), the aging leader of the Ukrainian Orthodox Church in the United States, patriarch of the Ukrainian Autocephalous Orthodox Church. When the Soviet authorities refused to grant Mstyslav a visa, Ioann Bodnarchuk, now metropolitan of L'viv and Volhynia, was named Mstyslav's deputy and acting head of the church.

Faced with the growing threat of the autocephalists, the Moscow Patriarchate resolved upon a new empire-saving initiative. On 31 January–1 February 1990, an extraordinary Bishops' Council was convened in Moscow in great haste. At the Council, it was decided to bring into existence a new ecclesiastical entity—a Ukrainian Orthodox Church, under then Metropolitan Filaret (Denysenko) of

Kiev.[35] The clear-cut intention behind this move was to convince nationalisti-cally inclined Ukrainians that there was no need for them to form an autocepha-lous church or to defect to the Unia; their needs would be cared for by the newly established Ukrainian church under Filaret. That body, however, was in fact what Orthodox canon law terms an *autonomous* rather than a fully independent, or autocephalous, church.

Once the Ukrainian populace had voted overwhelmingly for full indepen-dence from the Soviet Union on 1 December 1991 and the USSR had broken apart later that month, the specter of a breakaway Ukrainian church became especially worrisome to Moscow. Worse, from the Holy Synod's perspective, was the fact that the cause of a Ukrainian autocephalous church now had the fervent support of both Metropolitan Filaret of Kiev and then Ukrainian presi-dent Leonid Kravchuk, as well as Ukrainian nationalists generally. Filaret and Kravchuk, it should be noted, had enjoyed close contacts for many years, Kravchuk having served as Ukrainian Communist Party secretary for ideology while Filaret was exarch of Moscow's parishes in Ukraine.[36]

By March 1992, Filaret was pushing energetically for Moscow to grant autocephaly to his autonomous church, arguing that otherwise the Ukrainian church would prove helpless before the expansion-minded Uniates. For his part, President Kravchuk wrote a letter to Patriarch Aleksii requesting autocephaly. At a pivotal church Council held in Moscow from 31 March to 4 April 1992, the question of full independence for the Ukrainian church emerged as the central issue. The session devoted to Ukrainian autocephaly lasted seven hours, without a break, and concluded only in the early hours of the morning. Sixty-two individ-uals spoke on the issue of autocephaly, with a majority arguing that "Filaret was pushing the church in the direction of secular politics" and that therefore a "schism" (*raskol*) was imminent. Sharp criticism was also directed against Filaret's character.[37]

While on paper an Orthodox monk, Filaret, as everyone in the hall was aware—for it had been publicized widely in the Russian press—was de facto married and had fathered three children. The Council resolved nevertheless that Filaret could remain an Orthodox bishop, but only so long as he surrendered the key post of metropolitan of Kiev. Filaret appeared to concur with this decision, but when he returned to Kiev, he changed his mind and renounced the agree-ment, arguing in his defense that the local clergy and laity were imploring him to stay on. Filaret then transformed himself into a ferocious defender of Ukrainian autocephaly.

In an interview given to *Pravda Ukrainy* in August 1993, Filaret defended his decision to support the autocephaly drive.[38] "When the Supreme Soviet of Ukraine adopted its decision on independence on 24 August [1991]," he recalled, "I understood that the church, too, could not be held back [by Moscow]. . . . Any state, whether in the past or in the present, that has found independence has immediately raised the question of the independence of its church. A state that has a church that is dependent on another state is fragile." Filaret maintained that Patriarch Aleksii II had, like his predecessors Aleksii I and Pimen, been selected "in advance by state organs." The church Council that had chosen Aleksii patriarch in 1990 had, thus, been in effect a charade.

Filaret's account of Aleksii's elevation, it should be noted, accorded with materials unearthed by Russian parliamentarians in the KGB archives following the failed coup, which revealed that "during the preparation of the Local Council of 1990, [Vladimir] Kriuchkov, the head of the KGB ... dispatched a special encoded telegram to all directorates of the KGB, suggesting that they facilitate the election of Aleksii (Ridiger), the Metropolitan of Leningrad, to the patriarchal throne."[39] Because the Russian church had been and still was dependent on the Russian state, Filaret argued, Ukraine needed to have an autocephalous Orthodox church. "With the separation of the Ukrainian Orthodox Church from Moscow," Filaret argued, "Ukraine will forever leave Russia. It [the church] is the last but very important string which ties Ukraine to Moscow."[40]

Recognizing that Filaret represented a major threat—though also an easy target due to his well-documented arbitrariness and venality—the Moscow Patriarchate elected to take swift action against him. A Council of Bishops of the Ukrainian Orthodox Church was convened in Kharkiv on 27 May 1992, and Metropolitan Volodymyr (Sabodan) of Rostov and Novocherkassk, chancellor of the Moscow Patriarchate, was selected as head of the autonomous Ukrainian Orthodox Church. This choice was swiftly confirmed by the Moscow Holy Synod.[41] In mid-June 1992, a Council of ninety-four bishops met outside Moscow and reduced Filaret—who was not present—to the status of an ordinary monk; Bishop Iakiv of Pochaiv, who had supported Filaret, was also stripped of his rank.[42]

The selection of Volodymyr (to give the new metropolitan of Kiev the Ukrainian version of his name) was a shrewd one. An ethnic Ukrainian born in the Khmel'nyts'kyi region, Volodymyr had served most of his life in Ukraine in various posts: vicar bishop of Kiev, dean of the Odessa Seminary, metropolitan of Chernihiv, and editor of the Ukrainian Orthodox *Visnyk.*[43] Volodymyr's task was nevertheless a difficult one: as head of an autonomous church—and while continuing to serve as a permanent member of the Moscow Holy Synod—he was to convince Ukrainian believers that he, rather than the autocephalists, best represented their religio-national interests.

Volodymyr's strategy was to argue that he did not oppose autocephaly—to the contrary, he supported it—but that he favored a slow, steady path to church independence. The Moscow Patriarchate leadership, too, held out the carrot of eventual autocephaly, stating at one point that it would be granted "no later than 1995."[44] Volodymyr's task, in short, was to buy time until the "fever" of independence and nationalism had waned in Ukraine. By late summer 1993, evidence began to accumulate that that strategy was working. The severe economic dislocations in Ukraine were beginning to induce many Ukrainians to reconsider their relations with Russia.[45]

In March 1993, it was reported that Volodymyr enjoyed the support of 29 Ukrainian bishops and 5,400 Ukrainian parishes; the comparable figures for Filaret were 18 bishops and 2,500 parishes.[46] It should be noted in this connection that in June 1992, at the time that he had been reduced to the status of a simple monk by the Moscow Bishops' Council, Filaret had joined with a number of bishops and clergy of the Ukrainian Autocephalous Orthodox Church to found a new entity, the Ukrainian Orthodox Church—Kiev Patriarchate. While Mstyslav was named the head of this church, and Filaret merely his deputy, the U.S.-based Mstyslav refused to have anything to do with the tainted Filaret and rejected the proposed arrangement.[47] Mstyslav's death in June 1993 at the age of ninety-five put an end to this stand off, though some 500 autocephalous parishes in Galicia have refused to form ties with Filaret.

Another strategy followed by the Moscow Patriarchate has been to put pressure on President Kravchuk of Ukraine not to push too vigorously for an independent church. Thus, in August 1992, Patriarch Aleksii sent a letter to the Ukrainian president in which he emphasized that "The Ukrainian Orthodox Church [UPTs], independent in its administration, enters into universal Orthodoxy through the Moscow Patriarchate."[48]

A related tactic has been to isolate the Ukrainian autocephalists from other Orthodox patriarchs and other heads of Orthodox churches. Filaret of Kiev and Archbishop Volodymyr Romaniuk, who was selected as patriarchal *locum tenens* following the death of Mstyslav in June 1993, had sought to obtain autocephaly from the ecumenical patriarch of Constantinople, Bartholomew I. Bartholomew, however, has proclaimed that he "recognizes only one canonical Metropolitan of Kiev—His Eminence Volodymyr (Sabodan)." The patriarch of Alexandria has made similar public statements. These declarations brought to naught a visit paid to Constantinople by Archbishop Romaniuk and Arsen Zinchenko, the fervently pro-autocephaly chairman of the Ukrainian Council for Religious Affairs, as well as a letter to Patriarch Bartholomew from President Kravchuk of Ukraine.[49]

To sum up the situation to date, Metropolitan Volodymyr and the Moscow Patriarchate have so far held the line successfully against the Ukrainian autocephalists and their powerful Ukrainian state supporters. To be sure, there have been some painful moments, as Volodymyr noted during a September 1992 interview. On 12 August 1992, he recalled, the autocephalists had "seized by force" the cathedral, diocesan administration, and theological seminary in Luts'k. Attempts had also been made at that time to take over church buildings in Rivne, Vinnytsia, Ivano-Frankivs'k, Pereiaslav-Khmel'nits'kyi, and other locations.[50] In June 1992, one hundred activists associated with the Ukrainian National Self-Defense Organization, armed with lead pipes, clubs, and other weapons, had attempted to take the Kievo-Pechers'ka Monastery for Filaret by storm but had been halted by elite police forces.[51] Moscow had "bent" but not "broken" before the strong winds of Ukrainian ecclesiastical separatism and nationalism.

Moldova

Keeping the Moldovan Orthodox parishes in line has proven to be an even more difficult task for the Moscow Holy Synod. As early as April 1991, Moldova's minister of culture and religious affairs, Ion Ungureanu, had expressed Chişinău's discontent with the subordination of the Eparchy of Moldova to the Russian Orthodox Church. While Moldova had proclaimed political sovereignty, Ungureanu observed, "we still belong from the ecclesiastical point of view not only to the USSR, but even to Russia."[52]

In the autumn of 1992, the newspaper *Izvestiia* reported that conflict had become particularly sharp between the Moscow Patriarchate representation, headed by Metropolitan Vladimir of Chişinău and Moldova and the Moldovan Ministry of Culture and Religious Affairs. The Christian Democratic Popular Front of Moldova, it was reported, was also assailing continued Moldovan ecclesiastical submission to Moscow as "a betrayal of national interests."[53]

The attempt of the Russian-dominated "Trans-Dniester Republic" within Moldova to obtain full de facto independence from Moldova led to bloody armed clashes in May–June 1992 between Moldovan forces, on the one hand, and Trans-Dniester irregulars and the Russian Fourteenth Army, on the other. These clashes, in turn, put immense strain on Moscow–Moldova church relations. Metropolitan Vladimir of Chişinău issued a strong appeal to Russian President Yeltsin to stop the fighting, but his intercession was not enough to retain the allegiance of many Moldovan Orthodox.[54] In October 1992, at the request of Metropolitan Vladimir and the Orthodox populace of Moldova, the Moscow Holy Synod decided to declare the Moldovan Eparchy an autonomous church.[55]

Even this important concession seemed not to be enough. The Romanian Orthodox Church under Patriarch Teoctist moved in and established a Bessarabian metropolitanate on Moldovan soil, with Bishop Peter of Balti serving as its temporary administrator. The Romanian church apparently felt justified in taking this action because Bessarabia and the Bessarabian church had been part of the Kingdom of Romania between 1919 and 1940. A large number of Moldovan parishes soon went over to this new/old metropolitanate, and the center of Moscow-affiliated parishes shifted to the breakaway Trans-Dniester Republic.[56]

While the Moscow Synod had successfully prevented a linkup between Constantinople and Ukrainian autocephalists, it proved incapable of thwarting a move by the Romanian Patriarchate into Moldova. Patriarch Aleksii protested sharply to Patriarch Teoctist concerning the creation of the Bessarabian metropolitanate and the Romanian church's communing with Bishop Peter, "who is under ban by the Holy Synod of the Russian Orthodox Church." "The Romanian Orthodox Church," Aleksii complained bitterly, "has committed a coarse anti-canonical act of interfering in the internal affairs of another autocephalous Orthodox church, and has created the threat of a new schism."[57]

Unless the Russian state should prove capable of reincorporating Moldova into a new, expanded empire, the Moldovan church will likely be lost to the Moscow Patriarchate.

Latvia

A third troublesome area for the Russian church has been the Republic of Latvia. Like Moldovans, ethnic Latvians have been concerned over perceived attempts by Russians to dominate their republic. It is easy to see why this should be so. The 1989 all-union census revealed that 34 percent of Latvia's populace was composed of ethnic Russians, while so-called Russian-speakers amounted to 48 percent of the total population.

During the summer of 1992, the Latvian minister of justice, Viktor Skudra, had expressed strong reservations about granting Orthodox churches and other ecclesiastical properties in Latvia to the Moscow Patriarchate. The minister noted that "up until the [Soviet] occupation of 1940–41," the Orthodox churches in Latvia had submitted to the patriarch of Constantinople.[58] "Independent Latvia," Skudra declared, "will not accept Moscow's interfering in the activity of any organization on its territory, including that of a religious confession."[59]

These statements by the Latvian minister prompted a visit by Metropolitan Iuvenalii of Krutitsy, a permanent member of the Moscow Holy Synod, who assured Skudra that the patriarchate had no intention of interfering in the state affairs of Latvia.[60] In November 1992, there followed a second visit to Latvia by Iuvenalii, who was accompanied by Metropolitan Kirill of Smolensk, during which the two hierarchs had talks with the then chairman of the Latvian Supreme Soviet, Anatolijs Gorbunovs.

This second visit apparently did not settle matters in Latvia. According to the newspaper *Moskovskii komsomolets,* "After this visit, the Orthodox Church in Latvia split into four parts: parishes maintaining loyalty to the Moscow Patriarchate; those recognizing the Russian Orthodox Church Abroad; an Autocephalous Latvian Orthodox Church; and, finally, a Latvian Church in Exile, subordinate to the patriarch of Constantinople."[61] Unless Latvia were to be reincorporated into a new Moscow-dominated empire, the chances of the Moscow Patriarchate's retaining control of that republic's parishes seemed quite slim. Like the Orthodox Church of Finland, Latvia's parishes appeared likely to turn to Constantinople rather than Moscow for ecclesiastical legitimacy.[62]

Other Republics

Ukraine, Moldova, and Latvia are the three republics in which the Moscow Patriarchate has encountered particularly rough sledding in its empire-saving endeavors. Elsewhere, matters have proceeded relatively smoothly. A singular success story, at least to date, has been the key republic of Belarus. On 31 January–1 February 1990, an extraordinary Bishops' Council in Moscow created an autonomous Belarusian Orthodox Church under Metropolitan Filaret of Minsk, an ethnic Russian who had not been raised in Belarus.[63] This new church was, of course, an exact parallel to the Ukrainian Orthodox Church created at the same Bishops' Council. The Belarusian church's blitz-formation in early 1990 represented a kind of "preemptive strike" directed against autocephalist sentiment in Belarus. Up until now, the strategy appears to have worked. In the fall of 1992, at a press conference, Metropolitan Filaret of Minsk rejected accusations that his church represented "an instrument of Russian imperialism," arguing that priests were in fact being encouraged to use the Belarusian language in sermons.[64] The metropolitan's (and Moscow's) flexible stance on the Belarusian language issue has served so far to keep nationalist passions at bay.

Along with Ukraine and Belarus, Kazakhstan has been the former union republic of most interest to Russian empire savers. In January 1991, the Moscow Holy Synod angered President Nursultan Nazarbaev of Kazakhstan when it made a decision to open two new dioceses in Kazakhstan.[65] This act represented a clear-cut attempt to shore up the heavily Russian and Slavic northern tier of Kazakhstan. It did little, however, to halt the out-migration of Russians from that republic. At the time of the 1989 all-union census, Russians had constituted 38 percent of Kazakhstan's populace; today that figure has dropped to 35 percent, while the percentage of Kazakhs has increased from 40 percent to 43 percent.[66]

The Republic of Georgia boasts an ancient autocephalous church headed by Catholicos Il'ia II. That fact, however, has not prevented the Moscow Synod from injecting itself on occasion into the internal affairs of the Georgian church. Thus, in early 1991, Patriarch Aleksii II trespassed on the prerogatives of a sister church when he sent an appeal to Catholicos Il'ia and to Georgian believers criticizing "those responsible for the tense situation in South Ossetia."[67] A similar condemnatory statement was issued by Metropolitan Gedeon of Stavropol and Baku.[68]

The attempt of Russian political empire savers to encourage separatism in largely Muslim areas of Georgia such as Abkhazia and Ajaria has drawn fire from Georgian Orthodox believers, who have expressed outrage that Russians would choose to side with Muslims against their Orthodox brethren. One example of such sentiment was an open letter by a Georgian Orthodox woman, Nino Gorgodze, to then Russian Vice President Aleksandr Rutskoi, himself an Orthodox layman.[69]

Is the Russian Orthodox Church a Tool of the State?

It will have been noted that Ukrainian, Moldovan, and Latvian spokesmen arguing on behalf of severing ecclesiastical ties with Moscow have done so on the assumption that the Moscow Patriarchate remains an instrument of Russian state control. In some instances, these spokesmen have sought quite obviously to substitute Ukrainian, Moldovan, or Latvian state control for that of Russia. But is their contention that the Moscow Patriarchate is a state-controlled entity valid?

Certainly few today would seek to deny that prior to the collapse of the August 1991 coup the Russian Orthodox Church had been both tightly controlled and meticulously monitored. Konstantin Kharchev, chairman of the Council for Religious Affairs from late 1984 through early 1989, has confirmed that the Russian church was indeed rigorously controlled by the Central Committee of the Communist Party (especially its Ideological Department) and by the KGB.[70]

In early 1992, a former KGB agent, A. Shushpanov, gave an interview to the mass-circulation pro-democracy weekly *Argumenty i fakty* in which he described in detail his work as a secret police operative inside the Moscow Patriarchate's Department of External Ecclesiastical Relations.[71] A "majority" of the individuals working in that department, Shushpanov noted, were in fact agents working for either Moscow or the all-union KGB. There was also a full-time KGB "resident" or chief-of-station located at the department. Obligatory reports on contacts with foreign visitors had to be submitted in five copies: one copy for the department chairman, one for the Council for Religious Affairs ("in essence a *filial* of the KGB"), and three "submitted directly to the KGB." For his labors, Shushpanov recalled, he was paid "not at all badly," and the money supplemented his regular department salary.

His chief task while at the department, Shushpanov underlined, was to "work against" dissenting Orthodox priest Gleb Yakunin. "I not only kept track of his activities," Shushpanov noted, "but I also worked out an operation directed against him. The KGB tried to lead him into committing espionage." This attempt at entrapment was related to Father Yakunin's acquaintance with the Reverend Michael Spengler, Protestant chaplain at the American Embassy in Moscow. Fortunately, Shushpanov concluded, this intrigue—which might have led to Father Yakunin's being tried on a charge of treason—failed, partially as a result of his own efforts. Shushpanov later told Yakunin what he had done and received the priest's forgiveness.

While there can be little question, then, concerning the pervasive involvement of the Party and the KGB in Russian church affairs in the pre-August 1991 period, the question of the degree of state influence in the almost three years following the putsch is a legitimate one. As shall be seen, it is my belief that the degree of state meddling in church affairs has remained significantly high.

In assessing the extent of state involvement in present-day Russian Orthodox Church affairs, one confronts, first of all, the plain fact that the overwhelming majority of the current 119 bishops of the Moscow Patriarchate were ordained to the episcopacy prior to August 1991. This suggests that each of these bishops was carefully screened and vetted by both the ideological apparatus of the Communist Party and the KGB. It need hardly be noted that a flourishing of religion in the USSR was *not* an aim of those two bodies.

Candidates for elevation to permanent membership in the Moscow Holy Synod obviously received the closest possible screening and evaluation. Wherever possible, a "hook" into a candidate was deemed desirable. According to research done by the weekly *Moskovskie novosti,* Filaret (Denysenko) of Kiev had been approved by the KGB for ordination to the episcopate only after he had entered into a liaison with Evgeniia Rodionova, the woman who bore three children with him. The KGB "wanted to have a guarantee that the young bishop 'would obey.'"[72] One must assume that similar hooks served to obtain the "obedience" of other hierarchs eventually elevated to permanent membership in the Holy Synod.

Following the failure of the August 1991 coup, pro-democracy Russian parliamentarians were afforded a brief "window of opportunity" during which they were able to examine a number of KGB files, including some that shed light on that organization's frequent and wide-ranging intrusion into the life of the Russian church. This "window" coincided with Vadim Bakatin's tenure as chairman of the USSR KGB from August through December 1991. Bakatin's name, it should be noted, had figured on the August 1991 KGB arrest list, and that powerful official appeared determined to defang a totalitarian entity that had come close to putting him in prison. Bakatin's successor, Viktor Barannikov, chairman of the newly formed Russian Ministry of State Security, soon set about reversing Bakatin's policies. (Barannikov was himself, however, ousted from the chairmanship in late July 1993, apparently for siding with the anti-Yeltsin forces.)

Materials unearthed from the KGB archives indicate that four of the six current permanent members of the Moscow Patriachate Holy Synod are, or at least until recently were, KGB agents: Patriarch Aleksii II (agent code name "Drozdov"); Metropolitan Iuvenalii of Krutitsy ("Adamant"); Metropolitan Kirill of Smolensk ("Mikhailov"); and Metropolitan Filaret of Minsk ("Ostrovskii"). The head of the patriarchate's publications department, Metropolitan Pitirim of Volokolamsk ("Abbat"), was also revealed to be an agent.[73] It should be stressed that an "agent" of the former KGB was considerably more than an informer; he or she was an active operative of the Committee for State Security, in effect a nonuniformed officer of that organization. Successful agents were wont to receive official awards. In February 1988, for example, "agent Drozdov" (Patriarch Aleksii) was given a letter of commendation for his activities by the KGB chairman.[74]

It might be argued that all of this refers to the recent past and that the Moscow Patriarchate is now fully free of the influence of the Russian secret police. Such an argument presumes that former agents among the church hierarchy were churchmen first and operatives second. Given the route by which these men became bishops, however, it seems more likely that they would be agents and defenders of a strong state first and churchmen second. Evidence in favor of this hypothesis is provided by an extraordinary article, "Render Unto Caesar the Things That Are Caesar's: A Historic Apologia," which appeared in the Nos. 11–12, 1992 issue of *Zhurnal Moskovskoi patriarkhii* (Journal of the Moscow Patriarchate), well after the August 1991 putsch.

Authored by Deacon Andrei Lorgus, this article limned past cooperation between the Russian Orthodox Church and the secret police—Lorgus even had good things to say about the NKVD during the period of Stalin's Great Terror—and looked for future benefits from their close collaboration. The KGB's broad sources of information, Lorgus noted, could assist the church in both its domestic and foreign policies, while the church could keep the secret police well informed as to what was taking place in ecclesiastical circles and in society at large.[75] In a similar vein, an article by Archpriest V. Petliuchenko appearing in *Mezhdunarodnaia zhizn'* sought to demonstrate that the church's foreign policy and that of the Russian state were essentially the same.[76]

Some Western commentators have sought to downplay the political significance of leading Moscow Patriarchate hierarchs' serving as KGB agents. It should be noted, however, that the Russian secret service has taken the issue of the unveiling of the names of its agents exceedingly seriously. Thus on 14 February 1992, *Pravda* published a violent attack on Russian people's deputy Gleb Yakunin by four officers of the Ministry of Security of the Russian Federation—the successor organization to the KGB—for "de facto deciphering the [names of] agents of the former Fifth Directorate."[77] The use of such agents, the officers insisted, "is a sharp and necessary weapon in the hands of the special services." What, then, should be done with Father Yakunin? The authors noted (misleadingly) that in the United States the unmasking of a "secret agent" was punishable by a fine of $50,000 or by a prison term of up to ten years. Clearly, they had such a fate in mind for Father Yakunin.

At a closed session of the Russian Supreme Soviet held in July 1992, people's deputies Lev Ponomarev and Gleb Yakunin were accused of having committed "treason" (*izmena rodine*) by Viktor Barannikov, then chairman of the Russian Ministry for State Security.[78] The treasonable offense? De facto revealing of the names of the hierarch-agents. On 26 July it was reported that the Russian Procurator's Office was bringing legal action against Ponomarev and Yakunin for having disclosed the KGB Directorate "Z" materials.[79] In December 1992, however, the procurator general reversed course and effectively quashed the ministry's attempt to bring the two legislators to trial on charges of treason.[80]

The Russian parliamentary committee looking into the causes of the putsch—and especially into the role of the KGB in preparing it—was shut down in early 1992 by then Supreme Soviet chairman Ruslan Khasbulatov. Khasbulatov reportedly acted after receiving visits from both Patriarch Aleksii and Evgenii Primakov, director of Russia's Foreign Intelligence Service (the newly formed "Russian CIA"), urging him to suppress the committee.[81]

Russian religious rights activist and former political prisoner Zoia Krakhmal'nikova has aptly described the Moscow hierarchy's collaboration with the secret police: "It is a catastrophe. A national moral catastrophe. . . . This is a spiritual Chernobyl, an infection with the sin of Judas. The Lord said concerning Christians that they are the salt of the earth, the light of the world. And if we

Christians behave ourselves so shamefully, so immorally that our clergymen collaborate with the secret police, that our hierarchs turn out to be agents of the KGB, then what can we expect from our people, of whom we are a part? . . . [A] patriarch who has turned out to be a KGB agent cannot repent only before God. He must repent [publicly] before the church people."[82]

Toward A "Red-Brown" Church?

Until the bloody events of October 1993, Russia was being riven by *dvoevlastie,* dyarchy or dual power. One locus of power was the Russian president, Boris Yeltsin, and the pro-democracy, pro-market forces gathered around him. Another was the Russian parliament, headed by rightist leader Ruslan Khasbulatov. Another focal point was the powerful Russian Defense Ministry, generally allied with Yeltsin but at times adopting positions close to those of the "Red-Brown" (i.e., neo-communist and proto-fascist) coalition dominating the parliament. The parliament had, of course, emerged as a vociferous center of empire-saving sentiment, while the Defense Ministry also frequently adopted empire-saving positions, especially with regard to former republics of the Soviet Union.

Where did the Moscow Patriarchate leadership stand in all of this? Archpriest Viacheslav Polosin, then chairman of the Russian parliament's Committee on Freedom of Conscience, noted in August 1993 that Patriarch Aleksii had recently given President Yeltsin a direct ultimatum: either the president must sign a new law passed by the legislature restricting the activities of foreign missionaries in Russia, or "the Russian Orthodox Church would go into the opposition," that is, would officially link up with the Red-Brown coalition.[83] The Moscow Patriarchate—as the evidence of the already-discussed May 1993 All-World Russian Assembly suggested—had, however, already effectively begun to move in the direction of the so-called opposition.

Most graphic (and scandalous) were the words and actions of Metropolitan Ioann (Snychev) of Petersburg and Ladoga, a permanent member of the Moscow Holy Synod, who emerged as a great favorite of contemporary rightists and whose essays and interviews have been featured regularly on the pages of *Sovetskaia Rossiia* as well as in such publications as *Den', Molodaia gvardiia,* and *Pravda.* Ioann, it should be said unambiguously, was and is engaged in fomenting racial hatred directed against Jews, and he is arguably the most influential anti-Semite in Russia today. Among other activities, Ioann has asserted and defended the authenticity of the notorious fabrication *Protocols of the Elders of Zion.*[84]

As British scholar Norman Cohn, author of a pathbreaking book on the *Protocols* entitled *Warrant for Genocide,* has written, "the deadliest kind of anti-Semitism, the kind that results in massacre and attempted genocide, has little to do with real conflicts of interest between living people. . . . At its heart lies the belief that Jews—all Jews everywhere—form a conspiratorial body set on ruining and then dominating the rest of mankind."[85] Ioann is preaching precisely such a potentially genocidal form of anti-Semitism, since his message objectively serves to "demonize" the Jews.

Describing a single vast Jewish conspiracy extending from the time of Christ to the present, Ioann has warned, "Christ destroyed the myth of [Jewish] 'chosenness,' providing all surrounding peoples with access to his saving teaching. Convicting the satanic sources of the measureless pride of these false pretenders to world rule, Jesus said to them. . . : 'Your father is the devil.'. . . The 'Elders of Zion' could not forgive him this truth."[86] And Ioann then continued shrilly:

> Then war was declared against the Christian church. The haters of Christ were not able to wage it openly; they did not have the strength. So their weapon in this war became various secret societies and organizations, which, behind a veil of seemly activity, concealed their main goal: the casting down of Christianity and the destroying of national states, in this way preparing the "voluntary" unification of the world within the framework of a single international political structure, under the rule of one world government.

From the time of Christ to the present, according to Metropolitan Ioann, the satanic Elders of Zion, working through and within various shadowy organizations, such as world Masonry, have sought to achieve global rule. "All dark forces that are destroying the national Christian states," Ioann has cautioned sternly, "are working under the sign of the Masonic star. A Masonic hand took part in the destruction of Russia." A viperine Jewish-Masonic conspiracy thus looms large in Ioann's interpretation of world politics.

As Ioann sees it, the United States represents another focal point of world evil. "As deputies to the [December 1992] Seventh Congress remarked from the podium," he recalled, "a plan has been devised in the United States to cut back the world population and, first of all, that of the Russian populace. The task has been set to destroy approximately one hundred million [Russians]—more than half the ethnic Russians living in Russia. And this sinister plan will be carried out very simply—people will die of famine and illnesses."[87] By making such irresponsible statements, the metropolitan has been promoting hatred against the United States.

For Ioann, President Yeltsin and all Russian "democrats" represent yet another locus of world evil. The metropolitan has noted proudly that he urged his spiritual children to vote against Yeltsin and against the Russian president's social and economic policies at the time of the 25 April 1993 referendum.[88]

The Russian pro-democracy newspaper *Segodnia* has observed that, with Metropolitan Ioann, "a public apologia for the *Protocols* [*of the Elders of Zion*] is encountered for the first time" in the figure of a leading hierarch of the Russian church.[89] Speaking on behalf of the Congress of Jewish Religious Communities and Organizations in Moscow, the chief rabbi of Moscow, A. Shaevich, has accused Ioann of promulgating "undisguised anti-Semitism" and has asked the patriarchate to take disciplinary action against him.[90]

It should also be noted that the publishing house of the Troitse-Sergieva Monastery has issued a new printing of the works of prerevolutionary rightist Sergei Nilus, an edition that includes Nilus's edition of the fabricated *Protocols*.[91] During an August 1993 interview, people's deputy Ivan Shashviashvili, a leader of the Red-Brown coalition in the Russian parliament, revealed that the diocese of St. Petersburg and the Troitse-Sergieva Monastery had fully financed an anti-Yeltsin, anti-"democrat" campaign trip that he and like-minded activists had conducted throughout the Volga region.[92] This would seem to have been a flagrantly improper use of church funds.

The Union of Orthodox Brotherhoods (whose honorary patron is Patriarch Aleksii) sent a letter in August 1993 to the Russian Supreme Soviet, the procurator general, and the Ministry of State Security requesting that a prerevolutionary article defining "crimes on religious grounds" be returned to the Russian Criminal Code.[93] The Union of Orthodox Brotherhoods also assailed "books in mass printings that contain an apology for satanism and Masonry," "Western films" (which allegedly promoted demonism) and the democratic press for blocking attempts to "counteract Satanism." Metropolitan Ioann of Petersburg was vigorously defended as being the victim of a slander campaign.

The lamentable fact is that the Russian Orthodox Church as an entire body has been steadily shifting to the political right since approximately 1991. In the summer of 1992, two enterprising researchers, S.B. Filatov and D.E. Furman, published the results of a survey they had conducted on Russian religious mass consciousness both in the Russian Republic and in other former union republics.[94] To summarize their findings, the two researchers discovered that during the Gorbachev period a "religious boom" had taken place among ethnic Russians. During the period 1990–91, however, "there took place a sharp weakening in sympathy for Orthodoxy."

The percentage of respondents identifying themselves as Orthodox during this period had dropped precipitously from 46 percent of the total sample to 19 percent. The explanation for this drop, Filatov and Furman wrote, stemmed from the increasingly right-wing, antidemocratic orientation of the Russian church. Persons identifying themselves as Orthodox Christians held a more positive view of the Communist Party and of Stalin than did the populace as a whole. On the other hand, they had a less favorable opinion of the need to protect human rights than did the national average. In reaction to this growing conservatism of the patriarchate leadership and flock, large numbers of survey respondents chose to identify themselves as "Christians in general," rather than as Orthodox Christians.

Patriarch Aleksii's former associate, Deacon Andrei Kuraev, has unintentionally corroborated these findings in his recent essay "Orthodoxy Without Youth?" Noting that "the nationalistic ideology of the Union of Orthodox Brotherhoods" had come to dominate the ecclesiastical life of the capital, Kuraev defined that ideology as revolving around two obsessive themes: "the imminence of the Antichrist and the greatness of Russia."[95] A "hunt for heretics" was said to be another key aspect of the ideology.

This grim teaching, which focused on "fear" (*strakh*) rather than on "joy" (*radost'*), Kuraev concluded, had little appeal for today's Russian youth. For this reason, the youth were increasingly avoiding the church. In the future, Kuraev predicted sadly, Protestantism and not Orthodoxy could emerge as the dominant religion of Russia. "If the statement that our youth is our future is true," Kuraev wrote, "then the future of Orthodoxy in Russia will be to lead only a marginal existence."

By increasingly aligning itself with the Reds and Browns and with aggressive empire savers and empire expanders, the patriarchate leadership would ensure, as Deacon Kuraev foresaw, the church's diminishment and eventual irrelevance to the needs of contemporary Russians. The conjoining of *sergianstvo* (servitude to the state) and *iosiflianstvo* (an excessive emphasis on externals) would ineluctably serve to discredit the church in the eyes of the populace.[96]

The Patriarch Belatedly Takes a Stand

In April 1994, Patriarch Aleksii II, after nearly two years of silence during which the rightists had made marked inroads into the Russian church, decided to take an open stand against Metropolitan Ioann of Petersburg, the Union of Orthodox Brotherhoods, and other extremist elements within the church. (Earlier, in January 1993, the patriarch had reportedly sent a "private" communication to Metropolitan Pitirim of Volokolamsk, the long-serving head of the patriarchate's publications department, instructing him not to publish Ioann's writings in the official church press.)[97]

In an interview granted to *Moskovskie novosti,* Aleksii noted that "The position of Metropolitan Ioann troubles many."[98] While he, the patriarch, had been supporting the Memorandum on Civic Peace and Concord (promoted by President Yeltsin and Prime Minister Chernomyrdin), Metropolitan Ioann, he said, had been attacking it. Ioann, the patriarch underlined, "cannot speak for the church. That is the right of a Local Council and the Bishops' Council. In the interval between Councils, that right is possessed only by the Holy Synod and the patriarch. No one gave Metropolitan Ioann such a commission."

A soon-to-be-held session of the Holy Synod, the patriarch revealed, would discuss Ioann's statements. (Six months after the patriarch's statement, however, the promised session had still not been held.) Aleksii went on to distance himself from Ioann's virulent anti-Semitism. "The Russian Orthodox Church," he declared, "is free of racial prejudice. To whom is it not clear that to incite interethnic discord in our difficult time is madness? The opinion of one hierarch [i.e., Ioann] is, I repeat, not the opinion of the church." Aleksii explicitly rejected Ioann's call for a religious war against Jews and for the expulsion of unbaptized

Jews from Russian soil: "We categorically deny the inevitability of religious wars between any confessions."[99]

On the subject of the extremist Union of Orthodox Brotherhoods, Aleksii said, "At the last Congress of Brotherhoods, I witnessed the fierceness with which several persons spoke out. The speech of a woman representative of the Cheliabinsk brotherhood was openly mendacious and anti-ecclesiastical. . . . Truly Christian patriotism cannot be defiled by national pride, by a desire to monopolize the idea of patriotism for narrowly egoistic aims."

What prompted this open change of course by the patriarch? One factor, presumably, was the fact that Ioann and his supporters had begun openly criticizing Aleksii for alleged philo-Semitism. Ioann, for example, had drawn attention to the fact that Aleksii had met with a group of American rabbis during his fall 1993 visit to the United States and that a Bishops' Council of the Moscow Patriarchate had subsequently "de facto disavowed" the text of Aleksii's speech to the rabbis.[100] Another factor was undoubtedly that Aleksii, as he noted in the above-cited interview, was backing the "civic concord" initiative of Yeltsin and Chernomyrdin, while Ioann had thrown in his lot with General Rutskoi, the former Russian vice president, and his followers, who opposed the initiative.

Aleksii's apparent change of orientation, it should be stressed, concerned Russian domestic politics only. In its policies and activities toward the "near abroad," the Moscow Patriarchate remained firmly set on a course of energetic empire saving.

Postscript: Zhirinovsky and the Russian Orthodox Church

Despite being a self-professed religious "unbeliever," the leading Russian neofascist activist, Vladimir Zhirinovsky—whose deceivingly named Liberal Democrats won 22.8 percent of the party preference votes to the State Duma in December 1993—has recently begun to stress the role to be played by the Russian Orthodox Church in bringing about a realization of his vast imperial ambitions.[101] In his recent book, *The Last Thrust to the South,* Zhirinovsky repeatedly underlines a belief that the Moscow Patriarchate should function as a powerful state church within a Russian empire that would eventually extend from the English Channel to Vladivostok and from the Arctic Sea to the Indian Ocean.[102] During a January 1994 visit to the Bosnian Serbs, Zhirinovsky stressed his championing of "the Orthodox cause" and was rapturously hailed as "Zhirinovsky, Orthodox Savior."[103]

Notes

1. On Major General Sterligov, see "Patriot s Lubianki," *Argumenty i fakty,* 1993, no. 13 (April), p. 3; and "Skromnoe obaianie russkogo natsionalista," *Novoe vremia,* 1992, no. 42 (October). On the Russian Assembly, see *Pravda,* 4 January 1993, p. 1. For the Assembly's view of Russian Orthodoxy, see *Russkii sobor,* 1993, no. 7, p. 2.

2. *Nezavisimaia gazeta,* 5 June 1993, pp. 1–2. Vice President Aleksandr Rutskoi also addressed the Assembly, as did Vladimir Ispravnikov, who is known as "Khasbulatov's economist" (*Pravoslavnaia Moskva,* June 1993).

3. *Sovetskaia Rossiia,* 1 June 1993, p. 3.

4. *Nezavisimaia gazeta,* 5 June 1993. According to a report appearing in *Crossroads* (Jamestown Foundation): "Over the last year Kirill [of Smolensk] has 'evolved,' one source told us, into a more xenophobic stance, publicly encouraging reactionary organizations, such as the Russian National Assembly led by veteran KGB officer Aleksandr Sterligov" (15 August 1993, pp. 2–3).

5. *Krasnoiarskaia gazeta,* 11 June 1993, pp. 2–3. See also *Sovetskaia Rossiia,* 1 June 1993, p. 1.

6. *Krasnoiarskaia gazeta,* 11 June 1993.

7. Ibid.

8. Ibid.; and *Sovetskaia Rossiia,* 1 June 1993.

9. "Vesti," Russian television, 30 May 1993, in Radio Free Europe/Radio Liberty, *Russia and CIS Today,* 31 May 1993, p. 390/19.

10. Vladlen Sirotkin, "Svoboda sovesti bez Pravoslaviia i islama?" *Nezavisimaia gazeta,* 20 August 1993, p. 5. Due to his full-time work in the parliament, Polosin became a "retired" priest, that is, he was no longer rector of a parish.

11. For an excellent overview of the ideas of the interwar Eurasians, see Nicholas V. Riasanovsky, "The Emergence of Eurasianism," *California Slavic Studies,* 1967, no. 4, pp. 39–72.

12. Ibid., p. 57.

13. Florovskii's essay was republished by *Novyi mir* in early 1991: "Evraziiskii soblazn," *Novyi mir,* 1991, no. 1, pp. 195–211.

14. See *Den',* 1992, no. 15, p. 3; and Sergei Stankevich, "Derzhava v poiskakh sebia," *Nezavisimaia gazeta,* 28 March 1992, p. 4.

15. Metropolitan Kirill of Smolensk appeared to cautiously endorse this program in his keynote address to the All-World Russian Assembly. See *Rossiiskaia gazeta,* 18 June 1993, p. 14.

16. See "Gribnitsa," *Obshchaia gazeta,* no. 5 (20–26 August 1993), p. 9.

17. *RFE/RL Daily Report,* 14 September 1993. The interview appeared in the 5–11 September 1993 issue of *Den',* p. 1. Khasbulatov used the term "Eurasian parliament."

18. For Khasbulatov's statement concerning the hajj, see *Komsomol'skaia pravda,* 27 July 1993, p. 3.

19. *RFE/RL Daily Report,* 15 September 1993.

20. This section summarizes material appearing in John B. Dunlop, *The Rise of Russia and the Fall of the Soviet Empire* (Princeton: Princeton University Press, 1993), pp. 158–63.

21. *RFE/RL Daily Report,* 2 July 1990.

22. *Literaturnaia Rossiia,* 26 April 1991, p. 17.

23. For the text of Sergii's 1927 "declaration of loyalty," see Matthew Spinka, *The Church in Soviet Russia* (New York: Oxford University Press, 1956), pp. 161–65.

24. *Literaturnaia gazeta,* 28 November 1990, p. 9.

25. *Sovetskaia Rossiia,* 22 December 1990, p. 1. According to a version circulated by the patriarch's defenders, he was ill in bed and was misinformed about the content of the "Letter of the Fifty-Three" by one of the signatories who telephoned him and asked for permission to add his name to the document.

26. See "Slovo Patriarkha Aleksiia," *Otdel vneshnykh tserkovnykh snoshenii Moskovskogo patriarkhata,* 16 January 1991, in *USSR Today,* 18 January 1991, p. 54/01–02.

27. Radio Mayak, 13 March 1991, in *USSR Today,* 13 March 1991, p. 230/49–50.

28. *Novoe vremia,* 1991, no. 22, p. 13.

29. On this question, see Oxana Antic, "Church Reaction to the Coup," *Report on the USSR,* 20 September 1991, pp. 15–17; and Vladimir Moss, "The Free Russian Orthodox Church," *Report on the USSR,* 1 November 1991, pp. 8–12.

30. See Aleksandr Nezhnyi, "Nad bezdnoi," *Ogonek,* 1991, no. 37.

31. *Kontinent,* 1992, no. 31.

32. Cited in *Rabochaia tribuna,* 17 February 1993, p. 4.

33. Jaroslaw Martyniuk, "Religious Preferences in Five Urban Areas of Ukraine," *RFE/RL Research Report,* 9 April 1993, pp. 52–55.

34. See John B. Dunlop, "The Russian Orthodox Church and Nationalism After 1988," *Religion in Communist Lands* (winter 1990), pp. 294–98.

35. See *Ukrainian Weekly,* 4 March 1990, p. 8.

36. See *Nezavisimaia gazeta,* 27 June 1992, p. 6.

37. See the detailed account of the Council in *Rabochaia tribuna,* 17 February 1993, p. 4.

38. "Domysly i pravda," *Pravda Ukrainy,* 17 August 1993, p. 3.

39. See Archpriest Victor S. Potapov, "By Silence Is God Betrayed," Voice of America, Washington, DC, 1992, p. 37.

40. *Ukrainian Weekly,* 21 March 1993, p. 3.

41. See *Nezavisimaia gazeta,* 27 June 1992, p. 6; and *Ukrainian Weekly,* 21 June 1992, p. 4.

42. *Ukrainian Weekly,* 21 June 1992, p. 4.

43. See *Ukrainian Weekly,* 28 June 1992, pp. 1, 13.

44. See *Rabochaia tribuna,* 17 February 1993, p. 4.

45. See "Ukraine Over the Brink," *Economist,* 4 September 1993, pp. 45–46; and "Ukraine Questions the Price Tag of Independence," *New York Times,* 8 September 1993, p. A9.

46. *Ukrainian Weekly,* 21 June 1993, p. 3.

47. See *RFE/RL Research Report,* 9 April 1993, p. 53.

48. "Pis'mo Patriarkha Prezidentu Ukrainy," *Megapolis ekspress,* 26 August 1992, p. 19.

49. See the Russian-language newspaper published in Ukraine, *Nezavisimost',* 28 July 1993. On Arsen Zinchenko and his role in promoting Ukrainian autocephaly, see *Moskovskie novosti,* 11 October 1992, p. 20. In September 1993, a Church Council elected Archbishop Dmytro (Iarema) the new patriarch of the Ukrainian Autocephalous Orthodox Church. See *Ukrainian Weekly,* 19 September 1993, p. 3.

50. *Megapolis ekspress,* 9 September 1992, p. 6.

51. *Megapolis ekspress,* 1992, no. 26, p. 3.

52. See *RFE/RL Daily Report,* 26 April 1991.

53. *Izvestiia,* 10 September 1992, p. 2.

54. See "Obrashchenie Arkhiepiskopa Vladimira k El'tsinu," *Tsfatul tserii,* 27 June 1992, p. 1.

55. See *Nezavisimaia gazeta,* 20 October 1992, p. 6.

56. See *Nezavisimaia gazeta,* 25 December 1992, p. 1.

57. Ibid.

58. *SM—segodnia,* 7 August 1992, p. 1.

59. See *Megapolis ekspress,* 23 September 1992. In Estonia, a similar struggle has recently broken out between that republic's parishes that are subordinate to the Moscow Patriarchate and the Estonian Department for Confessional Affairs, which seeks to deprive the Moscow parishes of property rights. (See Russian radio, 9 March 1994, in *Russia and CIS Today,* 10 March 1994, p. 0173/11 and *Rossiiskaia gazeta,* 6 October.)

60. *Megapolis ekspress,* 23 September 1992.

61. *Moskovskii komsomolets,* 4 February 1993.

62. As Fr. John Meyendorff has noted, "When Finland won its independence from Russia in 1918 one of the first acts of the Finnish Orthodox . . . was to remove the stigma of being called 'Russians' by the vast majority of Lutheran Finns, who tended to view Orthodoxy as a 'Russian faith.' So under the leadership of Archbishop Germanos Aab, in 1923, the Church of Finland placed itself under the jurisdiction of the ecumenical patriarch of Constantinople. Moscow protested against this situation, but finally in 1958 recognized the autonomous status of the Finnish Church." John Meyendorff, *The Orthodox Church* (New York: Pantheon, 1962), pp. 181–82. See also Metropolitan John of Helsinki, "The Finnish Orthodox Church" in *Eastern Christianity and Politics in the Twentieth Century,* ed. Pedro Ramet (Durham, NC: Duke University Press, 1988), pp. 267–85.

63. *Ukrainian Weekly,* 4 March 1990, p. 8.

64. *RFE/RL Daily Report,* 2 October 1992. In a recent interview with the Polish-language journal, *Kultura,* Metropolitan Filaret of Minsk claimed that the Belarusian church had ten bishops, eight hundred parishes, and roughly seven million adherents. *Kultura* (Paris), July–August 1993. I am grateful to my Hoover colleague Maciej Siekierski for bringing this information to my attention.

65. "Patriarkh i politiki," *Moskovskii tserkovnyi vestnik,* 1991, no. 10 (June).

66. *Economist,* 4 September 1993, p. 38.

67. See *RFE/RL Daily Report,* 25 February 1991.

68. Moscow Radio–1, 25 February 1991, in *USSR Today,* 25 February 1991, p. 170/47.

69. *Svobodnaia Gruziia,* 10 November 1992, p. 2.

70. See John B. Dunlop, " 'Kharchev Affair' Sheds New Light on Severe Controls on Religion in USSR," *Report on the USSR,* 23 February 1990, pp. 6–9.

71. *Argumenty i fakty,* 1992, no. 8 p. 5. Archpriest Viacheslav Polosin has asserted that the Department of External Ecclesiastical Relations effectively had been turned into "a secret center of KGB agents among the believers." *Nezavisimaia gazeta,* 20 February 1993, p. 4.

72. In *Moskovskie novosti,* 12 July 1992, p. 20.

73. On this, see Potapov, "By Silence Is God Betrayed," pp. 26–28; and John B. Dunlop, "KGB Subversion of Russian Orthodox Church," *RFE/RL Research Report,* 20 March 1992, pp. 51–53. Patriarch Aleksii has been identified as agent "Drozdov" by Zoia Krakhmal'nikova in *Novoe russkoe slovo* (New York), 3 March 1992, and by journalist Mikhail Pozdniaev in *Stolitsa,* 1992, no. 36. See also Keith Armes, "Chekists in Cassocks: The Orthodox Church and the KGB," *Demokratisatsiya,* 1993, no. 4, pp. 72–83.

74. *Ogonek,* 1992, nos. 18–19, p. 13. To date, the only Moscow Patriarchate bishop to publicly admit that he has served as a KGB agent has been Archbishop Khrizostom of Vilnius. See the interview with him in *Moskovskii komsomolets,* 30 November 1993, p. 2. Concerning the KGB's extensive use of church funds to finance secret police operations, see the open letter of Fr. Gleb Yakunin to the patriarch in *Ekspress-khronika,* 1994, no. 4, reprinted in *Russia and CIS Today,* 30 January 1994, pp. 64/22–29. According to journalist Iurii Buida, monies from this so-called black cashbox may have been employed by the KGB to fund political assassinations. See *Novoe vremia,* 1994, no. 5, pp. 50–51.

75. On Lorgus's article, see Iakov Krotov, "Proslavlenie stukachestva," *Moskovskie novosti,* 1993, no. 14, p. 9B.

76. "Pravoslavnaia tserkov' i vneshniaia politika," *Mezhdunarodnaia zhizn',* March 1993.

77. *Pravda,* 14 February 1992, p. 6.

78. See *Megapolis ekspress,* 22 July 1992, p. 19.

79. See *RFE/RL Daily Report,* 30 July 1992.

80. See *Crossroads,* 1 January 1993, p. 1.

81. See the interviews with Fr. Gleb Yakunin in *Kuranty,* 8 August 1992, p. 4, and with Lev Ponomarev in *Ogonek,* 1992, nos. 18–19. For a useful discussion of the "Bakatin period" of leadership in the KGB, see the article by former KGB Lieutenant Colonel Aleksandr Kichikhin in *Sibirskaia gazeta,* August–September 1993.

82. *Ogonek,* 1992, nos. 18–19.

83. *Moskovskii komsomolets,* 18 August 1993, p. 2.

84. For a vigorous defense by Ioann of the authenticity of the *Protocols,* see *Sovetskaia Rossiia,* 11 June 1993, p. 3.

85. Norman Cohn, *Warrant for Genocide* (New York: Harper and Row, 1966), p. 16.

86. *Sovetskaia Rossiia,* 10 October 1992. Republished in *Molodaia gvardiia,* 1993, no. 1. For a discussion of the *Protocols,* the Jewish-Masonic conspiracy, and other obsessions of present-day Russian right-wing ideology, see Walter Laqueur, *Black Hundred: The Rise of the Extreme Right in Russia* (New York: HarperCollins, 1993).

87. *Russkii sobor,* 1993, no. 6, p. 1.

88. Ibid.

89. In *Segodnia,* 2 March 1993, p. 7.

90. Ibid.

91. *Moskovskie novosti,* 7 March 1993. On Sergei Nilus, see Cohn, *Warrant for Genocide,* pp. 89–107.

92. Russian radio, 17 August 1993, in *Russia and CIS Today,* 18 August 1993, p. 0586/10.

93. *Sovetskaia Rossiia,* 12 August 1993, p. 3. Patriarch Aleksii addressed a conference of the Union of Orthodox Brotherhoods in February 1993. See *Moskovskii tserkovnyi vestnik,* 1993, nos. 5–6, p. 6.

94. *Sotsiologicheskie issledovaniia,* 1992, no. 7, pp. 3–12. For other recent polling data on Russian Orthodox believers, see Intertsentr VTsIOM, *Ekonomicheskie i sotsial'nye peremeny, monitoring obshchestvennogo mneniia,* no. 8 (December 1993), pp. 5–7.

95. "Pravoslavie bez molodezhi," *Moskovskie novosti,* 4 July 1993, p. 7A.

96. On *iosiflianstvo* or "Josephetism," see John B. Dunlop, *The New Russian Nationalism* (New York: Praeger, 1985), pp. 86–88.

97. *Segodnia,* 2 March 1993, p. 7.

98. *Moskovskie novosti,* 17–24 April 1994, p. 11A.

99. For Metropolitan Ioann's summons to expel unbaptized Jews from Russia, see his essay "Tvortsy kataklizmov" in *Sovetskaia Rossiia,* 22 March 1994, p. 4.

100. *Otrada: Informatsionnyi vestnik Russko-amerikanskogo obshchestva* (Spring Valley, NY), no. 3 (March 1994), p. 8.

101. For Zhirinovsky's statement that he is a religious "unbeliever," see *Literaturnaia Rossiia,* 12 July 1991.

102. See Vladimir Zhirinovskii, *Poslednii brosok na iug* (Moscow: "LDP," 1993). For Zhirinovsky's references to the role of the church in a future Russian empire, see pp. 75, 78, 95, 104, and 112.

103. See "Bosnian Serbs Hail Russian Nationalist," *Washington Post,* 1 February 1994, p. A16.

3

The Russian Orthodox Church in the Postcommunist CIS

Dimitry V. Pospielovsky

Past and Present

By 1989 the Orthodox believers in Ivanteevka, a Moscow satellite town of over fifty thousand inhabitants, had been trying for over three years to reopen a single church for worship. Their struggle went on, despite the decision by the Council of Ministers of the USSR, to which the believers had appealed, to restore the church to religious use. Local officials repeatedly responded in the negative, using the pretext that the building, together with an adjoining factory club, was going to be converted into a local history museum and a "culture-propaganda complex, needed very badly not only by the town, but by the county as well." Only after more public protests supported by the local green movement, which, as in most places in Russia, coincided or overlapped with church activists, the church was finally handed over to the believers by the end of 1989.[1]

Surely, such scenes belonged to a past era, gone with the collapse of communism in August 1991. Not quite so. A similar duel took place in Moscow in 1991–92. It involved a church adjacent to the grounds of Trekhgornaia manufaktura, a large Moscow industrial plant. The newspaper report has two photographs: one shows a church in ruins, the other, a demonstration of grade school children with big posters, protesting that the return of the church to believers would deprive the children of a club, forcing them back into the streets and basements. The smiling faces of the children betray the affair as an adult action. In fact, the demonstration was organized by the plant's administration on 15 May 1992 to commemorate the fiftieth anniversary of the Seventeenth Party Congress's declaration of the Five-Year Plan to Overcome Religion.

In postcommunist Moscow the parish council and its priest, recently appointed to the new church by the patriarch, were being blamed by the plant administration for depriving children of a place for play and relaxation. But since its forced closure in the 1930s the church had not been used for any such purpose. It was only when a parish action group had been formed and requested the return of the church that the administration of the plant hastily began its reconstruction into a children's club. The plant adminstration continued to resist the church's return to believers even after a decision of the Moscow City Council, signed by its president, to restore it to religious use. And despite Yeltsin's statement of 5 December 1991 that all "shrines, churches, monasteries, and sacred objects [will be returned] to the believers to whom by right they should belong," the plant's administrators threatened to use violence against the clergy and church activists. The real reason for the sudden concern for children was that on the spacious grounds of the church private homes were to be erected for the plant bosses.

The dispute was resolved by a squadron of paramilitary Siberian Cossacks, who occupied the site on 4 May.[2] What is the difference between 1989 and 1992? (And difference there is.) First, whereas the Ivanteevka case had been typical for 1988–90, in 1992 the Trekhgornaia manufaktura story was, as the article remarked, a sensation. Second, the confrontation was solved within six months. Third, since the October 1990 Law on the Freedom of Conscience made the church a juridical person—although no normative act on how to proceed with the transfer of former church property to the church, as promised by Yeltsin, has ever been issued—the law and the president's statement have put the church in a strong legal position, unprecedented since 1918. But fourth, the whole affair indicates a dangerous power vacuum at the top that was expressed in the factory bosses' indifference to the laws and decrees of both the central and the Moscow city government and their compliance only due to illegal use of force—a private army (the Cossacks). If we remember that originally the factory bosses threatened to use force, and that they as well as most of the local administrators are former communist bosses, the existence of a propensity for a dangerous civil war cannot be denied.

The Postcommunist Era

The New Status and the Revival of the Church

What is the real meaning of the 19–22 August 1991 events in general and for the church in particular? They could be seen as the last stage in the disintegration of the old communist establishment under its proper name, the days when the nation witnessed the CPSU's senility: it was unable even to organize a coup d'état properly. At the same time it marked the replacement of some semblance of central power with an unstable power vacuum, setting in motion a centrifugal process of decomposition of the USSR.

As far as the church is concerned, the de facto postcommunist era began to dawn with the adoption of the new church statute at the Millennial Church

Council in 1988 and the statute's de jure confirmation as a result of the adoption on 1 October 1990 of the USSR Law on the Freedom of Conscience. The final version of this law was largely the result of revisions of the original version carried out by the June 1990 Local Church Council, which had elected the new patriarch and submitted the draft of the law to severe criticism. After the Council the newly elected patriarch, Aleksii II, went straight to Gorbachev, protesting that the draft law did not go far enough. Among the gains made by the church in subsequent joint deliberations in the Supreme Soviet were extensions of the rights of parish rectors and educational rights of the church. Having participated in the making of the USSR Law on the Freedom of Conscience, the church was even more successful with the RSFSR Law on the Freedom of Conscience of 25 October, which is not only more favorable to religion than the USSR law but also, with the abolition of the USSR, remains the only valid law on religion on the territory of Russia.[3]

The law establishes every registered religious association as a social organization with the full status of a legal person. In contrast to the Lenin-Stalin laws, believers and religious organizations have the right to disseminate their teachings. The law stipulates that Russia is a secular state in which both atheism and religion are separated from the state and may be financed only with private funds. The right of conscientious objection to military service is recognized as replaceable by alternative forms of service.[4]

In contrast to the USSR law, which banned the teaching of religion in state schools, the Russian law leaves to headmasters the decision of whether to permit the teaching of religion as an optional subject by personnel approved by the church (usually priests), while "the teaching of religion in an academic or epistemological framework, and of religious-philosophical disciplines, . . . not accompanied by rites and ceremonies and informative in nature, may be included in the educational program of state educational institutions." Believers are now protected by law from the use of their places of worship for the conduct of any "atheistic events." In contrast to the USSR and Ukrainian laws, the RSFSR legislation abolished its Council for Religious Affairs (CRA). However, in 1992 both the Moscow and St. Petersburg city administrations established offices for liaison with religious organizations staffed by former CRA officials, and the Russian government was moving in the same direction, over the protests of the Russian church.

Article 17 explicitly recognizes the charters and statutes of religious organizations as legal documents. Previously, the state recognized only groups of twenty lay persons as representing a local group of believers responsible for a church building leased by the state to that group of twenty. Now parishes, dioceses, and the central patriarchate have been granted full legal recognition in accordance with the 1988 statute.

The judicial organs have responsibility for registering the charter of a religious group within one month of its submission. If refused, the case goes "to the

Expert Review and Consultation Council of the RSFSR Supreme Soviet for its conclusions. In such event, the time frame for registration may be extended to three months. . . . Denial of registration of the charter . . . may be appealed in the courts." Churches receive the right to "conduct religious rites in military units," prisons, hospitals, and so forth.

Like most other social organizations, religions are allowed to engage in business, establish workshops, factories, and shops, and possess and cultivate land. The exorbitant taxation on the income and products of such enterprises has been reduced to the level of taxes imposed on such endeavors by any other social organization. Church employees, including clergy, are taxed on a par with state employees, while funds and donations used for charity or cultural preservation are tax-deductible. Social security and pensions of the clergy and other church employees are now the same as those of the rest of the population.[5]

The 1988 statute, in general, restored a canonical conciliar structure of the church roughly approximating, although not quite matching, the 1918 statutes. It put particular emphasis on the restoration of the self-governing parish as the basic unit for the revival of active participation by the laity. It also stressed the importance of church charity and educational work (both illegal prior to the state laws enacted October 1990).

In the spirit of the 1988 statute, though strictly speaking still illegal, lay church brotherhoods,[6] in all cases presided over by a priest, began to arise or come out of the underground in the course of 1989–90. Just before the passage of the new state laws permitting such activities, a congress of representatives of the brotherhoods, convoked in Moscow on 12–13 October 1990, formed the All-Russian Union of Church Brotherhoods, which was technically illegal prior to the passage of the Law on the Freedom of Conscience. A little later, on 25 January 1991, a congress of parish youth representatives gathered at Moscow State University under the joint honorary chairmanship of the patriarch and the university rector and formed an All-Russian Orthodox Youth Movement, which elected the then thirty-three-year-old Bishop Aleksandr of Kostroma as its chairman. Both groups are engaged in aiding church education, catechization, charity activities, and, particularly in the case of the Youth Movement, the restoration of churches and monasteries that were returned to the believers in ruins. In 1991 alone there were already fourteen Youth Movement summer camps at the sites of monasteries, and many more were formed in 1992.[7]

Within a month of the death of seventy-nine-year-old Patriarch Pimen in May 1990, the current patriarch, sixty-one-year-old Aleksii II, was elected by a secret ballot of the most democratic Local Council (*sobor*) of clergy and laity since 1918. It is with his ascent that the postcommunist era in the life of the church really began, with the August 1991 putsch and its collapse assuming the role of very important signposts. It is arguable, however, that as long as the Communist Party remained in power there could be no guarantee that the newly won legal rights of the church, or any laws in fact, would be respected and could prevail over the interests of the party. Indeed, since the putsch the process of restoring churches to their owners was initially quite swift, but it began to stall in about mid-1992. A local government would approve the return of a building to the church, but the actual transfer would take months, even years, or simply would not happen at all, because the firm, organization, business, museum, or theater group occupying the building had nowhere to go. This is even truer of secular buildings that had belonged to the church and whose return was being sought for use either as ecclesiastic educational or charity institutions or as rectories. The point is, with the process of privatization of property and the rise of private enterprise, many such buildings, and almost all uninhabited buildings, have been sold to enterprises by local governments starved for cash. Even President Yeltsin's decree of 23 April 1993, On the Transferring of Religious Structures and Other Properties to Religious Organizations, has had very little effect, owing both to the lack of a normative act on the subject and the already discussed reasons.[8]

The Patriarch Under Attack

The postcommunist era confronted the church with new problems. As long as the communist dictatorship remained, even in its watered-down version of the Gorbachev years, most opposition forces and dissidents tried to minimize their internal differences, or rather play them down in the face of the common enemy. The church was the embodiment of the only tolerated teachings contrary to Marxism. It was moreover the only surviving overt institution linking the present generations with the Russian non-Marxist cultural and historical heritage. To any thinking Soviet citizen it was clear that the church could survive under the totalitarian communist pressure only at the cost of considerable compromise and certain forms of cooperation of its leadership with the Soviet regime and its organs and that it was impossible to play such a visible role, particularly internationally, in the World Council of Churches and other organizations, without close contacts with the KGB. All this was suspected and whispered about in dissidents' kitchens until it became clear that the days of the communist regime were numbered, especially after the collapse of the putsch.

Two parallel processes appeared with the final decline of communism and the growing tide of revelations about the crimes of the regime in the ever freer mass media and the belated publication of Solzhenitsyn's works. On the one hand, the nation's eyes began to turn toward the church in the hope that it would bring Russia spiritual renewal, as reflected in numerous respectable public opinion polls of 1989–91. Polls showed an incredible increase of believers: from 27 percent in 1990 to 40 percent in 1992. Those who considered themselves Orthodox Christians likewise increased: from 19 percent in 1989 to 33 percent of the population in 1990. Yet only 3 percent of the alleged Orthodox sector took communion at least once a month in 1991; that is, from a strict theological point of view, fewer than two million citizens of Russia were true members of the church. Thus a 1992 poll in which only 15 percent of the population declared themselves Orthodox, while those calling themselves merely *Christian* grew from 22 percent in 1990 to 52 percent in 1992, may have put the low communicants' figure into its proper context. Another poll in 1990 showed that 64 percent of the population trusted the church, but only 5 percent trusted the CPSU.[9]

But elements critical of the Moscow Patriarchate's past record of relations with the communist authorities who had held their tongues in the past now came out with their attacks into the open. These forces included some dissidents who had been imprisoned directly or indirectly for religious activities criminally punishable prior to the new laws of 1990 and groups and individuals who began to claim, rightly or wrongly, that they had belonged to the severely persecuted so-called "True Orthodox" or "Catacomb Church."[10] At the same time the extremist right-wing monarchist émigré church group, the so-called Russian Orthodox Church Outside Russia (ROCOR), which has excluded itself from intercommunion with all local Orthodox churches that recognize the sacramental validity of the Moscow Patriarchate, decided to take advantage of the free-for-all situation in Russia.

On 15–16 May 1990 a Council of Bishops of ROCOR meeting in Jordanville, New York, with the participation of their formerly secret bishop from Russia, Lazarus,[11] resolved to establish parishes and even dioceses under their jurisdiction on the territory of the Soviet Union. Realizing the absurdity of parishes in Russia belonging to a "Church Outside Russia," the ROCOR now officially named its parishes in Russia the Free Russian Orthodox Church. The resolutions rationalized the decision to set up a parallel church network in Russia by claiming that the Moscow Patriarchate's sacraments lacked charisma, that therefore its clerics could join the ROCOR only through repentance for having served in the Moscow Patriarchate, and that no relations or even negotiations with the Moscow Patriarchate could take place until it fulfilled the following conditions:

1. Condemned Metropolitan Sergii's 1927 Declaration of Loyalty to the Soviet State and its subsequent subordination of the church to the atheistic communist government;
2. Its hierarchy and the whole clergy publicly repented for their collaboration with the atheistic and theomachistic state;
3. Exposed and carried out a purge of the most politically compromised members of the clergy;
4. Pulled out of all ecumenical bodies, primarily the World Council of Churches.

The first response, that of the Council that had elected Aleksii II as patriarch, was very modest and humble, appealing to the ROCOR faithful to reflect on the fact that the establishment of a parallel church of the same faith as the church of the Moscow Patriarchate but hostile to it would only harm the Orthodox common cause, and that by ignoring the Moscow Patriarchate as the legitimate local church of Russia the ROCOR excluded itself from the ecumenical family of Orthodox churches, of which the Russian Orthodox Church is a member.[12] A sterner message, contained in the October 1990 encyclical of the Council of Bishops of the Russian church to its clergy and laity, stated that the ROCOR, which had closely collaborated with the Nazis, had no moral right to condemn the Russian church for its involuntary collaboration with the communists.[13]

The patriarch responded to the ROCOR demand both implicitly and explicitly. He chose the anniversary of the Bolshevik "October Revolution" in 1990 to make the first moral-political statement of the church since the 1920s. He called the event "a bitter page" in Russia's history that should "remind us that not a single political, cultural, or national idea is worth more than a human life. . . . Do not let the spirit of mutual hatred and vengeance once again celebrate its victory in Russia! . . . Those who can, join me and the church in the following prayer: O Lord, renew, protect and make wise our nation, for in 'distress it sought thee, it poured out a prayer when thy chastening was upon it.' (Isaiah 26:16)."[14]

Responding directly to the ROCOR conditions, the patriarch declared that he took full responsibility upon himself for all the compromises and mendacious statements the historical church was forced to make during the past seven decades, whether committed before or during his archpastorate. As to Metropolitan Sergii's 1927 declaration, had he been there, he could only have wept together with the metropolitan, who had to issue it against his will in the hope of saving the lives of his imprisoned bishops. He agreed that ecclesiastically the declaration was wrong and therefore irrelevant to today's church, but at the time Sergii believed he was thereby saving the church from total destruction. And to those who say that the gates of hell cannot overcome the church, the patriarch replied that this is true of the Church Universal, but numerous historical churches of the past had disappeared, and this could have happened to the church of Russia, at least hypothetically, as well.

Then he reminisced about how he managed to save his own Estonian diocese from closing churches during Khrushchev's attack on the church by constant compromises on other issues. And he asked forgiveness of those Christians who may have been tempted by his political compromises. On another occasion he praised the "catacomb Christians" for their steadfastness and martyrdom and said that there were two roads during the persecution years: seek personal salvation and sacrifice by hiding the unblemished church in the catacombs, hidden not only from the KGB but from masses of believers as well; or by all sorts of compromises keep the church doors visible and open for those who seek.[15] On the issue of repentance the patriarch said that every Christian ought to repent for his sins all the time, but how can a church as a collective body repent before its people when it is the people? Besides, had a large part of the Russian people not joined the Bolshevik attack on the church and left it defenseless, it would not have been forced by the Bolsheviks to make the compromises for which now it is being denounced. Yet on Forgiveness Sunday (the last Sunday before Lent), the patriarch, after giving a sermon on the past sins of the church, dropped to his knees, facing the flock crowding his cathedral, and bowed to the ground three times, exclaiming, "Forgive me, my children! Forgive me, my dear ones! Forgive me!"

On the ecumenism issue he stood his ground by admitting that the World Council of Churches and other such international bodies have often been used politically, but "only those people who have lost the sense of duty to declare the truth of Orthodoxy to confessionally divided Christendom and to fulfill Christ's command on the unity within Him of all His followers can call for the end to the dialogue with Christians of other confessions in the twentieth century."[16]

On several occasions he warned against and condemned extreme nationalism and anti-Semitism. On the prospects of a new state-church symbiosis he said that a state church could flourish only if 100 percent of the population were practicing members of the church, not even 90 percent. Otherwise, nothing good comes out of a symbiosis where the church begins to be used as a weapon: "And when the church is used as a club, it disintegrates into sawdust." Addressing the intelligentsia, the patriarch pointed out that the church should not be seen only as a nostalgic remnant of the past; it is also a pointer to the future.[17]

The Church, Its Critics, and the KGB

No sooner had Aleksii been elected patriarch than one of his own leftist priests, Georgii Edel'shtein, named him a KGB informer on the basis of an internal Council for Religious Affairs report of the 1960s on a conversation with the young Archbishop Aleksii on the possible candidates for the patriarchate should the ninety-year-old Patriarch Aleksii I die. Archbishop Aleksii spoke about the individual characters and personal strengths and weaknesses of the two most likely candidates. There is not a single political element in his deposition, nothing that could lead any one of them to trouble with the KGB. Yet the story (available in the West since the 1970s)[18] reappeared periodically in 1990–92 in Russian democratic newspapers as incriminatory evidence against him,[19] whereafter every excuse was used by them to defame the patriarch.

On 10 July 1991 Yeltsin took the oath as the first democratically elected president of Russia in its history. He asked the patriarch to bless him at the ceremony, which the patriarch did with a brief exhortation:

> There is no sense today in searching for some personifications of evil in our country, thinking that having found them our country will rise to its feet. . . . Once the communist rulers of Russia thought that having gained power they would form a new . . . "human material," as they used to say.
>
> We are witnesses of the tragedy that is the result of their inability to appreciate where the true source of the sinful corruption of life is to be found. . . .

> Boris Nikolaevich! Forgive people! Be merciful to them! Human beings . . .
> cannot be changed overnight, or even in five hundred days. Our sick society,
> and people who have suffered so much, need understanding, love, and toler-
> ance. We ought to remind ourselves frequently of the Apostle's words: "Take
> up each other's burdens, and thus ye will fulfill the law of Jesus."[20]

No sooner was this speech printed than the Russian "democrats" began to
protest that this smelled of the restoration of a state church. The traditionally
secular, unchurched, and predominantly agnostic Russian liberal intelligentsia,
making no distinction between secular pluralism and church canons that allow
only one bishop in one place, and believing that there is safety in numbers and
that the ROCOR was politically unblemished, began to lend it support. The
patriarch replied to one such journalist that a church headquartered in the United
States may not establish its parishes on the territory of the bishop of Moscow,
just as much as the bishop of Tashkent cannot establish his parish in this diocese,
and vice versa. Moreover, he said, the Moscow Patriarchate is the sole legal inheri-
tor and descendent of the prerevolutionary Russian church through Patriarch Tikhon
and his successors. The ROCOR not only was made up of clergy who had abandoned their dioceses and parishes, and thus could have no legal claim on them again,
but by negating the validity of the Russian church and forbidding intercommunion
with all other local Orthodox churches, it had removed itself from the Orthodox
universe (*oikoumene*). This is not to deny its right to exist in a secular democratic
state. But in relation to the Orthodox Church its rights are no different from those of
the Baptist Church, for instance: it may establish and build temples for its faithful,
but it can have no claim on existing Russian Orthodox Church property.[21]

It should be noted that in the course of 1990–91 the attack on the Moscow
Patriarchate for its alleged intolerance of the ROCOR initiative on Russian soil
came simultaneously from the left and the right.[22] In fact, the leftist press constantly accused the church and the patriarch of preferring the rightist and "patriotic groups," claiming that the patriarch's admonitions of the latter have been
milder and more compassionate than his criticism of the left. An official summation of the patriarch's policies and statements during his first year in office drew
the critics' attention to several issues, including the patriarch's repeated warnings
against blind imitation of the prerevolutionary past, even in church life and
practices; his condemnation of chauvinism and anti-Semitism; and his comments
that once the threat of communist totalitarianism began to wither away, the
democratic journalists turned their wrath against the Orthodox Church,

> trying to convince themselves and others . . . that Orthodoxy is an impediment
> to a democratic development of Russia. . . . As a result of this, the democratic
> movement deprives itself of members with deep Orthodox Christian convic-
> tions; while lovers of personal and social freedom begin to shun the church.
> One of the forces on which Russia's greatness depends is the ability of the
> intelligentsia . . . to cooperate in a common effort for the renewal of the souls
> of our people.[23]

The summation also cites the patriarch's categorical protest against a Supreme Soviet member's suggestion to mobilize the clergy to rescue the state. Finally, both the summation and the patriarch drew attention to the paradox that the democrats have been supporting the most reactionary, antidemocratic, and rigid branch of the Russian church, the one that had caused all the émigré church schisms.

Although both the USSR and the Russian Supreme Soviets had rejected the proposal of church representatives to legitimize armed forces chaplains in their respective draft Law on the Freedom of Conscience, only a few months later top Soviet military commanders on their own initiative began to negotiate with the church leaders on the same subject; but the patriarch's word was that this was impossible as long as the armed forces were politicized and had communist political commissars. At the end of May 1992, in this author's presence, the patriarch confided this information to a mass audience at a public conference, adding that now, as the army has been depoliticized, it is the duty of the Orthodox Church to begin to train special pastors for the armed forces, hospitals, and other public institutions.

The logic of the link between his reaction to Soviet generals in 1991, prior to August, and the above statement of 1992 indicates his political vision, the genuineness of his support for the anti-coup forces in August 1991, and the unfoundedness of his many critics' claims that Patriarch Aleksii's statement of 20 August (published in *Izvestiia* on the next day) questioning the legitimacy of the coup, requesting the public appearance of Gorbachev, the legitimate leader, and appealing to the armed forces "to prevent the shedding of blood" so that the nation would be able to build its home "according to its freely chosen way and the universal norms of morality and justice" was but a forced, belated, and opportunistically oblique statement. To begin with, it was far from clear in the afternoon of 20 August who was going to prevail in the conflict, and the patriarch had to think about the future of his church in case the putsch succeeded. Second, his opposition to it was manifested already on 19 August, the Feast of the Transfiguration of Our Lord (according to the Julian Calendar), when serving the liturgy in the Kremlin Dormition Cathedral he ordered the clergy not to commemorate the government and the armed forces in the litanies.[24] Third, the patriarch showed on which side he was almost eight months before the putsch when he expressed his sympathy and condolences to the Lithuanian victims of the Soviet army attack in Vilnius in January 1991, protested against the brutalities, and appealed to the Soviet armed forces not to do this again; that is, he indirectly suggested insubordination to unjust commands.[25]

One of the consequences of August was the partial opening of the KGB archives. The result was the formation of the Supreme Soviet Commission to Investigate the Causes and Circumstances of the August 1991 Putsch. A special section of the commission, headed by Lev Ponomarev and Fr. Gleb Yakunin, acquired access to some KGB archives on its use of churchmen. On 6 March

1992 the commission submitted to the leadership of the Moscow Patriarchate a report detailing the methods of the KGB in hiring agents among bishops and other leading personnel of the church.[26] With no great difficulty it became possible to decipher some of the real personalities behind the KGB pseudonyms given them. These included Metropolitans Pitirim, Iuvenalii, and Filaret of Kiev, as well as the late Nikodim of Leningrad, and even the present patriarch when still a metropolitan. Among the documents there were some boastful reports of a junior KGB official to his boss that he had managed to recruit a very important agent who would do important work in demoralizing the World Council of Churches. The KGB seems to have held in particularly high esteem as its agents Filaret of Kiev, Pitirim, and Iuvenalii. And thus the dissidents' wrath fell especially heavily on these three heads. Members of the commission had just begun their investigation and had only for comparison's sake taken a quick look through other faiths, coming to the conclusion that all religions of the Soviet Union had been similarly infiltrated, Muslims more heavily than others, when Khasbulatov, chairman of the Supreme Soviet, ordered the investigation stopped, allegedly on Patriarch Aleksii's request. The vice-chairman of the commission, Fr. Gleb Yakunin, said that this act prevented a proper study of the situation with other religions, thus giving the Orthodox Church unjustly bad public-ity, as if its clergy alone cooperated with the KGB. In fact, Father Yakunin and his colleagues complimented themselves on the fact that only the Orthodox had mem-bers of sufficient moral power to make public their ills, while all other religions, no less implicated, have avoided such bad publicity about themselves and made no attempt to undertake similar investigations. Others argue that at this moment, when the nation is wholly disoriented and disturbed, it needs to see a pillar of moral force in the church, and such revelations achieve nothing except depriving many of that moral support and creating an even unhealthier atmosphere of more distrust and suspicion.[27] Such matters, they say, should be put off to more peaceful days.

But there were other flaws with the whole affair. First, the boastful reports of KGB officers to their superiors about the particular worth of the bishop-agents should be taken with a grain of salt: the reporting officer will more certainly than not try thereby to earn an extra star on his shoulder. Second, not a single one of the reports obtained by the commission contained any information on what the agents actually did; was any one of them guilty of denouncing anybody to the KGB? Without such information the documents were not real indictments, be-cause every person on whom there was a KGB file had an assumed name, for example, Solzhenitsyn's KGB name was Spider, Sakharov's, the Ascetic. Third, Yakunin admitted that the commission members were not allowed to browse through the KGB files freely, but were handed files by the KGB. The files could have been specially selected and compiled with some ulterior motive in mind, for example, to undermine the growing respect for religion by discrediting it with KGB connections, thereby continuing the seven-decades-old struggle against religion by new means. But whatever their faults, the fact remains that Metropol-itan Iuvenalii has been a very active and popular administrator of the Moscow provincial diocese; Pitirim has been a very controversial figure, hated by many, distrusted by most, yet prominent in public relations at home and abroad; the late Nikodim had been an extraordinary personality who, despite his external loyalty to the Soviet state and prominent assistance rendered to Soviet foreign policy propaganda, was never trusted by the CRA, which, not without reason, "accused" him of being a dedicated churchman actively hostile to Marxist ideology.[28] Patriarch Aleksii's merits have already been discussed. While attacking the above bishops there is a conspicuous silence on such notorious figures among the bishops as Metropolitan Mefodii of Voronezh, Archbishop Feodosii of Omsk, and several other morally and politically corrupt figures.[29] Further evidence that this may be part of a campaign to compromise the church, deviously guided by the old antireligious forces in the KGB and the former Agitprop, is the current hate campaign being conducted by the neo-Nazi Union of Orthodox Brotherhoods against the best-educated and most publicly active Russian Orthodox clergy, accusing them all of disseminating a Judaic heresy within the church. Besides the absurdity of the accusation, their choice of names leads one to the above conclusion. It includes personalities whose ages range from twenty to seventy and whose ideas are as diverse as can be within one church: from pro-Westerners to anti-Westerners, from monarchists to liberals. The only things they share are high erudition and intelligence, popularity, a high profile, a successful ministry, and missionary achievements. The list of these "Judaizers" is headed by the late Fr. Aleksandr Men', whom the Brotherhood Union names the chief perpetrator of the Judaic heresy and who was mysteriously and savagely murdered in September 1990. His murder was followed by similarly savage murders (preceded by torture) of two other prominent Moscow priests within five months following Father Men''s murder. Just as mysteriously, none of these murders has been solved by the investigative organs. These may be construed as an interconnected chain of acts aimed at liquidation or defamation of the most prominent or active clergy in order to render it as "harmless" as possible from the atheists' point of view and odious in the eyes of the general public.[30]

The KGB revelations caused a sensation. They became another pretext for former dissidents like Edel'shtein, Krakhmal'nikova, and such sensation-prone journals as *Stolitsa*[31] to unfurl new attacks on the patriarch and other bishops, bringing up again the 1967 CRA report. Even before the KGB documents, the popular Leningrad TV program "The Fifth Wheel," showing the funeral of Fr. Aleksandr Men'—a thorn in the side of the KGB and all atheists for many years, as he had brought literally thousands of intellectuals to the church (he had been called the chief pastor to the intelligentsia)—officiated by Metropolitan Iuvenalii, insinuated that Iuvenalii had arranged the murder. But lo and behold, Father Men''s widow asked Metropolitan Iuvenalii to preside over the written legacy and archives of her husband.[32]

Nevertheless, in response to the above report the All-Russian Council of Bishops of 30 March–4 April 1990 formed a commission to investigate the charges of the clergy's ties with the KGB. It is chaired by the thirty-five-year-old Bishop Aleksandr of Kostroma, consecrated in 1990, that is, in the post-KGB era, and known for his political integrity and his former troubles with the KGB. The commission is made up entirely of clergymen ordained and consecrated after 1989. The Council's address chastised the press for turning incomplete bits of information into sensations but welcomed an honest, critical public "discussion on the past and present of the church, conducted competently, honestly, responsibly, and with love for one's fellow man."[33] So far no visible results of the church Commission on Clergy-KGB Relations have transpired; and this author knows for certain of only one man engaged in such research in the KGB archives, a genuine scholar and integrally honest monk, Father Damaskin (Orlovskii).

The commotion subsided rather quickly, in no small measure thanks to the above address of the Council, but even more so thanks to confessions of some clergymen on what was often involved in such collaboration or how cooperation with the KGB was being avoided in their particular instances and thus may have been similar in most other cases as well. One of the most authoritative voices was that of Archbishop Khrizostom, currently of Lithuania, known for his independence and daring and for having therefore been demoted in the past from the post of deputy head of the church's external relations to the diocese of Irkutsk in eastern Siberia. He disclosed that in his case, being a KGB "agent" for eighteen years amounted to submitting written reports after each trip abroad. Thus, returning from Ethiopia shortly before the fall of the monarchy, he wrote in the report that the monarchy was about to fall and a radical revolution there was imminent. When this "prophecy" was fulfilled six months later, his prestige grew tremendously in the KGB. He believes most clergymen's cooperation with the KGB was as innocent as his. Another priest protested against Edel'shtein's claim that every second priest cooperated with the KGB. Another priest, Shargenov, vowed he always refused such cooperation from his student days at a foreign languages institute, wherefore he was never allowed to go abroad. At twenty-five he had converted, went to a seminary, and was later ordained. Again refusing to work for the KGB, he was prevented from teaching at a seminary until 1989. He knows about twenty priests very well and as many seminarians. All of them had been approached by the KGB prior to 1989, and all refused any cooperation. In conclusion, he believed that the maximum possible proportion of KGB collaborators among the clergy could not have been more than 10 percent, roughly corresponding to the percentage of traitors among the Apostles.[34]

As far as the patriarch is concerned, a recently discovered document tells more about his real self than the overt actions of the last, safe years. The document is a letter to Gorbachev, written on 17 December 1985 by then Metropolitan Aleksii, chancellor of the Moscow Patriarchate, who owing to Patriarch Pimen's senility was really running the patriarchate. Using Aesopian terms, the only acceptable language at that time, the metropolitan tries to convince the new general secretary that the separation of church and state does not at all mean the exclusion of the church from all public and social life. He writes, "The church could actively and decisively struggle against all sorts of vices and illnesses of our society, help improve the spiritual and moral health of the people." Gorbachev passed this letter on to the CPSU Central Committee Secretariat, which concluded that the metropolitan represented that part of the clergy "that wants to gain social influence for the church." This was intolerable, the secretariat ruled, and ordered the Council for Religious Affairs to take the necessary steps. And taken they were: on 13 March 1986, Aleksii lost the all-important job of chancellor and was transferred to Leningrad as its metropolitan.[35] This is not martyrdom, of course, but it shows that even in those years, in his quiet way, the patriarch was constantly struggling for the good of the church and always had in mind a moral-spiritual role for the church in society and independence from the state structures.

In his letter, he went on to say that however much the church is separated from the state, it will be linked to the nation by invisible threads. And indeed, despite all the anti-patriarchal and anti-Moscow Patriarchate propaganda in the media, in a poll carried out at the end of February 1992 on the popularity of public figures in the former USSR, of the sixteen most popular persons, the patriarch ranked second, with 47 percent positive support, compared to Yeltsin's 54 percent; but on the negative vote the patriarch had the best score: only 4 percent disliked him, compared to 19 percent who disliked Yeltsin.[36] But the continuing lack of official information from the Moscow Patriarchate on the subject of the clergy's involvement with the KGB does the church no good, and this has probably begun to reflect itself in the falling popularity of the patriarch and the church he heads, although not so long ago the church enjoyed enormous popularity as the spiritual core of the nation and the most important antipode to Marxist materialism. Thus, in a June 1993 list of one hundred leading politicians in Russia, the patriarch slid to fortieth place (poor consolation: the church-KGB link attacker, Father Yakunin, was in ninety-third place). When asked which leading personality influenced the respondent's turn to religion, Aleksii II took fifth place, with only 10 percent of the respondents naming him, after such lay persons as Solzhenitsyn, with 15 percent, and the Christian secular scholar Academician D. Likhachev, with 14 percent. This closely matches another question: "What is the main source of your religious weltanschauung?" Nine percent named the church and its clergy. For 39 percent the main religious informer was the media, and for 21 percent, the Bible and other religious literature.[37]

Despite this cooling off toward the national church and its leadership, the above poll revealed a continuation of "the religious boom." Not only has the proportion of believers increased in three years from 27 to 40 percent, but, what probably is more telling, the proportion of people who declare that religion plays no role whatsoever in their lives has decreased from 25 percent in 1990 to 14 percent in 1992; and, deducting the other 75 percent who expressed different degrees of religious influence upon themselves, we end up with merely 11 percent who apparently continue to express hostility toward religion. Generally one encounters a consensus in Russia of negative attitudes towards atheism, even among nonbelievers, as a weltanschauung with no place for absolute concepts of good and evil. This view has been typically reflected by Tat'iana Koriagina, a noted economist and member of the Supreme Soviet, when she linked economic problems of postcommunist Russia to atheism: "An atheist society is defenseless against evil," she said, against the monopoly of criminals in business. In her opinion, both communists, who have been the first to engage in money making, and democrats brought up on Marxist materialistic relativism defend the right of criminals to launder their capital and enter into legitimate business, thus creating a double standard: fraud and theft by the poor is punishable, but for the rich commendable.[38]

The Effect of Foreign Missions

It is precisely because of the high expectations from the church and from Christianity in general, which for the vast majority of Russians is personified in the Orthodox Church,[39] that all the above schisms and religious, or seemingly religious, conflicts have such a painful effect in Russia. The Orthodox Church may be tolerant and friendly toward other religions, but it will never subscribe to the Anglican branch theory. For the Orthodox there can be only one church, the Orthodox, with its direct succession from the ecumenical councils and denial of the right of any individual bishops, be they popes or Luthers, to establish new dogmas or doctrines. The more ecumenically minded Orthodox see Roman Catholicism as a part of that one church, although an erring part. As for Protestants, the Orthodox would at best agree that they may possess bits and pieces of the true Christian teachings, whereby Protestants who lead a true Christian life within their religions may be saved.

The influx of heterodox preachers from the West baffles both churched and unchurched Russians. Churches competing with each other, trying to outdo each other, taking advantage of the economic bankruptcy of the Orthodox Church and, as it were, buying converts by offering free English-language classes, credits to businessmen, and food parcels for converts, in which American fundamentalists are actively engaged, makes religions in the eyes of the average Russian no better than traders in the marketplace.

This aggressive influx of American Protestant fundamentalists of all kinds as well as plain non-Christians, such as Mormons or Jehovah's Witnesses, cannot be viewed in a friendly manner by the Orthodox. Indeed, they complain that the Protestant fundamentalists behave in Russia as if it had never known Christianity and was a country of pagan savages.[40]

Even more painful for the Orthodox was the unilateral decision of the current pope to establish Roman Catholic dioceses there. They may be justified, although not in such numbers, in Belarus and Ukraine, where there used to be several Roman Catholic dioceses before the revolution, but there have never been Roman Catholic bishops in Moscow, Novosibirsk, and Karaganda.

At numerous conferences of the Roman Catholic-Orthodox Dialogue, including the meeting of the leading theologians of both churches in Freising (Bavaria) in 1990, it was resolved that the two are sister-churches and that no proselytism would take place on each other's territory. Hence, it was to be expected that before sending bishops onto the historical territory of the Orthodox Church the pope would at least consult or inform the Russian Orthodox Church. But he did nothing of the sort, implying thereby that the former Soviet Union was a territory open for mission and Catholic conquest.[41]

Instead of helping the Orthodox sister-church schools and seminaries to survive these years of financial catastrophe due to the devaluation of the ruble, the Roman bishop of Moscow has established a Roman Catholic theological college in Moscow, and he is actively engaged, along with the Roman bishop of Novosibirsk, in converting Russian youth to Roman Catholicism, according to Russian sources.

The patriarchate's message to Western Christians is the following: Do you recognize us, Orthodox, as Christians or not? If you do, then instead of trying to outwit and outmaneuver us, causing moral harm to Christianity as such in the eyes of nonbelievers, many of whom are potential Christians and who are often turned away by this ugly competition, you ought to help the Russian Orthodox Church in this dire moment of economic collapse, shortages of clergy and theological schools, and temporary inability to open a sufficient number of schools owing to the lack of money and colossal expenditures on the restoration and building of churches. You ought to help the Orthodox Church to successfully carry out its mission on its native soil. Your versions of Christianity are alien to the Russian spiritual tradition and its whole culture. Therefore, to obtain converts for your faiths you have to spend umpteen times more effort and money than the Orthodox Church. The country now is in a general state of collapse; crime is on the rise. Your option is not between making Russia Orthodox Christian, Roman Catholic, or Baptist, because Russians will never convert to Protestantism or Roman Catholicism in great numbers. These religions can only hope to pick up fringes, and at very high cost to themselves, while causing bitterness toward such disorienting inter-Christian competition and hence to Christianity among the masses. Unchurched, living in a moral vacuum and an anarchic chaos (because without moral values democracy degenerates into anarchy) but with a nuclear arsenal, the country will be a greater danger to its neighbors than ever. The choice is between a totalitarian monster and an Orthodox Christian democracy.[42]

Internal Threats to the Church

The national-Bolshevik/neo-Nazi, fascist, and general right-wing pro-monarchist elements are gaining strength as the so-called forces of democracy (mostly consisting of former communists, at least in positions of importance) lose public support owing to, on the one hand, their colossal corruption, and on the other, "reforms" that sink the nation ever deeper into poverty. Thus the correctness of the patriarch's strong support for the democratic forces, especially during the putsch, is being questioned. Neither is the "democratic era" helpful to the church in the moral sphere. Besides corruption, the last two years have been marked by a salient depreciation of public morals: twelve-year-olds sell pornography openly and with impunity in metro passages; prostitution, striptease clubs, and porno-graphic films have literally inundated the country, along with rising crime. The "democrats," thinking of themselves as successors of the Russian prerevolution-ary Westernist secular intelligentsia, are predominantly agnostics or atheists; but as admirers of the Western way of life, they see the Western Christian churches as historical levers of the progress, democratic freedom, and social welfare prev-alent in the Western democracies (ignoring the fact that the West has had its share of Hitlers, Mussolinis, Latin American dictators, etc.). Hence, the media, largely controlled by the Westernists, tends to be critical and suspicious of the Orthodox Church but very benevolent to the Catholic and Protestant churches, including their incursions into Russia.[43] When they do turn closer to home, fearing renewal of the historical ties between the Russian Orthodox Church and the state, and repulsed by the past enforced cooperation of the church with the communist state (forgiving themselves for their own often slavish subservience to that regime in the past!), they prefer all sorts of splinter groups (including the ROCOR) to the mainline church.

As the so-called Free Russian Orthodox Church (FROC, the Russian branch of the émigré ROCOR) has increasingly allied itself with the Vasil'ev Pamyat, a neo-Nazi, anti-Semitic organization, even accepting physical support from their militant thugs in wresting away churches from the Moscow Patriarchate,[44] the democrats' sympathy and support for that schismatic group began to wither away. This cooling off occurred in particular after the ROCOR openly sided with the "Red-Browns." In October 1992 the Moscow fascist-national-Bolshevik weekly *Den'* published a lengthy interview with Metropolitan Vitalii, the head of the ROCOR, in which he gave full support to *Den'*'s contention that a world Zionist-Masonic plot was gathering forces to destroy Russia and the Orthodox Church. Vitalii called Yeltsin a "rascal" selling out Russia and appealed to "patriots" and the Russian army to rise against him, restore Russia "to its histori-cal borders," and install a tsar. Moreover, he declared that all religions except the Orthodox Church were satanic cults, wherefore any form of ecumenism was treason. Then two young ROCOR clergymen, Bishop Ilarion and Father Potapov, were sent to Moscow by Vitalii with written instructions to disavow his *Den'* interview as allegedly cited out of context and without his authority and to apologize to Russian readers for whatever pain and confusion it may have caused them. This the two ROCOR messengers duly did at a press conference in Mos-cow on 13 November 1992. Also on his and their Synod's behalf they condemned all forms of racism and anti-Semitism, as well as the anti-Semitic Pamyat and those FROC priests in Russia and the ROCOR bishop of Cannes, Varnava, who collaborated with and supported Pamyat. Then, also on Vitalii's authority, they temporarily banned those priests from performing public services and Varnava from visiting Russia, pending their investigation by a ROCOR legal commission. Of the FROC clergy only its bishop of Suzdal, Valentin, participated in the press conference supporting the condemnation of racism and Pamyat. No sooner had the clergymen returned to the United States, when Vitalii reprimanded them and disavowed their statements on his behalf in Russia. Subsequently, the ROCOR Synod of Bishops at its 9 February 1993 session praised Pamyat as a great patriotic organization, congratulated FROC clergymen in Russia, condemned Father Potapov for having criticized both Pamyat and the named priests, and threatened him with suspension from priestly duties should he ever again travel to Russia in a pastoral capacity and interfere in any Russian ecclesiastical matters. A general Council of all ROCOR bishops in May 1993 confirmed the February decisions and appointed Varnava of Cannes as the temporary head of FROC parishes in Russia while suspending Valentin and Lazarus for moral transgressions.[45]

In June 1993 the suspended FROC Archbishop Valentin assembled a conference of representatives of sixty-five FROC parishes that obviously did not recognize the validity of his suspension. The conference resolved to declare temporary autocephaly and to have nothing to do with the ROCOR as long as it cooperated with Pamyat.[46]

One would have thought that the above ROCOR scandal clarified the issues. The ROCOR enclave in Russia would syphon off the fascist-racist elements from the patriarchal church, making it easier for the liberal intelligentsia to respond to the patriarch's invitation to join the church and become constructively active there. However, as long as the fascist publications by Ioann, the Russian Orthodox metropolitan of St. Petersburg, in the Russian national-Bolshevik and neo-Nazi press, which in spirit do not differ from the above Vitalii's interview, and the racist hate-campaign statements by the Union of Orthodox Brotherhoods do not meet ex cathedra condemnations and bans from the patriarch and his Synod, these anti-Christian elements (camouflaged as Orthodox Christians) will have no reason to depart from the Moscow Patriarchate.[47] After all, that church, with its fourteen thousand communities, offers much greater opportunities than a few scores of ROCOR parishes in the CIS; especially since, according to oral information from a ROCOR source, their line in Russia has once again been changed: Lavrus, an American ROCOR bishop, visited Russia in the fall of 1993, restored Valentin as the ruling bishop of their parishes there, convinced him and his "Free Russian Church" to return to the ROCOR fold, and removed Varnava from the office of overseer of their Russian churches.[48]

On the other hand, as long as Metropolitan Ioann is not censured officially by the patriarchate, and as long as open criticism of his statements is made only by individual Orthodox laymen and the lower clergy, the Moscow Patriarchate will remain vulnerable to accusations of tacit agreement with the Union of Orthodox Brotherhoods, Metropolitan Ioann, and the extremist minority of the clergy. Moreover, the patriarch has not even dared to deny Ioann's untruthful assertion that "there are no differences of opinion between the patriarch and myself"; nor has he denied Ioann's claim that the patriarch's ban on the appearance of Ioann's writings in the official press of the Moscow Patriarchate pertains only to a single article.[49]

Even though now, after the patriarch's excommunication of those who would first use deadly weapons and the suppression of the Red-Brown revolt on 4 October 1993, Metropolitan Ioann and his ilk have kept a low profile; anything short of an official condemnation by the church of its extremists and their removal from leadership positions will hardly satisfy the liberal, democratic, and generally moderate elements in Russia. Moreover, should the patriarchal Synod make official pronouncements against the extremists, it would likely be interpreted, in view of its silence on the subject prior to the revolt, as another sign of conformism to the powers that be, which will hardly improve the public image of the church establishment or enlarge its flock among the intelligentsia.[50]

Such conformism has given rise to the liberal intelligentsia's fear of a re-emerging church-state symbiosis, despite repeated and emphatic rejections of such intentions by the patriarch. Deacon Kuraev, one of the patriarch's advisors, has appropriately chastised the democrats for looking the wrong way, while failing to see the real dangers creeping into Russian society:

> While the democratic press . . . was discussing whether the Orthodox Church would become the state religion, it is paganism that has virtually become the state religion. The nightly news program ends not with a prayer, but with an astrological prognosis; and it is pictures of Krishna, not Christ, that decorate the walls of the metro trains; while the organ of the Russian Supreme Soviet publishes not the sermons of Patriarch Aleksii but "the prophet Ioann."[51]

This Ioann Bereslavskii is a self-appointed "chief bishop and prophet" of the above-mentioned Mother of God Center, a Jewish convert, as he claims,[52] to "the only truly" Orthodox branch of the "Catacomb Church." All known "catacomb" branches, however, disown him and his sect. Indeed, while Orthodox believers generally feel very offended by the aggressiveness of the Western Protestant missionaries and their disrespect for and ignorance of Russian cultural and spiritual traditions, at least they preach the Gospel, however primitive and incomplete their teaching may be. Much more dangerous are the occult sects. Some are foreign imports, like Moon's "Universal Church," Scientology, the Jehovah's Witnesses, or "Krishnaites," but others are entirely homegrown, of which the most aggressive and widespread are the "Mother of God Center," which, apparently having moved its headquarters from Moscow to St. Petersburg, has renamed itself the "Church of the Transfiguring Mother of God"

(CTMG), and even more perverse, "The White Brotherhood," which promised the end of the world on 24 November 1993. Both engage in luring teenagers, moving them to a place very distant from their families, and turning them into propagandists of the faith by constant brainwashing achieved by such means as underfeeding, sleep deprivation, exhaustion from long days of work (walking long distances, distributing their literature, striking up conversations with other children for the purpose of recruiting them), and subjection to long daily occult religious services and hours of tape-recorded "sermons" by Bereslavskii or the "Prophetess Maria Devi Khristos." According to reports, these sermons are quite incomprehensible because of their lack of logic or consistency, deliberate use of wrong syntax, and "mystical" neologisms without sense (for example, the name of the "doctrine" of the White Brotherhood and its newspaper is Iusmalos). The whole purpose is to confuse the youngsters, to fascinate them by turning them into "prophets" of an incomprehensibly mystical faith. From ordinary schoolchildren, subordinate to and punishable by parents, they suddenly become angels of the true faith, destined for salvation after the approaching doomsday. In its letters to "prophets" (every member is a prophet, although there is a council of twelve senior prophets, of whom the eldest is twenty-six years old), Maria Devi has advised them to physically attack churches "to destroy altars of the Emmanuel-Satan." The command has been obediently fulfilled in numerous places. The "prophets" rush into the sanctuary, desecrating it, and shouting curses at the "Emmanuelite servants of Satan"—that is what they call the Orthodox Christians, obviously ignorant of the meaning of the word "Emmanuel."[53]

The atmosphere of general collapse in the country breeds eschatological expectations that are rampant also among members of the Orthodox Church. Therefore sects claiming direct knowledge (from the Virgin Mary, with whom Bereslavskii claims to be in constant communication, and from Jesus Christ, who has allegedly settled within the body of Maria Devi) of the coming of doomsday fall on fertile soil. Many believe that all the hardships of Russia today are the product of Satan gaining the upper hand on the eve of doomsday, and the Union of Orthodox Brotherhoods foments these fears. Not unrelated to that must have been the murder of three monks at the Optina Monastery at the end of the all-night Resurrection service on 18 April 1993 by a mad veteran of the Afghan War who chiseled out on the knife with which he stabbed his victims: "666—from Satan." When caught he declared he was instructed by Satan to kill monks. In another case youngsters belonging to another locally grown occult sect in Voronezh, instructed by their "spiritual mother," murdered a twenty-year-old engineering coed by hammering nails into her body.[54]

Nonetheless, the official Orthodox Church was more concerned with the proliferation of the Protestant missions than with the occult groups, which are much more dangerous for the human soul. For a while the Orthodox Church was not sure whether the Mother of God Center was another, if extreme, schism within the Orthodox Church or an outright occult heresy. After all, Ioann Bereslavskii claims to be an Orthodox catacomb bishop, wears an Orthodox cassock with an Orthodox pectoral cross, and his newspaper, *The Word of Christ,* appears with a picture of the destroyed Moscow Christ the Savior Cathedral. In fact several times Ioann fallaciously declared to the media that he was negotiating a reunion with the Orthodox Church, while his leaflets, widely distributed in Moscow metro stations, called Orthodox priests sorcerers. It was only in June 1993 that the patriarchal Synod at last officially excommunicated the White Brotherhood and the CTMG, publicly declaring that these sects had nothing to do with Orthodoxy or any form of Christianity.[55] Both sects reject marriage and family life. Ioann condemns conception and birth as the greatest sins of lechery and calls upon his followers to disown and damn their mothers as whores.[56] Probably it was also a question of numbers: there are currently about one thousand foreign religious missions and mission points of all kinds in Russia[57] and, according to one report, U.S. fundamentalists are planning to have 200,000 Evangelical schools, missions, and chapels in the whole CIS by the end of this century; the two occult sects, however, may have only some twenty thousand members. Not only the Orthodox, but even Russian Evangelicals are unhappy with the influx. The director of the Protestant Radio-TV Center in Tula, Kulakov, viewed mass-produced "Christianity" as negatively as compulsory atheism of the past: "Western preachers, as a rule, are ecstatic, very far removed from the Russian culture and our traditions. A jumping and twisting pastor on the podium with a microphone at his mouth causes revulsion not only in Russian Christians, but even in the unbelievers."[58] Also, the aggressive behavior of the missionaries, their clear aims not only to evangelize the nonbelievers but to tear away members of the Orthodox Church, has badly compromised ecumenism, in which the Moscow Patriarchate has been actively engaged since the 1960s. Orthodox believers are bewildered: "Is this the behavior of brothers-in-Christ?" they ask. All this weakens the position of the patriarchate in general and the patriarch in particular, while strengthening the Orthodox "fundamentalists," who preach that ecumenism is a part of a Masonic-satanic plot to destroy Russia and its church.

Conclusion

One month before the church Council that elected Aleksii, a group of young, active clergymen and prominent Orthodox lay intelligentsia had addressed to the Synod of Bishops an appeal to restore a true *sobornost'* on all levels of the life of the church.[59] It is known, and the patriarch has stated this several times, that he is a strong supporter of restoration of *sobornost'* along the rules adopted at the Moscow Council of 1917–18. In fact, he has given the blessing for a full multivolume publication of all documents pertaining to that Council.[60] The establishment of the Orthodox Youth Movement and the Union of Orthodox Brotherhoods is a move in the right direction. However, as discussed above, the Union of Orthodox Brotherhoods has been usurped by the Red-Browns, particularly the two most extremist groups, the "St. Sergius Brotherhood" of Sergiev Posad and the Moscow "Union of Christian Regeneration," whose newspaper appears with portraits of Hitler, quotations from *Mein Kampf,* and a cross and swastika on its masthead. The confrontation between them and other extremists from the periphery, on the one hand, and the church-dedicated Christian brotherhoods, on the other, at the third congress of the Union in St. Petersburg in June 1992 resulted in the departure of some of the latter from the Union after the loud extremist minority denounced the patriarch and all the ecumenically active bishops as Judeo-Masons. Surprisingly, the patriarch did not react, nor was he defended by the Union's chairman, Archimandrite Kirill (Sakharov). On the contrary, on the eve of the above congress Kirill stated that he had sent a letter to the patriarch reprimanding him for his statement to the Jewish rabbis in New York in November 1991 in which the patriarch stressed the common biblical heritage of Christianity and Judaism and hence deep mutual ties between Christians and Jews.[61] It was that encounter with the rabbis that led to the outburst at the congress. Moreover, even a movement of "non-commemorating clergy" appeared: these were priests who refused to mention the name of the patriarch in the litanies chanted at each liturgy. The movement seems now to have subsided, with some of that clergy deserting to the ROCOR. The fourth congress of the Union of Orthodox Brotherhoods, held in Moscow in February 1993, stressed its loyalty to the patriarch, which has been achieved at the expense of his total silence on controversial subjects and his failure to censure the extremists in the church he heads, all for the sake of avoiding an open split. But was it worth it, especially if one looks at the resolutions of that congress demanding the canonization of Tsar Nicholas II with a formulaic "ritually killed by the Jews," the canonization of Ivan the Terrible as a true fighter against Judaism,[62] and the restoration of that tsar's bloody Oprichnina in order to stamp out the alleged Judaic heresy within the contemporary Russian Orthodox Church?

The organization of the Union of Orthodox Brotherhoods, which was the first act blessed by the patriarch toward activating the laity, may have put him and his Synod on guard against further experiments with *sobornost'* at this stage. On the other hand, the potential of another attempt at usurping power by the so-called Red-Brown forces, which are now much better organized than in 1991, may have convinced some of the more opportunistic members of the church leadership to take a "wait and see" position vis-à-vis the extremists inside the church, who are clearly linked to the Brown elements in that "unholy alliance," especially since they have at least one spokesman in the patriarchal Synod, namely Metropolitan Ioann of St. Petersburg.[63]

However, not everything is at a standstill. Reports on the 1992 general Councils of Bishops of the whole church indicate that at last the effects of the post-August freedom are manifesting themselves in the behavior of the participants: they expressed their opinions more openly than ever before and dared to criticize the church leadership and propose new ideas. As one participant commented, freedom of discussion has been there since the 1990 Council, with its secret ballot and truly democratic election of the patriarch, but the effects of the previous seventy years were still too mentally repressive to untie the delegates' tongues. The outspokenness of 1992 has really opened a new page in internal church relations and in bishops' behavior and moods. The daringness of erudite young clergymen to openly and critically discuss internal church problems and to criticize with impunity their bishops and their policies in the secular press are additional hopeful signs of new and healthier times in the life of the church.[64]

Come 1993 and the impression is that, having begun his tenure with determination and a definite vision, the patriarch became confused about how to react to the controversial pressures on him from the increasingly polarized society in general and his flock and probably advisors as well. This confusion was reflected in several acts of 1993.

The year began with continuing attempts by the Bolshevik-dominated Supreme Soviet to gain control over the media and the church. The freedom and independence of two such crucially important opinion-forming institutions were too much for the parliament's Bolshevik mentality to tolerate. By the end of January, draft amendments to the RSFSR Law on the Freedom of Conscience were made public. They proposed to create a parliamentary "representative organ of inspection" that would have the right to receive all necessary information on the life of religions and to send their representatives as juridical persons to all official events and conferences of a religious body. That was to be a parallel body to the Department of Social Organizations and Confessions of the Ministry of Justice. Like the latter body (formed over and against the protests of the church), which is staffed by former officials of the CRA, the parliamentary organ was likely to be chaired by Iu. Rozenbaum, the former chief legal advisor of the CRA and a militant atheist (at least in the very recent past). Metropolitan Kirill sharply criticized the proposed amendments as introducing (Article 11) in fact detailed control over all activities of the church and said that such an organ was totally unnecessary owing to the existence of a department in the Chief Procuracy that supervises the legality of aspects of religious life and the church's relations with the state within the context of the 1990 law. He added that no church representative was ever invited to participate in the preparation of that draft.[65] Due to the protests of the church the draft amendments appear to have been at least temporarily scrapped.

But then suddenly on 28 April 1993 the same patriarch who had repeatedly supported the separation of church and state addressed a letter to the government proposing that there be formed at the Ministry of Justice a "joint commission of state officials and representatives of religious organizations . . . and that that commission be granted powers for a period of five to seven years to veto the licensing and activities of foreign religious organizations." The Supreme Soviet got busy again, although it was not asked.

In between there was the First All-World Russian Assembly, organized by the nationalists and rightists with a heavy admixture of national-Bolsheviks. The church, under the prodding of Metropolitan Kirill, who hoped to achieve moderation and separate the more moderate and reasonable nationalists from the extreme ones, agreed to cooperate with that Assembly. In fact, the conference part of the Assembly took place at the patriarch's official residence in the Danilov Monastery from 26 to 28 May. And in his speech at the Assembly and in press interviews Metropolitan Kirill stressed that the Assembly occurred not under the auspices of the church, but that the church merely agreed to participate in it.[66] Whether the church achieved the formation of a moderate patriotic bloc and its separation from the extremist bloc is very doubtful. In fact, most vocal at the Assembly were national-Bolsheviks of different hues. But the tone of the church leaders, Patriarch Aleksii and Metropolitan Kirill, was indeed one of moderation. The patriarch warned against any hostility toward other nations or attempts to forgive and forget the sins of one's own nation.[67] Metropolitan Kirill spoke about a Christian patriotism of love and protection of one's national flock with a friendly openness to the whole world and the rest of Christendom. Several speakers and resolutions of the Assembly demanded that the foreign missionary invasion be placed under control and that the state ought to intervene in limiting or banning their activities. In other words, the Assembly was another spur for the Supreme Soviet's action.

On 14 July it adopted new amendments to the Law on the Freedom of Conscience, creating a parliamentary liaison commission consisting of members of the Committee on the Freedom of Conscience and some representatives of the registered religions of Russia. Moreover, the Law now made preaching and missionary activities by foreigners illegal unless they were solicited by local religious organizations, and even then a license from this committee was required in order to begin any activities. It ought to be noted that the amendments offered no special privileges to the Orthodox Church, only equal privileges to all registered religions of Russia, including Russian Evangelicals and others. Indeed, the amendments were welcomed at first by the patriarch, the chief Muslim mufti of Russia, and the chief rabbi of Moscow, but criticized by Russian Protestants, Roman Catholics, and the democratic Russian press, as well as numerous Russian Orthodox laymen and lower clergy. Eventually Yeltsin vetoed these amendments as incompatible with freedom of conscience. Nevertheless, the whole episode was symptomatic of widespread moods in the country, and probably the story is not yet over.

The participation of the patriarch in the affair may not have been entirely voluntary and certainly went against his deeply held ideas of separation of church and state and freedom of conscience. Setting a time limit on the proposed measure, the patriarch's initiative could be compared to a free-market state temporarily resorting to state protection of some of its industries by high customs tariffs on imports. The problem is that the church is too precious to a state as a tool of ideological influence and control to be sure that once gaining control over it the state would be willing to relinquish it in a few years. Russia's seventeenth-century experience of state-church cooperation in suppressing the Great Schism, which led half a century later to Peter the Great's enslavement of the church by the state, is telling enough to dare repeat it now.

The patriarch must have had similar doubts when he addressed his 28 April petition, because almost simultaneously he began to stress the nonpolitical profile of the church by calling on the church to keep out of politics and asking his clergy to refuse to be candidates to parliamentary bodies in future elections and not to join any political parties: "We should not join any political parties or movements and be equally fair to our parishioners whatever their political views."[68] Responding to this call, Bishop Manuil of Karelia withdrew his membership from the republican parliament.

Apparently the patriarch concluded that in the current circumstances the church could do very little in direct participation in politics to improve the situation in the country and turned wholly to moral issues, appealing for mercy for Russian soldiers caught by Azerbaijani government troops while fighting on the Armenian side and condemned to death. Writing to the minister of the press and mass information about his concern with the moral effect on the population, and on youth in particular, of the flood of pornography from abroad in the media, the patriarch stressed his strong belief in "the inviolability of human freedom granted by God." The minister's reply shared the patriarch's concerns and put all hopes in the eventual passage of laws that would introduce some moral limitations and legal responsibility on the media and entertainment business and thus help educate the nation morally.[69] In the same light of caring for the moral and political survival of the Russian state, the patriarch and his Synod addressed themselves "To the Citizens of Russia, to Brothers and Sisters" to end the duality of power and the duel between the executive and legislative bodies, that paralyzes governance of the country. He accused those involved of putting their personal ambitions above national interest, warned against any return to the past and past dictatorship, and sought to preserve "freedom of the human person and the nation." During the 25 April referendum the Patriarchate kept strict neutrality.[70]

But to return to the subject of the patriarch's proposal of limitations on foreign missions, why did he specify the five-to-seven-year time limit? Obviously he hoped that during that period the church would be able to brace itself for proper missionary work and religious enlightenment of the nation, create enough theologians to carry out such activities, and improve its financial situation to allow mass religious publications, charity institutions, schools, youth camps, and so forth. However, with the present cadres at the top of the church, the inertia of most of its bishops, the confrontation between the Red-Browns using the church for their political ends, and the reform-minded clergy and laity who want to see their church as a moral leader speaking in the contemporary idiom to the nation, it is very doubtful that, deprived of competition from the foreign missions, the church would fully rise to its calling in that short span of time.

To avoid confrontation and splits, the patriarch has chosen to avoid direct exposure and chastisement of the extremists within the church, concentrating instead on preaching morality, moderation, and tolerance to the whole nation and its leaders, believing that as the church is a part of the nation, its pacification will have a positive effect on his flock as well. But should not the church set the example and thus lead the nation rather than follow it? It is very doubtful that such policies would be able to raise the national prestige of the church. A surer way to restore the church to the status of moral leader of the nation would be, it seems, to adopt the following steps.

First, the church should honor its 1992 promise to reveal all available archival data on the past (and present?) links between the KGB and the clergy, making public the nature of such contacts. Clergy found guilty of, say, denouncing people to the KGB, should be tried by church courts. Lesser offenders should publicly repent to their parishioners in a procedure similar to the one by which the repenting Renovationist clergy had been received back to the patriarchal Orthodox Church in the past.

Second, it seems it would be necessary to restore the ancient church practice of electing bishops with the participation of diocesan clergy and laity, restored once already by the Moscow Council in 1918. The elections should be preceded by reapproval or deposition of the current bishops by diocesan councils of clergy and laity, as had so successfully been done in the summer of 1917.

Third, with this renewed college of bishops a national Council of bishops, clergy, and laity should be called to restore the administrative structure of the church along the 1918 model; that is, with the diocesan-elected Higher Church Council and partly elected Synod of bishops.

The renewed supreme ecclesiastic bodies, mandated by the whole church, commanding the respect and support of the flock, would then be able to take a stand, condemn extremism and racism, and ban dissemination of hatred by any groups within the church. Should this lead to some of the perpetrators of hate propaganda joining the ROCOR or some other esoteric sect, it would not hurt the church as a whole; on the contrary, it would purify it and assure it of the position of spiritual leadership in the nation.

Moreover, it is only then that the more moderate majority of the ROCOR membership would likely reunite with the mother church, and whatever might remain of the ROCOR would become irrelevant as a small extremist sect.

Notes

An expanded version of this chapter with full documentation has been published in *Modern Greek Studies,* vol. 9.

   1. *Vestnik Khristianskogo informatsionnogo tsentra* (Moscow, Samizdat), no. 11 (18 July 1989) pp. 3–4, and oral information in September 1989. A note indicates that the cultural center idea was but a last-minute excuse to prevent the repossession by the believers. The church was confiscated from the believers in 1938 and at first turned into a

Pioneers' club. Then it was turned into a storage facility, which later was also liquidated, whereupon the church had been standing empty and falling apart for decades, despite repeated appeals by believers to restore it for worship.

2. E. Strel'chik, "Spory u sten khrama," *Moskovskii tserkovnyi vestnik,* 1992, no. 9 (June), p. 7.

3. See criticisms of the draft law in "Zaiavlenie pomestnogo sobora," *Zhurnal Moskovskoi patriarkhii,* 1990, no. 9 (September), pp. 9–11. Other republics have likewise adopted their republican laws, which in most cases are less liberal than the Russian one. Ukraine even retained its Council for Religious Affairs under the same communist personnel as before, whereas the Russian legislature abolished the institution.

4. The law on alternative service, however, remains practically a dead issue, for lack of a normative act.

5. Translated from *Sovetskaia Rossiia,* 10 November 1990, p. 5, by JPRS-UPA, 18 December 1990, pp. 92–95.

6. We are using the original Russian term *bratstvo,* although both women and men are members. Hence, the more accurate English equivalent would be *fellowship.*

7. N. Karpov, "Soiuz bratstv," *Moskovskii tserkovnyi vestnik,* 1990, no. 23 (October), pp. 4–5; "S''ezd pravoslavnoi molodezhi," *Moskovskii tserkovnyi vestnik,* 1991, no. 2 (January), p. 3.

8. Ilmira Stepanova, "Da ne otnimet ruka daiushchego," *Russkaia mysl'* (Paris–Moscow), 12–25 August 1993, p. 9. See also "Konfessional'nyi landshaft Rossii," a report by the Department of Social Organizations and Confessions of the Russian Ministry of Justice. *Put',* 1993, nos. 3–4; cited in *Podborka po presse* of the Moscow Patriarchate's Department of External Ecclesiastical Relations, 1993, no. 103, p. 25.

9. D. Pospielovsky, "Russkaia pravoslavnaia tserkov' segodnia i novyi patriarkh," *Vestnik russkogo khristianskogo dvizheniia,* 1990, no. 159, p. 213; Aleksandr Kyrlezhev, "Bog v epokhu 'smerti Boga'," *Kontinent* (Moscow–Paris), 1992, no. 2 (72), p. 265. S. Filatov and L. Vorontsov, "Kak idet religioznoe vozrozhdenie Rossii?" interview, *Nauka i religiia,* 1993, no. 5.

10. Most of the groups that had broken with the Moscow Patriarchate in the late twenties and early thirties over a number of issues returned to the patriarchate's fold during the 1940s, particularly after the election of Patriarch Aleksii I in 1945 and the appeal of the most revered leader of the Catacomb Orthodox Christians, the then imprisoned Bishop Afanasii (Sakharov), to his flock to rejoin the church headed by Aleksii I. Thereafter only tiny groups of the most fanatical adherents remained in the catacombs. They were mostly without clergy, and lacking theological education they degenerated often into eschatological sects quite far removed from the genuine Orthodox theology, as revealed, for instance, in the contemporary Moscow "Mother of God Center," which claims to have direct communication with the Virgin Mary and condemns Orthodox clergy as he-witches in brochures widely distributed by their agents in the Moscow metro stations. Very few genuine catacomb groups survived the KGB nets, and they were widely dispersed; now the number of people who claim to have come out of the catacombs is suspiciously high. See Dmitry Pospielovsky, *The Russian Church Under the Soviet Regime* (Crestwood, NY: St. Vladimir's Seminary Press, 1984), pp. 203–4 and 365–86. Also Mother of God Center's brochures, *Koldun v agape,* 11 June 1991; *Bozhestvennyi sud narodam,* etc.

11. According to Father Amvrosii (Sivers), a young monastic scholar belonging to a branch of the "Catacomb" Church that refuses to leave "the Catacombs" to the present day, Lazarus had been secretly consecrated by bishops of the ROCOR despite a warning from the Catacomb hierarchy (then it had been a true underground; now insisting on remaining underground is specious) that Lazarus was a KGB informer who denounced

several Catacomb bishops who were subsequently imprisoned. As the ROCOR Synod ignored their warnings, the Catacomb group broke with that émigré church. Father Amvrosii, "Katakombnaia tserkov' ot osnovaniia i do nastoiashchego vremeni" (presented at the Memorial Society conference, "Istoricheskii put' pravoslaviia v Rossii posle 1917 g.," St. Petersburg, 31 May–2 June 1993). Finally the May 1993 Council for all bishops of the ROCOR defrocked Lazarus, apparently on moral grounds: the above Amvrosii accused Lazarus also of sodomy. R. Vershillo, "Zarubezhnaia tserkov' podelilas' na chistykh i nechistykh," *Segodnia,* 6 July 1993; also see a note in *Russkii vestnik,* 1993, no. 16.

12. "Poslanie pomestnogo sobora," *Zhurnal Moskovskoi patriarkhii,* 1990, no. 9, p. 4.

13. "Vozzvanie arkhiereiskogo sobora," *Moskovskie eparkhial'nye vedomosti,* 1991, no. 1, pp. 5–13.

14. *Zhurnal Moskovskoi patriarkhii,* 1990, no. 12, p. 2; reprint from *Izvestiia,* 5 November 1990.

15. Patriarch's introduction to publications of material on the Catacomb Church of the past in *Sovershenno sekretno,* 1991, no. 7, p. 5. During his visit to the United States in November 1991 he said in one of the press conferences that he shudders from the thought of what would have befallen his Estonian diocese had he chosen during Khrushchev's persecutions the road of personal martyrdom rather than a give-and-take struggle for the survival of the churches and the diocesan monastery, originally earmarked by Khrushchev's administration for destruction.

16. Patriarch Aleksii II, "Hate Sin, But Love the Sinner," interview, *Nezavisimaia gazeta,* 10 June 1992, p. 5.

17. Patriarch Aleksii II, interview by G. Alimov and G. Charodeev, *Izvestiia,* 10 June 1991; Patriarch Aleksii II, "V parlament strany," *Rossiiskaia gazeta,* 9 May 1991; idem, "Taina very," *Literaturnaia Rossiia,* 31 May 1991; idem, "Kazhdaia dusha po prirode khristianka," interview, *Rossiiskaia gazeta,* 11 June 1991; idem, "Vesna patriarkha," interview, *Moskovskie novosti,* 9 June 1991; Deacon A. Kuraev, "Patriarkh Aleksii II: 'Piatyi sovetskii' ili 'piatnadtsatyi rossiiskii'?" *Rossiia,* special issue, 1991.

18. See, for example, Pospielovsky, *Russian Church Under the Soviet Regime,* vol. 2, p. 390 n.

19. Edel'shtein, "Vybory patriarkha: Na rasput'e ili v tupike?" *Russkaia mysl',* 8 June 1990, pp. 6–7; V. Voina, "Otets Zvezdonii iz RpTs," *Nezavisimaia gazeta,* 21 March 1991. The patriarch is defended by S. Averintsev in "Pravo zastupit'sia za patriarkha," *Nezavisimaia gazeta,* 18 April 1991.

20. *Argumenty i fakty,* 1991, no. 27 (June).

21. V. Senderov (democratic centrist, religious believer), "Gosudarstvennaia religiia?" *Russkaia mysl',* 14 June 1991, pp. 6–7, and 28 June 1991, pp. 9–10; idem, "Put' k edineniiu?" *Novoe russkoe slovo,* 19 October 1991; idem, "Otvet Alekseiu Zalesskomu," *Russkaia mysl',* 17 July 1992. A. Nezhnyi (democrat, Orthodox believer), "O chem zabyl episkop Evlogii," *Moskovskie novosti,* 2 June 1991; idem, "Bitva za khram," *Moskovskie novosti,* 28 July 1991. V. Potapov (VOA religious broadcaster, priest of the ROCOR), "Pomekhi," interview by I. Stepanova, *Vechernii Leningrad,* 13 August 1991. The patriarchate's position was stated by Father Ioann (Ekonomtsev), chairman of the church's Department of Christian Education, to representatives of the democratic press at the end of May 1991.

22. See, for example, A. Chelnokov, "Pravoslavnye strasti," *Golos* (a monarchist paper), 1991, no. 11. There were plenty of other similar articles in the right-wing press, but I did not collect them.

23. Kuraev, "Patriarkh Aleksii." Summation of patriarch's statements in *Rossiia,* special issue (n.d. but 1991), p. 6. Quotation from *Rossiiskaia gazeta,* 11 June 1991.

24. According to unofficial sources, Metropolitans Pitirim of Volokolamsk, the head

of the church's Publications Department, and Iuvenalii of Krutitsy and Kolomna went on the same day to see Pugo, the late minister of internal affairs and one of the key figures in the putsch. Most people think that the patriarch was not aware of that, but he might have been. Whatever his own feeling about one or the other side in the conflict, as leader of the national church he had to think about the church and its faithful's future in both eventualities. This would have been also in the tradition of Patriarch Tikhon and the 1917–18 Council. They minced no words criticizing the massacres, but kept their neutrality in the Civil War, and did negotiate with the Bolshevik leaders whenever given a chance. Zoia Krakhmal'nikova attacks the patriarchate in "Skandal v blagorodnom semeistve," *Novoe russkoe slovo,* 3 March 1992.

25. "Slovo patriarkha Aleksiia," *Izvestiia,* 15 January 1991.

26. Prezidium Verkhovnogo soveta RSFSR, "Chastnoe opredelenie komissii po rassmotreniiu prichin i obstoiatel'stv GKChP," 6 pp. + 7 pp. of documentary excerpts.

27. See, for example, E. Volochkov, "Ne otnimaite veru u veruiushchikh," *Moskovskii tserkovnyi vestnik,* 1992, no. 8 (May), p. 8. The author is a veteran of World War II, as well as Nazi and Stalin's concentration camps.

28. V. Furov (CRA's deputy chairman), "Iz otcheta Soveta po delam religii chlenam TsK KPSS." *Vestnik russkogo khristianskogo dvizheniia,* 1979, no. 130, p. 278. It has now transpired (apparently unknown to the CRA at the time) that Nikodim, along with Metropolitan Ioann of Iaroslavl', also placed in the middle category by Furov—political collaborators and ideological enemies—secretly ordained several hundred priests when they feared that Khrushchev might destroy the visible church as thoroughly as Stalin did in the 1930s.

29. This is based on numerous publications, including an interview of Father Yakunin in *Argumenty i fakty,* 1992, no. 1 (January), and the press conference of Yakunin and Lev Ponomarev, chairman of the commission investigating the KGB's subversive work in Soviet public organizations, organized by the Ethics and Public Policy Center and the Jamestown Foundation on 20 March 1992 in one of the U.S. House of Representatives' subcommittee office halls.

30. V.K. Diomin (from the Christian Renewal group), "O eresi zhidovstvuiushchikh," *Vestnik soiuza pravoslavnykh bratstv,* 1993, no. 43, pp. 15–25 (followed by a resolution of the fourth congress of the Union confirming the article's theses, pp. 26–29). See also Iurii Klitsenko, "Iznemogli v protivoiudeiskom stoianii," *Vecherniaia Moskva,* 7 July 1993. To name but a few: Fr. Vitalii Borovoi, a scholar, theology professor, and the chief ecumenist of the ROC (with strong anti-Roman sentiments, however); Fr. Georgii Kochetkov, the single most successful missionary in the Moscow Patriarchate, runs a large missionary parish in the center of Moscow, celebrates mostly in Russian rather than the poorly understood Slavonic, expelled from the Leningrad Theological Seminary by the KGB some ten years ago for secretly running a catechism school for adults, now directs a four-year theological evening school for adults with over four hundred attendee, and recently defended a D.D. dissertation on cathechization at the St. Serge Theological Institute in Paris; Fr. Vsevolod Chaplin, an official of the ROC's Department of External Ecclesiastical Relations, a very intelligent and erudite scholar whose articles on the Orthodox Church with criticism of the extremists often appear in the media; Deacon Andrei Kuraev, a moderately conservative theologian and philosopher (graduated in "scientific atheism" from the Moscow University Faculty of Philosophy), heads the philosophy department at the Moscow Orthodox University and is a very popular lecturer in Christian philosophy and theology at the University of Moscow, in the media has made enemies for himself both on the left and the right for attacking the "Brown-Red" elements, the church monarchists, Protestant and Roman Catholic activities in Russia, and the theology of the late Fr. Aleksandr Men'; and Fr. Vladimir Vorob'ev, a right-wing monarchist, very con-

servative cleric, morally impeccable pastor of great influence and popularity, a brilliant organizer who runs the biggest Sunday school in Moscow and directs the Moscow Theological Institute with its over one thousand students in diverse theological programs of four to five years duration.

31. M. Pozdniaev, "Okromia ego arkhiereistva," *Stolitsa,* 1991, no. 26, pp. 4–7; Fr. G. Edel'shtein, "Chekisty v riasakh," interview, *Argumenty i fakty,* 1991, no. 36; Fr. G. Edel'shtein, "Chitaia i perechityvaia klassiku," broadsheet, 7 December 1991.

32. "Komissiia Moskovskoi eparkhii po tserkovo-bogoslovskim trudam protoiereia Aleksandra Menia," *Moskovskii tserkovnyi vestnik,* 1991, no. 20 (December), p. 8. In fact the metropolitan might have used his KGB contacts to preserve Father Men' in the same parish for twenty years, whereas "normally" such a prominent clergyman would be moved about by the KGB from parish to parish and pushed out to a less geographically accessible one. See A. Kuraev, "Posmertnyi triumf komiteta," *Moskovskien ovosti,* 8 March 1992. Between September 1990 and March 1991 there were three mysterious and equally brutal and tortuous murders of outstanding priests in the Moscow area. First Father Men' was murdered on Sunday morning, 9 September, while walking toward his village's suburban railway station to travel to his parish for the Sunday liturgy. His skull was broken with the back of an ax. Then during the night of 26–27 December, Father Lazar', a priest-monk, was killed with a heavy metallic object in his flat. He had been entrusted by Metropolitan Iuvenalii to investigate corruption around the late Patriarch Pimen that involved the KGB. The murder was accompanied by the disappearance of all his electronic aids and his briefcase. In March 1991 a thirty-three-year-old priest-monk, Father Serafim, was brutally murdered, his body mutilated while he was still alive. He had just returned from the Russian Orthodox Mission in Palestine, had many baptized Jews in his parish and (Father Men' was himself a baptized Jew) openly preferring them to a group of Pamyat activists who constituted the other part of his parish. Suspiciously, although (or because) at the time Gorbachev personally ordered that the murders be investigated by the KGB, not a single one of them has been solved.

33. "Obrashchenie Arkhiereiskogo sobora Russkoi pravoslavnoi tserkvi," *Russkaia mysl',* 17 April 1992, p. 7.

34. Archbishop Khrizostom, "KGB platil komplimentami," interview by Iu. Tubinis, *Rossiiskaia gazeta,* 4 March 1992; Archpriest Aleksandr Shargunov, "Eshche raz o KGB i tserkvi," *Moskovskii tserkovnyi vestnik,* 1992, no. 1 (January), p. 4.

35. A. Kuraev, "Neizvestnoe pis'mo patriarkha," *Izvestiia,* 2 March 1992.

36. E. Chekalova, "Tele khochet videt'," *Moskovskie novosti,* 8 March 1992, p. 15. Since then Yeltsin's popularity declined to about 28 percent by the end of 1992.

37. "100 vedushchikh politikov Rossii v mae." *Nezavisimaia gazeta,* 3 June 1993, p. 1; Filatov and Vorontsov, "Kak idet religioznoe vozrozhdenie?"

38. Tat'iana Koriagina, "Ateisticheskoe obshchestvo bezzashchitno," interview by E. Zabavskikh, *Moskovskii tserkovnyi vestnik,* 1991, no. 9 (May). What she is referring to is the Marxist rejection of universal moral principles, the assumption that anything that serves the interest of the given class is moral.

39. I remember overhearing a conversation of a well-dressed intelligentsia family strolling in the park of the St. Petersburg Aleksandr Nevskii Monastery. Pointing at the main cathedral, the head of the family explained, "This is a Christian church, Orthodox. Then there the other, non-Christian religions: Catholics, Protestants."

40. The insensitivity toward, ignorance of, and lack of respect for local tradition by some of these Baptist and Pentecostal preachers from the United States are astounding. Thus, according to Patriarch Aleksii, they wanted to lease Red Square from the Moscow city government for the 1991 Orthodox Easter night for a large sum of money in order to floodlight it and St. Basil Cathedral and organize a pageant in the square with music,

animal performances, and presumably some play or other on the theme of Jesus' resurrection. The patriarch managed to stave off that affair by intervening with the city authorities at the last minute. For the Orthodox, the paschal night is the holiest and most solemn night of the year; the pageant would remind them of the days of the Union of the Militant Godless Easter night parades to draw believers away from the churches.

41. John Ericson, "A New Crisis in Catholic-Orthodox Dialogue," *Ecumenism* (Montreal), no. 107 (September 1992).

42. Official position of the Moscow Patriarchate as stated by Hegumen Ioann (Ekonomtsev), chairman of the Moscow Patriarchate's Department of Christian Education and Catechization in his negotiations with the Anglicans, Lutherans, Episcopalians, and Methodists in the course of 1991–92. Metropolitan Kirill, head of the External Ecclesiastical Relations Department of the Moscow Patriarchate, an ecumenist, and a friend of both Roman Catholics and Protestants, expressed the same idea while criticizing the arrogance of Western missionaries in Russia today. Metropolitan Kirill, "Russkaia pravoslavnaia tserkov' budet otstaivat' traditsionnye v otkrytoi Zapadu Rossii," interview by N. Babasian, *Nezavisimaia gazeta,* 5 June 1993.

43. See, for example, A. Nezhnyi, "Katoliki v 'Tret'em Rime'" *Moskovskie novosti,* 30 June 1991, p. 15; idem, "Gde doroga k Novomu gradu?" *Moskovskie novosti,* 1 March 1992, p. 10; idem, "Protestant obustraivaet Rossiiu," *Izvestiia,* 4 September 1992. D. Shusharin, "Na zerkalo necha peniat'," *Nezavisimaia gazeta,* 30 August 1992; idem, "Drug svobody i vrag unyniia: Takim vidiat Ioanna-Pavla II mnogie russkie," *Nezavisimaia gazeta,* August 1992.

44. M. Pozdniaev, "Kak protopop Averianov s patriotom Vasil'evym prezidenta El'tsina na um nastavliali," *Russkaia mysl',* 27 March 1992, p. 6. In May 1992 Varnava, the ROCOR titular bishop of Cannes who spends most of his time in Russia residing in Vasil'ev's flat, staged with Vasil'ev and his Pamyat thugs demonstrations in the Manezh Square and elsewhere in Moscow calling for the resignation of the Yeltsin "Judeo-Masonic" government.

45. For the Vitalii interview see "Lish' pravoslavie izluchaet liubov'," *Den',* 11–17 October 1993; A. Nezhnyi, "Nevesta Agntsa vstupaet v 'Pamiat'?" *Ogonek,* 1992, nos. 47–49 (November); S. Bychkov, "Voskreshenie mifa," *Moskovskie novosti,* 7 March 1993; "Russkaia zarubezhnaia tserkov': Dva dokumenta," *Russkaia mysl',* 21–27 May 1993; Z. Krakhmal'nikova, "Moi byvshii drug Varnava," *Novoe russkoe slovo,* 11 June 1993; an item on the suspensions and defrockings in *Russkii vestnik,* 1993, no. 16, in *Podborka po presses,* no. 101, p. 2. The ROCOR had been warned by this author on the low moral profile of Valentin and his long KGB connection but was rebuffed by the ROCOR press as a slanderer. See Pospielovsky, "Russkaia pravoslavnaia tserkov' segodnia i novyi patriarkh," pp. 211–28.

46. Vershillo, "Zarubezhnaia tserkov'." Once again this act is being justified on the basis of Patriarch Tikhon's decree of 20 November 1920 permitting individual dioceses of his church to declare themselves temporarily autocephalous should communication with Moscow become impossible. This has been used by the ROCOR as grounds for their own legitimization. But the decree could refer only to the historical territories of the Moscow Patriarchate, being absolutely irrelevant to clergy departing from that territory, especially those landing on territories belonging to other patriarchates, for example, Serbia, Bulgaria, or Constantinople. Even less can that decree excuse the formation of Valentin's diocese now that communication with the Moscow Patriarchate is wholly available. See this excuse in V. Senderov, "V Rossii dolzhna byt' svoia tserkov', a ne zarubezhnaia," *Russkaia mysl',* 1–7 July 1993. According to Father Potapov's oral testimony, since then the ROCOR Russian policy has been reversed once again: their American bishop Laurus went to Russia in the fall of 1993, restored Valentin and Lazarus, removed Varnava from

inside-Russia affairs, and Valentin's parishes were restored to unity with ROCOR. The Moscow ROCOR community requested Vasil′ev of Pamyat to remove the word "fascism" from his programmatic list of "spiritual values." As Vasili′ev refused to comply, "the Moscow office of the ROCOR declared its parting with Pamyat." *Moscow Patriarchate External Church Relations Department Information Bulletin,* 20 August 1993, pp. 3–4.

47. The patriarch banned the publication of Ioann's diatribes in the official publications of the Moscow Patriarchate. He did this in a private letter to the head of the patriarchate's Publications Department. It would, however, be wrong to think of Ioann as a pure and simple supporter of national-Bolshevism or neo-Nazism. In fact, he condemned those "patriots" who do not care about Orthodox Christianity or who appeal to telepathy, astrology, and the like. "These people love another country invented by themselves," not Russia, which is inseparable from Christian Orthodoxy. As for the reason why Ioann lets his diatribes be published in communist and fascist newspapers, these papers alone, he said, agree to publish him, while he does not care where they appear as long as they are printed and become available to the reader, as he is trying, he says, to save Russia and to wake up Russians to the moral threat to their country from the flood of demoralizing pornography, satanic sectarian teachings, and attempts at disintegrating the country—all allegedly a part of the anti-Russian Zionist-Masonic plot as laid out and predicted in the *Protocols of the Elders of Zion.* Ecumenism (the World Council of Churches), according to him, is also a part of that satanic plot. What is rather peculiar about Ioann is that in the above-cited Furov's CRA report Ioann is listed in the category of bishops most hostile to the Soviet socialist system who cannot be trusted by the regime, and in August 1991 he was the first Russian bishop (one day ahead of the patriarch) to condemn the putsch and to call on his flock to unhesitatingly support Sobchak and Yeltsin. Yet, in his writings he confuses anti-communism with Russophobia, condemning the post-1945 U.S. policies toward the USSR as proof of its plans to destroy Russia (quoting or misquoting an unfortunate single statement by Allen Dulles in 1945, in which there is a confusion of Russia and communism, and misrepresenting it as standing for the whole U.S. Soviet and Russian policy for all times). He also attacks Reagan for the term "Evil Empire," which was clearly and exclusively aimed at the communist dictatorship, not Russia. There are numerous such incongruities. Thus, Ioann idealizes the pre-revolutionary Russia as a true Orthodox society in one place, and in another quotes from his favorite mid-nineteenth-century Russian saint, Ignatii Brianchaninov, describing the decline of Orthodox Christianity and general Christian morality in Russia of his time in very alarming terms. A similar contradiction in terms is contained in Ioann's repetition of the Union of Orthodox Brotherhood's claim that the murder of the Russian royal family was a ritualistic act (the Brotherhood's formula is "ritually killed by the Jews"—Ioann does not spell it out) in which the idea was to kill the heir and deprive Russia of a future, writes Ioann, forgetting that according to the medical diagnoses of the time the tsarevich was not to live to see his twentieth birthday because of his acute hemophilia. So what future for Russia did he symbolize had he not been murdered? See Ioann's writing in *Sobesednik,* 1993, no. 1 (3), entire issue; idem, "Tvoreniem dobra i pravdy," *Sovetskaia Rossiia,* 15 March 1993; idem, "Da smushchaetsia serdtse vashe," *Pravda,* 23 June 1993.

48. Oral information from Father Potapov, 10 November 1993.

49. Metropolitan Ioann, "U nas s patriarkhom net raznoglasii," interview by A. Shchipkov, *Nezavisimaia gazeta,* 16 April 1993.

50. S. Averintsev, "Dostoinstvo ierarkha est′ dostoianie tserkvi," *Izvestiia,* 13 March 1993; Iu. Buida, "Pochemu zovut gorodovogo . . ." *Nezavisimaia gazeta,* 28 May 1993; A. Kuraev, "Pravoslavie bez molodezhi," *Moskovskie novosti,* 4 July 1993; S. Bychkov, "Vozhd′ raskola," *Moskovskie novosti,* 25 July 1993; D. Pospielovsky, "Vzgliad

izdaleka," *Moskovskii komsomolets,* 17 July 1993. The list would be incomplete without mentioning the St. Petersburg mayor, Sobchak, who, addressing a conference "on church and society" organized by Metropolitan Ioann in early May 1993, castigated Ioann's writings by warning that "there is a danger that the reviving Russian Orthodox Church can become an aid of yesterday's communists . . . this danger is clearly visible in the collaboration of many bishops with communist movements that hide under the flag of Russian nationalism." A. Shchipkov, "Tserkov', Sobchak, politika," *Smena,* 25 June 1993. Metropolitan Kirill, one of Russia's brightest bishops, dared only very indirectly to criticize the isolationist trends of antagonisms and a priori suspicion of all things foreign, without, however, naming any names. See Kirill, "Russkaia pravoslavnai tserkov'," n. 42.

51. A. Kuraev, "Nuzhno otlichat' podlinnyi svet ot religioznogo kitcha," *Rossiiskaia gazeta,* 14 August 1992.

52. See Metropolitan Ioann, "Ia zhazhdal poznat' istinu," interview, *Nauka i religiia,* 1992, no. 3 (March), pp. 48–49; idem, "Vo Gospode my ediny," interview by V. Solodovnikov, 1992 (clipping from an unnamed and undated paper).

53. There is a host of articles on both sects. See, for instance, Oleg Karmaza, "Komsomol'skaia boginia," *Komsomol'skaia pravda,* 26 June 1993; A. Shchipkov, "Bran Bogorodichnogo tsentra s 'Belym bratstvom,'" *Nezavisimaia gazeta,* 16 June 1993; "Seminar po problemam t.n. 'Bogorodichnogo tsentra.'" *Infobiulleten' OVTsS,* 25 March 1993, pp. 3–7. According to *Iusmalos,* Maria Devi is a deity containing Jesus and married to Ioann Svami, sometimes referred as John the Baptist, and their child will be Khristos Iusmalos, a new deity. In reality Maria Tsvigun (her real name) was a minor Komsomol functionary in Kiev and had a family of her own. Then appeared Ivan Krivonogov on the scene, a former *Znanie* lecturer and a toolmaker who tried his hand at private business but went bankrupt. One day he declared himself to be "Adam and the Sun" all in one, left his family, married Maria, and built up the whole myth. They found the religion business more profitable. They own two houses in Kiev now but have moved to Poland, as Ivan Krivonogov is wanted by the police for regular crimes. The sect has at least ten thousand followers, promised a global catastrophe for 1 July 1993, and the doomsday for 24 November.

54. A. Pavlov, "Serdtse d'iavola," *Rabochaia tribuna,* 4 June 1993.

55. Vsevolod Chaplin, "Oni ne pravoslavnye," *Moskovskie novosti,* 20 June 1993.

56. Kuraev, "Nuzhno otlichat' podlinnyi svet ot religioznogo kitcha."

57. "Konfessional'nyi landshaft Rossii"; and Pavlov, "Serdtse d'iavola."

58. *Infobiulleten' OVTsS,* 28 April 1993, p. 9. A. Kuraev in "Propast' ne tak uzh velika," *Moskovskie novosti,* 29 August 1993, writes that the influx of the American preachers has split Russian Protestants into a minority who approve of American methods and a majority of "nativist" Protestants raised in the Russian spiritual traditions, that is, in the Orthodox culture, who disapprove. The latter, represented, for instance, by the Odessa Baptist Seminary periodical, which publishes works by the Eastern church fathers and Orthodox theologians, disapprove of the Americans. In their theology they are moving closer to Orthodoxy, have lately begun to refer to their prayer houses as churches, decorate them with icons, place crosses on their domes, and call their chief regional presbyters bishops. He even muses that disapproving of their American brothers' missionary methods, these Russian Evangelicals might one day begin to establish their missions in America, almost unwittingly thus inculcating elements of Orthodox theology into American Evangelism.

But perhaps there is some confusion in Kuraev's observation: the changing of the name of prayer houses to churches may also be an American terminological influence, as may be placing crosses on church spires; even "bishops" may be an importation from American Pentecostalism.

59. "Otkrytoe obrashchenie k sviashchennomu sinodu Russkoi pravoslavnoi tserkvi," flier, 12 May 1990, signed by, inter alia, Averintsev, Nezhnyi, Senderov, and Zalesskii.

60. Nothing has been done so far: *no money*!

61. Metropolitan Kirill, "Soiuz pravoslavnykh bratstv—'redut' Tserkvi," interview; and D. Shusharin's comment: "Ibo o tom, chto oni delaiut taino, stydno i govorit'," *Nezavisimaia gazeta,* 21 May 1992. Also: oral deposition to this writer by A.M. Kiperovskii, leader of the Brotherhood of the Meeting of the Icon of the Theotokos (Moscow, August 1992). On the patriarch's address to the rabbis, see "Vashi proroki—nashi proroki," *Moskovskie novosti,* 26 January 1992, p. 24. But see also Ol′ga Gazizova, "O chem umolchali proroki," *Den′,* 1992, no. 13 (41), p. 5. She makes an idiot out of the patriarch, who allegedly reads out like a machine whatever such perfidious advisors as Kuraev hand him.

62. In fact, it was during the reign of his grandfather, Ivan III, that the Judaic heresy had appeared and was quashed by iron and fire, not under Ivan IV.

63. *Vestnik soiuza pravoslavnykh bratstv,* nos. 40 and 43. See also Ia. Krotov, "Dvoinoi standart," *Moskovskie novosti,* 7 March 1993; and Shchipkov's interview with Ioann, "U nas s patriarkhom net raznoglasii," where Ioann assures the interviewer that in his diocese he does not permit non-commemoration of the patriarch and yet hints at his own sympathy for the ROCOR and its leader Vitalii, deviously hinting that should there be pressure on him from the patriarchate he might switch to the ROCOR.

64. A. Nezhnyi, "O podlinnom tserkovnom dostoinstve," *Russkaia mysl′,* 10 April 1992, p. 8; E. Komarov, "Lish′ by tserkvi byla pol′za: Zametki posle Arkhiereiskogo sobora," *Moskovskii tserkovnyi vestnik,* 1992, no. 8 (May), p. 6. Also this writer's conversation with Fr. Dimitrii Smirnov, a priest, lawyer, and legal advisor to the patriarch. The articles cited above by Deacon Kuraev, Fr. Vesvolod Chaplin, and others. Also A. Kuraev, "Ne boites′," *Moskovskie novosti,* 12 January 1992; and V. Chaplin, "Subbota dlia cheloveka," *Moskovskie novosti,* 12 April 1992.

65. A. Shchipkov, "Popravki k svobode sovesti," and Metropolitan Kirill, interview by N. Babasian, both in *Russkaia mysl′,* 5 February 1993.

66. Metropolitan's oral testimony to this author, and his interview by Babasian, "Russkaia pravoslavnaia tserkov′."

67. S. Nikonov, "Russkii sobor: Popytka dialoga," *Moskovskie novosti,* 6 June 1993.

68. "Aleksii II: Politicheskie strasti ne dlia Tserkvi," *Rossiiskie vesti,* 22 May 1993.

69. "Bogu-bogovo, a kesariu?" *Rossiiskie vesti,* 10 June 1993.

70. *OVTsS-Fax,* 23 March 1993; "Raz′iasnenie Biuro kommunikatsii OVTsS MP," *Infobiulleten′-OVTsS,* 28 April 1993, p.5.

4

Civil Society and Religion in Traditional Political Culture

The Case of Russia

Mikhail Sivertsev

A modern state needs a democratic culture within which political parties can freely function. The absence of any inherent multiparty tradition turns the Russian parliament into a ministry for the output of laws and the parliamentary commissions into departments and trusts, each monopolizing the production of a certain variety of laws and (as was the custom in a monopolist ministry) producing laws for itself.

Russia's multiparty system is making its appearance in a political space inherited from a single-party culture, where the model for a party, in the political awareness of the masses, is the authoritarian party-state. At the same time, a parliamentary party presupposes a culture of civic interaction with other parties both in parliamentary debate and in the struggle for votes.

The Difficulties of the Burgeoning Russian Multiparty System

There are several factors that complicate the development of a multiparty system in Russia: (1) the absence of a civil society; (2) steady resentment and suspicion vis-à-vis the institution of political parties as such; (3) totalitarian habits of political and partisan thinking (there are too many sincere ongoing causes to foster political "consolidation" and "unity"); (4) disintegration of an imperial political space and the loss of political identity; and (5) the absence of a stable law-based state and the recurring spectacle of several parliaments "suspending" each other's laws in their territory—a multipower structure equaling an effective lack of power.

Russia's multipower system is developing under the influence of social, economic, and political modernization processes, adopting standards of party build-ing and parliamentarism that are novel for Russia's political culture but tradi-tional for developed countries. There is a high number of "derived" parties that are busy copying certain examples from domestic or world history.

Russia's Multipartisan Space

The emerging multipartisanship in Russia may be visualized as "stretched out" along a broad spectrum. This space is being created by the increasing numbers of issues and positions over which political groupings continual unite or divide.

The communists-versus-democrats opposition, which dominated the political scene up to the middle of 1991, continues to exist. Suspension of the activities of the communist parties has not put an end to their effective influence on ideologi-cal and political polarization. Not as a single organization, but rather as several competing organizations (complete with the communists-versus-democrats op-position), the Communist Party is still there. Of the causes, let us for the moment concentrate on a simple circumstance: most of the present-day political activists have limited experience, generally restricted within a communist-anticommunist dimension, largely because political socialization materialized within the Com-munist Party of the Soviet Union (CPSU) without any alternatives.

The existing alignment is complicated by a confrontation within the state supporters–state opponents dimension. Disintegration of the political space has sharply aggravated the supporters-opponents confrontation, tempting party lead-ers to make this confrontation pivotal in their party building.

The habitual from-a-movement-to-a-party pattern is being complemented with a from-a-party-to-a-movement model. This feature of Russia's multi-partisanship is a product of the absence of a civil society and of a general perception of the partisanship phenomenon as an authoritarian party. When a movement becomes a party, it usually disappoints its members. What follow are splits, crises, a merger of several parties into a bloc, and, finally, a return to the movement model. Fixed membership—a feature that distinguishes a party from a movement—is an important element of Russia's multipartisan space.[1]

A special and ever-increasing role in Russia's multipartisan space is played by the special groups that existed in both totalitarian and post-totalitarian times. Nonregistered movements of "intellectual kitchen groups," although distancing themselves from participation in the struggle for political power as a matter of principle, have continued to exert a significant influence on political culture.

At issue are religious and spiritual-ecological movements. One substantive feature of these is the combination of two contradictory but extremely important peculiarities: extraterritoriality (the interests of these movements are not con-fined to state borders, new or old) and the renunciation of political activity as a matter of principle. Because of this, these movements have developed a resis-tance vis-à-vis political crises and the disintegration of the political space. So, a religiousness-secularity dimension is a major component of the multipartisan space.

Invariables of the Russian Multipartisan Space

Despite the often unbridgeable differences historically existing between different points in the Russian multipartisan space, it is possible to identify certain common elements proper to all movements and parties, regardless of their position on the ideological and political spectrum:

- Policy and constituent documents contain many common topical and structural elements.
- Many activists bring political habits into the new parties that were gained when they underwent political socialization in structures of the party-state.
- The parties are not numerically strong. There is a desire for broad coalitions as a consequence of their small numbers.
- Parties oriented exclusively toward the leader appear; without the leader, the party disappears.
- Parties oriented toward resolving specific local issues by lobbying the appropriate economic structures (single-problem or single-issue parties)are formed.
- In party structures, a trend toward lumpenization emerges.
- The party comes to be regarded as a corporate structure that has no ideological ambitions and tackles the task of protecting party members.
- To the extent to which it is deemed necessary for the functioning of the party and its authority with mass consciousness, party ideology is ancillary as a matter of principle. Instead there are either parties of historical continuity (heirs to the decimated parties), parties of geopolitical continuity (representatives of international structures), or parties allying themselves with the heirs and the representatives in order to obtain part of their legacy or representation.

Models of Russian Parties

The Russian culture comprises several party models and several party-building patterns. The models considered below are not a definitive list, and more can be added. Incidentally, the existing parties are combinations of several models rather than any single model.[2]

Parliamentary Party

A parliamentary party has a clear-cut electorate, and it takes into account the local specificities. The party strives to form parliamentary rolls, achieves the success of its candidates during elections by permanently working with the electorate, and creates factions in parliament. A parliamentary party is a party of a civil society.

Party-State

A party-state strives to assume responsibility for the state as a whole. Political power and the state's political structures are regarded as components of intraparty power. The party-state has for a long time been a reality of the consciousness (and, indefinitely, the subconsciousness) of the political culture. And for a long time to come, political thinking will keep the habit of associating a party (as an institution of parliamentary democracy) with the model of a party-state. Thanks to this association, there appears a possibility (totally beyond the comprehension of the Western mind) of the coexistence of several parliaments— parallel parliaments and parallel government structures.[3]

A situation is possible in which a party or a bloc of parties will not be fighting for an electorate and parliamentary majority but will form their own parliament and their own government. In the process, the existing parliament will be pronounced "illegal." The emergence of several parliaments in a single political space is a continuation of the situation in which a single space is fragmented into chunks and every chunk comes up with a parliament of its own.

A parliament is a source of legitimacy. Fighting for parliament seats is fighting for a source of legitimacy. The traditions of political culture are such that the source of legitimacy is created by self-nomination.

Parties of Renaissance

At initial stages of their existence, renaissance parties emphasize their status as nonpolitical clubs and assemblies of intellectuals with narrow professional, often "museum," objectives. But the clubs and societies are becoming polarized with sufficient rapidity to create an ideological basis for broad and strong mass movements. Systems of long-term goals evolve in the clubs that may be shared by many political movements. For this reason, renaissance parties are potentially ones around which broad coalitions may be formed.

Parties of Geopolitical Continuity

Parties of geopolitical continuity incorporate themselves in the structures of international organizations, invoking the rights of local affiliates. There may be differing degrees of strength of organizational links, from complete independence to complete dependence. The parties of geopolitical continuity make it possible to obtain status from international structures, thus obviating the need for recognition from the local electorate. Upon receipt of the status of a regional affiliate, the leader begins to enroll members into the local organization by attracting supporters and new members; this provides the candidates for party membership with the special status of a member of an international entity.

Parties of Lobbying Orientation

Parties of lobbying orientation are created to accomplish specific objectives. Broad coalitions of political forces may be formed to stage mass actions, their levels ranging from the electorate to deputy intervention to sponsorship of draft laws.

Party-Family/Clan

As a party-state, a party-family/clan adopts a paternalistic attitude toward party members. The legal culture is nonexistent. Power is obtained by extraparliamentary means. The parliament is an instrument of ratification. The party is the source of legitimate action, and its paternalistic character is a real tradition of party awareness and party thinking. The party-state and party-family models are stable components of Russian political culture. At the level of individual consciousness, and the subconscious, these models become transposed into the Russian multipartisan space.

What features of partisan thinking and self-awareness are inherited by the political subconsciousness, regardless of their position in the new political spectrum?

A party-state and a party-family create a sense of unlimited power and cannot be compared with the parliamentary parties of the European type. European-style parties have a specific personnel policy for the party-state: leaders are continually shifted from region to region. A leader has no time to "overstay his welcome," to establish firm local relationships; the leader is hostilely alienated from the region, in which he or she exercises total authority. A party functionary ascends the rungs of the party hierarchy in the party-state to the extent to which the functionary proves his or her alienation from the local population and his or her subjection to the center. In a word, the situation is opposite to that of the new model of the deputy, who is, at least to some extent, dependent on the population. A party-state and a party-family are models remote from parliamentary parties. But people with experience in political socialization within these parties transpose them into the new political space.

Motives of Party Membership: Expectations and Answers

What expectations attract a person to a party in periods of changing value systems, uncertainty, and loss of social status? What parties answer these expectations?

Membership in a party is expected to restore inner certitude and give a person a stable position in the party structure. A person's position in the party replaces the lost socially definite position. Party membership releases one from the extremely oppressive sense that one is not needed. In other words, party membership helps to overcome a sense of alienation. In the absence of a civil society and a law-based state, overcoming the alienation presupposes that the party affiliation will provide answers to individual requirements in civil society and the law-based state. This is because party membership is called upon to resolve an important social and psychological problem: to give a lost and forgotten (often literally forgotten) person a sense of certainty. In this way, fixed membership turns out to be more natural and desirable than the freedom of "unfixed" presence in a movement.

A party that provides the answer to the expectations of certainty and attention, and restores a purpose to life, is hierarchical and closed. Leaders of such parties, responding to the expectations of certainty and confidence, are authoritarian and have a propensity for quite definite and rigid assessments and programs. In other words, they are prepared to impose concrete and clear ideologies (black-white, ours-theirs). A key feature of these parties is that the leaders are accepted only from within their ranks. Strangers, albeit sympathizing with it and serving it, are not admitted to the "inner" party.[4]

What groups are constantly provoked by the situation to accept the formula of an authoritarian party? They are the refugees and the jobless. The unemployed, especially after they have ceased to receive their unemployment benefits, also find themselves in the status of forgotten refugees in their own region and, psychologically, already strangers. That is why a party of the unemployed and refugees is regarded as a single phenomenon.

A party of the jobless evolves as a party of social protection. For refugees, programs of social protection are complemented with ethnic protection programs.[5]

A party of ethnic defense and a party of social protection are interlinked, have a mass character, and create a special context for the development of Russia's multipartisanship. The unusual and novel nature of the situation lies in that the many millions of refugees entering Russia and the many millions of the Russian diaspora have, during several months, turned into a nonindigenous Russian-language population in need of protection from the Russian government. A legal mechanism to protect the rights of the diaspora Russians is nonexistent in the Russian political culture, and at the present stage of the exodus it is simply impossible for lack of a developed legal awareness. Russian authorities, both central and local, are demonstrating a helplessness and impotence in resolving the refugee problem. In addition, the refugees themselves understand the helplessness of the authorities and are gradually ceasing to pay heed to the existence of authorities as such. In short, by their lifestyle and awareness, the many millions of refugees are already crossing over the bounds of that legal space that is controlled and legitimized by the official Russian authorities.

One substantial feature of this crossing over beyond the bounds of legal space is the mass conviction that it is useless to seek protection from the authorities. The protection of people of the diaspora and refugees thus becomes the task of a party, but one that will be unconstitutional as a matter of principle. From the outset, such parties of social and ethnic protection will assume the functions of authorities (local and central) in order to carry out what official authorities are incapable of doing. The rise of parties lacking constitutional authority is a natural answer to the need for social and ethnic protection in a situation in which the government is unable to ensure this protection by constitutional means.

**Parties and Parliament: Power and Law
Are in Different Spaces**

Parties of ethnic protection and parties of social protection may exist in parallel in Russia's political space, both as constitutional parliamentary parties striving for power by constitutional means and as unconstitutional parties bent on taking power by replacing the existing parliament. Unconstitutional parties may not necessarily seek the violent overthrow of the existing parliament; they may simply deny the parliament's right to be the legitimizing center and, by the technique of self-nomination, take over power in those compartments of political space where the official authorities cannot "reach," uniting with other unconstitutional (antiparliament) parties. Upon their unification, they create a parliament of their own (sobor, duma, constituent assembly, veche, and so on), which becomes the new center of legitimacy. Inside the new center, the unconstitutional parties behave in quite a parliamentary fashion. In the process, disavowing the other (so far official) center is a major component of the activity of the new center of legitimacy.

The enduring existence of constitutional and unconstitutional, parliamentary and antiparliament parties is hard to imagine within the political culture of European parliamentarism, given the law-based nature of the European political space. The legal political culture does not admit even of thinking about, let alone permitting, the parallel existence of several parliaments, that is, of several legal spaces and several centers of political legitimacy.

The absence of a legal political culture, of the inchoate legal awareness of individuals and civil society, gives rise to thoughts of rightful and wrongful, lawful and illegitimate parliament. This approach is even more likely in Russian political culture, in which, for a long time, effectively "illegal" structures that were affiliate structures of a party-state were described as "parliament."

The absence of a law-based state and civil society generates consciousness stereotypes, which in turn tend to support and strengthen the absence of a civil society and law-based state. Thus, the lack of confidence in authority, traditional in Russian culture, and the desire to avoid at all costs contact with authority in deciding one's private problems (which, from the point of view of a law-based state, requires the participation of the authorities) tend to harden the practice of resolving conflict situations out of court. The tradition of "deciding it among ourselves" makes going to court and to the authorities something shameful and patently hopeless. Let us recall a maxim, characteristic of Russian culture: "There is no truth in a court of law." The curious thing is that this approach to the institutions of power, including a court of law, is shared at the level of everyday life (at the level of advice "to avoid a court of law") by the direct administrators of the functions of authority. With this legal awareness, parties are thought of as community assemblies, where matters, including those pertaining purely to community affairs, are decided according to conscience (or according to party conscience).

Institutions of power have also traditionally been concerned with emphasizing the distance between the authority and the "subjects" and, relying on aggressiveness as such, demonstrating to the people the actual absence of rights. It is a tradition of power that regards the lack of rights as a positive value.

In this way, power and law have diverged in the Russian political tradition. That is why, unlike the culture of parliamentary democracies, power in Russian political culture is perceived in such terms as "Can one obtain this or that?" whereas law is concentrated in the tradition "to decide by conscience." Hence the notion, quite accessible to Russia's mass political consciousness, of the possibility of several legal and illegal parliaments exercising their lawmaking activity over one territory. According to this view, a bloc of parties that fails to achieve their ends in the parliament will build a new legal parliament rather than fight for a place in an illegal parliament.

So Russian political culture permits the notion of extraparliamentary centers of legitimation and permits the notion that the parliament (being in reality only the center for ratifying decisions already taken) may be nongenuine and must be replaced by the true and correct one. Given the basic mistrust of authority by both the people and the authorities themselves, however, and given the mistrust of the legal aspect of any authority, an indefinitely long existence of an illegal authority and an illegal parliament turns out to be quite possible.[6] In terms of the in-depth levels of the political tradition at issue, any authority is fundamentally illegal, but it nevertheless exists, and it ought to be taken, despite its illegality, as an unavoidable evil. The result is the prolonged existence, in the absence of any true authority, of the authority represented. There is a gray area in the power space (a multiplicity of legitimation centers), utterly intolerable and incomprehensible, that characterizes a developed parliamentary democracy with its presumption of confidence in the parliament. The space, however, has long existed in Russian political culture as "beyond the limit" and "Russian lawlessness," notions quite well understood by the people as habitual and not offensive to the legal tradition.

Parties and party blocs become centers of legitimacy. In the process, the parliament is seen not as a coming together of different forces and parties, but as a regular, new party that has seized power and is incapable of delivering on its promises.

Multipartisanship and Geopolitics: Parties of
New Regionalism and New Federalism

The outlook for Russia's multipartisanship is largely determined by the geopolitical situation: the disintegration of a single imperial space (legal, economic, cultural, and political). The emergence (or reconstruction) of legal, cultural, and political entities stimulates the rise of parties whose key task is to come to power precisely through the process of the formation of these regional entities. Hence the appearance of parties that may be described as parties of "new regionalism."

The new regionalism parties are busy tracing new frontiers in the geopolitical space, or restoring the old ones. But principally they are looking for new regional or geopolitical centers of power and ought to get their cue from their daily work with party members and the electorate. The parties of new regionalism take a careful attitude to the sovereignty of their local spaces and react with extreme indignation to any actual or imagined belittling of the independence of these spaces.

The parties of new regionalism are opposed by parties of new federalism, which strive to preserve the unitary economic and political space and appeal to history and culture with the vigor of the new regionalists. Parties within the regionalism-federalism dimension have one basic common feature: they are busy dividing geopolitical space. Their conflict is due to the parties' being linked with different centers of geopolitical areas. The center of the Baltic cultural space, the center of the Islamic geopolitical zone, and the center of the Far Eastern cultural area lie beyond the bounds of the space to which the new federalists gravitate.

The new regionalism parties differ from the new federalism parties by the geopolitical centers of cultural and political influence to which the parties are attracted. Over the long haul, one may assume that the leaders and activists of the new regionalism parties will undergo a political socialization in centers of different geopolitical areas, which will complete the emerging political and cultural entities and give them civilized forms.

The new regionalism and new federalism parties can be included in a common group of geopolitical zoning parties. And although a dialogue between those parties is an important condition of their activity, stable structures of a political dialogue are a thing of the future. Now one can speak only about a dialogue between the new regionalism parties only within sufficiently limited bounds.

An Industrial Party: Technocratic Neoconservativism

The emergence of new political movements and parties will increasingly be influenced by the leaders of industrial and overall economic activity. The desire for stability and foreign ties forces them to appeal to political parties as instruments to influence the political stability. There is also a narrower and more specific interest that prompts not only sharing in political influence but also the need to create one's own parliamentary party. This interest has to do with the need to have one's deputy rolls and parliamentary factions capable of pursuing lawmaking activity with sufficient independence.

An industrial party is the vehicle of the economic circles that have already understood that the major economic problems are political issues. One variety of an industrial party is a party of technical lobbying, intended to promote legislative initiatives on major technical and scientific programs.

An industrial party is subdivided into a party of major economic managers and a party of small business. Small business parties will be those of economic protectionism, linked with those of social and ethnic protection.

Industrial parties have a future in the Russian political space. The fact is that Russian political culture needs parties with a rich heroic history and a developed and exclusive ideology, such as industrial parties have. It is the ideology of technocracy, in sufficiently refined variants, converging with that of neoconservatives. As happens in political history, experiments that were absolutely aimless and ineffective in the utilitarian and rational sense produced a rich and strong ideology. In the case of Russian technocracy, the tremendous scale, utopian nature, and tragic aimlessness of the "projects of the century" help to discover a notable potential for technocratic ideologies in political culture. For the purposes of this chapter, it is important to stress the geopolitical scale of the Russian technocratic thinking and to remind the reader that today's industrial parties will inherit not only the vast scale of the ideology but also a *heroic* history of a decimated party. Heroic is used in the narrow sense of a working ideology.

Spiritual-Ecological Movements: Personal Autonomy, Self-Realization, and Political Exterritoriality

One substantive element of the Russian political space are movements brought together by the common theme of spiritual and ecological revival. This includes movements espousing personal improvement and self-realization and movements whose members and participants seek the way toward better forms of personal piety closely linked with the natural forces.

These movements aim at the individual person, the person's inner world, and the transformation of his or her consciousness. Through a network of schools, clubs, and seminars the movements help to bring out a person's potential so that the person can adapt his or her personality to resist an aggressive and hostile environment.

At their very inception, the spiritual-ecological movements develop into small exclusive groups with their own doctrines and spiritual practices of self-concentration and personality integration. They sincerely distance themselves from politics, regarding it as the concentration of the "evil of the world."

Despite their declared apolitical nature, these movements exercise an important influence on the alignment of the Russian political space and are sources of many political lines of force, especially in periods of strife and upheaval. Several reasons combine to make the spiritual-ecological movements a serious political force.

First, the closed groups of spiritual and ecological revival foster a certain type of personality and consciousness, so necessary for leadership of political movements in times of crisis. These personality features are the ability to maintain balance in sharply changing situations, independence, spiritual "exterritoriality," and, finally, the ability not to break, to hold steady for a long time in a situation of uncertainty. Politicians who have made their appearance in the present situation, hailing from well-off and stable structures that did not foster independent political thinking and conduct, lack all this. Leaders who received their political socialization in hierarchies of stable political structures swiftly break in extreme or uncertain situations. Leaders who received their socialization far from the stable political structures, for instance, in movements of spiritual and ecological revival, have important personality advantages in situations of conflict and uncertainty. In addition, they possess a broader, panoramic vision of the state of the world.

Second, the spiritual and ecological movements possess a higher penetrability over the barriers erected by social and state borders. These movements spread in a landslide fashion. Ecological ideas and those of personal change are universal, simple, and comprehensible. The movement has the nature of education and so does not require a complex organizational structure. An autonomous and independent personality is the aim of the movement. That is why the political movements for human rights and freedom of conscience frequently comprise activists from spiritual revival communities: these people possess a heightened sensitivity toward infractions of human rights.

Third, the specific objectives of an ecological character turn out to be platforms on which many movements may unite to carry out effective and purely political actions, such as the change of local authorities.

Ecological movements develop programs that are then adopted by many political movements, regardless of their niche in the ideological and political space—ranging from conservative to democratic.

Religious Movements and Parties: New Consensus and New People for Political Opposition

The spiritual and ecological movements are, naturally, linked with religious and national parties.

In the first stages, religious parties become formalized in accordance with the religious affiliation of their members. Development of the movement causes the religious base to expand, thus leading to numerous splits. This latter circumstance is equally a feature of movements that developed in the Russian political space on the basis of Islam and Christianity, although these religions do not exhaust the possibilities for creating confession-based parties.

The fate of religious parties is usually complicated by the fact that spiritual leaders tend to stress their distance from politics and see their participation in politics solely through vicariously influencing the society with their religious, priestly service. Nevertheless, despite substantial limitations of a doctrinal nature, religion outside politics has, with religious parties, serious promise in Russian politics. This is due to several reasons.

As the unitary geopolitical space of the empire disintegrates, an increasing ascendancy is acquired by social and sociocultural institutions with solid organizational, spiritual, and ideological links of long standing with the European and American cultural space and no ideological links with the previous regime. One ought to stress the importance of the absence of precisely ideological links. The organizational links of all sociocultural institutions with the former regime of the party-state are common knowledge. Of importance in this case, however, is the absence of ideological links (a different article of faith and a different education culture, that is, non-Marxist). Why is this circumstance important in the new process of party building? It is because, despite the clear possibility of being compromised personally (say, a hierarch who collaborated with the regime) or of a social institution being compromised (the church as a political entity that collaborated with the regime), it is impossible to compromise a religion that was always opposed to the ideology of the regime. Consequently, a party developing an ideology for its movement will be confident that at least at the level of ideology the party will not be compromised by allegations of links to the former regime.

Religious parties, being parliamentary parties, will operate on the basis of a different parliamentary role than do the nonreligious parties. The religious ones have a different reserve cadre of deputies, as compared with the deputy corps that developed as a result of an early history of democratic movements. One ought to stress a feature that is important from the point of view of programs of intraparty development of the religion-based parties. While in the general democratic movements and parties massive changes of allegiance by rank-and-file communists and nomenklatura (including the leading nomenklatura) and the joining of new movements and parties were natural, possible, and sometimes simply inevitable, the joining of confessional parties by communists was relatively rare. We witnessed the maturing, within CPSU structures, of several new parties of democratic and social-democratic orientation that formalized themselves both organizationally and ideologically while still inside the party-state in the form of platforms and elections. But it is impossible to imagine the emergence of a Christian or Islamic party as a full-fledged structure inside the CPSU. The complexity of communists joining religion-based parties has to do with serious psychological and ideological difficulties, about which I have been repeatedly informed by democratic movement activists who underwent their political socialization within the CPSU.

This amounts to saying that the religion-based parties may recruit their mass social base and deputy corps out of those who, prior to 1985, were at least spiritually opposed to the regime. The danger of "infiltration" by former apparatchiks, which, incidentally, is a recurring subject of debate in the democratic parties, is minimal, given the difficulties of mastering a religion-based system of values. The cultural barrier is especially visible in Islamic parties. According to my observations, knowledge or ignorance of the Arabic of sacred writings is a significant factor in selecting the elite of the religious party. This formal barrier prevents a possible influx of former communists wishing to return to power through the structures of the victorious parties. The return to power, however, through the structures of an Islamic democratic party not equipped with the fine filters of confessional knowledge turns out to be possible and actually takes place. A similar, albeit less pronounced, situation is observed in Christian movements and parties. The confessional parties possess a significant integrating potential.

Case Study: Islamic Movements and Parties in Dagestan

In Dagestan, Islam exists not only as a religion and a form of personal piety but also as a mode of daily life, a factor organizing the village commune, and a structure of real authority.

Under the repressive regime, in many Islamic regions of the former USSR mosques were blown up, there were very few places where one could learn Arabic, and religious education was nonexistent. At present one can often hear the *alim* in a Central Asian mosque read the Koran in Russian or reproduce a ritual text without knowing Arabic. But in the difficult-to-reach mountain villages of Dagestan, a living tradition of Muslim learning and knowledge of Arabic have survived.

Needless to say, as elsewhere, mosques and madrasahs were closed down, holy books were destroyed, and alims were exiled. And yet even a cursory acquaintance with the state of affairs in the mountain villages of Dagestan reveals that persons born there (first-generation intelligentsia) demonstrate very high rates of survival, preservation, and spiritual resistance of Islam to the repressive regime. The great stability of Islamic culture is a determinative factor in the evolution of the political situation in Dagestan.

A direct consequence of the uninterrupted tradition of Islamic education is the good knowledge of Arabic common among the rural population. At the moment, the centers of Islamic spirituality and Islamic piety, centers that boast highly qualified Arabic scholars, with pupils and schools, are located away from the capital of Dagestan. There is a stable and traditional system of transmitting holy knowledge from the teacher to the pupil. For a teacher of a rural school, to pass on knowledge, to teach Arabic to everyone wishing to learn, is a sacred duty, a necessary part of religious service. The teaching is free; to offer money is an insult. It is therefore quite possible to establish a wide network of Arabic classes at rural schools (although there is a shortage of teachers).

Quite often Islamic learning and holy books are passed on from a grandfather (a surviving alim) to a grandson, who assimilates Islam and goes on to, or wants to, attend an Islamic university in a recognized center of the Islamic world. This process does not involve the urban intelligentsia, which, according to Abdurashid Saidov, leader of the Islamic Democratic Party, "used to be thrown crumbs by the communists, has been orphaned and is waiting for a new sponsor."

A consequence of the uninterrupted tradition of living Islam is a particular identity structure, which is giving rise to a large number of conflicts.

Mountainous Dagestan is heterogeneous ethnically and linguistically, and Islam has long provided a cultural common denominator, a source of firm personal identity. The feeling of community with the Islamic world (Islamic identity) implies gravitation toward the holy Islamic centers and, more specifically, a chance to make a pilgrimage (hajj) to those places. Over several previous decades another type of identity came into being, a sense of community with the imperial center that had different holy objects and pilgrimage places. The generation of politicians who are now middle-aged was taught to want a pilgrimage to the center of the empire.

The conflict between these two types of cultural identity in the local population's political consciousness has recently become more pronounced. The clash around the issue of the hajj that broke out in the summer of 1992 was one of its external manifestations. One of the reasons why the conflict sharply escalated was that the local party nomenklatura decided, as the saying goes, "to change horses in midstream": they hoisted up the air and railway fares and the price of exit visas and tried to embark on the pilgrimage themselves, leaving Islamic activists behind.

As is known, a person who has accomplished a hajj receives a higher community and political status upon return. The party functionaries' intention to use the hajj to regain a position of authority was quite transparent. Having collaborated with the nomenklatura, the Department of Religions for the North Caucasus was abolished as a body and its heads dismissed on the insistence of the new Islamic leaders. It was replaced by the Department of Dagestan Muslims, which is headed by different people.

A living and constantly reproduced tradition of Muslim education creates a special context for the established political movements, turning Dagestan into a fervent Islamic zone and determining the evolution of new movements. Several influential political trends affected by the Islamic context can be identified: the Islamic Democratic Party of Dagestan; the Islamic Renaissance Party; the Department of Dagestan Muslims, which advocates traditional Islam; the Shamil Popular Front of Dagestan; and the nomenklatura party bodies.

There is a persistent impression that the chief distinction between various political movements and between factions inside them is, above all, involvement in international Islamic culture (specifically, the knowledge of Arabic, a clearly defined parameter). The ability to read and interpret holy texts gained by long years of apprenticeship is an indicative characteristic.

The young followers of Islam are not overly concerned about the problems of the middle-aged with their eternal collision between the atheistic Communist Party and traditional Islam. Knowing Arabic and having made a hajj despite the odds, they become aware of themselves as a part of the great world of Islam. After making a hajj, young people feel they have a mission in their native areas to resurrect Islamic culture. Their primary task is to set up a secondary and, in the future, a university Islamic educational infrastructure.

The future local Islamic leaders are not unduly worried about the current conflicts, making it a point to stay aloof and steer clear of meetings and clashes. Their plans and ambitions have a long-term character; they view Dagestan as a section of the Islamic world, they are standing outside party confrontations, and this is where their strength lies.

The division into democrats and fundamentalists is a convention, and may even be quite erroneous. But the self-assumed names of the parties seem permanent enough.

Among the issues held important by the Popular Front are their relations with the Terek Cossacks. The first issue of the newspaper *Call of the Ancestors* appeared voicing a typically unfavorable attitude toward the cossacks. The party nomenklatura keeps dreaming Bolshevik dreams containing an unexpectedly high quota of overt neo-Stalinism (the personal experience of belonging to the top echelon in a great power must be dear indeed to these people) but is also trying to fit into the new Islamic power structure, although there it cannot hope to enjoy the same amount of power and the old status.

Special mention must be made of the section of the nomenklatura that has come up against the issue of the economic conversion of military plants. This is a serious problem. In a region with a large redundant workforce, the closing down of several factories may sharply accelerate lumpenization; the emergence of lumpen parties and movements is practically unavoidable. This is why it is essential to take due account of the specifically Islamic features of the region when drawing up conversion programs.

In the past few years, in the region's rural areas, the local Islamic leaders were obliged to perform the functions of both religious and secular authority. Thus, formal legitimation of decisions is also becoming Islam's prerogative, and this baffles the former secular leaders and causes them to rebel, albeit sporadically.

What do the prospects of Islamic geopolitics in the North Caucasus imply? The transfer of a significant part of this region from the zone of Russian cultural and political influence to that of Islam. This means that strategic geopolitical prospects are beginning to be determined by a new cultural and religious orientation: the leaning toward the imperial center is being replaced by gravitation toward the religious centers of the Islamic world.

The chief sign of the change of geopolitical zones is the change of the places where the future local and religious leaders are getting their political, religious, and cultural instruction. In the not-too-distant past, such leaders were trained at the imperial center or in a hierarchy oriented toward it. A condition of a successful career was the rejection of Islam and the prospects of advancement within the Islamic political tradition. At present, a substantial number of the young people inheriting the posts in the local and regional power structures are getting this sort of instruction in the world centers of Islamic culture and politics, far away from the Commonwealth of Independent States.

What are the causes and consequences of the progressing transfer of a large part of the North Caucasus to the Islamic geopolitical zone? One of the chief causes is the amazing intactness of the live tradition of Islamic learning. The exceptional survival capacity of Islamic culture is crucial for the current and future situation in this region.

A direct sign of the live and, most important, continuous tradition of Islamic learning and education is the widespread knowledge of Arabic among the country people. An important consequence of this situation is an identity conflict unknown to the central regions of postimperial Russia. As mentioned above, the sense of community with the world of Islam (Islamic identity) implies gravitation toward the holy centers of the Muslim world, which is realized in the opportunity to make a hajj, to confirm one's Islamic identity to oneself and others. Meanwhile, for several decades another type of identity, that with the imperial center, has been shaped. The conflict between these two identities has recently become sharper and has to be reckoned with, because the opportunities for the old nomenklatura to find a place for themselves in the new power structures in the Islamic regions are much more restricted than those of their colleagues in the postimperial center.

The future religious leaders in the region perceive the North Caucasus as part of the world of Islam. In view of this, they are interested in stability and are not inclined to let the Russian authorities into their local problems, justly believing that they are able to settle their own accounts. The old elite, on the other hand, tries to involve the Russian authorities in local conflicts, which is making the transition to new geopolitical identity less stable.

The Idea of a Monarch in Party Building

Considering the crisis state of Russian political culture, as well as a certain sense of confusion before realities of a geopolitical nature (disintegration of the traditional imperial space), one ought to understand the opportunities and complexities of the monarchical idea that is being implemented in the monarchical parties and some of the confessional and liberal currents of political thought and practical political action.

The monarchical idea is shifting into the realm of political reality in direct proportion to the transition from crisis to hopelessness. The monarchical option appears to be most likely if several Russian-language states emerge in Russia's territory, divided by Turkic-language, Islamic (theocratic or Soviet) republics (states). Central Russia will become isolated socially, economically, and culturally (but not politically)[7] and will acquire the status of a regional center of power, remote from the mainstream lines of force of the present-day geopolitical space. In this case, the internal Russian experiments will no longer be of concern to the external areas along the perimeter, and they will become less resistant to monarchical changes (were they to take place). Restoring the monarchy with this turn of events is possible, however, not in the form of the imperial model but as an institution of tsarist power of the preimperial world (which, as a rule, is not taken into account by the neomonarchical programs, which tend to visualize the return of the monarchy only in the form of the imperial period).

Although one witnesses a certain revival of the monarchical idea and monarchical parties in European political culture as well, the Russian monarchy has some features that make parallels with Europe a remote prospect.

The idea of a wholly tsarist power is an important component of national Orthodoxy, and consequently, any program to restore Orthodoxy (except the Old Believer program) eventually raises the need to restore the institution of the monarchy as part of the institution of the church, which exists for full-fledged spiritual and religious practice in the first place, and as an institution of temporal power, in the second. For Catholics and Protestants, the institution of the monarchy lies outside the church, is not part of the positive doctrine, and is quite temporal. In short, the nature of Catholicism and Protestantism as full-fledged institutions, doctrines, and individual spiritual practice is not connected with the monarchy as an institution.

The idea of Russian monarchy is linked with that of autocracy, with the idea of the absolute and indivisible power of the autocrat differing from the European idea of constitutional monarchy, which presupposes distribution of power. The stability of the autocratic interpretation of tsarist power (as distinct from constitutional monarchy) indicates a delimitation of the notions of power and administration that characterizes Russia's neomonarchical thinking. If we assume administration to mean something that can and must be delegated and distributed, power is viewed to be in principle indivisible and undelegatable and capable of belonging in its totality only to the autocrat.

The mounting internal confusion in terms of values and psychology—assuming that the remaining elements of the Russian political space shrink to a smaller size and become ethnically and religiously (with the prevalence of Orthodoxy) more homogeneous—may put the idea of monarchy on the plane of practical politics, meaning the advent of strong monarchical parties and the creation of a parliament (*sobor*) that will call (not elect) the tsar. In any case, the problem of monarchy on the ideological plane is being discussed not only in the monarchical parties but also within liberal movements, to say nothing about Orthodox-oriented movements.

Despite a certain reasonable prospect for the idea of a monarchy in present-day conditions, the political implementation of a program to restore a hereditary autocratic monarchy will have to face a number of practical difficulties, the principal being the dynastic disputes and contradictions that have latently raged during the entire three hundred years of the reign of the house of the Romanovs. Add to this the unique propensity of Russia's political culture for the impostor phenomenon, the constant splits in the monarchical parties, and the arguments over the genuineness of the aspirants, and the influence of the monarchical parties on mass consciousness will be significantly weakened. That is why it is possible to restore the monarchy within the framework of a bloc of liberal and Christian movements, for whom the idea of monarchy is an important, but not central, part of their programs.

The special complexity and uncertainty of the monarchical parties has to do with the fact that traditionally monarchical movements were linked to the general state of Russian officers. The political independence of a monarchical movement (or party) has traditionally rested on the respectable activity of officers in the public arena in the form of a party representing the special interests of this exclusive and corporate institution of an estate. The crisis of the system of professional values of the present-day officer corps, its rapid lumpenization in the past decades, the lack of traditions of an estate, and the officers' perception of themselves as the defeated party, however, have deprived the officers of their role as the backbone of monarchical parties for the foreseeable future. This latter circumstance is added proof of the possibility of the idea of monarchy as part of the programs of liberal and Christian parties and of relatively little probability of vigorous political action by the monarchical parties proper.

Socialist and Social Democratic Parties: The Return to the Russian Tradition of Redistribution of Property

An examination of the prospects of Russia's multiparty system would not be complete without taking into account the possibilities of socialist and social democratic parties and movements.

Although socialist and social democratic movements are associated in the mass political consciousness with the defeated communist regime and are thus discredited, still the movements have potential. The potential is sufficiently high, if one removes from the titles of the parties of socialist and social democratic orientation the discredited components but keeps the socialist approaches related to social protection.

What are the factors that again make Russian political culture open for socialist and social democratic ideas and parties? Rapid impoverishment and unemployment, the absence of social guarantees, waning credibility in the government, and the people's growing awareness of themselves as a developing country with people living below the poverty line are all factors. The habit of freeloading has developed only recently; previously there was a (mass) feeling of honest earnings and dependence on results of work. Now the people are in the position of a sponger, hoping only for international assistance. As a developing country in social distress, Russia is becoming a target for specialized relief programs of international socialist centers and parties. Another factor is the return of earlier forms of Russian socialist thinking, complete with doctrines of redistribution of property, including the return of criticism of the institution of private property.

The current socioeconomic situation will rapidly restore the psychological experience, concentrated in the Russian version of the socialist doctrine of a class society. Unlike the situation at the turn of the century, there will be no problem in adapting a Western version of socialist doctrine to Russian conditions. Suffice it to activate the ethic of hatred and revenge in order to recall the criticism of the institution of private ownership and interpret the current situation as a realistic illustration of theories that for decades have been a dull subject drilled in schools and higher education institutions. When the past decades saw the appearance of societies to study and restore the primary truth of Marxism, the regime mercilessly persecuted and eradicated those societies. Now there are no ideological or political obstacles in the way of reviving socialist teachings. And there have appeared social segments that will find in such societies answers to their vital questions. The process of education will be all the more rapid, as they will not have to learn everything again but rather will have to rethink past knowledge, using convincing and simple examples.

Problems of Neocommunism

One ought not to regard the fate of the communist movement as finished in the Russian political space. Numerous variations of communist parties, which will differ substantially, are possible, depending on regional features. The tenacity of the communist idea in Russian political culture is tied to the fact that, historically, the communist movement assumed the character of a messianic, scholastic movement, religious in its doctrinal and practical components. This is a classic neopagan religion of salvation with a developed civilian cult and a powerful theocratic history of an order.

That is why purely temporal measures (banning or suspension of activity) go hand in hand with the religious energy contained in the messianic and salvation themes of communist ideology. They strengthen (or restore) the ideological potential of the communist movement.

A significant integrating and restoring role will be played by the Chinese brand of communism, keeping its geopolitical potential as one of the world's ideological systems. For mass consciousness of the young, the defunct communist empire will become an inspiring example of a larger-than-life heroic past and a direct pointer to vast Sino-communism, especially against the backdrop of a paltry life of scarcity and blind alleys in personal curricula vitae. This was the case with the French worker-intellectuals of the 1960s and 1970s, who demonstrated sympathies for Chinese communism.

The Religious Dimension of Russian Political Culture

In the future Russia will be a constitutional law-based state, but for now it is a traditional (religious) law-based state. For Dagestan it is traditional Muslim law—the *shari'ah*, or traditional pagan (pre-Muslim) law (*udut*). For central Russia it is "law and grace" in opposition. This opposition is a result of traditional state-church political culture—law under grace. In the deepest level of the Russian political culture, church and state are inseparable.

The history of Russian party building is a history of party-church-order building. When there was one party it was obvious. But the model and tradition of thinking party leaders of a one-party system have been inherited by the new multiparty system.

Now there exist many small party-orders. And in the new multiparty space law submits to grace. That is why one of the main dimensions of political thinking and political culture is the religious one.

Notes

1. "Fixed membership" in a party means that an individual must formally enroll as a party member, pay dues, identify himself or herself with party leaders, and have personal responsibility for party policy.

2. Parties may change their ideologies twice in a week. It is a myth to talk of a constant constituency under the name of party at the present time.

3. The model of the party-state is responsible for the concept of a party based on the "factory plant" that prepared *all* members of parliament. In this sense the parliament is a legislative structure of the party-state.

4. There are examples of authoritarian parties in all places of the ideological spectrum, from the Democratic Party of Russia to the monarchical party. Authority is a style of party building.

5. Public opinion surveys seem to contradict the idea of party membership as an important solution to psychological identity; few Russian respondents identify themselves with any political party. Refugees entering Russia and Russians of the diaspora, however, belong to illegal, unregistered organizations and avoid discussion of them. In addition, the mass political consciousness lacks a tradition linking party to this problem.

6. An alternative illegal parliament was formed on the basis of unregistered parties and a trade union movement that denied the legislative power of the legal parliament.

7. The enormous diaspora in all of Russia's territories will mandate political interdependence with central Russia.

5

The Church and Politics in Contemporary Russia

Vsevolod Chaplin

Contemporary Russia is a country of rapid change. These changes, which touch all aspects of state and societal life, are also naturally reflected in the church's relations with the state and society. At times, the dynamic of change is so swift that it is difficult to follow and analyze its development. Nevertheless, the processes brought forth by recent events in the area of relations between the church and the world of Russian politics can be discerned, and they deserve our consideration.

As is well known, until the beginning of perestroika the potential for Russian Orthodox Christians living in Russia to participate in political processes was extremely limited. Decrees of the All-Russian Central Executive Committee and the Council of People's Commissars of 1929 limited church activity, for all practical purposes, to conducting services, though this merely legalized the de facto situation. Any attempt by the church to undertake any sort of political activity was mercilessly terminated and resulted in exile, incarceration, condemnation to labor camps, and, sometimes, the death penalty. The situation changed somewhat after 1943, when Joseph Stalin, frightened by the war and searching for the support of the Russian Orthodox Church in those difficult days for the government, met Metropolitans Sergii, Aleksii, and Nikolai in the Kremlin and promised to improve the church's position in the Soviet Union. From that moment on the church had the opportunity to state its position on social problems. It is not difficult to understand, however, that this was allowed only within the framework of calls to struggle against foreign enemies and expressions of support for the existing state order and leadership in the USSR. Despite this severe limitation on the ability of the church to express itself on social problems, the very fact of the appearance in the press and on the radio of speeches by priests was very positive at that time. People who not long before spoke of the final death of religion could see that the church was alive and that its representatives were not the evil renegades that atheistic propaganda made them out to be.

The church's voice began to be heard a little more clearly in the early 1960s. Nikita Khrushchev, then leader of the country, took a somewhat ambiguous position toward the church. Being a convinced Communist and sincerely believing that in the early 1980s it would be possible to show the people the "last priest" on television, Khrushchev needed a certain external cover for his policy and had to create a civilized facade for it. Strange as it may seem, it was this very individual who, having closed an enormous number of churches, seminaries, monasteries, and the like, once again allowed the Russian Orthodox Church to undertake international activities, join the World Council of Churches, and establish contacts with the Roman Catholic Church and other foreign religious communities, as well as with a series of peacemaking institutions.

This activity, even if it did not go beyond the bounds of permissibility during the Khrushchev, and later Brezhnev, years, was extremely important for the internal development of the Russian Orthodox Church. In the first place, international contacts prevented the church's religious and social theory from stagnating completely, shut up in a circle of problems limited by the borders of the ghetto created for the church in the Soviet Union. Second, the attention of foreign brothers and sisters to the problems of Christians in the USSR, skillfully attracted by the church hierarchy, sometimes helped to ease repression and save churches, monasteries, seminaries, and other church institutions from being closed. Third, and perhaps most important, the hierarchy, clerics, theologians, and teachers at spiritual academies and seminaries suddenly had the opportunity to discuss contemporary social problems with foreign Christians (for example, within the framework of the World Council of Churches), study potential courses of action, and realize the role of the Christian community in the social *diakonia*. In those years the Russian church was forced to concentrate its social attention on problems very far from Russia (for example, the rights of blacks in South Africa or the Middle East conflict), while at the same time it could not openly say even a word about what was happening in Russia itself. The experience it gained, however, was not lost. It came in very handy when the church in Russia obtained its freedom and immediately came in contact with the multitude of problems festering throughout the territories of the former Soviet Union, problems that in many respects were similar to those in other areas of the world and had been discussed in the World Council of Churches with the participation of Russian Orthodox representatives.

It must be noted, however, that the then organs of state power were unable to limit the activity of church people solely to the participation of official representatives of the Moscow Patriarchate in international Christian activities or in the official Soviet peace movement. Many priests, and especially laypersons, people who as a rule were educated, attempted to involve themselves informally in the life of society. They established circles that discussed questions of Christian policy, undertook seminars, created samizdat journals and collections, and sometimes even simply gathered at somebody's apartment to talk about what pained them. Until the beginning of perestroika, however, and in certain cases during its first years, such activities were completely and absolutely prohibited and resulted in the most severe repression. Many of the informal church activists were incarcerated, sent into exile, deprived of jobs, or subjected to persecution solely because they dared openly to argue, whether in writing or out loud, that Christian policy in Russia was not a thing of the past and could be resurrected. Individuals from this circle became, in the years that followed, the founders and leaders of many Christian political unions.

As is known, 1988—the one-thousand-year anniversary of the baptism of Russia—was the turning point in church-state and church-societal relations. From this moment on the state stopped publicly declaring its enmity toward the church. Areas of church service, common in any society but forbidden in the USSR, began to be reestablished. Little by little church charity revived, the first Sunday schools appeared, and the church began to consider the establishment of its own system of education. New churches and monasteries were opened, and a variety of Christian cultural activities began to be held: exhibitions, concerts, lectures. All this took place in conditions of great enthusiasm, allowing the priests and believers to open any door and feel for themselves the new social forces and, in a sense, to be almost capable of moving mountains. Unwisely, however, not long after the thousand-year anniversary, attempts to create a Christian political structure came to light.

In 1989 the Christian Democratic Union of Russia (CDUR) was created. Aleksandr Ogorodnikov, at that time a well-known defender of rights and recently released prisoner of conscience, became its leader. Ogorodnikov's organization, the first of its kind, did not remain alone for long. In 1990 the Russian Union of Young Christian Democrats (RUYCD), whose leader was Dmitrii Antsyferov, and the Russian Christian Democratic Party (RCDP), whose leader was Aleksandr Chuev, split off from the Christian Democratic Union. That same year saw the creation of yet another large (by Russian standards) Christian democratic political structure: the Russian Christian Democratic Movement (RCDM). Among the leaders were figures well known in the world of unofficial religious activism: Viktor Aksiuchits, Gleb Anishchenko, Vitalii Savitskii, and the priests Gleb Yakunin and Viacheslav Polosin. In 1992, however, two organizations split off from the RCDM as a result of disagreements over positions taken by Aksiuchits and other leaders of the movement. They were the Russian Christian Democratic Union (RCDU), headed by Fr. Gleb Yakunin, Valerii Borshchev, and Vitalii Savitskii, and the Moscow Christian Social Union (MCSU), headed by Dmitrii Khanov. Not long afterward the RUYCD allied itself with the MCSU.

These organizations, all of which are currently in existence, are still not playing a significant role in the political life of the country, and as a rule, attempt to act in blocs with more influential political forces. Their political orientations vary greatly. The RCDM and the MCSU, for example, are self-described centrist parties, close to the state-conservative sections of Russian society. In the recent political crisis the RCDM completely supported the parliament. The MCSU has very clearly stated its monarchist sympathies. Chuev's party, the moderate-conservative RCDP, supported the course set out by President Yeltsin and traditionally identified with liberal circles. As a whole, however, it follows a political line traditionally identified with Western Christian democratic parties. The RCDU and the CDUR hold to a Western view of Russia's future and traditionally support the more liberal-democratic blocs. Membership in the Christian democratic parties is not large. According to the yearbook *Parties and Unions of Russia with Religious Priorities,* published by the Parliamentary Center of the Russian Federation, membership is as follows: RCDM, 2,000 to 2,500; RUYCD, approximately 200; RCDU, approximately 800; and RCDP, not more than 50 active members. (This information, as far as can be determined, was supplied by the organizations themselves and therefore should be considered a rough approximation only.) It is obvious that up to now Christian democratic structures have not had a significant number of followers. One cannot deny, however, the existence of a significant interest in the Christian element in politics and the possibility that support for the above-mentioned parties might increase following elections for the new Russian parliament, the Federal Assembly, on 11–12 December 1993.

With the Christian democratic structures somewhat in place, political organizations oriented toward the reestablishment of a monarchy in Russia—constitutional or absolute—began to form. In 1992, at a congress of thirty-four monarchist organizations, the All-Russia Monarchist Center (ARMC) was created. The supporters, as a rule, recognize the right to succession to the throne of the descendants of Grand Duke Kirill Vladimirovich (after the death in 1992 of his son, the Grand Duke Vladimir Kirillovich, the inheritors to the throne are considered to be his daughter, the Grand Duchess Maria Vladimirovna, and his grandson Georgii). A better known monarchist organization is the Union of Christian Rebirth (UCR), the followers of which do not recognize the unconditional right to the throne of the descendants of the Grand Duke Kirill. They believe that the question of who should occupy the throne is best decided as it was in the seventeenth century, in the Land Council, an assembly of popular representatives. Both the ARMC and the UCR are supporters of nationally oriented conservative forces and, as a whole, disagree with the policies of the current government of Russia. The ideologies of the ARMC and the UCR are clearly tied with the tradition of Orthodox Christianity. Among the supporters of these organizations are significant numbers of priests and active laypersons of the Russian Orthodox Church of the Moscow Patriarchate and the Russian Orthodox Church Abroad, a church structure created after the postrevolutionary emigration and today having no canonical ties with the Moscow Patriarchate.

Religious motivation, mainly connected with Orthodoxy, is present in the activities of radical nationalist associations such as the National Patriotic Front (NPF), founded in 1986, and numerous structures that have sprung from it as independent organizations (one such organization, the All-World Anti-Zionist and Anti-Masonic Front, today calls for the rebirth of ancient Russian paganism). The NPF finds itself in close contact with representatives of the Russian Orthodox Church Abroad, who, however, have recently had a falling out with the leadership.

Having begun through dissident and other informal means, the rebirth of Christian political activity within Russia has gradually affected official church structures and broader layers of church society.

In 1989 events took place in the Soviet Union that were unthinkable even two to three years earlier. Pimen, the patriarch of Moscow and all Russia, Aleksii, the metropolitan of Leningrad and Novgorod (who is the patriarch today), Pitirim, the metropolitan of Volokolamsk and Iurovsk, and Petr Buburuz, the archpriest from Moldova, were elected people's deputies of the USSR. Patriarch Pimen wrote in his political program:

> Today the center of a renewed system of values in our country is occupied by the individual. And each individual himself must carry out the great transformation, beginning with himself, through moral cleanliness, through the renewal of the internal "I," and through internal peace. The church calls on its children to actively follow Christian ideals, to preserve and strengthen in the family such undying spiritual treasures as love, chastity, and mutual charity. We know that in such families the new generation is being raised with love for God and neighbors, with devotion for our motherland. . . . True social justice, the goal toward which we all strive, will undoubtedly assist in overcoming social conflicts, the most direct causes of which are economic hardship, the dissolution of the health system, undervaluing of the importance of culture in the life of the individual and society, as well as other negative phenomena. In connection with this we should end the discrimination in pay against many professional groups, increase state expenditures for the defense of the family, motherhood, childhood, and old age, for the development and improvement of the means to protect the public health, for the stimulation of the spiritual development of the individual, and for the defense of nature and historical monuments and culture. . . . The church does have something to offer in contrast to today's spiritual bankruptcy. Christian tradition is oriented toward the individual, his uniqueness and moral responsibility. The church can oppose the growth of mass culture with a rich spiritual legacy centuries old; it can oppose the consumer's attitude toward life with self-sacrifice for neighbors; it can oppose the culture of violence, cruelty, and war with sermons of mutual love and peace in the world.

The selection in 1990 of Metropolitan Aleksii as patriarch of Moscow and all Russia coincided with a period of unusual interest in the church, Christianity, and everything else connected with religion on the part of political groups. A certain weakening of the old political structures and the rise of sharp struggles of ideas and political groups on the internal Russian stage forced many political forces to look for an alliance with the Orthodox Church. This situation became characteristic of the relationships between the church and political structures in the following years.

The year of election and enthronement of Patriarch Aleksii was also the year of the creation of the Russian parliament, at that time the most radical democratic force among the structures of power of the USSR. The popularity of the church at that time was higher than at any time before or after. Everything connected with Orthodoxy was received by popular opinion with great euphoria. The media and society seriously discussed the possibility of the instant assistance of the church in any sphere of state life, from agriculture to subsidies for independent artists. Naturally, the election potential of candidates who proclaimed Christian values as their credo and those who served as priests was incredibly high. Many priests wanted to run for election to the Russian parliament and organs of local government, with victory seemingly awaiting the majority. It was at that point that the Bishops' Council of the Russian Orthodox Church made a very wise decision. It declared that none of the priest deputies could speak in the name of the church, only in their own name, and that the candidacies of priests should be permitted only after receiving the church's blessing (a priest would have to receive the blessing of the bishop of the diocese, and the bishop would have to receive the blessing of the synod).

In the elections for the Russian Federation parliament four priests were elected people's deputies: Bishop Platon of Yarolslavl and Rostov, Archpriest Aleksei Zlobin of Tver', Archpriest Viacheslav Polosin, and Fr. Gleb Yakunin of Moscow. Incidentally, the last was nominated and elected without the blessing of the bishop of his diocese, although no disciplinary measures were brought against him. Polosin soon became the chairman of the parliamentary Committee on the Freedom of Conscience. Several priests and church activists were elected deputies of local organs of legislative power. Many representatives of Christian democratic associations also became deputies at different levels.

The social position of the church only began to be worked out in a quickly changing Russia. Nevertheless, within a year Russian Orthodox Christians found themselves caught in a whirlpool of stormy and dramatic events demanding of them a clear understanding of the problems of society and the corresponding responses.

The first of these events was the tragically famous attempt to overthrow the government on 19–21 August 1991. In the first hours of the putsch Patriarch Aleksii II asked for President Mikhail Gorbachev's opinions on the events to be made known; the originators of the putsch had said he was ill. On the night of 20–21 August, as military equipment was moving toward the barricades that had arisen around the so-called Moscow White House, the patriarch made the following plea:

Brothers and sisters! Our fragile civil peace has been destroyed. According to the news we have received, military actions are beginning and blood is being spilled. Under these circumstances my duty as patriarch is to warn all those to whom the word of the church is important and dear: anyone who takes up arms against his neighbor, against unarmed people, commits a very grave sin, excommunicating himself from the church, from God. Those individuals will be in greater need for tears and prayers than the victims themselves. Save us God from the horrible sin of killing our brothers.

Several days after the elimination of the threat of a coup, Patriarch Aleksii II and the Holy Synod of the Russian Orthodox Church appealed to the bishops, the clergy, and all its believers with the following words:

History is being judged. And each of us could produce a bill before the legal party and state circles for the unparalleled suffering that has fallen on us or on our loved ones over the last seventy-three years. However, let it not be that the completion of the trial will lead to the planting of the devilish seeds of evil and bitterness in our hearts. Let there be a transformation of our minds and a liberation from the totalitarian consciousness that made millions of people in our motherland willing and unwilling participants in lawlessness. . . . A new page has been turned also in the history of the church. We believe that the last external fetters that held back the church's free conciliar development [*sobornost'*], as willed to us by our glorious forefathers, and through their decisions at the Council of 1917–18, are falling off. . . . It does not follow, however, that the path before the Russian Orthodox Church is an easy one. The church itself will be forced to act in an environment of spiritual ruin—the bitter inheritance left us by previous leaders.

Life, unfortunately, has shown the prophetic truth of these words: the removal of the totalitarian control of the church has not made the position of priests and believers easy. Newer and greater problems are standing before the church, among which the problems of intranational relations and national conflicts in the territory of the former USSR deserve special mention.

On 27 December 1991, after the signing of the Belovezhsk agreement, which put an end to the existence of the USSR, the Holy Synod of the Russian Orthodox Church examined the situation:

The self-determination of the republics that were part of the former Soviet Union is a reaction to the many years of the domination of the totalitarian nationalities policy, under which the natural desires of the peoples to live according to their own traditions and aspirations were repressed. However, the reestablishment of what has been lost and destroyed in the lives of the peoples should be accomplished by worthy and morally justified means. Therefore, in defending one's own freedom one must not encroach on the freedoms of one's neighbors. One must not commit another sin—the creation of artificial barriers of misunderstanding and alienation among the peoples united by a multiplicity of ties, historical, religious, and cultural in nature. . . . Not long ago the majority of the republics that had made up the Soviet Union created the Commonwealth of Independent States. We believe the Commonwealth to be a realistic manner in which to maintain the community of peoples under existing conditions. However, the fate of the documents signed in Almaty will be determined by the manner in which they are fulfilled. "If what he has built survives, he will receive his reward. If it is burned up, he will suffer loss" (1 Corinthians 3:14–15). The process of creation of the Commonwealth is of use to all only when the positive principles of the signed agreement are fulfilled by real content. In the opposite case, it is the worsening of intranational conflicts, chaos, and social economic shocks that will bring losses to each and every one of us that await. . . . Without pretending to a special position in the state, nor to ideological and political privileges, our church will carry out its mission, entrusted to it by God, of pastoral concern for people, particularly for those who have fallen on especially hard times now. The Russian Orthodox Church hopes that the new relations between the states of the Commonwealth will be built on principles of law and generally accepted morals, will assist in the dissemination of national traditions, will guarantee the freedom of religion and will exclude attempts to create a state dominated by religion or ideology.

Unfortunately, the call of the church to avert intranational conflicts went unheard. As is well known, in many regions of the former Soviet Union intranational contradictions have become dramatically sharper, leading to the creation of a great many "hot spots." For the Russian Orthodox Church such a state of affairs has become especially problematic, for it is Russian although it unites people from many nationalities and has its canonical structure spread throughout the entire territory of the former Soviet Union, including Georgia. In Ukraine there is the Ukrainian Orthodox Church, a part of the Moscow Patriarchate. This church, whose adherents are the majority of Orthodox believers of the country, is independent in its internal affairs. Its ties to the church hierarchy in Moscow are practically limited to the participation of the metropolitan of Kiev and all Ukraine in the meetings of the Synod of the Russian church and with the blessing of the newly elected first-hierarch of the Ukrainian church by the Moscow patriarch. Complete independence in matters of finance, administration, enlightenment, and church-societal relations is enjoyed by the Belarusian Orthodox Church, the Orthodox Church in Moldova, the Latvian Orthodox Church, and the Estonian Orthodox Church. Dioceses of the Russian Orthodox Church operate in Kazakhstan, Lithuania, and Uzbekistan, while parishes connected to the nearest diocese centers operate in Azerbaijan, Kyrgyzstan, Tajikistan, and Turkmenistan. (It is also interesting to note that the Japanese Autonomous Orthodox Church, as well as a whole series of dioceses and parishes on all five continents, is also under the jurisdiction of the Moscow Patriarchate.)

The situation of the Moscow Patriarchate, with the major part of its congregation scattered throughout several states, has forced the church to approach carefully and with special concern the national conflicts that have arisen in the territories of the former USSR, taking into consideration the lawful interests not only of the population of Russia and the Russian-speaking populations of other states but all people, including both those who are and who are not part of the Russian Orthodox congregation. Especially tragic for the church are the conflicts in which representatives of peoples historically connected with the Russian Orthodox Church find themselves on different sides of the front. Such is the case in Moldova, where historically Orthodox people of a single church have taken arms against each other.

Under these circumstances the church has unwaveringly strived to assist the process of reconciliation through the efforts of the clergy, the parishes, and the church hierarchy. Practically every nationality conflict taking place in the territories of the former Soviet Union was noted in the special documents of Patriarch Aleksii II, in which the head of the Russian Orthodox Church called for peace and understanding among the peoples.

When the bloody conflict in Moldova flared up, Patriarch Aleksii addressed the Orthodox Christians in this country with the following words:

> Remember that God, according to St. John Chrysostom, "ordained retribution for sin now and in the age to come." Do not burden your souls with a deadly sin! Stop the bloodshed immediately, stop immediately the disastrous strife that takes away the lives of your relatives and friends, your brothers and sisters in humanity! You must know that no political, national, social, or human differences can give anybody the right to kill others. If we do not understand this, we shall become enemies to our own selves. I, the patriarch, whose faithful live in many states and belong to many nations, share the pain and feelings of all people in your country— Moldovans, Russians, Gagauzes, Ukrainians, Belarusians, and sons and daughters of other peoples. You are to be blamed equally, and you equally deserve a better life. I am deeply aware of the aspirations of the Moldovan people who have gained independence and now wish to consolidate their sovereignty. But it is my conviction that other ethnic groups in Moldova should also enjoy all the civil rights and have a say in its ordering.

A similar position was expressed in the patriarch's documents regarding the conflicts between North Ossetia and Ingushetia (North Caucasus), Georgia and South Ossetia, and Georgia and Abkhazia. The conflict between Georgia and Abkhazia was one of the key points in the joint declaration of Patriarch Aleksii and Il'ia II, the catholicos of all Georgia. The conflict over Nagorno-Karabakh figured in a joint declaration signed after meetings between Patriarch Aleksii, the supreme catholicos of all Armenia, Vazgen I, and the chairman of the Clerical Council of the Peoples of the Caucasus and head of the Azerbaijan Muslims, Sheikh ul-Islam Allakhshukur Pasha Zade. Patriarch Aleksii and the Holy Synod of the Russian Orthodox Church have also addressed a number of other external problems, specifically, the situation in the former Yugoslavia. All sides in the conflict, to each of whom the Russian church expressed its warm feelings in these documents, were unfailingly called to peace and harmony on the basis of mutual blessings.

Nevertheless, there remain other issues of contention, closer to home, to which the church has yet to respond that are not diminished by the situation in the so-called near abroad. Russians are worried about the plight of their fellow nationals living in other republics. In their desire to learn the opinion of the church on matters of political life, political forces have searched for ways to ally themselves with the church.

Under present conditions the Orthodox Church needs to develop its own social thought, something that until now has not existed in the form seen in, for example, the Roman Catholic Church. Until the revolution the social thought of the church, which had developed in the strict framework dictated by the state of justifying the existing order, could not communicate anything to the people except teachings about the God-given absolute monarchy and about the messianic significance of Russian tsarism as a governmental structure that defended the Orthodox faith and was the protector of the church. Subsequently, after 1917 any developments in Christian social theory were limited by the borders of a narrow ghetto of thinking clergy, who did not have the opportunity to speak with broad masses of the people or with underground groups of Christian intelligentsia. It must be noted, however, that attempts at Orthodox Christian exploration of contemporary social ideas and the place of the Orthodox Church in society were undertaken by many Russian religious philosophers and publicists during the end of the nineteenth and beginning of the twentieth centuries, some of whom continued to work after emigration. Among them were such well-known authors as Nikolai Berdiaev, Bishop Sergei Bulgakov, Fr. Pavel Florenskii, Ivan Il'in, Aleksei Khomiakov, Ivan Kireevskii, Vasilii Rozanov, and Vladimir Solov'ev.

The revival of religious social theory in present-day Russia began at a time when broad strata of society were for all practical purposes deprived of knowledge in this area, and the development of Christian views on social life was not freely forged. When the fetters were removed, the ideas of Christian society were compelled either to return to prerevolutionary ideas or to borrow from foreign sources, including Russian émigré sources. As a result, today there is a fairly significant number of active priests and laity oriented toward the ideal, traditional for the monarchical period of Russian history, that the Orthodox autocratic reign is the only form of government worthy of the church's blessing; but there are also many people—mostly members of the Christian democratic parties of the so-called liberal tendency—who believe that the modern Russian Christian social doctrine should be adopted from Western sources. These two tendencies at times are utterly polarized and frequently are expressed in extremist viewpoints. Thus in the secular press one can find, on the one hand, articles by Christian activists calling for the excommunication from the church of anyone who does not support the idea of the revival of autocratic monarchy and, on the other hand, articles calling for the rejection of Orthodoxy because it supposedly interferes with the establishment of a market economy and the reform of the Russian political structure. The overwhelming majority of Russian Orthodox priests and laypersons, however, are sufficiently apolitical, and the debate on the future of the social doctrine of the Russian Orthodox Church is taking place inside a fairly narrow stratum of those among the clergy and church people interested in political matters.

It seems that the extremist point of view, relying blindly on copying pre-revolutionary or foreign ideas, does not have vital force. Experience shows that Russian Orthodox social theology will look for its own original, new path in the stormy waves of the worldly sea. Naturally, on this path it is impossible to get by without taking into account the experience of predecessors in Russia and abroad, as well as followers in other countries. This experience, however, needs creative sensibility.

The first attempt to form the view of the church on social problems in contemporary Russia was the address of the Bishops' Council of the Russian Orthodox Church, held from 31 March to 4 April 1992, in Moscow. Following are excerpts from this address that reflect the church's current position on political matters:

> Our word to the powers that be is about people who think today about their daily bread with alarm—orphans and invalids, elderly people and families with many children, the unemployed and those who have abandoned their homes involuntarily. The authorities should be very concerned about them. After all, their suffering is the suffering of all people, in which, as in a person's body, "if one part suffers, all parts suffer with it" (1 Corinthians 12:26). We should not forget that the care of the orphaned and the wretched is the highest obligation of society, the measure of the worthiness and moral health of a nation. The state should not throw its citizens to the tyranny of fate. Otherwise the bitter cup of suffering will inevitably spill over onto all of us.
>
> We appeal to the leaders of political parties and social movements. We are troubled that sometimes people want to see in the church only a political fellow traveler, the guide of some sort of plans and ideas. The mission of the church is to serve the Lord, to save souls, and to preach the Gospel among the people.
>
> We appeal to the peasants. Remember that your labor is extraordinarily important; after all, the stability of society, the harmony of the people's existence, and human life itself depend first and foremost on it. Revive the spirit and tradition of our glorious agriculture, be zealous masters of the land, labor alone or together with others in the name of your prosperity and that of your neighbors. Treat the earth, which has been cultivated by many generations of your ancestors and which, in the words of the psalmist, is the Lord, with love and care.
>
> We appeal to entrepreneurs—to those who by their energy, talent, and labor turn to the matter of reviving the economic structure, ruined by decades of totalitarianism. Keep in mind that the path you have taken requires a firm moral foundation, the absence of which can lead to the sin of moneygrubbing. Do not forget about mercy and charity in order to win God's blessing for your labors.

We appeal to all working people. In your hands is the future of the people, the well-being of whom today depends not so much on the system as on the individual, his actions and internal content. Do not permit yourself to be used for the perpetration of unjust political acts. Set aside your vital interests, be concerned not only about your material prosperity but also the all-round good of society.

We appeal to the people who are occupied with the upkeep of the monuments of Orthodox culture. The church shares this concern and with all its power will assist the revival of cultural heritage. We are prepared to cooperate with the genuine caretakers of the upkeep of the monuments of the past.

We appeal to public figures, employees of the press, radio, and television, people of culture and arts, teachers, anyone who is not indifferent to the moral aspect of the people. Our society flouts moral norms without circumspection. Immoral behavior in the economy, politics, and human relations has become habitual. The propaganda of eroticism and pornography, exploiting instincts for commercial and ideological purposes, destroys the individual, the family, and society.

We appeal to our compatriots. Both the church and society have to liberate themselves from the legacy of totalitarianism. But we should not pretend that we have freed ourselves from internal enemies. Every one of us—bishops, clerics, laypersons, every person desiring good for the country, the people, and themselves—has to change our lives. The Holy Scripture commands us to be made new in the attitude of our minds (Ephesians 4:23), to live a new life (Romans 6:4). Repentance, changing the attitude of the mind—only this can save us from repeating the lessons of history. The renewal of the church and the renewal of society begin with the spiritual renewal of every heart under the influence of the Holy Spirit. We believe that God will help us on this path.

Still another important document disclosing the view of the head of the Russian Orthodox Church on social issues was an interview with Patriarch Aleksii in October 1992 in the Moscow weekly *Megapolis Express*:

The church is not only clerics and monks. A Christian can be a worker, tiller, scholar, journalist, politician—and he will not be less of a Christian because of it. In any free society it is normal and natural that Christians, concerned about the state of this world, play some role in political processes. The church does not hinder its offspring in participating in social life. But the developed tradition is that a bishop, priest, or layman who participates in political activity on his own initiative expresses only his own personal opinion. The opinion of the entire church, where there are people of different cultures, nationalities, and political, theological, and philosophical views, can be expressed only by the Bishops' Council or those empowered by the Council.

I consider that nevertheless not the clergy but the active laity should be the basic formulators of Christian principles in politics. The task of the clergy is to educate such laypeople, and not to aspire to take upon themselves a burden that is not canonically placed on the clergy. The more laypersons there are who are capable of soberly, wisely, and truly ecclesiastically engaging in politics, the sooner, I hope, pastors will be able to devote more time to their age-old service.

The political activity of church offspring should bring peace, accord, truth, and justice to people. No current human "interests," about which it is fashionable to speak today, should be the reason for hurried actions and decisions, the more so toward enmity and discord. God's servant—whether bishop or layperson—should be, in his service, above the personal, above the social, above the national, even above the narrowly ecclesiastical. The good of every person—near or far—should be his main concern. And not only material good, but first and foremost spiritual good.

Absolutism in present-day Russia is impossible and dangerous. Considering the grave moral state of the people, we are not insured against the usurpation of power by a person who, in the guise of an Orthodox autocrat, begins to undertake dark deeds. Whether it will be a constitutional monarchy or republic is largely unimportant. The main thing is that this structure, this state system, guarantees in fact a free and just social structure in which all people in the country could find a place of dignity and could live in accord, helping one another.

The creation in Russia of Christian political organizations is the first increase of participation of laypersons in this sphere of life. Of course, the tradition of Christian politics in our country again begins from nothing, and the first attempts cannot be complete. I personally do not like that our Christian political associations constantly fragment because of personal differences; moreover, at times each small group claims to reflect general church opinion. But I am convinced that with time, with experience, and with a higher level of discussion, petty discord will yield to the unification of efforts. And here a genuine Christianization [*votserkovlenie*] should help—not the ability to bow correctly and read Slavonic, but an understanding that we all, however different, are a part of the Body of Christ and his united Church.

Christian democracy in Russia, like in any other place, is possible. But have we matured enough for it? I am afraid that still much time will pass before a realistic conception of Russian Christian democracy, one that people can understand, appears. And the realization of this conception is still further in the future.

The Orthodox Church always supported genuine patriotism; the Christian is called upon to love his earthly home and his neighbors, to adorn the earth with his labor, to defend his compatriots from dangers. But Christian patriotism cannot have anything in common with nationalism—that is, hatred of other peoples, feelings of national superiority, blaming people of a different nationality for one's own misfortunes, and calls to violence. The activity of national movements truly arouses apprehension. What they sometimes try to bring out in the name of the church is incorrect. But the doors of our temples are open to them, as they are open to all. To excommunicate from the church, to silence them, is the easy way, but this way is not Christian. Let people come to us, and if they truly want to become Christ's pupil, then we accept them with love and will cure their wounded hearts.

I am not a supporter of the idea of state religion. I suppose that the majority of the clergy and believers think the same. I have said repeatedly that the best relations of the church with the state are relations of free cooperation. The destinies of the church and state are different. But they are called to mutual assistance—without pressure on one another, without replacing one another, without red tape, without attempts to limit the freedom of the church, the state, society, or the individual.

That summarizes the position of the church hierarchy on social and political problems.

In recent times the Department of External Ecclesiastical Relations of the Moscow Patriarchate has attempted a rapprochement between the social activity of official church structures and the work of Christian associations. At the end of 1992 in Moscow, in the Danilov Monastery, a roundtable entitled "Christian Associations in Contemporary Russia" took place in which the head of the department, Metropolitan Kirill of Smolensk and Kaliningrad, participated, along with other department employees and the heads of RCDP, RUYCD, RCDU, RCDP, MCSU, and ARMC. In the course of the discussion, an agreement in principle was reached on the possibility of conducting regular meetings of the representatives of the department with workers of the Christian social structures with the aim of mutual assistance toward working out the Christian approach to contemporary social problems. The first of such meetings was the two-day seminar "Christianity, Patriotism, National Problems," which took place in March 1993 in the Danilov Monastery. Participants in the seminar—among them priests, theologians, secular specialists, representatives of RCDP, RUYCD, RCDM, RCDU, MCSU, ARMC, UCR, and several other Christian social organizations—gave reports that reflected a highly varied palette of views on the problems of relations of the Christian to the national question.

The other direction of the activity of the department—the structures for church relations not only with foreign countries but with all "foreigners," that is, the secular, the worldly—is contact with political and social associations of the most varied orientation and participation in measures taken by them. This contact and participation, however, does not have a political character but rather is an attempt to bring the position of the church hierarchy, on these and other issues, closer to political circles and the public. Such work today requires a serious intensity of forces and the utmost clarity in the understanding of the genuine role of the church in society. The latter is particularly necessary in connection with attempts to use the participation of representatives of the church in political measures for demonstrating church support of a particular political force, which in the end can split the church body.

One of the large social undertakings that took place recently with the active participation of the Russian Orthodox Church was the First All-World Russian Assembly, which called on the initiative of social organizations of a patriotic direction and placed as its goal not the acceptance of political declarations but the scrutiny of issues of the national existence of the Russian people on the basis of dialogue with people of the most varied political convictions. The leaders of political parties and movements were not among the speakers at the Assembly;

they attended only as guests. The most important result of this undertaking was that, within church walls, assisting the reconciliation of differences, people professing widely varied political doctrines—from communists to monarchists— could agree with one another on many problems that the Russian people face, particularly with reference to their historical conscience.

The unifying and conciliatory role of the church, very clearly demonstrated at the All-World Russian Assembly, is beginning to have an impact on Russian social life. The peacemaking activity in the country, however, is not something new for the Orthodox Church: in the fourteenth century, for example, two famous Russian saints—Aleksii, the metropolitan of Moscow, and Sergii of Radonezh—did much for the reconciliation and unification of broken and hostile Russian principalities. In the process of reconciliation of opposed social forces, the church does not strive to give political prescriptions or to teach politicians and social leaders how to act; it does not take sides; and it does not evaluate the acts leading to confrontation from a purely political perspective. The church strives simply to call the sides in the conflict to peace and agreement, to the search for mutually acceptable decisions, and does so with a readiness to make its mediation possible in dialogue. Namely, such a position makes church mediation acceptable for all sides in the conflict, even when all other ways have been exhausted.

The critical confrontation of legislative and executive powers, which has complicated political life in Russia in recent months, has not remained outside the field of view of the hierarchy of the Russian Orthodox Church. In the work of the Ninth Congress of People's Deputies of the Russian Federation (March 1993), when the real danger of violent conflict appeared, the church appealed to the contenders to begin a dialogue, to reject political ambitions, and not to permit violence. A special appeal was made to the army that called for nonparticipation in the conflict. A lessening of the confrontation after the March crisis did not last, however. As is well known, in late September 1993, after the signing by Boris Yeltsin of the decree on the step-by-step constitutional reform, the Supreme Soviet of the Russian Federation, dissolved by the president, and other social forces refusing to submit to this decree began an armed confrontation with the executive power.

From the very beginning of this dramatic crisis, the head of the Russian Orthodox Church called for restraint from any actions that could lead to the spilling of blood and incite civil war. The address of the patriarch containing this call was sent on 22 September from San Francisco (where he was at the time) to Moscow and quickly disseminated by the Russian mass media. Leaflets with the text of the patriarch's address were disseminated near the Moscow White House as well. Cutting short his visit to the United States, Patriarch Aleksii addressed Russians in these words:

> Russia is on the edge of an abyss. Currently we have a choice: either stop this madness or bury any hope for a peaceful future for Russia. It is particularly

tragic that today Russian power can collapse. If this happens, future generations will damn us. . . . One bullet fired near the White House can lead to
catastrophe, the bloody echo of which will reverberate throughout the entire
country. That is why I am calling for a lessening, by all peaceful means, of
armed confrontation.

Having mentioned the necessity of treating every person kindly, the patriarch
said that no political goals could hinder the provision to those in the White
House of medicine, food, water, and medical assistance, for it should not be
permitted that physical exhaustion lead people to uncontrolled violent acts. The
first-hierarch of the Russian Orthodox Church also called the conflicting sides to
a dialogue and suggested any form of necessary mediation.

On 1 October the Holy Synod issued a declaration in which it warned against
the dangers of civil war and Russia's collapse, dangers that became real during
the crisis. "He who resorts to violence first," the Synod document read, "will be
doomed inevitably to defeat and damnation. By the power granted by God, we
declare that he who raises his hand against the defenseless and spills innocent
blood will be excommunicated from the church and anathematized."

The initiative of the patriarch on mediation in the conciliation of the conflict
brought approval from both sides. On 1 October, in the Danilov Monastery,
negotiations began in which several state and church leaders took part: Patriarch
Aleksii; Metropolitans Kirill and Iuvenalii; Sergei Filatov, the head of the
president's administration; First Deputy Prime Minister Oleg Soskovets; Ramazan
Abdulatipov, chairman of the Council of Nationalities of the Supreme Soviet; Iurii
Voronin, deputy chairman of the Supreme Soviet; Iurii Luzhkov, the mayor of
Moscow; as well as one of the judges of the Constitutional Court. The negotiations, in the words of one of the participants, proceeded under very difficult
conditions. On 2 October, however, the participants in the dialogue managed to
agree that a bipartisan commission of experts would work out a plan for the
gradual disarmament of the people gathered in and around the White House, with
the simultaneous removal of the government's armed formations. There appeared
real hope for resolving the armed conflict. But the next day was different. Soon
after the supporters of the dissolved parliament began violent activity in the streets
of Moscow, the parliamentary side placed on the negotiations conditions that were
deliberately unacceptable for the presidential side. Then several hours later the
capital of Russia, as one journalist expressed it, "was awash in blood."

On the morning of 4 October a document titled "Entreaty of the Patriarch"
was disseminated in Moscow. Patriarch Aleksii wrote:

> My brothers and sisters! God's anger has spilled over onto Russia. Christ died
> for our sins. People did not listen to the church's appeal, they raised their
> hands against their neighbors. Innocent blood has been spilled. Now every
> hour can lead the country to new suffering. When blood is spilled, there is a
> great temptation for revenge, a temptation for cruelty and for flouting the

freedom of neighbors. At this moment I implore all those who have weapons in their hands: Be kind to your neighbors! Do not permit the demon of hatred and revenge to deprive you of your senses! Do not permit the death of women and children, of the wounded and unarmed who turn up in the area of the conflict, of all those who are not involved in the violence! Do everything possible to stop the spilling of blood.

The appeal of the church for peace and agreement was not heard. And today the church grieves for the victims of political strife. Simultaneously, it believes and hopes that society will again be revived and that Russia will rise from the ashes and will finally be able to become a country living freely and peacefully.

On 8 October, the day of remembrance of Saint Sergii of Radonezh, the gatherer and peacemaker of the Russian land, Patriarch Aleksii, members of the Holy Synod, and other hierarchs, at the Troitse-Sergieva Monastery in Sergiev Posad (outside Moscow) for the holy day, issued an address in which they made the following statement:

> In spite of the fact that the mediating mission of the church was accepted by the sides of the conflict, people flouted moral principles and spilled innocent blood. This blood cries to heaven and, as the holy church warned, becomes the indelible mark of Cain on the conscience of those who inspired and carried out the murders of our innocent neighbors. God renders them their due in this life and on Judgment Day. Now, as quickly as possible, it is necessary to return to peaceful life, to guaranteeing human rights and civil freedoms, and the establishment of law and order in the country. It is necessary to set aside all discord and to create the life of our fatherland.

As Russia prepared for new elections to the federal parliament to be held in December 1993, the question was again put to the church hierarchy about the possibility of priests taking part in the elected organs of power. At the 8 October meeting of the Holy Synod, the following decision was made:

> Taking into account that the work of several organs of representative power, first and foremost on the federal level, will be carried out on a permanent basis or will require a full commitment of time, which excludes the possibility of the fulfillment by a priest, in case of his election, of his pastoral obligations laid upon him by God; recalling that such work of priests in the higher organs of state power already has aroused confusion and division among believers—to direct priests to refrain from participating in elections as candidates for deputy in the organs of representative power operating on a permanent basis and, first and foremost, on the federal level. According to the determination of the Synod, priests who do not submit to this decision will be defrocked.

This decision by the Holy Synod had many critics. Nevertheless, it seemed timely. When the demand for the activity of politicians in cassocks is unusually high, but the voice of the majority of priests and believers not inclined to political extremes is drowned in extraordinarily loud exclamations of a small number of radically oriented priests, such as the "conservatives" and the "liberals," there is a great danger of substituting, in the eyes of the public, the genuine opinion of the church with the opinion of its politicized radical stratum. In addition, the clergy is called upon to play a particular role in the church and society. A pastor, responsible before God for the souls of all the people that come before him, cannot reject a person for his political convictions, cannot politically oppose someone from his flock, and cannot alienate a person with too sharp an adherence to political views that that person may not share. One wants to believe that Christian political activity will become a sphere for the application of responsible efforts of laypeople who can, without qualms, represent in society the interests of the most varied, even diametrically opposed, political forces, if only the activity of the latter does not directly contradict their faith and Christian morality. Pastors are called upon to stand above political divisions, to make peace and bring people together for their good. Pastors of the church should not remove themselves from the problems of "this world." But they should evaluate these problems, including political problems, not by political but by moral criteria. Their actions are not a political struggle but rather the word of God's truth and service to God and people. Their weapon is not the sword, not the machine gun, and not sharp words. Their strength is in God and faith in Him.

Before Orthodox Christians of Russia stands a long and seemingly difficult search for their place in the social and political life of a changing Russia. At this stage, this search will be conducted under conditions of gradual abatement of the religious boom that characterized Russian life in the past few years. In spite of the fact that the mass explosion of religiosity, which the Russian press wrote about not long ago, has not occurred and, by all accounts, will not occur, the Russian Orthodox Church remains the largest faith in Russia, to which ten million people belong, at least nominally.

How will relations of Orthodox priests and the laity develop toward political life? What will be the future of new Christian political structures? The answer to these questions probably only God Himself knows. One wants to believe that Russian Orthodox Christians, learning from the mistakes of their predecessors and from the experience of foreign believers, can avoid two ruinous temptations: on the one hand, the temptation of power, the temptation of the possibility of acquiring influence and winning over one's opponents with purely peaceful political means; and on the other hand, the temptation to leave the increasing difficulties in some ghetto fenced off from the complicated and contradictory contemporary world by a wall of isolationism, justified by some sectarian thesis of selection.

God willing, they will avoid both. For only then will the Russian Orthodox Christian community be able to carry out its social service through service to God, liturgy after liturgy, proclaiming Christ to people through the example of the life of His followers. Only then will it be able to help, by word and deed, its rulers, its people's leaders, and all of Russian society to live life gently and serenely in all piety and purity, for this is good and pleases our God the Savior (1 Timothy 2:2–3).

6

Glasnost and the Gospel

The Emergence of Religious Pluralism

Michael Bourdeaux

A British resident in Moscow, where he is successfully establishing the first Quaker meeting since before the Revolution, wrote recently:

> Seldom in human history have so many people been tested with such traumas as in the former Soviet Union, whose totalitarian regime has had far more shattering and catastrophic effects than we ever imagined before we set up our home here, however well seasoned we were by our previous experiences of communism. We do not mean to paint a simplistic black and white picture of communism versus capitalism, but we admit that we had underestimated the damaging and stultifying effect of 70 years of totalitarianism. "We have been left like children," said a woman to us today, "our people are without values, the worst of the West is plaguing us, criminality and nihilism are soaring to previously unimaginable heights." She returned to her Moscow flat a few weeks ago and found her 17-year-old son strangled. "Suicide," insisted the police. "Never," she said, but no one took notice of this, and Russia still has no inquests.[1]

Apart from being surprised that he was surprised, one notes that the point is well made. No society has ever experienced communism before, therefore there are no guidelines for the emergence from it. It is, in its relentless way, only logical that a system that so disregarded human values and made no provision whatsoever for any transition to democracy or pluralism should contain within its broken power an unquantifiable threat to human well-being, possibly to the globe itself. The outbreak of uncontrolled violence in the former Yugoslavia is the best-known example, but there is a less reported though comparable threat of catastrophe in numerous places in the former Soviet Union.

There is, at the same time, optimism to set alongside the pessimism. Religion, unfettered by the bands that confined it for three generations, is already playing a positive role in rebuilding the morale of many people who have witnessed the collapse of the former ideology.

Although little noted by the journalists and rarely acknowledged by diplomats and academics, religion played a remarkable role in holding on to values that, in the long run, the Kremlin was not so mistaken in viewing as "anticommunist." Here almost alone, within communities where Islam and Judaism as well as Christianity exerted their semiclandestine influence, an alternative set of values prevailed. Preserving them was a task for the human spirit, and in so doing individuals exhibited a quality of moral bravery that inspired others to follow.[2]

It is not therefore accurate to attribute the rebirth of religion in the former Soviet Union to Mikhail Gorbachev's glasnost and perestroika. As we saw in the introduction, there were considerable forces at work even as far back as Nikita Khrushchev's violent antireligion campaign of 1959–64, and not only where this religious motivation was allied with nationalism. Repression often drove the faith underground, but deep in the soil it intensified and sprouted shoots that eventually broke the surface.[3]

During Gorbachev's brief period of ascendancy, every aspect of religion began to flourish with vigor. At first conventionally, but mildly, he called for atheism to combat religion more effectively, just as his predecessors had done in stronger language. He was too preoccupied with other agendas to promote a new policy on religion, but by 29 April 1988 he had come to see that the church was a powerful force that could, if harnessed, possibly move forward the limping process of perestroika at a more rapid rate. Consequently, he met the leaders of the Russian Orthodox Church in the Kremlin on that day and addressed them in these words:

> Believers are Soviet people, workers, patriots, and they have the full right to express their convictions with dignity. Perestroika, democratization and openness concern them as well—in full measure and without any restrictions. This is especially true of ethics and morals, a domain where universal norms and customs are so helpful for our common cause.[4]

Never before in history had the ruler of a communist state spoken in anything remotely resembling these terms, but for Gorbachev the word was a prelude to action. This meeting took place just six weeks before the Russian Orthodox Church was due to celebrate its millennium, marking one thousand years since the baptism of St. Vladimir in the river Dnieper in Kiev. Gorbachev's action opened up a short period of intensive interaction between church and state during which the former was given access to, sometimes even domination of, the media and allowed to populate some of the most hallowed domains of the Soviet empire, such as reception halls in the Kremlin and the Bolshoi Theater. For a few weeks it seemed as though the Communist Party had yielded primacy to Holy Russia, which was being reborn before the eyes of an astonished populace.

Gorbachev's New Law

At the April 1988 meeting, Gorbachev stated that, in return for its effort on behalf of perestroika, promised by church leaders in the name of some forty or fifty million believers, there would be a new law on religion that would restore to people their rights, of which they had been deprived since Lenin's first antireligion decree of January 1918. Later, in 1929, Stalin's Law on Religious Associations removed even the theoretical protection believers had retained while the constitution still proclaimed the right to "religious propaganda." The legal fiction of the separation of church and state remained, but the law itself even went so far as forcing every would-be congregation to register with the state (which could and usually did refuse) and expressly allowing secular veto over the membership of the governing body of any local group that did manage to register.

Worse still, there was an undefined corpus of secret decrees and local KGB instructions that secured even more severe restrictions, leading, for example, to the total ban on the existence of the Ukrainian Catholic (Eastern Rite) Church in 1946, after the Soviet Union had conquered a huge tract of western Ukraine, where this church predominated. Nowhere was there provision for seminary education, though after 1945 the Russian Orthodox Church managed to reestablish a minimal amount after negotiations with Stalin on 4 September 1943, a "thank you," as it were, for support in the war effort. De facto, the totality of religious activity was reduced to worship within the four walls of a registered church, permitted in any place only on the say-so of the Soviet authorities.[5]

These laws remained in force until the fulfillment of Gorbachev's promise in 1990. The debate on a new law after all those years was bitter; it took place behind closed doors and was not formally reported, but there were numerous leaks. It is easy to imagine, for example, the horror felt by the old guard at the prospect of seeing Christian teaching in schools, something they must have thought had been banished forever, but it became a reality as a result of the law the Russian Federation passed (the Soviet version never went this far).[6]

The new religious practice began to operate in the towns and villages throughout the Soviet Union well before the promulgation of the new law. In fact, religious restrictions simply fell away from the time of the millennium celebrations of 1988, and the last religious prisoners gained their freedom the next year. A new law on publishing began to operate from 1988, removing censorship and by implication freeing the religious bodies from one of the most massive restrictions they had endured. In some places, notably Estonia, Christian publishing houses immediately sprang up.[7]

The new property law of March 1990 conferred on religious communities the right to own buildings, which had been abolished in 1918 and had been the state's most effective tool in curbing their activities. This, of course, left open the question of reparation for the damage done to, often the total destruction of, churches, mosques, and synagogues throughout the territory of the Soviet Union. Nevertheless, places of worship began to reopen everywhere, a process that continues today.

A further early gain was the repeal in April 1989 of the secret laws. Therefore, as well as the reemergence of the Ukrainian Catholic Church from the underground, the major cities witnessed burgeoning activity from Pentecostals, Jehovah's Witnesses, and dozens of other foreign imports—Hare Krishna, Scientologists, Moonies, and so on. Their unrestrained activities, after the failed coup of 1991, would soon stimulate a rapid reassessment of needs in the area of legislation.

These piecemeal changes were accompanied by secret talks on the formulation of a full body of new laws. It is typical of the chaos that accompanied Gorbachev's last days in power that not one, but two—or potentially sixteen— new laws emerged in the fall of 1990. Individual Soviet republics had always had their own laws, but these were slavishly in harmony with Soviet master versions. As soon as the republics began to exercise muscle, the scope for anomalies immediately became apparent. The Soviet Union passed the Gorbachev version, while the individual republics, notably the Russian Federation, began to pass their own, with scant regard to the Kremlin's decrees. The collapse of the Soviet Union a year later, of course, saw the end of Soviet legislation and put a certain amount of logic back into the process.[8]

The short-lived Soviet law would be considered satisfactory according to international norms (including real provision for the separation of church and state), while the Russian version—especially regarding religious education in state schools—is more "liberal" than, for example, its American counterpart. It is one of history's more satisfying reversals that the new Russian law was guided through the parliament by no less a figure than the recently elected deputy, Fr. Gleb Yakunin, who had suffered imprisonment under the old law for eight and a half years.[9] The whole procedure of evolving new legislation was more tortuous than can be set out here.

Both versions forbid any incursion of atheist activities into the religious sphere, while the church (as well as Judaism and Islam) is officially allowed access into what had up till then been hallowed communist territory: the media, clubs, lecture halls, prisons, even the army. Religious activities at once began in all of them, reinforcing the impression that Holy Russia really had been reincarnated on the territory of the Soviet Union. Religious festivals would be properly marked, with the major ones becoming public holidays. However, there is no specific provision for Muslims to keep Friday as their holy day or for Jews to keep shabbat sacred (nor for that matter for Christians to observe Sunday).

One major difference between the two is that the new Soviet law preserved, at least in name, the old and widely hated vehicle of repression, the Council for Religious Affairs. It was not mentioned in Stalin's 1929 law, for the good reason that it did not exist until after World War II, when Stalin needed a body to control the permitted degree of religious activity. There was no emendation of the 1929 law to take its controlling role into account. It is difficult to see, had the Soviet Union lived on, what part this body could conceivably have played when there was supposed to be separation of church and state. However, a bird born and bred in a cage when freed will often be willing to return to its confinement, as events of the last year illustrate.

Khasbulatov, Yeltsin, and the Evangelists

It is self-evident that the new liberal law on religion of the Russian Federation, passed in September–October 1990, did not have the space to prove itself in practice before the collapse of the Soviet system a year later. Naturally, Russia inherited the new law from its predecessor.

It comes as something of a surprise, therefore, to find that, less than a year after Russia's new independence, its legislators were already attempting to find a way of restricting the freedoms so recently acquired. The explanation of this is not far to seek, and it tells us a great deal about the current drift of Russian society.

Freedom proclaimed under the law meant freedom for all—not least for the world's rich evangelists. It is astonishing to observe how, after the world had by and large ignored or misrepresented the religious needs of the Soviet Union over several decades, suddenly these needs became a fashionable cause. Embedded in this was the goodwill of innumerable people who humbly and genuinely wanted to help Russia reestablish the roots of its faith. Their quiet dedication was often swamped by the insensitivity of others. Cohorts of disparate foreign preachers were to be found roaming the streets of the major cities, employing brash evangelistic methods and backed by what to Russians seemed limitless reserves of capital. Religion was now permitted on the airwaves; however, not satisfied with the resulting opportunities, foreign agencies bought not just air time, but sometimes even whole radio stations. Foreigners who had never learned a word of Russian, who did not know the history, the classics of literature, or the particular richness of the Russian Orthodox tradition, suddenly launched themselves at an unsuspecting public genuinely eager for something spiritual to fill the void left by communism but totally unable to distinguish between witchcraft, Eastern philosophy, and the Christian gospel. This made life especially difficult for those who had been mentally, spiritually, and linguistically preparing for just such an opportunity for decades.[10]

There are many hundreds of Western evangelists and missionary groups active in Moscow alone. It would be invidious to attempt to separate them all into sheep and goats, but among those who had prepared for decades, and therefore were spiritually attuned to the tasks ahead, were groups of German Lutherans, the Swiss churches through their publication *Glaube in der 2. Welt* (Zurich), the Roman Catholic society Aid to the Church in Need, Peter Deyneka Russian

Ministries, and the Quakers. The Salvation Army and Mother Teresa of Calcutta's Sisters of Charity quickly responded to the challenge to set up aid and relief programs to help fill the immense social needs left behind by communism.

What was the result? Very rapidly, considering prevailing conditions, an influential body of opinion began to proclaim that the freedoms had gone too far, that they threatened the true traditions of Russia, and that something must be done to curb them. Such attitudes are to a certain extent understandable and justifiable, though the methods attempted to bring some control into the anarchy were unbelievably crude.

In November 1992 Ruslan Khasbulatov signed a decree establishing an "Experts' Consultative Council," though such a body had already been mentioned in Article 12 of the 1990 law. This new step immediately sounded warning bells among the Russian intelligentsia. As defined by Khasbulatov, it looked only too much like the old Council for Religious Affairs redivivus, especially as its chairman (appointed before the body met) was to be an old warhorse of the communist struggle against religion, the lawyer Iurii Rozenbaum, whose activism in the field went back at least thirty years. The twenty-two other members of the team flaunted a spurious balance. Thirteen, nine of them named, were officials of the former communist state, not one of whom had any known religious commitment, and one member, unnamed, was to come from the Ministry of Security (the successor body to the KGB). Nine others were to be nominated by individual religious bodies, which were listed in alphabetical order. Adventists, Jews, Buddhists, and Pentecostals were represented alongside the Russian Orthodox Church. There was no explanation of the criterion by which nine (rather than eight or twenty) religions/denominations were to be represented. Curiously, Aleksandr Torshin, advisor on religious affairs in President Yeltsin's private office, said in London on 28 September 1993 that fourteen was the recognized number. The original list was in alphabetical order, thus giving the odd impression that the small Adventist Church somehow had precedence over the massive Russian Orthodox.[11]

It was immediately obvious that the primary task of the new Experts' Consultative Council was not so much to consult as to draft new legislation modifying the freedoms enshrined in the Russian Parliament's Law on the Freedom of Conscience of two years earlier. A draft emendation of Article 11 read:

> [The relevant state] bodies and agencies shall have the right to receive essential information from religious associations and attend events sponsored by religious associations.[12]

There follows a long and complicated section giving the secular authorities the right to suspend religious bodies if they break the law.

The specter of renewed government control over religion had clearly begun to haunt the edifice of church life once again. A new version of Article 18 would, if passed, considerably tighten the obligations connected with registration (such an instrument of persecution under the old system). This would seem to give the new body a strong voice in the act of registration, that is, inter alia, influence the decision on which bodies coming in from the outside should be considered legitimate and which not.

Aleksandr Shchipkov, a young democrat with impeccable credentials, at a conference in Moscow in February 1993, quoted the department for registration at the Ministry of Justice:

> Under the control of the Ministry of Justice and its organs in the localities come the following: making sure that statutes are observed; the right to issue warnings; the right to go to court to forbid religious organizations to operate; the right to suspend the activities of religious organizations prior to court decisions; the right to demand and receive information and explanations; the right to be present at events organized by the churches.

Shchipkov reacted in these words: "These are harsh provisions, to say the very least. Imagine what a meal they will be making of them in the provinces!"[13]

There was here already the possibility that Russian religious activities would be automatically registered, while others would not. The patriarch would shortly write a letter saying that this draft was too mild in the restrictions it could enforce upon foreign activities. He wrote in December 1992:

> It is a fact that none of the additions related to the registration of foreign religious organizations in Russia seeks to impose limitations on their increased religious activity and/or expansion. In fact, they seem to make legal their increasing invasion. . . . A special committee at the Ministry of Justice must be organized . . . [with] the right to put "vetoes" for five to seven years on the registration and activity of these foreign religious organizations.[14]

The draft legislation was already sailing into stormy and uncharted waters. How would the patriarch view the religious activities of citizens of the former republics perhaps still resident in Russia? Would the Roman Catholic Church, for instance, be judged to be a foreign body? Common sense says no, and there are numerous non-Russian Catholics scattered over Russian territory and across the expanses of Siberia, many of them there as a result of deportation or imprisonment. The Roman Catholic archbishop in Moscow, Tadeusz Kondrusiewicz, is Belarusian-Polish by birth, a representative of the "near abroad." It is clear that if the patriarch's request should become law, it would be unworkable. Undesirable evangelists or propagators of strange cults from abroad might be kept out by refusing them entry or residence permits (as indeed can be done in a democratic society), but it would clearly be impossible to do the same in respect to non-Russian citizens of the former Soviet Union, many of whom were resident in the Russian Republic long before the collapse of communism.

It is impossible for state legislation, per se, to distinguish between evangelists who exert a positive or a negative influence or between sects and religions that can be tolerated and those that cannot. A democratic society like Britain watches results, prevents, for example, a sect from abducting minors from their parents, and refuses entry to foreign religious extremists who advocate illegality or practices that are clearly socially undesirable. There are also (at the moment) regulations on the use of airwaves and television channels.

It was suspected by some observers that the hierarchy of the Russian Orthodox Church, feeling beleaguered by the multifarious activity of the new sects, might have been behind the establishment of the Experts' Consultative Council. It soon became apparent that this was not so—at least in the form in which Khasbulatov promulgated it. Metropolitan Kirill, head of the Department of External Ecclesiastical Relations and usually regarded as the second most powerful figure in the Russian Orthodox Church after Patriarch Aleksii II, launched into a powerful attack against the new body and the revisions it was drafting in February 1993:

> The amendments [to the legislation] have been prepared without our participation. In general, we cast doubt on the expediency of these amendments at this particular time, because a law is already functioning that we consider to be a good one. . . . [It] embodies the clear wish to reanimate the defunct Council for Religious Affairs, to reintroduce a state body that would have the right to interfere in the internal affairs of religious institutions. . . . I have consulted with representatives of the Catholics and Baptists on this matter and they state unanimously: we will not allow these people in; we did not do so when they had no legal right and now, under conditions of democracy, we certainly shall not do so.[15]

However, as we shall see later, the situation was not quite as clear-cut as it seems from the metropolitan's words.

The International Academy for Freedom of Religion and Belief is an association of American academic lawyers with immense expertise on church-state relations in their own country. They heard of what was afoot and moved with muscle and rapidity to request a meeting with the Experts' Consultative Council. Most of the eighteen members who went to Moscow in March 1993 are believers, representing a wide range of commitment, from Baptists to Roman Catholics and Jews to Mormons. They had persuaded an apparently reluctant Iurii Rozenbaum to set up a conference on "Freedom of Religion in a Modern World," a generic title to accommodate discussion of the new draft legislation, and I received an invitation to accompany them as an advisor. A reception for a broad swathe of Moscow intelligentsia took place in the Praga restaurant, Moscow, on the evening of Sunday, 21 March, after which about forty people decamped to a former Central Committee rest home at Lesnye Dali, about an hour's drive outside the city.

It would have been hard to find a less congenial venue than the hall in which the conference took place for sixteen unremitting hours over the next two days. The room was built to hold three hundred. The speakers were hopelessly elevated on the dais above the scattered audience: distance and formality were a disincentive to any intimate discussion or give-and-take.

The first session saw a discussion of the Experts' Consultative Council itself. Alfred Blaustein, of Rutgers University, read a brief *Izvestiia* article criticizing its formation and saying that the old Soviet ideals were alive and on the way back. Rozenbaum exploded, retorting that it was unhelpful to embitter the discussions in this way and citing the multifarious benefits the churches had experienced since the collapse of communism. He cited some local American fiscal document that he claimed exerted closer government oversight over churches than ever existed in Stalin's Soviet Union.

There was no programed slot for an overview of church-state relations from the Stalin era to the present, which was a serious handicap for those American participants who were less than fully briefed. However, a discussion of the new draft legislation was unavoidable, though it was confined strictly to one two-hour session, after which the conference moved on to consider many other less contentious issues. Rozenbaum never relinquished his role as chairman for one second of the two days (the conference did not break up into smaller discussion groups) and looked the very embodiment of an old-style communist functionary trying to control proceedings. However, he did not try to impose limits on freedom of speech, though it was obvious there had been a prior agreement imposing restrictions through the formulation of the agenda.

One might have expected Metropolitan Kirill, six weeks after the publication of his views, to have represented them, or caused them to be represented, at this conference. As it was, Father Innokenti (Pavlov) was the sole representative of the Moscow Patriarchate, and he attended only for a few hours on the first day, sitting silently during this debate and speaking only later on the topic of religion and national minorities.

There were representatives of the Adventists and the Pentecostals present, who spoke decisively against the new draft of Articles 11 and 18. Curiously, there were no Jews, Muslims, or Baptists in attendance, even though they were officially represented on the Experts' Consultative Council and had been at the opening banquet the previous day. Another notable absentee, though he was listed by name on the program, was Fr. Viacheslav Polosin, a priest, formerly a lawyer, who was then a member of the Russian parliament. He had played a role, possibly the leading one, in formulating the draft put forward by Rozenbaum's council, but he excused himself on the grounds that the parliament was in emergency session to discuss the possible impeachment of President Yeltsin.

The dominant voices during this session of the conference were the Americans, all of whom opposed any state restriction on religious activity, saying that the American model of complete separation of church and state was the only one for Russia to follow. Safeguards would be in place because no criminal activity, including financial impropriety, would be permitted under existing laws, but it would not be necessary to emend them in order to make them explicitly refer to the sphere of religion. To allot to the state the right or duty to differentiate among various types of religious activity, whether originating from outside Russia or not, was putting on it a wholly inappropriate burden, one that it could never carry without crossing the demarcation line between church and state.

At the end of the conference two representatives from each side, Russian and American, conferred and agreed on a declaration that, of course, had no official status but which received the unanimous assent of the participants. In rather general terms it upheld the separation of church and state in its fullest sense and affirmed the place of religious liberty as a fundamental human right. Rozenbaum concluded by stating that the draft emendations should go back to the drawing board and that no further versions would be produced except after informing the International Academy.[16]

Rozenbaum failed to carry out this promise, or may have been prevented from doing so. Between the end of March and the summer much activity, including lobbying and changing of sides, took place. On 23 June there was a debate in the Soviet of Nationalities (one house of the Russian parliament). On 30 June Rozenbaum spoke at a symposium, warning of what was to come and dissociating himself from the latest draft of the new law, stating that it was badly formulated and internally contradictory. He was obviously upset that his own version had been ignored.

The earlier Article 18 had now become number 15 and then 14; it unambiguously forbade foreign-based religious organizations from engaging in missionary activity on Russian territory unless they first obtained accreditation from the state authorities.

Metropolitan Kirill had done a volte face and now no longer considered the 1990 legislation to be satisfactory. He had come around to the patriarch's view that it was the obligation of the state to put a curb on the unrestrained missionary activity of the many cults, Christian and non-Christian, that were spreading their influence from outside. Viacheslav Polosin now emerged as the chief spokesman for the change in law and seems to have been principally responsible for the final version.

On 14 July the Russian parliament debated and passed amendments and additions to the Law on Freedom of Conscience. Now widespread international consternation and criticism greeted the changes, with foreign agencies claiming that they infringed on religious liberty and international agreements such as the Universal Declaration of Human Rights.

Father Gleb Yakunin, in a telephone conversation with Keston Institute, called the new law "discriminatory and antidemocratic." Heads of the Russian Protestant denominations sent a joint letter to President Yeltsin complaining of the development and asking him to withhold his signature from the decree, the last step before it passed into law. The Russian branch of the International Religious Liberty Association predicted that the new law would lead to state censorship of religious literature published abroad, the jamming of foreign broadcasts, and a worldwide lack of confidence in Russia's commitment to reform.

President Yeltsin responded to this pressure (in the midst of what must have been an extraordinary work schedule at the time), clearly conscious of the importance of his reputation abroad, and sent the legislation back with his amendments to the parliament for further consideration, as was his right. On 27 August parliament debated yet further emendations, and the new version was passed (156 for, 3 against, and 2 abstentions).

Now it seemed certain that the bill would receive Yeltsin's final assent, but a recess intervened. Then on 17 September he returned it again unsigned. Before anything else could happen, Yeltsin dissolved parliament on 21 September.

An interesting sidelight on this was provided in London by Aleksandr Torshin, who said that it had been his job to gather together these expressions of foreign intervention and pass them on to Yeltsin. However, he had done so with the recommendation that the president should sign and had been surprised when this did not happen. "The Moscow Patriarchate approved, so what more do you want?" he asked his audience. "That's just the problem," came a reply.

During the tense days that followed the dissolution of parliament, Patriarch Aleksii and Metropolitan Kirill put themselves forward as mediators between President Yeltsin and the Rutskoi-Khasbulatov faction. Few details of what occurred have emerged, but they met representatives of both sides for two sessions. It has been suggested, though there is no proof of this, that the Rutskoi group agreed to this step as a diversionary tactic while the assault on the television tower, which initiated the violence, was being prepared in secret. The destruction of the Russian White House itself assuredly saw the end of any unfinished parliamentary business.

There is no reason to doubt the good faith of the patriarch when he brought the two sides together. This was a unique departure in Russian church history, and no blame can possibly fall on the shoulders of the church leadership for the failure of the initiative. Had the patriarch succeeded, this would have given a considerable boost to his public image and the status of the church. If he had brokered a peaceful agreement, President Yeltsin would have been enormously in the patriarch's debt, and very likely the latter would then have suggested to the president that his signature on that document would have been a fitting quid pro quo.

It soon became clear that, following the elections of December 1993, the issue of new legislation on religion would soon come back before the Russian parliament. A very small drafting conference, including American lawyers, Iurii Rozenbaum, and myself, convened in the Netherlands in late January 1994. The carefully crafted results were circulated to all members of the new Duma. However, as early as May discussions were on again in the relevant parliamentary committees concerning a further unsatisfactory draft produced by, among others, Viacheslav Polosin.

Interchurch Relations

It is outside the scope of this chapter even to attempt to summarize an overall account of the present life of any of the religious communities, Orthodox, Catholic, Protestant, Jewish, or Muslim. Every one of these has groups of fellow believers in one or more members of the Commonwealth of Independent States. Contacts across these borders exist and are likely to play a role in future relations among these states, whether or not they follow a path toward further political disintegration.

By far the greatest concern here is the situation of millions of Russians outside the country's borders, among whom, naturally, there is a high proportion of members of the Orthodox Church. Before the collapse of Soviet power all these fell neatly under diocesan administration. It has come as a psychological blow to the Moscow Patriarchate to find that, as the church could begin to spread its wings in Russia, so its direct influence declined not only in the Baltics but also in other states of the CIS. Ukraine offers an especially complex picture and is treated elsewhere in this volume.

Where the Orthodox Church forms a small minority of believers, such as in Lithuania or the states of Central Asia, local bishops now have the complicated task of evolving a new relationship with the majority and with the new governments. Independently minded bishops such as Khrisostom of Vilnius can develop their own relations with the Roman Catholic majority of Lithuania without having to refer back to Moscow.

However, the underlying nationalist attitude that Russians should be Orthodox is a significant factor in the development of Christian life since the abolition of the constraints of communism. Whoever leads the Kremlin has a card to play here: the Russian Orthodox Church leadership can potentially be called on at any time to legitimize "protection" for Russian nationals in the near abroad, whatever form this might take. So far this has not happened, nor has the Moscow Patriarchate called for the political leadership to support the Orthodox Serbs in the former Yugoslavia, but there is always the chance that such factors might come into play.

It is extremely hard for the Orthodox Church to come to terms with the fact that Russia is now a pluralistic society. The debate on the new laws illustrates this, but there is not the remotest chance that the Moscow Patriarchate will be able to arrest the spread of cults and Christian denominations new and old, except possibly by the power of its own teaching and evangelical zeal, unassisted by legal constraints on rivals.

This is not for a moment to imply that the explosion of foreign sectarianism is essential for the future development of Russian society, but it is a fact of life that is virtually impossible to counter under present conditions. It would surely be better if the Moscow Patriarchate could make a real effort to seek out the goodwill and enter into dialogue with those foreigners who feel called to active long-term involvement with Russian Christians.

At this point, too, one should emphasize that in such fields as education, publishing, administration, and technical know-how, both foreign Protestants and Catholics have a great deal that is positive to offer. They can help over a period of time to make good the losses of decades in these areas. Therefore one might expect, as Russia faces difficult days ahead, that cooperation rather than rivalry might be the order of the day.

Persecution in the worst days had the effect of calling a halt to interdenominational hostility, and there are many known examples of Christian companionship across the divisions—and indeed of Orthodox-Jewish friendship—flourishing in the camps.

The USSR did not permit the establishment of a council of churches. Individual denominations and religions were sometimes brought together in conferences or to sign documents in support of Soviet policies, but this was an entirely artificial and mainly propagandistic exercise that basically had nothing to do with ecumenical initiative. Given the prerevolutionary role of the Orthodox Church, there was not even a dormant tradition of sensitivity to other denominations to resurrect.

The Moscow Patriarchate is certainly not coterminous with the Russian Orthodox Church. Its policies are in the hands of a small group of hierarchs, the composition of which has been largely unchanged since the collapse of communism. There are many strands within it: for example, the parish clergy who have had a theological education; their (mainly) much less well-educated flocks; and the younger urban intellectuals. While the believer in the parish may feel love for his or her parish priest and respect for the office of bishop, the policies of the Moscow Patriarchate itself are often something distant and of little practical relevance, except insofar as they help provide regular worship in the parish churches. Some bishops, inevitably, are now beginning to adopt a more independent line and to look into the specific needs of their local areas in a way that was not possible under the dominance of the KGB and the Council for Religious Affairs. There are intellectual circles in the major cities, consisting mainly but not solely of the laity, where there is acute criticism of the patriarchate not only for its past collaboration with the Soviet regime but also now for its alleged failure to make best use of the new opportunities and for not looking for fruitful possibilities in ecumenical cooperation.

As it is, the patriarchate spends time and energy on worrying about the role of Catholics, Protestants, and non-Christian cults. Relations with the Anglican (Episcopal) Church provide an interesting note. This community consists of no Russians at all in Moscow (as far as is known), and the pastorate was reestablished on a full-time basis only in May 1993 solely to fulfill the needs of the foreign community. The chaplain, Canon Chad Coussmaker, had as one of his tasks the regaining of full rights over the old Anglican Church, from which the community had been expropriated after the Revolution (as a result of glasnost, Sunday use had been restored some time earlier). In order to comply with the law, the community has to apply for registration: the patriarch would give his approval (!) only if the application were in the name of "the Anglican Church *in* Moscow" (not "*of* Moscow"). The difference must reflect the intention of the Orthodox Church that there should be no missionary work emanating from the community.[17] Yet, in essence, Anglicans everywhere are good friends of the Orthodox and are earnestly seeking ways of working together with them.

It will obviously take decades of effort before the climate is right in Russia for the establishment of an effective council of churches. Meanwhile, various mainstream Christian denominations are set on rebuilding their lives independently of each other. In all its aspects, the task is formidable.

Conclusion

For all religious communities in Russia, these are times of opportunity, but also of great uncertainty. It remains to be seen how, with the abolition of the old parliament, the Russian Orthodox Church will once more address the issue of new legislation aimed at controlling non-Russian missionary activity. It is likely that the next time around the task will prove more difficult because of heightened awareness worldwide of what was attempted the last time. It is certain, however, that the attitudes of mind formerly expressed by the parliament-patriarchal axis will not quickly change, and therefore the collapse of the attempt to control certain aspects of religious life by legislation will not prevent future attempts to achieve the same goal.

Notes

1. Roswitha and Peter Jarman, *OPS Journal Letter* (London: Quaker Peace and Service) 1993, no. 1, p. 7.

2. Michael Bourdeaux, *Risen Indeed* (London: Darton, Longman and Todd, 1983), passim.

3. See, e.g., Michael Bourdeaux, *Religious Ferment in Russia* (London: Macmillan, 1968); and Jane Ellis, *The Russian Orthodox Church: A Contemporary History* (London: Croom Helm, 1986).

4. Michael Bourdeaux, *The Gospel's Triumph Over Communism* (Minneapolis: Bethany House, 1991), p. 44.

5. Jane Ellis, ed., *Religious Minorities in the Soviet Union,* 4th ed. (London: Minority Rights Group, 1984), pp. 5–6; and idem, *Russian Orthodox Church,* p. 25.

6. See Bourdeaux, *Gospel's Triumph Over Communism,* pp. 72–73.

7. Ibid., pp. 151–52.

8. See Michael Bourdeaux, *The Role of Religion in the Fall of Soviet Communism* (London: Centre for Policy Studies, 1992), passim.

9. Bourdeaux, *Gospel's Triumph Over Communism,* p. 72.

10. On cults in the former Soviet Union, see *Frontier* (Keston, Kent), May–June 1991, pp. 1–2, 12–15.

11. Michael Bourdeaux, "Old Games, New Rules," *Frontier,* July–August 1993, pp. 15–16.

12. Unpublished dossier of materials for conference in Moscow, March 1993. Copy in Keston Institute archive.

13. Aleksandr Shchipkov, "Attempts to Revive the Council for Religious Affairs in Russia," *Religion, State and Society* (Oxford), vol. 21, nos. 3–4 (1993), p. 372.

14. Letter no. 3488 from Patriarch Aleksii II to Archpriest Viacheslav Polosin, 8 December 1992. Copy in Keston archive.

15. Metropolitan Kirill, interview, *Russkaia mysl'* (Paris), 5 February 1993, p. 9.

16. Bourdeaux, "Old Games, New Rules."

17. Canon Chad Coussmaker, Anglican Chaplain in Moscow, letter to Keston Institute.

II

The Western Newly Independent States

7

Politics and Religion in Ukraine

The Orthodox and the Greek Catholics

Bohdan Bociurkiw

Introduction

With the attainment of independence, the chief problem that came to confront the Ukrainian government in the realm of religious policy was the continuing allegiance of the majority of the Orthodox in Ukraine to the Moscow Patriarchate, which remained opposed to the separation of Ukraine from Russia and intent on pursuing their eventual political reunion through ecclesiastical unity of the two.

The traditional dependence of Orthodox churches on the state had contributed in the context of nearly three centuries of Russian rule over Ukraine to the Russification of the church and the denationalization of its faithful, the legacy of Moscow's domination that could not be overcome either during the short-lived Ukrainian statehood in 1917–19 or under German occupation in 1941–43. For the third time in the twentieth century, the large Russian minority and a significant number of linguistically and culturally Russified Ukrainians have so far prevented the Orthodox Church in Ukraine from unified action for ecclesiastical independence from Moscow; each time the minority within the church pleading for autocephaly was driven into schism. For Orthodox churches within sovereign states, autocephaly—independence of the jurisdiction of a patriarchate in another country—has been a historical norm. Jaroslav Pelikan noted that the concept of "autocephaly" in Orthodoxy

> is connected with the Eastern concept of the church, which is neither monarchical nor federative (both of which require a central authority), but represents an aggregate of national churches that subsist alongside one another, are organized in their own hierarchies, and are independent of one another.[1]

While the majority of the church in an independent state (usually speaking through their church's national [local] Council, and including the majority of its bishops) would normally address a request for autocephaly to its "mother church," historically the latter have as a rule refused to grant autocephaly to national churches under a variety of pretexts, and it was the intervention of the national state that was decisive in securing autocephaly, with the respective patriarchate only later recognizing the given church's independence.[2] Just as the patriarchate of Constantinople remained an "imperial church" even after the conquest of Byzantium by the Ottoman Turks, so too the Moscow Patriarchate retained its traditional function of an "imperial church" under Soviet rule.[3]

The distinct history of Galicia, where, after its Austrian annexation, the fusion of Greek Catholicism and Ukrainian national consciousness made it into a bulwark against both Polonization and Russification, ensured the survival of the Uniate Church in the catacombs for more than forty years after Stalin's forcible "dissolution" of the Union of Brest and the so-called reunion of the Greek Catholics with the Russian Orthodox Church. It also ensured that until the collapse of the USSR, the "reunited" church in Galicia, in contrast to the rest of Ukraine, retained its Ukrainian character, which eventually contributed to the rise from its midst of a Ukrainian Autocephalous Orthodox Church to counter the revival of the Greek Catholic Church in 1989. The Russian Orthodox Church in Ukraine, renamed in 1990 the Ukrainian Orthodox Church, retained an almost total hold on the allegiance of Orthodox believers in the rest of Ukraine until the proclamation of Ukrainian independence seemingly opened the prospects for state-supported autocephaly of the reunited Orthodox Church in Ukraine. The confrontation between Kiev and Moscow over the independence of the Ukrainian Orthodox Church, which ironically resulted in further division within the church, will be discussed at length in this chapter.

Historical Perspective

The most important factor in shaping Ukrainian religious and ethnic identity has been Ukraine's location on the historical fault line between Orthodoxy and Catholicism, and for several centuries on the boundary between Orthodoxy and Islam as well. Kievan Rus´ had not broken with the Catholic West after the Great Schism of 1054, and its interaction with Poland, Germany, Hungary, and other Catholic nations of medieval Europe did not end until after the plunder of Byzantium by the Latin Crusaders in 1204 and the installation of a Roman Catholic patriarch in the see of Constantinople.[4] With the Mongol conquest in 1240 and the subsequent transfer of the Kievan metropolitan see to the north, the political and ecclesiastical continuity in Ukrainian history (except for the Galician-Volhynian principality in the west) was interrupted, facilitating the appropriation by Moscow of the ethnoreligious myth of "Holy Rus´."

The most potent of myths underlying Ukrainian national identity has been the

Cossack myth of fearless defenders of Christendom against the recurring raids of Muslim Crimean Tatars and Turks looting Ukraine of its wealth and people. The myth sustained Ukrainian Orthodoxy against Polish Roman Catholic expansion, but not against Russia. In fact, claims of the "Orthodox tsardom" facilitated Russian expansion into Ukraine.

Of decisive importance in delaying the crystallization of Ukrainian ethnic identity and inhibiting the formation of the modern Ukrainian nation was the loss of the country's political independence, only briefly revived after the victorious Cossack rebellion against Polish rule in 1648, and the subsequent partition of Ukraine between Poland and Russia in 1667. Poland, which eventually displaced the benevolent post-Mongol Lithuanian rule over Ukraine after the 1569 dynastic union of Poland and Lithuania, had progressively weakened the metropolitan see of Kiev through discrimination against the Orthodox, Polonization of the Ukrainian elite, and growing pressures for a union of the Orthodox hierarchy with Rome.

The fall of Byzantium in 1453 placed the patriarchate of Constantinople under Ottoman rule, weakening its authority over the Orthodox in the Polish-Lithuanian Kingdom, with the Moscow Patriarchate, established in 1589, challenging Constantinople's jurisdiction over Ukraine and Belarus. In Ukrainian cities, inconsistent policies of the patriarch of Constantinople further aggravated tension between the lay brotherhoods formed to defend Orthodoxy, and the bishops were tempted by Polish promises of equalization of their status with that of the Latin hierarchy should they enter into a union with Rome. These were some of the factors[5] that led the majority of the Orthodox hierarchy in Ukraine and Belarus to enter into the negotiations with the papacy that culminated in the Union of Brest in 1596. In return for submission to the pope and the acceptance of Catholic dogmas, Rome granted the Uniate Church a number of rights, including the retention of its Eastern rite, the Church Slavonic liturgical language, Eastern canon law, married clergy, and administrative autonomy.[6] Theoretically, the Uniate Church would have best protected the religious and ethnic distinctiveness of Ukrainians and Belarusians against both Orthodox Russia and Roman Catholic Poland. But as some bishops and nobles and, most importantly, Ukrainian Cossacks refused to accept Catholicism, the Union of Brest brought about permanent religious division and interconfessional struggle in Ukraine that was ultimately overcome after the partition of Poland in the late eighteenth century, with the tsars eventually forcing the Uniates to "reunite" with the Russian Orthodox Church.

The Uniate Church (renamed the Greek Catholic Church), however, survived and flourished in Austrian-annexed Galicia (as well as in Hungarian-ruled Transcarpathia), thanks to the Habsburgs' desire to strengthen it as a barrier to Russian expansionism and a counterbalance to Polish irredentism. In the land deprived of its traditional elites through centuries of Polonization, where Ukrainian ethnicity was literally reduced to Uniate priests and peasants, the educated stratum of empowered Greek Catholic clergy eventually supplied national, political, and cultural leadership to Austria's Ukrainians until the late nineteenth century. By then, the secular intelligentsia—mostly sons and daughters of the Uniate pastors—took over national leadership in Galicia.

Ironically, the Greek Catholic and Orthodox churches exchanged their roles as guardians of Ukrainian ethnic identity and culture. Having annexed the Kiev metropolitan see from the patriarchate of Constantinople in 1685, Russia progressively denationalized it, incorporating individual dioceses into the Russian Orthodox Church (ROC). By the early nineteenth century, the Orthodox Church in Ukraine was transformed into the most potent instrument of Russification and a major obstacle to the Ukrainian national revival movement. The Uniate Church, once viewed by the Cossacks as a Polish-inspired device for destruction of Ukrainian identity and freedom, emerged under enlightened Habsburg rule as the bearer and defender of Ukrainian indentity and, eventually, as a major force in nation building. The short-lived experience in building Ukrainian statehood between 1917 and 1921 demonstrated the profound difference in the attitudes of the two churches to Ukrainian independence. After the collapse of tsarist rule, the Russian Orthodox episcopate, monasteries, and theological schools in Ukraine became the most implacable enemies of Ukrainian political independence and autocephaly, equating them with betrayal of Orthodoxy.[7] In contrast, the Greek Catholic Church, led by the great Metropolitan Andrei Sheptyts'kyi from 1901 until 1944, gave its full support to the cause of Ukrainian statehood. After the West Ukrainian Republic was defeated in the 1918–19 war with Poland, the church supplied moral leadership and its protective umbrella to the Ukrainian national movement under Polish occupation. In eastern Ukraine, finally conquered by the Bolsheviks by 1921, the Russian Orthodox Church continued to oppose a popular movement for the Ukrainization (i.e., de-Russification) and autocephaly of the local Orthodox Church, provoking a schism. As not a single member of the ROC hierarchy would ordain a Ukrainian bishop for the parishes celebrating services in the Ukrainian language, the national church movement seceded from the Russian Orthodox Church, proclaiming itself the Ukrainian Autocephalous Orthodox Church (UAOC). At its founding council in October 1921, the UAOC resorted to a Protestant practice of laying on of hands by the rank-and-file clergy and laymen to create its own hierarchy, allowing married parish priests into the episcopal office and adopting a lay-dominated, conciliar church structure. At the same time, the UAOC retained Orthodox ritual enriched by religious folk customs and "ecclesiastical creativity."[8] However, the hold of the old "state church" on the ecclesiastical loyalty of conservative Orthodox clergy and believers proved to be too strong for the UAOC to attract more than a handful of ROC priests and a minority of faithful in Ukraine.[9]

The Ukrainian Autocephalous Orthodox Church was wiped out by 1930,[10] while the Moscow Patriarchate, which by 1927 pledged absolute loyalty to the regime, was reduced by 1939 to a handful of parishes without a single bishop in Ukraine. It was the outbreak of World War II and the Soviet occupation of western Ukraine and Belarus, and subsequently in 1940 of Bukovyna, Bessarabia, and the Baltic states, that gave a new lease on life to the moribund Moscow Patriarchate. Reduced by 1939 to four bishops, the Russian Orthodox Church suddenly became indispensable to the Kremlin as an instrument of integrating, Sovietizing, and Russifying the populous Orthodox dioceses in the annexed territories. The ROC resumed its prerevolutionary role of an "imperial church," guarding the unity and absorbing the territorial gains of the Soviet empire.

Even during the wartime German occupation of Ukraine (1941–43), when the Ukrainian Autocephalous Orthodox Church was revived, this time with a canonically ordained episcopate,[11] the majority of Orthodox bishops,[12] clergy, and parishes opted to remain under the jurisdiction of the Moscow Patriarchate in Soviet-controlled Moscow, assuming a temporary designation as the Ukrainian Autonomous Orthodox Church.

In return for its loyalty, Stalin granted in September 1943 a number of special privileges to the Russian Orthodox Church (except for its internal freedom)[13] and once again employed it in reconquering Ukraine as a vehicle for absorbing the remnants of the wartime UAOC.[14] From early spring 1945, after Stalin secretly ordered the liquidation of the Ukrainian Greek Catholic Church in the USSR on 16 March,[15] the Moscow Patriarchate obediently joined the regime in a campaign of "reunion" of the Greek Catholics with the ROC following the arrests of the entire Uniate episcopate and leading clergy. Conspiratorially conducted by Stalin's secret police (NKGB/MGB), this campaign of intimidation and blackmail (and terror against the active opponents of "reunion") culminated in the pseudo-Council of L'viv in 1946, at which the intimidated "representatives" of the Uniate clergy "abolished" the 1596 Union of Brest and "voted" to "return" to their alleged "mother church"—the ROC. A similar "reunion" was conducted in Transcarpathia in 1949, after the local Greek Catholic Bishop Romzha was murdered by the MGB.[16] However, nearly all the "converted" clergy remained Greek Catholics at heart, as were their faithful.

Hundreds of the "recalcitrant" clergy and monks were shipped to the gulag, followed by the imprisoned pastors' families and some 200 to 250 nuns who were exiled to the Asian parts of the USSR. The remnants of the clergy, monks, and nuns who managed to elude arrests and deportations formed a catacomb Greek Catholic Church. This clandestine church gained in strength following Nikita Khrushchev's amnesties in the mid-1950s, and from then it was once again administered by two surviving bishops.[17] After the metropolitan of the Greek Catholic Church, Iosyf Cardinal Slipyi, was released from captivity by Khrushchev in early 1963 (as a result of joint intercession by Pope John XXIII and President Kennedy), he resumed the leadership of the church in the USSR and in the Ukrainian diaspora from Rome.

Soviet suppression of the Uniate Church was ultimately aimed at breaking up the symbiotic relationship that had developed since the nineteenth century between Greek Catholicism and intense national consciousness in Galicia. It was also directed at undermining armed resistance in western Ukraine, led by the 90,000-strong Ukrainian Insurgent Army[18] and the nationalist underground, which initially offered shelter to the catacomb church.

Ultimately, the Greek Catholic Church—the largest underground religious organization in the Soviet Union (and indeed in the world)—remained the only *free* expression of Ukrainian ethnoreligious identity under communist rule. Its grassroots support enabled it to survive underground until Gorbachev's reforms.

Gorbachev's Reforms and Religious Developments in Ukraine

Gorbachev's first years in power witnessed a growing rapprochement between the regime and the Moscow Patriarchate that culminated in the lavish joint celebration in 1988 of the "millennium of Russian Orthodoxy" (which largely ignored the fact that the 988 baptism of Rus´ occurred in Kiev, and that Christianity spread from today's Ukraine to present-day Belarus and Russia).[19] Legal and secret restrictions on religious practices were somewhat relaxed during 1985–87, and by 1989 virtually all religious prisoners and deportees were allowed to return home—among them a number of Uniate priests and activists who soon assumed the leadership of a public campaign for the recognition and rehabilitation of the Ukrainian Catholic Church.

In August 1987, a group of bolder Greek Catholic clergymen and lay activists, led by the Committee for the Defense of the Ukrainian Catholic Church, declared their emergence from the underground and appealed to the pope for help in the restoration of the church's rights.[20] The emergent group undertook a campaign of public religious services, pilgrimages, religious demonstrations, and mass collection of believers' signatures on petitions for the return to the Greek Catholics of their closed or confiscated churches. Increasingly frequent confrontations between Ukrainian Catholics and the militia and the KGB publicized the Uniate protests at home and abroad and encouraged those catacomb bishops and priests who had so far been intimidated by the past repressions to speak out publicly for their religious rights. Helped by the Ukrainian Catholic Church in the diaspora, sympathetic human rights supporters, the mass media, and political figures in the West, as well as by such Russian human rights spokesmen as Andrei Sakharov, Fr. Gleb Yakunin, Aleksandr Ogorodnikov, and Vladimir Poresh, and above all by the rapidly growing national democratic movement in Galicia, the issue of the relegalization of the Greek Catholic Church now emerged on the international East-West agenda (particularly at the Vienna CSCE review conference and in Moscow-Vatican relations). This issue has come to figure also in the domestic forces and the conservative-chauvinist camp with which the Moscow Patriarchate has become increasingly identified.[21]

The Shcherbyts´kyi regime in Ukraine tried to buttress the Russian Orthodox

Church in Galicia by anti-Uniate propaganda and administrative countermeasures, as well as a hasty transfer to the Moscow Patriarchate in the winter of 1988–89 of hundreds of hitherto "closed" churches—the very ones that were either illegally used by Greek Catholics or were petitioned for by them.[22] By the spring of 1989, it became clear that the process of disintegration of the Russian Orthodox Church in Galicia had begun. Contributing to it were semifree elections to the Congress of People's Deputies, which in Galicia were won by some open supporters of the Ukrainian Catholic Church and national revival; the departure of individual Ukrainian Orthodox priests from the ROC to either the Greek Catholic or the Ukrainian Autocephalous Orthodox Church (UAOC); and in Moscow, a four-month-long public hunger strike by rotating groups of Uniate priests, nuns, and lay believers calling for the return of their constitutional rights that began to gather open expressions of support in the Soviet press.[23]

Moscow's Strategy Vis-à-Vis the Ukrainian Catholic Church

After denying for four decades the very existence of an underground Ukrainian Greek Catholic Church, the patriarchate and the regime now (since winter 1988–89) sought to disqualify the former as a religious organization, so as to declare it "ineligible" for any benefits arising from the planned Law on the Freedom of Conscience and Religious Organizations. They attempted to portray the Uniate Church as an "unchurchly, extremist, nationalist" organization that, under the "guise of religion," was aiming at a violent takeover in Galicia, preparing a "pogrom" against Orthodox Ukrainians and Russians, and threatening to turn western Ukraine into another Nagorno-Karabakh or Ulster.[24]

The Moscow strategy also aimed to split a former ethnoreligious monolith in Galicia along the traditional tensions within the Uniate Church—between "Easterners-ritualists" and "Westerners-Latinizers"—by attracting the former into the Orthodox or at least an "autocephalous" Greek Catholic Church, while pushing the latter into the Roman Catholic Church, even a Ukrainian-speaking one.[25]

Threatening otherwise to break off its "ecumenical dialogue of love" with the Roman Catholic Church, the Moscow Patriarchate (acting also as a proxy for the Kremlin) demanded that the Vatican repudiate the practice of Catholic proselytism among the Orthodox and abandon the principle of a "one-sided" union (under the pope) including the 1596 Union of Brest and its child—the Greek Catholic Church. In return, Moscow offered to allow registration of individual congregations of "Eastern Catholics," provided, however, that all other questions—the allocation of church buildings to such congregations, their future ("noncompetitive") canonical organization and hierarchy—would be decided by consensus between the Moscow Patriarchate and the Roman Catholic Church, with the Soviet government acting only upon their *joint* recommendations.[26]

Such was the outcome of protracted and difficult negotiations between the patriarchate and the Curia (August–October 1989), which was confirmed during the meeting between Gorbachev and Pope John Paul II at the Vatican on 1 December 1989. Details of this agreement were worked out at the Moscow meeting of the papal and patriarchal delegations in January 1990 and ratified by the pope and the ROC Synod of Bishops later that month.[27] Moscow's insistence on treating Ukrainian Uniates not as a continuation of the Greek Catholic Church forcibly "reunited" in 1946 but as a "new" denomination—"Eastern Catholics" within the *Roman* Catholic Church[28]—was very likely also motivated by the patriarchate's desire to undermine the Greek Catholic Church's claim to its pre-1946 property confiscated by Stalin's government and turned over to the loyal Russian Orthodox Church. "Normalization" of Moscow-Vatican relations culminated in the establishment of regular diplomatic relations between the USSR and the Holy See.

The Resurgence of the Greek Catholic Church and the UAOC

Before long, Moscow and its loyal republican authorities in Kiev lost control over ecclesiastical developments in Galacia, where in March 1990 the Ukrainian Greek Catholic Church rejected the January ROC-Vatican agreement and turned for aid in restoring its rights to the newly elected local and oblast authorities dominated by supportive Rukh deputies. The rapid resurgence of the Uniate Church led the patriarchate to change its tactics: while unleashing a campaign of disinformation about the alleged "persecution" of the Orthodox in Galicia by Uniate "extremists" and the new "separatist"-led local authorities, the Russian Orthodox Church began increasingly to call upon Gorbachev's leadership and the "law and order" agencies to intervene directly in western Ukraine to "re-store" order, remove Greek Catholics from the churches they had repossessed, and unseat the pro-Uniate "nationalist" authorities.[29] At the same time, seeing the rapid collapse of its church organization in Galicia (despite the recent renam-ing of the ROC's Ukrainian Exarchate the "Ukrainian Orthodox Church"), the Moscow Patriarchate and its allies in the republican organs had come to view the emergent Ukrainian Autocephalous Orthodox Church—as long as it confined itself to Galicia—as a "lesser evil" than the Uniate Church. Indeed, the early autocephalist activists in Kiev found themselves marginalized as several hundred Orthodox parish priests in Galicia rushed to join the UAOC in order to keep their parishes and livelihood; co-opting the symbols from Ukrainian nationalists and anti-Uniate rhetoric from the ROC, they mounted a different kind of campaign against the Greek Catholic Church, accusing it of serving as a tool of the Polish pope and Polish "revanchists" trying to reannex western Ukraine to Poland.[30] The patriarchate-regime's strategy deepened interconfessional conflict in Galicia, deflecting much of the energies of the Uniate and Autocephalous Churches from combating Moscow to internal competition for parishes, churches, and the faithful.

By June 1990, 1,592 congregations were formed by the Greek Catholics in Galicia and 1,303 churches reclaimed, while the number of Uniate clergy increased to 767, including 370 former Orthodox priests. The Ukrainian Greek Catholic Church was organized in two dioceses, headed by Archbishop Volodymyr Sterniuk, a *locum tenens* of the L'viv archbishop major, and Sofron Dmyterko, the diocesan bishop of Ivano-Frankivs'k, who were assisted by five auxiliary bishops.[31] In Transcarpathia, where there was no mass lay movement for the church's legalization, only some 129 parishes under Bishop Ivan Semedii and two auxiliaries were reestablished during 1990.[32] As of 1 January 1991, the Greek Catholic Church reached a total strength of 2,001 congregations within the republic,[33] gaining an absolute majority of parishes in two of the three Galician oblasts and a plurality in the third. Of its 854 priests, the majority were now converts from Orthodoxy.[34]

In January 1991, the pope confirmed all diocesan and titular bishops in Ukraine,[35] and in late March, Archbishop Major Myroslav-Ivan Cardinal Liubachivs'kyi returned to his L'viv see. On 28 May 1991, under the new republican law on religion, the statute of the Ukrainian Greek Catholic Church was registered at the republican level, and the statute of the L'viv archdiocese, on 15 June.[36]

By 1 January 1992, the Greek Catholic Church grew to 2,144 congregations;[37] in the beginning of 1993, it totaled 2,807 parishes and 2,214 churches organized in three dioceses, with three diocesan and eight auxiliary bishops, 1,128 priests, forty-three monasteries and convents with 1,118 monastics, three diocesan and three monastic theological seminaries with 1,469 students, 475 Sunday schools, and five periodicals.[38]

On 12 July 1993, the pope approved the establishment of four new dioceses in Galicia and Bukovyna and nominated one more bishop for the new diocese of Zboriv,[39] but he has not responded to the Greek Catholic Synod's request for an additional diocese in central Ukraine to administer 34 parishes in the traditionally Orthodox oblasts. Despite repeated requests by the Ukrainian Greek Catholic Church to raise its status to that of the patriarchate (as promised by the pope, once the church would reestablish itself in its home territory in Ukraine), Rome has still to make good on its promise. The Vatican's reluctance to establish a Greek Catholic diocese in east-central Ukraine may reflect recently adopted changes in Rome's strategy in the Orthodox regions of the former USSR.[40]

Thus, after more than four decades of forced underground existence, the Greek Catholic Church reestablished its public presence in Galicia, albeit without regaining the title to all of its nationalized property,[41] however sympathetic the democratically elected local and oblast authorities are to its cause. But the pre-1945 Galician ethnoreligious monolith is no more, with the divided Orthodox Church controlling 1,674 Galician parishes in 1993,[42] primarily, it seems, due to its prevalence in the numbers of established parish clergy.

The Autocephalous and Autonomous Orthodox Churches

Though the first initiative group to revive the Ukrainian Autocephalous Orthodox Church surfaced in Kiev in February 1989,[43] the real impetus for the appearance of the UAOC came in the summer of 1989 from L'viv's SS. Peter and Paul
parish (once a Uniate congregation), headed by Fr. Volodymyr Iarema. Unlike
the Kievan initiative that looked back to the anti-Muscovite tradition of Metropolitan Lypkivs'kyi's UAOC of the 1920s, the movement from ROC to the
UAOC in Galicia invoked the legacy of Fr. Havryil Kostel'nyk's "reunion" with
Orthodoxy in 1945–46, which was now conveniently reinterpreted as a patriotic
action for an independent Ukrainian church that was "betrayed" by the MGB
agentura within the Moscow Patriarchate.[44] Hence an initially anti-Uniate theme
emerged in the Galician UAOC as a way to "save Orthodoxy" in Galicia with the
collapse of the Russian Orthodox Church's defenses against Greek Catholic
revival. In the fall of 1989, the UAOC was joined by a former ROC bishop of
Zhytomyr, Ioann Bodnarchuk, a Galician native, who ordained several more
bishops for the new church. The canonicity of these ordinations has been denied
by the ROC.[45] At its All-Ukrainian Council in Kiev in June 1990, the UAOC
proclaimed itself a patriarchate and elected *in absentia* as its first patriarch
Metropolitan Mstyslav Skrypnyk, primate of the Ukrainian Orthodox Church in
the United States and the only surviving hierarch of the wartime, "second"
UAOC.[46] His arrival in Ukraine in October 1990 coincided with the official
recognition of the UAOC by the republican authorities, who nevertheless continued their preferential treatment of the Moscow Patriarchate's UOC.[47] By 1 January 1991, the Autocephalous Orthodox Church in Ukraine totaled 939
congregations, of which 96 percent were located in Galicia.[48] On 1 January
1992, the UAOC had 1,490 parishes, organized in fourteen dioceses under ten
bishops.[49] The much larger Ukrainian Orthodox Church had 5,031 parishes as of
January 1991[50] and 5,473 congregations a year later,[51] organized in twenty-two
dioceses, with twenty-three bishops, thirty-two monastic institutions, and three
theological seminaries.[52]

Unlike both the Greek Catholic and Autocephalous churches, with their
monoethnic flocks, the UOC has been a territorial and multiethnic (but predominantly Ukrainian-Russian) subdivision of the Moscow Patriarchate that, under
the pressure of developments in the republic, was accorded broad autonomy in
October 1991.[53]

On the basis of this grant by the Local Council of the ROC of "independence
and self-government" in its internal affairs, the Ukrainian Local Council (22–23
November 1990) adopted a Statute on the Administration of the Ukrainian Orthodox Church that was approved by the Moscow Patriarchate; it also adopted
the corresponding Civil Statute of the UOC, which was duly registered with the
Council for Religious Affairs in Kiev.

The "independence" of the UOC was limited by several provisions of its statute: it remained an integral part of the Russian Orthodox Church; the primate of the UOC (metropolitan of Kiev and all Ukraine), though "elected for a life term by the Ukrainian episcopate from among the Ukrainian (UOC) hierarchy," was subject to the "blessing" (approval) by the patriarch of Moscow and remained a permanent member of the ROC Holy Synod. The primate is responsible for convening meetings of all governing bodies of the UOC: its Holy Synod, Council of Bishops, and Local Council. In case of complaint against the primate, chairmanship of the Holy Synod goes to the next senior member of the hierarchy; were he to be brought to ecclesiastical trial, the UOC Holy Synod, chaired by the next senior hierarch, would elect at once a *locum tenens* who would temporarily take over the administration of the Kievan diocese. The statute did not clarify such important issues as the validity of the decisions by the patriarch of Moscow (other than approving the election of the UOC primate) and the ROC's Holy Synod and Council of Bishops for internal affairs of the Ukrainian church; the right to hear appeals from Ukrainian bishops against decisions by the primate and the UOC Synod and Local Councils; or the ROC's right to try the Ukrainian primate before its own ecclesiastical courts.[54]

The Churches and Ukrainian Independence

The collapse of the reactionary coup in August 1991 and the subsequent proclamation of Ukraine's state independence has fundamentally affected the situation of the churches in the republic and their relationship with each other and with the state. Like its powerful political ally, the Communist Party of Ukraine, the UOC emerged compromised by its leaders' support of the coup.[55] Its hopes for Moscow's intervention in defense of its interests against the Autocephalist "schismatics," the Uniate "extremists," and their national "patrons" in Rukh and in the local government in Galicia ended with the banning of the party and the collapse of the central repressive structures.[56]

By then Metropolitan Filaret had come under attack in the uncensored media for his scandalous private life (living for many years with a common-law wife and fathering three children).[57] There were revelations from the now opened secret party archives about his long intimate association with the KGB (along with other leading figures in the Moscow Patriarchate).[58] Neither were Filaret's guilty secrets unknown to the ROC and UOC episcopate; he nevertheless was elected *locum tenens* after the death of Patriarch Pimen of Moscow in 1990 and remained a senior member of the ROC Holy Synod. Nor were the authorities unaware of Filaret's family life. Though his protector, the Communist Party, had now collapsed, Filaret still enjoyed the confidence and support of the head of Ukraine, Leonid Kravchuk, formerly chief of the CPU propaganda apparatus.

A sudden "conversion" of Filaret to the idea of autocephaly for the UOC came at the strong urging of President Kravchuk. It was therefore not surprising that the metropolitan did not reject outright the offer made by the UAOC Council of Bishops in early September to begin negotiations about the merger of both churches in the Ukrainian Patriarchate already proclaimed by the UAOC.[59] On 10 September Metropolitan Filaret announced the agreement of the UOC to conduct negotiations with the UAOC, but qualified it with the condition that such talks should "proceed from the interests of peoples residing in the territory of Ukraine and observe apostolic rules and decisions of ecumenical councils governing the life of the Orthodox Church."[60]

The Local Council of the Ukrainian Orthodox Church, which met in the Kievo-Pechers´ka Monastery on 1–3 November after much arm-twisting by Filaret, endorsed the episcopate's decision to seek autocephaly for the UOC from the Moscow Patriarchate as "canonically justified" and "historically inevitable" and so that the UOC would exist "not only in unity with the Russian Orthodox Church, but also with all local churches." In the words of Metropolitan Filaret,

> [T]his will assist in the liquidation of the existing Autocephalist schism, prevent Uniate and [Roman] Catholic expansion, and serve to reconcile the hostile [factions].[61]

As for the "merger" offer from the UAOC, the Council resolved that

> while the UOC does not recognize the arbitrary declaration of autocephaly, it fights, however, for the unity of Orthodoxy and, therefore, appeals to all those who call themselves the Ukrainian Autocephalous Orthodox Church to return into the bosom of the canonical holy church—the UOC.[62]

At the same time, the Council decided to retain Church Slavonic as the liturgical language, with its "eastern" (Russian) and "western" (Ukrainian) pronunciations, allowing, as before, the use of Ukrainian, Russian, or other living languages, "depending on the wishes of the local flock and pastors."[63] Claiming to speak for "thirty-five million [UOC] believers,"[64] Metropolitan Filaret at first voiced his optimism that Patriarch Aleksii II and the ROC episcopate would not refuse the UOC's request for autocephaly: "If they would not give us full independence, this would mean that they want to push the Orthodox believers in Ukraine into an independent autocephalous schism."[65] However, after his return from Moscow, where he presented the UOC Council's documents to the patriarchate, with a strong letter of support from Kravchuk, Filaret reported that "a lot of untruth is now accumulating in Moscow in order not to grant us full independence."[66] Indeed, on 22 November, the mouthpiece of the patriarchate—the Union of Orthodox Brotherhoods—appealed in Moscow to citizens of Ukraine to vote against independence in the approaching 1 December 1991 referendum, as "Slavic peoples of Russia and Ukraine have 'one history, one fate,'" and called upon the voters "not to allow the enemy of our salvation to separate us."[67] Clearly the Russian Orthodox Church has thrown its lot to the nationalist forces in Russia eager to preserve or to restore the unity of the empire.

Meanwhile, the importance of the churches' support for a pro-independence vote in the referendum moved the leaders of the republic—both Leonid Kravchuk (soon to be popularly elected president of Ukraine) and a democratic opposition leader, Ihor Iukhnovs'kyi—to convene an interconfessional conference, the "All-Ukrainian Interreligious Forum," on 19–20 November. The gathering served both to minimize any organized religious-based opposition or abstention in the coming referendum on independence and to diffuse interchurch conflicts, while opening the prospects of a direct involvement of religious organizations in the shaping of the Ukrainian state's confessional policy.[68] The forum, which brought together representatives of ten major confessions in Ukraine, also provided a public occasion for confronting not only the two Orthodox conceptions of a "national church" in independent Ukraine but also a Greek Catholic proposal for a single Orthodox-Catholic Patriarchate of Kiev, Halych, and all Rus', in communion with the Orthodox patriarchates and the Catholic Church, which, not unexpectedly, was deemed unrealistic by the UOC and the UAOC.[69] Significantly, the leaders of Protestant denominations (most notably the Evangelical Christian-Baptists) opposed any discrimination between "national" and other churches and pleaded for the government's adherence to the statutory principle of the separation of church and state.

The Futile Quest for Autocephaly from the Moscow Patriarchate

The process of Ukraine's emancipation from the imperial control of Moscow, culminating, if not ending, in the overwhelming popular endorsement of Ukrainian state independence on 1 December and followed by international recognition of the Ukrainian state, has for the first time since the annexation of the Kievan church by the Moscow Patriarchate led the former Russian Orthodox Church in the republic not only to assume autonomy as the Ukrainian Orthodox Church but eventually to request canonical autocephaly from the Moscow Patriarchate. After the collapse of the Soviet Union, Metropolitan Filaret convened a Synod of Bishops in January 1992 to plead again for autocephaly of the Ukrainian Orthodox Church.[70] By then, however, the Moscow Patriarchate managed to divide the Ukrainian episcopate with threats and promises, helped by the heavy-handed methods used by Filaret to bring the bishops in line.[71] Meanwhile, the leaders of the Russian Orthodox Church proceeded to redefine the traditional notion that independent states should have an autocephalous church. On the contrary, they argued, the new situation demanded greater unity, and the Moscow Patriarchate was, after all, not a Russian but a supranational ecclesiastical authority.[72] At the same time, the patriarchate issued guarantees to those bishops and dioceses in Ukraine that would not support autocephaly of continued "canonical pastoral nourishment" by the Russian Orthodox Church (i.e., an offer to secede from the UOC, should it "unilaterally" embrace autocephaly and to remain under the direct jurisdiction of Moscow).[73]

Prior to and during the Council of ROC Bishops in Moscow (31 March–5 April 1992), which was to consider the Ukrainian petition for autocephaly, the patriarchate orchestrated a rebellion of most of the UOC bishops against Filaret.[74] Despite protest by six Ukrainian bishops that the ROC Council of Bishops was violating the internal autonomy of the UOC by sitting in judgment of the activities of Metropolitan Filaret and other UOC bishops rather than limiting itself to the question of autocephaly, the gathering accused Filaret of seeking independence for the Ukrainian church for his own "egotistical" ends and attacked the Ukrainian government for "interference" with the church's freedom (by addressing to the Council a letter supporting the UOC's petition for a grant of autocephaly). All but six of the participants attacked the very prospect of Ukrainian autocephaly as a step toward "schism" and Uniatism, a blow to the "unity" of the three East Slavic peoples, and an invitation to Russian Orthodox in Ukraine to secede from the UOC and for Belarusians and the ROC in the Baltic states to follow the Ukrainians in separating themselves from Moscow.[75] Intense pressure was put on Filaret to resign "voluntarily" from the primate's position for the sake of "peace" and "unity" in the church, and proposals were made at the Council for his immediate removal. Filaret bought time by promising to convene a council of Ukrainian Bishops after the Moscow gathering and to submit to it his resignation.[76] It became clear that the Moscow Patriarchate would never part with its Ukrainian component, which is larger than the remaining part of the ROC.[77] However, for tactical reasons the official response of the Moscow Council was to declare that it was not in principle opposed to Ukrainian autocephaly and to postpone a final decision on this matter until the next Local Council of the ROC (not due until 1995) because, it concluded, the majority of the UOC bishops, clergy, and faithful were not in favor of complete ecclesiastical independence "at this time." In fact, at least two bishops threatened to secede from the Ukrainian Orthodox Church and return to the jurisdiction of Moscow in the event the patriarchate granted of autocephaly to Ukraine.[78]

The Split in the Ukrainian Orthodox Church and the Ukrainian Government

However, upon his return to Kiev, having reassured himself about continuing support from President Kravchuk, Metropolitan Filaret publicly repudiated his Moscow pledge as involuntary, uncanonical, and contrary to both the UOC statute and governmental regulations, arguing that under the government-registered statute of the church he was elected primate for life.[79]

In a quick and angry response, the Moscow Patriarchate sanctioned an "assembly" of anti-Filaret bishops, clergy, monks, and brotherhoods in Zhytomyr on 30 April. The Zhytomyr gathering expressed no confidence in Metropolitan Filaret, because of "his deliberate attempt to deceive the Fathers of the Bishop's Sobor [Council] of the Mother Church."[80] Though attended by only six bishops (with two more cabling their support), the "assembly" insisted on convening without delay a Council of Ukrainian Bishops to accept Filaret's resignation and elect a new primate.[81] On 7 May, an "enlarged meeting" of the ROC Holy Synod issued an ultimatum to Filaret "to convene the Sobor [Council] of Bishops of the Ukrainian Orthodox Church before 15 May and to hand in to it his . . . resignation from the post of the UOC Primate." At the same time, the Holy Synod, clearly violating the autonomous statute of the Ukrainian church, prohibited the metropolitan from exercising his powers, except for convoking the Bishops' Council for the sole purpose of his resignation and replacement. The Holy Synod also declared "null and void" any punishments imposed by Filaret on bishops, clergy, and laity for supporting Moscow's decisions. Should he fail to carry out its orders, declared the Holy Synod, Filaret would be brought to trial before the ROC Council of Bishops.[82]

As Filaret ignored Moscow's ultimatum, the Holy Synod, acting again in violation of the UOC statute, declared the primate's Kievan see vacant and named the next senior Ukrainian hierarch, Metropolitan Nykodym of Kharkiv, "temporary primate." It instructed him to call and conduct a Council of UOC Bishops to elect a new primate.[83] To prevent the Ukrainian government's intervention, Nykodym deliberately misinformed the authorities that he would be convening a "pre-Council conference" in Kharkiv on 27–28 May 1992.[84]

On 25 May, Metropolitan Filaret informed Patriarch Aleksii II of Moscow that he considered the decisions of the Holy Synod "ungrounded and invalid."[85] On the next day, Filaret convened, with the support of the Ukrainian government, an "All-Ukrainian Conference for Safeguarding the Canonical Rights of the Ukrainian Orthodox Church."[86] The conference rejected the Moscow Patriarchate's decisions and condemned the actions of bishops who remained obedient to the Russian "mother church" as "betrayal of the Church and the Orthodox people in Ukraine."[87]

Predictably, the Kharkiv Council of UOC Bishops loyal to the Moscow Patriarchate voted on 27 May to remove Filaret from the primate's Kievan see and suspended him as bishop pending the decision of the next ROC Council of Bishops in Moscow. In his place, the Kharkiv gathering elected as the new metropolitan of Kiev and primate a Moscow nominee, Volodymyr Sabodan of Rostov and Novocherkask, who had served until then as chancellor of the Moscow Patriarchate.[88] Though the new primate was an ethnic Ukrainian, he was not a member of the Ukrainian Orthodox Church's episcopate, and his past career left no doubt about his loyalty to Moscow. On 28 May, the Russian Holy Synod ratified Metropolitan Volodymyr's election.[89]

As the Ukrainian government refused to recognize the validity of the Kharkiv Council and rejected Moscow's right to intervene in the affairs of the UOC, the split of the Ukrainian Orthodox Church into a minority "autocephalist" faction led by Filaret (later called the UOC—Kiev Patriarchate) and the majority pro-Moscow faction led by Metropolitan Sabodan (UOC—Moscow Patriarchate) became complete. There were now two Ukrainian Orthodox Churches and two metropolitans of Kiev (i.e., two primates), and the Kiev government, insistent on the autocephaly of the Orthodox Church in Ukraine, made its choice. It recognized the minority UOC headed by Metropolitan Filaret as the legal heir to the hitherto single Ukrainian Orthodox Church and its assets and funds, and it barred the pro-Moscow UOC from access to the government-owned mass media.[90] As Metropolitan Volodymyr pledged his loyalty to the Ukrainian state and expressed his hope that eventually his church would be granted autocephaly by Moscow, the government relented by declaring that individual parishes, monasteries, convents, and theological seminaries could decide by majority vote which of the two churches they wished to belong to without risking their respective assets.[91] However, central facilities and funds of the "old" UOC were left in Filaret's hands, including the primate's official residence and headquarters of the church and the primate's St. Volodymyr Cathedral.[92] Metropolitan Sabodan was compelled to make his headquarters in the Kievan Monastery of the Caves (Kievo-Pechers'ka Lavra), which, incidentally, Filaret's new ultranationalist supporters had earlier unsuccessfully tried to occupy.[93]

Meanwhile, Patriarch Aleksii II summoned Filaret to Moscow to stand ecclesiastical trial before the ROC Council of Bishops on 11 June.[94] While Filaret ignored the summons, the Moscow Council, on submission of the loyal UOC bishops, condemned him for a "cruel and arrogant attitude"; "diktat and blackmail" with regard to clergymen in his jurisdiction; violation of monastic vows of chastity in his private life; "perjury" (i.e., failing to carry out his pledge to step down as primate); "public slander and abuse of the Bishop's Sobor" [Council]; "performance of religious rites, including ordinations, while interdicted"; and "causing a schism in the Church."[95] The Council resolved to divest Filaret (and his vicar, Bishop Iakiv Panchuk) of all degrees of priesthood and to declare null and void all his ordinations and all penalties imposed by him.[96] In a message to the Ukrainian Orthodox Church, the patriarch and the Council's Presidium declared that "all believers who will enter into ecclesiastical communion with former Metropolitan Filaret (Denysenko) and former Bishop Iakiv (Panchuk) shall be subjected to excommunication, and clergymen—to the divestiture of holy orders."[97] The message denied that the patriarchate's actions were motivated by its unwillingness to grant autocephaly to the Ukrainian church, which would be given if it were requested in canonical manner by "the people of the Church" "freely and clearly with no political or other pressures."[98] The document charged that "Filaret and other ecclesiastical law-breakers are misusing the topic of autocephaly exclusively for their own selfish interests, inculcating the false impression of themselves being victims of their autocephalist convictions."[99]

On 16 June, the Presidium of the Ukrainian parliament (Supreme Council) issued a declaration on interconfessional relations that reiterated its support for Metropolitan Filaret and his adherents as the legitimate Ukrainian Orthodox Church and for the Ukrainian Autocephalous Orthodox Church.[100] Following

Metropolitan Volodymyr's arrival in Kiev on 20 June, Filaret addressed a letter to the chairman of the Ukrainian parliament, Ivan Pliushch, charging that Metropolitian Sabodan's church by its unquestioned submission to the "illegal decisions" of the ROC's Holy Synod had reverted to the status of the "Ukrainian Exarchate of the Moscow Patriarchate."[101]

The "Merger" of the UOC and the UAOC and Patriarch Mstyslav

In anticipation of the Local Council of the pro-Moscow UOC called by Metropolitan Volodymyr for 26 June 1992, Metropolitan Filaret and Patriarch Mstyslav's administrator in Kiev, Metropolitan Antonii (Masendych), hastily convened a "joint" Local Council of the pro-Filaret UOC and the Ukrainian Autocephalous Orthodox Church a day earlier. Though they were given full government backing, the two organizers of this gathering failed to inform Patriarch Mstyslav—the canonical head of the UAOC—in advance, or to secure his blessing for a Local Council (which, as far as the UAOC was concerned, could not otherwise be convened).[102] With some Autocephalist bishops staying away, the joint Local Council proclaimed a "unification" of both churches into a single "Ukrainian Orthodox Church—Kiev Patriarchate" (UOC—KP), elected in absentia Patriarch Mstyslav as its head, and named Filaret "deputy patriarch."[103] The governmental Council for Religious Affairs, under its new chairman, Arsen Zinchenko, promptly recognized the new church and proceeded to "de-register" the Ukrainian Autocephalous Orthodox Church, despite the fact that only some 350 UAOC parishes joined the UOC—KP. This left without the rights of a legal person an overwhelming majority[104] of UAOC congregations loyal to Patriarch Mstyslav and opposed to Filaret, who, until his sudden "conversion" to autocephaly, was the fiercest enemy of Ukrainian political and ecclesiastical independence. They now "disappeared" from the official statistics of religious organizations in Ukraine.[105]

All in all, only a small minority of the "old" UOC joined the Ukrainian Orthodox Church—Kiev Patriarchate. According to manipulated statistics released by the Council for Religious Affairs, the new church totaled 1,665 congregations on 1 August 1992[106] and 1,763 parishes as of 1 January 1993;[107] included in this total were 672 parishes "that have not amended their statutes" (presumably a veiled reference to UAOC congregations that refused to join the UOC—KP).[108]

The Ukrainian Orthodox Church subordinate to the Moscow Patriarchate has retained the majority of Orthodox parishes: 5,658 on 1 August 1992, and 5,590, headed by twenty-nine bishops, at the beginning of 1993.[109] The chairman of the Council for Religious Affairs, Arsen Zinchenko, subsequently recalculated the January 1993 totals for the UOC of Metropolitan Sabodan as 5,449, and for the UOC—KP as 1,904.[110] To be sure, an unknown number of UOC and UAOC congregations are divided in their attitude toward the UOC—KP, as attested by sporadic violence erupting in some (especially Volyhnian) parishes.

In the meantime, the UOC—KP suffered a major blow when its nominal head, Patriarch Mstyslav (Skrypnyk), after some procrastination, repudiated the 26 June "unification" Council as uncanonical and removed from the UAOC episcopate Metropolitan Antonii (Masendych), one of the chief organizers of "unification." He asked the so-called deputy patriarch, Filaret, to leave the church, since he seemed too compromised to ever be recognized by other Ortho-dox churches.[111] Mstyslav's repeated requests to the Ukrainian government to lift its "de-registration" of the Autocephalous Orthodox Church have remained unheeded, raising charges of the government's violation of international stan-dards of religious rights and freedoms.[112] For its part, the UOC—KP responded to Patriarch Mstyslav's actions by convening on 15 December 1992 its Council of Bishops, which virtually stripped Mstyslav of all powers, except those ex-pressly delegated to him by the Synod.[113]

The long-ailing Patriarch Mstyslav—the most outstanding figure in Ukrainian Orthodoxy and its living link with the wartime ("second") UAOC—passed away on 14 June 1993. The two Orthodox churches that considered Mstyslav their canonical head—the UAOC and the UOC—KP—each elected its respective *locum tenens*: Archbishop Petro (Petrus') of L'viv and Halych, and Metropolitan Volodymyr (Romaniuk) of Chernihiv and Sumy.[114] Surprisingly, the UOC—KP bypassed its "deputy patriarch," Filaret. On 7 September, the Ukrainian Auto-cephalous Orthodox Church elected at its Local Council in Kiev a new patriarch, the recently ordained bishop of Pereiaslav and Sicheslav, Dmytrii (Iarema).[115] As pastor of the L'viv Church of SS. Peter and Paul, Iarema was the first ROC priest to bring his parish into the revived UAOC in 1989; he was also instrumen-tal in having Bishop Ioann (Bodnarchuk) of Zhytomyr, who defected from the Russian church, assume archpastoral leadership of the Autocephalous Church. Hailed at one time as the "father of Ukrainian autocephaly," Iarema later turned against Ioann and had him expelled from the UAOC by Patriarch Mstyslav.[116] At its September Council, the UAOC claimed to have eight dioceses, with five bishops, two theological seminaries, and 1,500 parishes with "de-registered" statutes. The Council pleaded, so far in vain, to have the Ukrainian government restore the UAOC's legal status.[117]

Reacting to the Local Council of the UAOC, the UOC—KP launched a smear campaign against the "operetta patriarchate" of the UAOC, accusing its leading figures of "Russophilism" and circulating an alleged KGB "document" intended to compromise Patriarch Dmytrii (Iarema) and Archbishop Petro (Petrus') as KGB "agents" and "collaborators."[118]

On 20–21 October, the Ukrainian Orthodox Church—Kiev Patriarchate held its "All-Ukrainian Orthodox Council" in St. Sofiia Cathedral in Kiev. After Metropolitan Antonii (Masendych) was disqualified from the nomination be-cause of his age (thirty-two),[119] the Council, choosing from four remaining

ORTHODOX AND GREEK CATHOLICS IN UKRAINE   149

candidates, elected the church's *locum tenens* Metropolitan Volodymyr Romaniuk[120] as its new patriarch of Kiev and all Rus'-Ukraine.[121] Invoking its constant support for the independence of Ukraine, the Council asked the government to "return" to the UOC—KP the historical church-museums—of St. Sofiia Cathedral and the St. Andrii and St. Kyrylo churches in Kiev. The Council also asked the government to transfer to the UOC—KP the principal monasteries of the UOC under the jurisdiction of the Moscow Patriarchate—the Kievo-Pechers'ka Monastery and the Pochaivs'ka Monastery in Ternopil' Oblast—as well as a number of historical churches throughout Ukraine and diocesan administration buildings in seven oblasts.[122] The UOC—KP thus openly called for state intervention against the rival Orthodox churches in violation of the Ukrainian law on Freedom of Conscience and Religious Organizations. On the eve of the "All-Ukrainian Council," the Ukrainian government made an unsuccessful attempt to have Patriarch Bartholomew of Constantinople recognize the UOC—KP.[123]

The All-Ukrainian Council, despite its election of a new patriarch, did not resolve the internal problems of the UOC—KP. With Metropolitan Filaret continuing to run the church, "humiliating in every way Patriarch Volodymyr (Romaniuk),"[124] internal opposition to Filaret crystallized around Metropolitan Antonii (Masendych) of Pereiaslav and Sicheslav (Dnipropetrovs'k). This was not unnoticed by the pro-Moscow UOC and the Moscow Patriarchate. In the last days of December 1993, Metropolitan Volodymyr (Sabodan) convened the "Second Conference of the Ukrainian Orthodox Church" at the Kievo-Pechers'ka Monastery. Attending the conference were representatives of the UOC—KP and the UAOC, who were invited by Metropolitan Sabodan to discuss the problems of interchurch relations. Behind the scene, negotiations were apparently taking place between Metropolitan Volodymyr and Metropolitan Antonii (Masendych) about him and his anti-Filaret fellow bishops joining the pro-Moscow UOC, presumably in return for their recognition (more likely, later reordination) as canonical bishops. As the conference ended on 29 December, Antonii immediately took a "leave for health reasons" just as the news was leaked that he had defected to the Moscow Patriarchate.[125]

On 5 January 1994, the Russian Kiev newspaper *Nezavisimost'* brought into the open the split in the UOC—KP by publishing a joint declaration of Metropolitan Antonii (Masendych) and four other hierarchs—Archbishop Spiridon of Vinnytsia and Bishops Sofron of Zhytomyr, Roman of Kharkiv and Poltava, and Ioann of Iahotyn. Announcing their union with the UOC under the jurisdiction of the Moscow Patriarchate, the five bishops declared that "the UOC—KP is noncanonical and lacking in divine grace, and is not guided by the canons of the Orthodox Church." They accused Metropolitan Filaret of continuing "persecution" of bishops within the UOC—KP. At the same time they declared:

> We [are] patriots of our independent state and are striving towards an independent Ukrainian church. By our prayers and intense efforts we are trying to

accelerate the granting of independence [autocephaly] to our Ukrainian Orthodox Church.[126]

Without losing any time, Patriach Aleksii of Moscow addressed a letter to the
Ukrainian minister of justice, Onopenko, "explaining" the status of the pro-Moscow UOC with a view to regaining for it the "old" UOC property. Ignoring the
1993 split in the UOC and the removal (and defrocking) of Metropolitan Filaret
engineered by the Moscow Patriarchate, Aleksii assured the minister that the
pro-Moscow UOC

> [is] canonically independent and entirely self-governing in its [internal] af-
> fairs . . . the Moscow Patriarchate has no claims on the movable and real prop-
> erty of the Ukrainian Orthodox Church.[127]

The defection of five bishops, who had undoubtedly led at least some of their
parishes back to the pro-Moscow UOC, created a major crisis in the UOC—KP
and placed before the Ukrainian government the dilemma: should it continue to
favor Metropolitan Filaret and treat the UOC—KP as a quasi-state church; or
should it assume a more neutral position in the inter-Orthodox conflict and end
its discrimination against the "deregistered" UAOC? Unless the government
withdraws its backing from Filaret and brings about his "retirement" now that a
new patriarch (Romaniuk) has been elected, there is strong likelihood of further
defections from the UOC—KP.

Conclusion

Thus Ukraine now has *two* patriarchs of Kiev and *three* Orthodox churches: an
ethnic and predominantly Galician Ukrainian Autocephalous Orthodox Church;
a quasi-state church, the Ukrainian Orthodox Church—Kiev Patriarchate, with
mostly Ukrainian and partly Russian membership;[128] and the largest of the three,
the territorial Ukrainian-Russian church, the UOC—subordinated to the "imperial church"—the ROC.

In the westernmost regions of Ukraine, the Greek Catholic Church, another
ethnic church—now the second-largest religious organization in Ukraine—represents a "national" church with a regional base, but with a slowly expanding
Greek Catholic diaspora in the rest of Ukraine and beyond. In Kiev and some
other centers of the country, the emergent Greek Catholic communities, despite
their "registration," have been for a long time denied the use of empty Orthodox
churches on the grounds that they were once built by the Orthodox. Thus in the
capital of Ukraine, the local Greek Catholic services had to be celebrated for
over two years in the open, *outside* closed or empty Orthodox churches, and
attempts by the Uniate hierarchy on rare occasions to conduct services with
government permission in state-owned museum-churches were prevented by

well-organized UOC "protesters," without the local authorities' enforcing public order. When after long pleading the Greek Catholic Church was returned the plot of land on which the Kiev Uniate Church was once located, the same "protesters" attempted to disrupt the blessing ceremonies on the site, on which a Greek Catholic church will be built.[129]

Despite its image of unity and stability, the Greek Catholic Church has problems of its own: tensions between the former "catacomb clergy" and the priests who defected from the ROC, as well as between the "native" clergy and the émigré priests who dominate the administration of the archbishop major, Cardinal Liubachivs'kyi. Moreover, it faces a problem in the refusal of the Transcarpathian diocese of Mukachiv-Uzhhorod to integrate in the single Ukrainian Greek Catholic Church in Ukraine. Closely identified with the regional "Ruthenian" identity, the eparch of the diocese and one of his two auxiliary bishops opted instead for direct subordination to the Vatican.[130] Another problem has been the unwillingness of the Vatican to approve the creation of additional Uniate dioceses, especially in eastern Ukraine, where the Polish Roman Catholic Church has been given free reign.

Together, the divided Orthodox churches and the Greek Catholic Church represent an overwhelming majority of believers in Ukraine, though the percentage of religious people in the total population of Ukraine remains a matter of conjecture. It is admittedly much higher in western Ukraine than elsewhere, and it may be far less than half of the urban population in east-central oblasts where Soviet systematic destruction of institutional religion and atheist indoctrination, as well as the policy of denationalization, lasted much longer than in the western oblasts.

According to a survey conducted by the National Institute of Strategic Research in October 1992, only 20 percent of the representative national sample declared themselves Orthodox; 5 percent, Greek Catholic; and 2 percent, adherents of other faiths. Of the remainder, 42 percent identified themselves as "unaffiliated believers," and 32 percent as "atheists."[131]

This chapter has deliberately omitted the discussion of religious organizations other than the Orthodox and Greek Catholic in Ukraine. There are fifty-six such organizations, most of them with minuscule followings.[132] The third largest denomination in Ukraine—the Evangelical Christian-Baptists with a total of 1,297 congregations—comprised on 1 January 1993 the Union of the ECB of Ukraine (1,194) and Religious Congregations of the Former Council of Churches of ECB (103), not counting 6 congregations of unaffiliated Evangelical Christians and 2 communities of "Pure Baptists." The Pentecostals (808 congregations) are divided into the majority "Union of Christians of Evangelical Faith (Pentecostals) of Ukraine" (575 congregations) and the minority "Union of Free Churches of Christians of Evangelical Faith of Ukraine" (18); there are also 197 unaffiliated Pentecostal communities. Two organizations of Seventh-Day Adventists total 342 congregations, and there are 10 Reformed Adventist communities, apart from 47 congregations of Evangelical Christians—"Sabbath-Keepers." Jehovah's Witnesses have 411 congregations, móstly in Transcarpathia. There are as well 9 unaffiliated Protestant congregations.[133]

The old "ethnic" Protestant churches are represented in Ukraine by the Hungarian Calvinist (Reformed) Church in Transcarpathia (94 congregations), German and Swedish Lutheran Churches (10 and 1 congregations, respectively), and 1 Ukrainian Evangelical-Reformed congregation, as well as 3 Korean and 2 Hungarian Methodist congregations.[134]

There are also numerous religious cults, ranging from the International Society for Krishna Consciousness to the recently notorious "White Brotherhood" and a neopagan nationalist religious cult—"Native Ukrainian National Faith" (RUNvira)—imported from the Ukrainian diaspora in the West.[135] The chief common concern of "cosmopolitan" Protestant sects in Ukraine is possible discrimination from local authorities and from the established Orthodox and Greek Catholic churches. On the other hand, religious minorities, for example, the Roman Catholics,[136] are favored against the Uniates in east-central Ukraine, while the republican government has been particularly vigilant against any manifestations of ethnoreligious discrimination against Jews.

The overall religious picture of contemporary Ukraine is that of religious pluralism more publicly tolerated than in Russia.[137] This challenges the traditional view of Ukraine as an Orthodox-Uniate country. It reflects, on the one hand, the more complicated ethnic composition of Ukraine—a product of both forcible transfers of various nationalities and greater demographic mobility. On the other hand, it attests to the active proselytizing activities, especially of moderate Protestant sects, which, with their cosmopolitan attitudes, found it easier to evangelize the ethnically uprooted "new Soviet men and women," with their use of Russian as a lingua franca. The Ukrainian government has made a modest start in encouraging interconfessional dialogue and ecumenism; it needs to do much more in this respect.

To conclude, in aiming for the autocephaly of the Orthodox Church in Ukraine, both Metropolitan Filaret and the Ukrainian government made a strategic mistake in rushing, in the face of expected hostility from the Moscow Patriarchate, without first educating the UOC clergy and faithful in the advantages and inevitability of an independent Orthodox Church in an independent state. By his concentration on the episcopate and by using questionable methods to get their "unanimous" vote for autocephaly, Filaret made it easier for the patriarchate to subvert the unity of Ukrainian bishops. The reasons that were advanced by the UOC in Moscow in pleading for autocephaly—that it would stem the spread of the UAOC and the Uniate Church, as well as a Roman Catholic "invasion" of Ukraine—were easily countered with arguments that the continued unity with the Moscow Patriarchate would strengthen the position of the UOC vis-à-vis the Catholics and, in particular, the Ukrainian government's pressure on the local Orthodox Church.[138] No positive arguments for autocephaly from Moscow—that it will help the Ukrainian church to mature, revive the ancient traditions of the Kievan church, regain its national character (i.e., help to de-Russify the church), and elevate it to full-fledged participant in ecumenical intra-Orthodox and inter-Orthodox relations—were advanced at the Bishops' Council in March–April 1992. The openly threatened Russian-Ukrainian split in the UOC should it acquire autocephaly was a clear enough indication that the Moscow Patriarchate would under no circumstances part with the Ukrainian dioceses and monastic and theological institutions with strong Russian or Russified Ukrainian presence[139] (as happened in 1917, when Moscow proceeded to split away Russian Orthodox parishes from the revived Georgian Patriarchate in the Georgian Republic until Stalin compelled the ROC in 1943 to recognize Georgian autocephaly and its territorial jurisdiction). Having proclaimed the entire territory of the former USSR as "canonical territory" of the Moscow Patriarchate, the ROC has embraced the Commonwealth of Independent States as the political framework for its jurisdiction and a stepping-stone to greater future "unity" of the three East Slavic peoples.[140] As in the past, the Russian church is likely to use every "canonical weapon" in its arsenal to prevent a diminution of its ecclesiastical empire.

The Ukrainian government had other options than unconditionally supporting Filaret in 1992–93. It could have built its policy in favor of autocephaly around the Ukrainian Autocephalous Orthodox Church, whose patriarch Mstyslav (Skrypnyk), could not have been defrocked by the ROC and who may have found a better reception in the patriarchate of Constantinople. Alternatively, the Kiev government could have followed the precedent set by the Directorate government in January 1919, when it declared the autocephaly of the Ukrainian Orthodox Church by state law, applying administrative sanctions against bishops who refused to embrace Ukrainian autocephaly.[141] The experience of the reborn Polish state in the early 1920s in setting up, in the face of the Moscow Patriarchate's and Kremlin's opposition, an Autocephalous Orthodox Church in Poland (recognized in 1924 by the patriarchate of Constantinople, which in its *tomos*, incidentally, declared Moscow's annexation of the Kiev Metropolitan see in 1685–86 null and void)[142] could have also been of some relevance to the new Ukrainian state.

President Kravchuk's apparent unwillingness or inability both to disturb the "old nomenklatura cadres" entrenched in the Ukrainian parliament and administration and actively promote Ukrainization may have contributed to his difficulties in the ecclesiastical realm. Finally, the failures in Kiev's church policy reflect on the qualities of the clergy—once "weaned" by the communist authorities on the principle "the worse, the better"—and now intimidated by the bishops selected by the security organs in the past on the basis of their servility to Moscow and their "iron-hand" control over the priests. The quality of the politicians trying to "run" church affairs also complicates Ukraine's church policy. Many, if not all, of them may be paying lip service to the importance of religion, but their view of it tends to be instrumental as a convenient means of advancing political objectives. As in the other areas of contemporary Ukrainian politics, the long shadow cast by decades of Bolshevik rule extends to the realm of church-state relations as well.

Notes

1. Jaroslav Pelikan, *Confessor Between East and West: A Portrait of Ukrainian Cardinal Josyf Slipyi* (Grand Rapids, MI: William B. Eerdmans, 1990), p. 43.

2. In the case of the Orthodox Church in Muscovy-Russia, it took 141 years and the imprisonment of the patriarch of Constantinople, who happened to visit Moscow in 1588, to gain the recognition of Russian autocephaly in return for the patriarch's release by Tsar Boris Godunov in 1589.

3. For an elaboration of the concept of an "imperial church," see the typology elaborated in Bohdan Bociurkiw, "Institutional Religion and Nationality in the Soviet Union," in *Soviet Nationalities in Strategic Perspective,* ed. S. Enders Wimbush (London: Croom Helm, 1985), pp. 182–86.

4. Pelikan, *Confessor*, p. 56.

5. See Borys Gudziak, "Istoriia Vidokremlennia: Kyivs'ka mytropoliia, Tsarhorods'kyi patriarkhat i heneza Beresteis'koiunii," in *Kivotos,* vol. 1, ed. Iaroslav Hrytsak and B. Gudziak (L'viv: Instytut istorychnykh doslidzhen' LDU and Instytut istorii tserkvy, 1993), pp. 6–15. Among the factors motivating the pro-Union bishops was also the spread of reformation into Ukraine and Belarus.

6. Ibid., pp. 17–19; cf. Johannes Madey, *Kirche zwischen Ost und West* (Munich: Ukrainische Freie Universitat, 1969), pp. 27–30.

7. See Bohdan Bociurkiw, "The Issues of Ukrainianization and Autocephaly of the Orthodox Church in Ukrainian-Russian Relations, 1917–1921, " in *Ukraine and Russia in Their Historical Encounter,* ed. P.J. Potichnyj, M. Raef, J. Pelenski, and G.N. Zekulin (Edmonton: Canadian Institute of Ukrainian Studies Press, 1992), pp. 244–73.

8. Leading Ukrainian composers and artists who joined the UAOC in the 1920s created a number of religious and quasi-religious services and spectacles marking anniversaries of great national figures (e.g., Taras Shevchenko) or major historical events that were incorporated into the rituals of the Autocephalous Church.

9. Thus by 1 September 1926, there existed 894 registered Autocephalist congregations within Soviet Ukraine (a year later—1,904 congregations), with 17 active bishops, 645 parish priests, 5 monastic priests, and 155 deacons presiding over, according to very low Soviet estimates, 700,000 active parishioners, amounting to 13 percent of Orthodox believers in the Ukrainian SSR. *Fond* 5 (NKVD), *op. 2, spr. 213, ark.* 31; *spr.* 2168; *op. 3, spr.* 751, *ark.* 37–38; *spr.* 399; *spr.* 2169, *ark.* 2; *op. 2, spr.* 2170, *ark.* 17–51, Central State Archive of the October Revolution of the Ukrainian SSR, Kiev.

10. Bohdan Bociurkiw, "The Soviet Destruction of the Ukrainian Orthodox Church, 1929–1936," *Journal of Ukrainian Studies* (Edmonton), no. 22 (summer 1987), pp. 3–21. After the so-called self-dissolution of the UAOC, its remnants were allowed to continue under a new name, the "Ukrainian Orthodox Church," and the few remaining bishops considered "trustworthy" by the GPU-NKVD remained until the total suppression of the church in 1936 and the execution of most of its bishops.

11. The first hierarchy of the wartime UAOC was ordained with the blessings of the primate of the Orthodox Church in *Generalgouvernement Polen* (German-occupied Poland), Metropolitan Dionizii (Valedinskii), by Metropolitan Aleksandr (Inozemtsev) of Pinsk, and Archbishop Polikarp in interwar Poland.

12. I.e., bishops ordained both during the Polish rule and Soviet occupation of Volhynia: the only exceptions were Archbishops Polikarp and Aleksandr.

13. See M. Odintsov, "Drugogo raza ne bylo . . ." *Nauka i religiia* (Moscow), 1989, no. 2 (February), p. 9, based on a memorandum by G.G. Karpov (the chief of the secret NKGB department on religion *and* chairman of the soon-to-be created governmental Council for the Affairs of the Russian Orthodox Church), *fond* 6991, *op.* 1s, *d.* 1, *listki* 1–19, Central State Archive of the October Revolution of the USSR, Moscow,

14. With all but one UAOC bishop (Metropolitan Buldovs'kyi of Kharkiv) escaping with the retreating German troops, only 500 Autocephalist parishes were left behind to be "reunited" with the ROC.

15. Cited in an unpublished manuscript by Ivan Bilas, "Virolomstvo derzhavy i trahediia tserkvy" (1991), based on another Karpov memorandum prepared on Stalin's and Molotov's request (CAROC's document collection at the Central Archive of the October Revolution, Moscow), pp. 33–45.

16. See an eyewitness account by a Basilian nurse, "Iak pomer Iepyskop Romzha," in *Litopys neskorenoi Ukrainy: Dokumenty, materiialy, spohady,* ed. Iaroslav Lial'ka et al. (L'viv: Prosvita, 1993), pp. 353–59. See also Bohdan Bociurkiw, "The Suppression of the Ukrainian Greek Catholic Church in Postwar Soviet Union and Poland," in *Religion and Nationalism in Eastern Europe and the Soviet Union,* ed. Dennis J. Dunn (Boulder, CO: Lynne Rienner, 1987), pp. 97–119.

17. Among the amnestied clergy were two surviving Greek Catholic bishops, Mykolai Charnets'kyi from L'viv and Ivan Liatyshevs'kyi from Ivano-Frankivs'k, who secretly resumed their archpastoral duties. See Bohdan Bociurkiw, "Ukrains'ka Hreko-katolyts'ka tserkva v katakombakh (1946–1989)," in Mrytsak and Gudziak, eds., *Kivotos,* pp. 113–52.

18. V. Davydenko, "Ne stanut' ahntsiamy voky," *Radians'ka Ukraina* (Kiev), 28 November 1988.

19. See John B. Dunlop, "Gorbachev and Russian Orthodoxy," *Problems of Communism,* vol. 38, no. 4 (July–August 1989), pp. 96–116. On the reaction in Ukraine, see an open letter "Moskovs'komu patriiarshomu ekzarkhovi na Ukraini" by L'viv priest Volodymyr Iarema, dated 27 February 1989, reproduced in *Ukrains'kyi pravoslavnyi kalendar na 1990 rik* (South Bound Brook, NJ: Ukrainian Orthodox Church of the U.S.A., 1990) pp. 105–8.

20. Cited in *Ukrainian Press Service* (Rome), no. 9, September 1987, p. 5. The appeal was signed by 1 bishop, 36 priests, monks, and nuns, and 174 laymen. Earlier, in February 1987, the *Chronicle of the Catholic Church in Ukraine* reported that Ukrainian Catholics addressed petitions to the Supreme Soviet of the USSR and Gorbachev personally, pledging their loyalty to the Soviet state and calling for the church's legalization. Ibid., p. 4.

21. B.R. Bociurkiw, "The Ukrainian Catholic Church in the USSR Under Gorbachev," *Problems of Communism,* vol. 39, no. 6 (November–December 1990), p. 10. Note in particular a statement on the subject by Ambassador Iurii Kashlev (who headed the Soviet delegation to the Vienna CSCE conference) in *Moscow News,* 5 November 1989.

22. See interviews of M.P. Kolesnyk, chairman of the Council for Religious Affairs in Ukraine, in *Izvestiia,* 1 February 1989, and *Radians'ka Ukraina,* 28 March 1989.

23. Of particular importance were publications in three mass circulation liberal periodicals: Alexander Petrov's interview with the USSR deputy from L'viv, writer Rostyslav Bratun', "Western Ukraine—A Hot September," *Moscow News,* 1 October 1989, p. 13; M. Odintsov, "Uniaty," *Argumenty i fakty,* 7–13 October 1989; and Georgii Rozhnov, "Eto my, Gospodi," *Ogonek,* 1989, no. 38, pp. 6–8. *Argumenty i fakty*'s print run at the time was 22.1 million, and *Ogonek*'s—3.3 million.

24. See P.I. Iarots'kyi and O.I. Utkin, "Uniats'ka tserkva: Pravda istorii i suchasnist'," *Pid praporom leninizmu* (Kiev), no. 23 (December 1988), pp. 72–77; Kolesnyk, interview, in *Izvestiia,* 1 February 1989; and Metropolitan Filaret, interview, *Visti z Ukrainy,* no. 23 (June 1989).

25. See the account of Metropolitan Filaret's May press conference in L'viv (attended also by CRA chairman M.P. Kolesnyk) in *Pravoslavnyi visnyk* (Kiev), no. 8 (August 1989), and *Vechirnyi Kyiv,* 8 September 1989.

26. This discussion of the Vatican-Moscow negotiations is based on a report entitled "The Activities of the Holy See for the Benefit of the Catholic Church of Ukrainian Rite," presented by the Vatican secretary for relations with states, Archbishop Angelo Sodano, at the meeting of Ukrainian Catholic bishops in Rome convened by the pope on 25–26 June 1990; as well as the accounts published in the Pontifical Council for Promoting Christian Unity, *Information Service,* no. 71 (1989) (III–IV), pp. 130–33; *Pravda Ukrainy,* 6 February 1990; and conversations with Ukrainian Catholic bishops in Ukraine and the diaspora during 1990.

27. According to *Pravda Ukrainy* (6 February 1990), the pope ratified the Moscow "Recommendations for the Normalization of Relations Between Orthodox and Catholics of Eastern Rite in the Western Ukraine" on 25 January, and the ROC Council of Bishops on 31 January 1990. However, the PCPCU *Information Service* (no. 71 [1990], p. 133) published the text of the Holy See's approval of these "Recommendations" dated 19 February 1990, voicing the pope's reservations concerning historical judgments contained therein, especially with respect to the Union of Brest of 1596. The "Recommendations" of which the Ukrainians learned first from *Pravda Ukrainy* on 6 February 1990 (one month before the Vatican published them) astonished and enraged Ukrainian Catholic activists in western Ukraine and supplied anti-Uniate ammunition for the UAOC, which was totally ignored in the agreed-upon allocation of church buildings contested by the two denominations.

28. Official communiqué adopted by the "Meeting Between Representatives of the Roman Catholic Church and the Russian Orthodox Church, Moscow, January 12–17, 1990," reproduced in PCPCU *Information Service,* no. 71 (1990), p. 131.

29. See Metropolitan Filaret of Kiev, "Liudy, bud'te oberezhnym," *Pravoslavnyi visnyk,* 1990, no. 5, pp. 26–27; a declaration of 10 April 1990 by the ROC Holy Synod concerning developments in western Ukraine, in *Pravoslavnyi visnyk,* 1990, no. 7, pp. 10–11; and an appeal for donations to help victims of "religious extremists" in western Ukraine, "Dopomozhemo nashym bratam," *Pravoslavnyi visnyk,* 1990, no. 8, 1990, p. 24. See also N. Protribnyi, "Respublikans'kyi komitet zakhystu prav viruiuchykh Ukrains'koi pravoslavnoi tserkvy," *Pravoslavnyi visnyk,* 1990, no. 6, pp. 30–31, originally published in *Pravda Ukrainy,* 30 March 1990.

30. Metropolitan Ioann, "Metropolitan Ioann Discussed the Ukrainian Autocephalous Orthodox Church Today," interview by M. Kolomayets, *Ukrainain Weekly,* 14 October 1990, pp. 3, 14. See also V. Lyubats'ky, "Where is the Split?" *News from Ukraine,* no. 37 (September 1990); Viktor Bondarenko, "Mizhkonfesiinyi konflikt na Ukraini: Vytoky, stan i shliakhy podolannia," *Liudyna i svit,* 1991, no. 3, p. 6; and T. Starak, "Kil'ka dumok pro avotokefaliiu," *Vira bat'kiv* (L'viv), no. 19 (4 November 1990), pp. 9–10. See also R. Hladysh, "Oberezhno—provokatsiia!" *Halychyna* (L'viv), 27 June 1990.

31. Reports by Archbishop Volodymyr Sterniuk and Bishop Sofron Dmyterko at the meeting of the Ukrainian Catholic bishops with the pope in the Vatican on 25 June 1990.

32. "Dovidka pro kil'kist' relihiinykh orhanizatsii v Ukrains'kii RSR . . . na 01.01.1991." This report of statistics on religious organizations in Ukraine was issued by the republican Council for Religious Affairs (CRA) in Kiev in connection with the Ukrainian Supreme Soviet's considerations of a draft Law on the Freedom of Conscience and Religious Organizations.

33. Ibid.

34. Letter from Ivan Hrechko of L'viv, 25 February 1991; and Msgr. Ivan Dátśk. (Dacko), "Nainovisha pastyrs'ka sytuatsiia UHKTs v Ukraini," *Svitlo* (Toronto), vol. 54, no. 3 (1991), pp. 107–9.

35. For the Vatican announcement, see *L'Osservatore Romano,* 21 January 1991.

36. *Tserkovnyi visnyk* (Chicago), no. 13 (30 June 1991). The resurgence of the Ukrainian Greek Catholic Church was helped by changes in the procedure for "registration" of religious congregations, which had required final approval by the Council for Religious Affairs in Moscow and discriminated against the UGCC. By a republican government decree of September 1990, final decision about "registration" was transferred to the oblast plenipotentiaries of the Ukrainian CRA. On 23 April 1991, the Ukrainian Supreme Soviet adopted the republican Law on the Freedom of Conscience and Religious Organizations, which was more "statist" than the Russian law; it retained a "state organ for religious affairs"—the old CRA (which was abolished in the Russian Federation). It was made responsible for "registration" of statutes of religious centers, diocesan administrations, monastic and theological institutions, and brotherhoods, without which they could not acquire the rights of juridical persons, including property rights. As will be seen later, this provision made the CRA an arbiter in cases of splits and mergers of religious organizations and was used to legitimize government intervention in the affairs of the UOC and the UAOC.

37. *Za vil'nu Ukrainu* (L'viv), 10 December 1992.

38. Council for Religious Affairs (Ukraine), "Dani pro kil'kist' relihiinykh hromad, v nykh sluzhyteliv kul'tu . . . na 01.01.1993," pp. 2–3; idem, "Dani pro kil'kist" relihiinykh orhanizatsii, shcho diiut' v Ukraini . . . na 01.01.1993," p. 3; idem, "Dovidka pro kil'kist' kul'tovykh sporud, iakymy korystuiut'sia relihiini hromady . . . na 01.01.1993"; idem, "Dani pro kil'kist nedil'nykh tserkovnykh shkil . . . na 01.01 1993." I am grateful to Arsen Zinchenko, chairman of the Council for Religious Affairs, for supplying me with a complete set of statistical tables on religious groups in Ukraine for 1992 and 1993.

39. *Svoboda* (Jersey City, NJ), 7 August 1993.

40. On 15 January 1993, Pope John Paul II established the interdicasterial Commission for the Church in Eastern Europe to centralize the coordination of the Catholic Church's activities in former communist states, including Ukraine. Pontifical Council for Promoting Christian Unity, *Information Service,* no. 83 (1993) (II), pp. 81–82.

41. Of the 2,214 church buildings of the Ukrainian Greek Catholic Church, only 1,693 were made the church's property; the remaining 521 were assigned for use by the state, which retains the title to these churches. CRA (Ukraine), "Dovidka pro kil'kist' kul'tovykh sporud."

42. "Dani pro kil'kist' relihiinykh hromad," pp. 1–2.

43. For the founding documents of the initial Committee for the Restoration of the Ukrainian Autocephalous Orthodox Church in Ukraine, see *Nasha vira* (Kiev), no. 1 (September 1989), p. 2.

44. Iarema, "Moskovs'komu patriiarshomu Ekzarkhovi na Ukraini," pp. 5–8.

45. See "I snova samosviaty," *Moskovskii tserkovnyi vestnik,* 1990, no. 2; and Metropolitan Filaret (Denysenko), "Do pytannia pro istoriiu Kyivs'koi mytropolii," *Pravoslavnyi visnyk,* 1991, no. 4, pp. 48–50. Cf. Bishop Antonii (Masendych), V. Bondarenko, "Zarady sluzhinnia Bohovi ta poriatunku liudyny," *Liudyna i svit* (Kiev), 1991, no. 10 (October), pp. 15–16. Bishop Ioann would not reveal the identity of his two co-consecrators. One of them was reportedly a pseudo-bishop of the Russian Orthodox Catacomb Church, an impostor Vikentii "of Tula."

46. "Pershyi Vseukrains'kyi sobor UAPTs v Kyievi (Skorochenyi opys soboru)," *Visnyk* (Winnipeg), 1990, no. 8 (August), pp. 6–8. Cf. Ihor Hulyk, "Sobor: Notatky z

pershoho Vseukrains'koho soboru Ukrains'koi avtokefal'noi pravoslavnoi tserkvy," *Za vil'nu Ukrainu* (L'viv), 3 July 1990.

47. "Pryizd Vladyky Mstyslava do Kyieva," *Radians'ka Ukraina* (Kiev), 21 October 1990; Valery Lyubats'ky, "Patriarch Mstyslav Calls to Unity," *News from Ukraine,* no. 45 (November 1990). On 28 October 1990, during the second congress of Rukh, the Moscow Patriarchate and its Ukrainian Exarchate (Ukrainian Orthodox Church), the central authorities, and hardliners in the Ukrainian party and government leadership apparently orchestrated a confrontation between the adherents of ROC/UOC and those of the UAOC was subsequently employed by the authorities and the UOC as a propaganda weapon against the Rukh supporters of the UAOC ("nationalist extremists"). See "Tak oni sobliudaiut svobodu sovesti . . . ," *Pravda Ukrainy,* 30 October 1990; "Press Konferentsiia Mitropolita Filareta," Ibid., 2 November 1990; "Drama u Sofii Kievskoi," Ibid., 7 November 1990; and with M.P. Kolesnyk (chairman of the Council for Religious Affairs in Ukraine), interview by S. Volnianskii, "Ne meshat' veruiushchim ulazhivat' svoi konflikty," Ibid., 21 December 1990. On 4 November 1990, *Radians'ka Ukraina* published a vicious personal attack on Patriarch Mstyslav Skrypnyk (V. Andriievs'kyi and V. Troits'kyi, "Kar'iera petliurivs'koho ad'iutanta").

48. "Dovidka pro kil'kist' relihiinykh orhanizatsii v Ukrains'kii RSR . . . na 01.01.1991."

49. *Liudyna i svit,* 1991, no. 10, p. 15; *Ukrains' kyi holos* (Winnipeg), 23 September 1991.

50. CRA (Ukraine), "Dovidka pro kil'kist' relihiihykh hromad . . . na 01.01.1992."

51. CRA (Ukraine), "Dani pro kil'kist' relihiihykh hromad . . . na 01.01.1992."

52. Ibid.

53. See "Postanovy Arkhyiereis'koho soboru Rus'koi pravoslavnoi tserkvy" and "Hramota Aleksiia II mytropolytu Kyivs'komu i vsiei Ukrainy Filaretu," *Pravoslavnyi visnyk,* 1991, no. 1, pp. 3–5; "Postanovy soboru Ukrains'koi pravoslavnoi tserkvy, 22–23 lystopada 1990 roku, m. Kyiv," Ibid., 1991, no. 2, pp. 2–3; as well as Z. Havrylenko, "Pershyi sobor Ukrains'koi pravoslavnoi tserkvy," Ibid., pp. 7–10.

54. "Status pro upravlinnia Ukrains'koi pravoslavnoi tserkvy" and "Hromadians'kyi status Ukrains'koi pravoslavnoi Tserkvy," *Pravoslavnyi visnyk,* 1991, no. 5, pp. 2–19.

55. Metropolitan Filaret had reportedly welcomed the coup in his sermon on Monday, 19 August 1991, according to Vladimir Moss, "The Free Russian Orthodox Church," *Report on the USSR,* vol. 3, no. 44 (1 November 1991), p. 11, Cf. *Glaube in der 2. Welt,* vol. 19, no. 10 (1991), p. 8.

56. In September 1992, a section of the KGB Fourth Department, which had controlled religious organizations, was abolished. *Glaube in der 2. Welt,* vol. 19, no. 10 (1991), p. 7. The subsequent publication of documents found in this section's archives exposed Metropolitan Filaret of Kiev and several other senior ROC hierarchs as regular collaborators of the KGB. See M. Dobbs, "As Economy Fails, KGB-Agent Hunt Takes Backseat," *International Herald Tribune,* 12 February 1992.

57. Aleksandr Nezhnyi, "Ego blazenstvo bez mitry i zhezla," *Ogonek,* 1991, nos. 48 and 49.

58. John B. Dunlop, "KGB Subversion of the Russian Orthodox Church," *RFE/RL Research Report,* 20 March 1992.

59. Radio Kiev–3, 1:40, 17 September 1991. Significantly, the "merger" offer was made without prior knowledge or approval of Patriarch Mstyslav, who was then in the United States.

60. A Report from Kiev by Ukrainform-TASS, Radio Kiev, 22:00, 10 September 1991.

61. N. Svichkolap, "Sobesedovanie s Bogom: Ukrainskaia pravoslavnaia tserkov' prosit nezavisimosti," *Pravda Ukrainy,* 6 November 1991.

62. V. Hruzin, "Vid samovriadnosti do avtokefalii: Z press-konferentsii Blazhennishoho Mytropolyta kyivs'koho i vsiiei Ukrainy Filareta," *Demokratychna Ukraina,* 7 November 1991.

63. Radio Kiev–3, 1:30, 5 November 1991.

64. Hruzin, "Vid samovriadnosti."

65. Radio Kiev–3, 1:30, 5 November 1991.

66. Radio Kiev, 1:00, 20 November 1991.

67. A. Burdis, "Pravoslavnye bratstva prizyvaiut k edinstvu Ukrainy i Rossii," TASS, 22 November 1991, in *USSR Today,* no. 397 (22 November 1991), p. 23.

68. Radio Kiev–2, 21:00, 14 October 1991; "Vseukrains'kyi relihiinyi forum," *Sil's'ki visti,* 26 October 1991; "Religious Representatives Meet," *Ukrainian Weekly,* 27 October 1991; Radio Kiev–2, 23:15, 20 November 1991.

69. See "Zvernennia Ukrains'kykh hreko-katolyts'kykh vladyk" of 8 November 1991, reproduced in *Nasha meta* (Toronto), 25 January 1992. Radio Kiev–2, 23:15, 20 November 1991.

70. "Zvernennia iepyskopatu Ukrains'koi pravoslavnoi tserkvy do Sviatishoho patriiarkha Moskovs'koho i vsiiei Rusi Aleksiia II, Sviashchennoho synodu ta vsikh arkyiereiv Rus'koi pravoslavnoi tserkvy," *Pravoslavnyi visnyk,* 1992, no. 3, pp. 8–9.

71. See "Postanovy Sviashchennoho synodu Ukrains'koi pravoslavnoi tserkvy," *Pravoslavnyi visnyk,* 1992, no. 3, p. 8, disciplining three diocesan bishops and condemning insubordination by retired Metropolitan Agafangel of Vinnytsia, a well-known Russian chauvinist, who has been subverting the clergy of his former diocese against the UOC, calling it "illegal, schismatic, Filaretist, without divine grace and salvation," and threatening to secede under a direct jurisdiction of Moscow. See also Viktor Bondarenko, "Pravoslav'ia v Ukraini: Rozkol zamist' avtokefalii," *Liudyna i svit,* 1992, nos. 9–10, p. 3.

72. Metropolitan Filaret, interview by V. Bondarenko, "Ia pidu svoieiu dorohoiu," *Liudyna i svit,* 1992, no. 4, pp. 2–7.

73. Bondarenko, "Pravoslav'ia v Ukraini," p. 4.

74. Ibid.

75. "Iz vystuplenii uchastnikov Arkhiereiskogo sobora Russkoi pravoslavnoi tserkvi," *Zhurnal Moskovskoi patriarkhii,* 1992, no. 7, pp. 11–19; and no. 8, pp. 3–8.

76. Ibid., no. 8, pp. 7, 8.

77. See Evgenii Komarov, "Tserkov' sokhranila edinstvo," ibid., no. 8, pp. 4–11.

78. "Iz vystuplenii uchastnikov Arkhiereiskogo sobora," pp. 7–8. See also "Decisions of the Enlarged Session of the Holy Synod," in Moscow Patriarchate, Department for External Ecclesiastical Relations, *Information Bulletin,* no. 12 (16 May 1992), pp. 1, 3.

79. In response, the diocese of Odessa and Izmail, including the Odessa Theological Seminary, petitioned the patriarch to come under his direct jurisdiction. *Information Bulletin,* no. 12 (16 May 1992), p. 17. "Message from Patriarch Alexy II of Moscow and all Russia and the Holy Synod of the Russian Orthodox Church to the Episcopate, Clergy and Lay Believers of the Ukrainian Orthodox Church" of May 7, 1992, *Information Bulletin,* no. 12 (16 May 1992), p. 3. See also Bondarenko, "Pravoslav'ia v Ukraini," p. 4.

80. "Decisions of the Enlarged Session."

81. Ibid.

82. Ibid.

83. "Decisions of the Bishops' Council of the Russian Orthodox Church," 11 June 1992, *Information Bulletin,* no. 16 (16 June 1992), pp. 2–3.

84. Bondarenko, "Pravoslav'ia v Ukraini," p. 5.

85. "Decisions of the Bishops' Council," p. 3.

86. Ibid.

87. Ibid.

88. Ibid.

89. Ibid.

90. Metropolitan Volodymyr, "Za namy til'ky babtsi i Boh," *Moloda hvardiia* (Kiev), 7 August 1992.

91. *Robitnycha hazeta* (Kiev), 8 July 1992.

92. V. Anisimov, "Predstavitel' prezidenta v pravoslavii," *Nezavisimost'* (Kiev), 27 June 1992.

93. "Khto i chomu shturmuvav lavru?" *Holos Ukrainy* (Kiev), 3 July 1993. The ultranationalist group that assumed protection of Filaret was the "Ukrainian National Self-Defense"—a paramilitary outgrowth of the Bandera wing of the OUN.

94. "Decisions of the Bishops' Council," p. 3.

95. "Legal Action of the Bishops' Council of the Russian Orthodox Church, 11 June 1992," *Information Bulletin,* no. 16 (16 June 1992), pp. 5–6.

96. Ibid., p. 6.

97. Ibid.

98. Ibid.

99. Ibid.

100. Bondarenko, "Pravoslav'ia v Ukraini," p. 6.

101. Ibid.

102. K. Kindras', L. Kokhanets', V. Labuns'kyi, "Ne prynosyt' trukhliave derevo dobrykh plodiv," *Holos Ukrainy,* 10 October 1992.

103. Bondarenko, "Pravoslav'ia v Ukraini," p. 6. The most damaging criticism of the Local Council absorbing the UAOC into the UOC—KP came in a "Declaration" addressed after the gathering to Metropolitan Antonii (Masendych) by the leadership of the UAOC's Brotherhood of St. Apostle Andrew—the First-Called *(Prozvanoho).* It charged that the 26 June 1992 meeting that was held in Metropolitan Filaret's residence was *not* a Council for the following reasons: it violated the procedure for convocation of a Council spelled out in the UAOC statute; the patriarch was neither notified about it nor gave his consent to it; no pre-Council commission was convened to set organizational rules and procedures for it; three bishops attending were not entitled to speak for twenty-six dioceses of the UOC; according to the UAOC statute, a Council requires a quorum of two-thirds of the bishops (out of eighteen Autocephalist hierarchs only seven attended); and there were no delegations from dioceses and parishes. "Zaiava Keruiuchomu Kantseliariieiu Mytropolytu Pereiaslavs'komu i Sicheslavs'komu Antoniiu." On the "Declaration" are handwritten the date (28 June 1992) and registration number (56). A photocopy of this document is in the author's possession. The subsequent split in the Brotherhood and the later attack by the UOC—KP on its L'viv leader, Bohdan Rozhak, as a "KGB agent" and "traitor" may be attributed to this "Declaration."

104. Marta Kolomayets and Borys Klymenko, "UOC of Kiev Rejects Patriarch's Demands," *Ukrainian Weekly,* 20 December 1992. Some 1,300 parishes of the UAOC refused to join the UOC—KP. See also Vladyka Petro (Petrus'), "Iierarkhiia tserkvy musyt' buty ideinoiu ta moral'no chystoiu," *Vysokyi zamok* (L'viv), 6 February 1993.

105. See CRA (Ukraine), "Dani pro kil'kist" relihiinykh hromad.

106. *Za vil'nu Ukrainu* (L'viv), 10 December 1992; and CRA (Ukraine), "Dani pro kil'kist' relihiinykh orhanizatsii, shcho diiut' v Ukraini," p. 2.

107. Ibid.

108. Ibid.

109. Ibid.

110. Ibid.

111. "Churches: Spheres of Influence," *Ukrainian Weekly,* 27 December 1992; Petro, "Iierarkhiia tserkvy."

112. See Ukrains'ka pravnycha fundatsiia, *Svoboda sovisti v Ukraini: Porushennia prav liudynk* (Kiev, 1993), pp. 3–4.

113. Ukrains'ka pravoslavna tserkva, *Kyivs'kyi patriiarkhat,* press release, no. 3 (December 1992), pp. 3–4.

114. *Novyi shliakh,* 28 August 1993.

115. *Svoboda* (Jersey City, NJ), 16 June 1993.

116. Ibid., 3 April 1993; *Ukrainian Weekly,* 19 September 1993.

117. *Ukrainian Weekly,* 19 September 1993. The total of the UAOC parishes remaining outside the UOC—KP may have been somewhat inflated by the September Council. A leading member of the UOC in Canada (in the jurisdiction of the ecumenical patriarchate) who was sent with his church's delegation to Ukraine to examine prospects for reconciliation between the three churches, Mythred Archpriest Tymofii Minenko, reported in Toronto on 21 February that by mid-December 1992, only 350 UAOC parishes joined the UOC—KP, while *1,300* Autocephalist congregations failed to register under the statute "merging" the two churches. Tymofii Minenko, "Suchasnyi stan Pravoslavnoi tserkvy v Ukraini ta stanovyshche Ukrains'koi pravoslavnoi tserkvy v Kanadi," *Nasha meta* (Toronto), 13 March 1993.

118. See "Zvernennia Ukrains'koi pravoslavnoi tserkvy kyivs'koho patriiarkhatu do pravoslavnykh ukraintsiv, uchasnykiv zboriv 7 veresnia 1993 roku," dated 7 September, and signed by the UOC—KP *locum tenens,* Metropolitan Volodymyr (Romaniuk). The author has in his possession rather suspicious-looking photocopies of the alleged "KGB document" in question and alleged correspondence between Archbishop Petro (Petrus') and the UOC—Moscow Patriarchate about his intention to rejoin the ROC, as well as slanderous and demogogic leaflets signed by the "St. Michael Brotherhood" and the "Orthodox Brotherhood of Ukrainian *Samostiinyki*" that were circulated in Ukraine.

119. The church statute set forty as a minimum age for a patriarch; attempts by younger delegates to change this provision in the statute so as to allow Antonii's candidacy were defeated by the Council majority. *Dukhovna akademiia* (Kiev), 1993, no. 2.

120. Metropolitans Volodymyr (who received eighty-five votes), Filaret (thirty-four votes), Ioann Bodnarchuk (who petitioned for readmission to the Russian Orthodox Church in 1992) (twenty-four votes), and Archbishop Iakiv (Panchuk) of Ternopil' (two votes). *Dukhovna akademiia* (Kiev), 1993, no. 2, p. 6. Filaret, however, retained his title of "deputy patriarch."

121. A native of the Hutsul region in western Ukraine, Vasyl' Romaniuk, sixty-eight, was sentenced in 1944 to ten years of forced labor for participation in the Ukrainian nationalist resistance movement. He was ordained in 1964 as a priest in the Russian Orthodox Church and served in his native region until his arrest in 1972 for links with dissidents. After serving his sentence of seven years in a concentration camp and three years exile (during which he achieved international recognition as a human rights fighter and member of the Ukrainian Helsinki Group), Father Romaniuk was barred from the priesthood within the Russian Orthodox Church until he wrote a repentant letter to the archbishop of Ivano-Frankivs'k, Makarii (Svystun), which was promptly published by the Soviet authorities. He was then assigned a parish in his region. Allowed to come to Canada in 1987, Romaniuk returned to Ukraine to join the UAOC and was ordained in April 1990 as Bishop Volodymyr of Uzhhorod and Vynohradiv (but failed to win over a single Russian Orthodox or Uniate parish in Transcarpathia to the UAOC). Known for his hostility to the "Polonophile" Ukrainian Greek Catholic Church, Romaniuk was elevated to archbishop in 1991, and in 1992 was one of the UAOC hierarchs who joined with Metropolitans Filaret and Antonii (Masendych) in establishing the Ukrainian Orthodox Church—Kiev Patriarchate.

122. *Dukhovna akademiia* (Kiev), 1993, no. 2.

123. Ibid.

124. Declaration of the five bishops, "V UPTs KP diishlo do rozkolu," *Svoboda* (Jersey City, NJ), 13 January 1994.

125. Ibid.

126. Ibid.

127. Ibid.

128. At a Kiev conference on "Ukrainian Orthodoxy" (20–21 October 1993), it was reported that the UOC—KP did not make any efforts to Ukrainize the church; on the contrary, some of the former UAOC parishes replaced Ukrainian liturgical language with a Russified version of Church Slavonic. *Novyi shliakh,* 12 November 1992.

129. V. Tsymbalistyi, "Posviachennia ploshchi pid patriiarshyi sobor v Kyievi," *Svitlo* (Toronto), vol. 56, no. 9 (1993), pp. 292–95.

130. Archbishop Antonio Franco, Apostolic Nuncio in Ukraine, "To All Priests of the Greek Catholic Mukachiv Eparchy" (Kiev, 7 February 1993), in *Nasha meta* (Toronto), 22 May 1993.

131. V. Ielens'kyi, "Relihiini hromady Ukrainy," *Ukrains'ke slovo* (Kiev), 17 September 1993. Thus while in Ternopil' Oblast in Galicia there is one religious congregation per 800 inhabitants, in the Dnipropetrovsk Oblast the ratio is one congregation for 17,000 inhabitants.

132. CRA (Ukraine), "Dani pro kil'kist' relihiinykh orhanizatsii, shcho diiut' v Ukraini," pp. 1–20.

133. Ibid., pp. 4–9, 11, 14.

134. Ibid., pp. 12, 16.

135. Ibid., p. 12. RUNvira had ten congregations as of 1 January 1993.

136. In January 1993, there were 531 Roman Catholic (predominantly Polish and Hungarian) parishes in Ukraine.

137. Serge Schmeman, "Russia May Curb Foreign Religions," *New York Times,* 16 July 1993. See also "Watering Russia's Spiritual Desert," presentation by Archbishop Tadeusz Kondrasiewicz of Moscow at the Ethics and Public Policy Center in Washington, D.C., in the center's *Newsletter,* no. 42 (spring 1993), p. 3.

138. See "Iz vystuplenii uchastnikov Arkhiereiskogo sobora."

139. Ibid.

140. Komarov, "Tserkov' sokhranila edinstvo."

141. See Bohdan R. Bociurkiw, "The Politics of Religion in the Ukraine: The Orthodox Church and the Ukrainian Revolution, 1917–1919," Kennan Institute for Advanced Russian Studies, Occasional Paper no. 202 (Washington,D.C., 1986), pp. 32–34.

142. See Orest Kupranets', *Pravoslavna tserkva v mizhvoiennii Pol' shchi, 1918–1939* (Rome: "Analecta OSBM," Series 2, Section 1, 1974), p. 31.

8

Politics and Religion in Ukraine

In Search of a New Pluralistic Dimension

Vasyl Markus

Ukraine is presently undergoing a complex process of transition from historical domination by Eastern (Orthodox) rite national churches serving the needs of a state-controlled society to a pluralist and secular religious and social model. This contribution to the present volume intends to examine the most recent changes in the main religious bodies, that is, the Orthodox and Ukrainian Greek Catholic churches, as well as to explore the religious landscape of Ukraine by dealing with other newly established denominations and a number of older ones.

Contrary to popular belief (or the wishful thinking of some people), Ukraine is not a land of one or two national religions. Orthodoxy, which prior to 1917 could have claimed a prevailing presence and a privileged status throughout Russian-dominated Ukraine, does not now possess that exclusive position in eastern, central, or even the traditionally Orthodox areas of northwestern Ukraine. In a similar sense, the Greek Catholic Church (the Catholic community of the Ukrainian-Byzantine rite), which exclusively dominated in the Ukrainian lands held by Austria-Hungary before 1918 and then by Poland and Czechoslovakia, cannot today either manifest itself as or pretend to be the only religion of western Ukrainians.

Ukraine is now a nation of many religions, Christian and non-Christian (Jewish, Muslim), as well as a country in which a large segment of the population does not profess any religion. It is, in terms of religious beliefs and practices, a pluralistic society in which both the positive and negative effects of Soviet-Marxist socialization are visibly present. Therefore, Ukraine must be viewed as a modern secular state, in whose formation the religious factor historically played a significant role and where even now, in the postcommunist environment, religion cannot be underestimated.[1]

Also, it must be noted that certain religions in Ukraine's history either fulfilled a positive function in nation building or tended to hamper that process. The Ukrainian case illustrates well the effects of diametrically opposed religious influences, and this aspect too will be examined.

The Orthodox and Catholic Churches

For centuries, two traditional churches, both taking their roots from the same source, namely the Orthodox Church and the Greek Catholic (Uniate) Church, have been particularly important nation-building agents. The branch of Eastern Orthodox Christianity that four centuries ago (1595–96) had been united with Rome (thereafter also called the Uniate Church) strongly emphasized the separateness of Ukraine and Belarus from Moscow, thus cementing spiritual and cultural elements of Ukrainian national identity. On the other hand, the Orthodox Church, especially after the fall of Ukrainian Cossack autonomy in the eighteenth century, tended to weaken Ukrainian separatist trends by serving the imperial designs of Moscow. The rebirth of Ukrainian identity among the Orthodox in this century was, to a great extent, due to the influence of the nationalist movement on that church, contrary to what has occurred in western regions. In the latter case, the Greek Catholic religion (Uniate Church), being separate and indigenous, largely contributed to the national revival.

The social dynamics and political functions of the two religious communities circumscribed their distinct roles in the past and predetermined their peculiar fate in the last four decades under Soviet rule. Three Ukrainian Orthodox Church (UOC) jurisdictions now in existence are the successor churches to the Russian Orthodox Church (ROC), which in certain senses enjoyed special treatment under the old regime. The Ukrainian Greek Catholic Church (UGCC) reemerged in 1988–90 in a quasi-revolutionary manner from illegal status to a legalized institution. It resurrected itself from the secrecy of catacombs to a free social and moral entity with an aura of martyrdom.

On the other hand, Orthodoxy had to live with the stigma of being subservient and obedient to the regime and therefore having preferential treatment. Additionally, it had been viewed by some as an institution hostile to the Ukrainian national cause. Contrary to Orthodoxy, the Greek Catholic Church prided itself as a national patriotic church that from 1945 to 1990 carried the burden of a hard struggle against Russian communism for religious and national survival. This consideration explains many vicissitudes of religious relations, internal and external, in Ukraine in the last three to four years that have brought about the results discussed in the following paragraphs.

First, the recent rise of the autocephalous movement (i.e., the aspirations of the church for independence) among the Orthodox, mostly in western Ukraine, can be explained not only by religious and nationalist motivations but also by purely psychological ones. As a result of recent political changes, former Uniate priests and the younger generation of Orthodox clergy in western Ukraine in the ranks of the official ROC attempted to prove their Ukrainian patriotism in the most obvious way. They did it by allying themselves with the nationalistic branch of Orthodoxy, which enjoyed a public image of being a church equally persecuted in the 1930s and 1940s. That church, however, survived outside the USSR and even has flourished among the Western diaspora. Preferring to remain Orthodox, its priests in Ukraine wanted to move beyond the status of second-rank churchmen vis-à-vis those Greek Catholics who did not convert to the ROC after 1946.[2]

Thus, the new movement in 1989–90 for Ukrainian autocephaly originated in western Ukraine and finally conquered not only some grassroots but also segments of the establishment of the ROC in parts of eastern Ukraine. That was a noteworthy achievement that later predetermined the further fate of Ukrainian Orthodoxy, including its present problems.

Second, the Greek Catholic Church emerged almost like a phoenix from the ashes after a long period of clandestine existence in the USSR. Presently in three Galician oblasts in western Ukraine, it is numerically the largest and most dynamic denomination.

To sum up the extraordinary phenomenon of the Greek Catholic revival, one has to consider the following important circumstances:

- The church has survived, albeit in fragmentary structures, in the underground throughout the entire period of Soviet rule in the region.
- Its branches continued to exist and flourish in Western exile, particularly under the leadership of the late Cardinal Iosyf Slipyi, who remained a living symbol of the perseverance of that church.
- The Roman Catholic Church extended its moral support and protection to the suppressed church of Ukraine, and the church's aspirations were included in the universal human rights movement.

Some Catholic maximalists feel that the victory (restoration of the UGCC in 1989) was only partial and that it has been overshadowed by a sizable switch of many former Uniates to Orthodoxy (first to the Autocephalous Orthodox Church, and now to that branch that created the UOC—Kiev Patriarchate). To this author, such a development has been a phenomenal success for both the Ukrainian Catholic and the Orthodox churches, and even more so for the national cause, since the latter was able to gain force from the spiritual values of religion. Rumors in Ukraine that the movement for autocephaly in Galicia might have been inspired and favored by the KGB, with the aim of weakening the nationalist cause in Ukraine, do not undermine this assessment of the church's restoration.[3] Even if some secret police or Communist Party quarters desired to counteract resurgent Catholicism by spreading such rumors, the measure fell short of its goal. The switch of some followers from the ROC to autocephaly strengthened what the KGB wanted to weaken. So, whether intended or not, the religious revival in western Ukraine resulted in a nationalist boomerang that also spread, though to a lesser degree, to eastern regions of Ukraine, where nationalist consciousness was not very high.

Ukraine's Orthodox Church on the Road to Independence

The drive toward church independence made significant inroads in the established Orthodox Church, later causing its split. The UOC—Kiev Patriarchate joined in support of an independent Ukraine. Again, an alliance was forged between the pro-independence postcommunist leadership and the formerly obedient, pro-regime church elite in Ukraine. The alliance undoubtedly had an impact on the results of the 1 December 1991 referendum on independence. The ideology of a new separate national church, expressed on several occasions by Metropolitan Filaret Denysenko of Kiev, was simple: in an independent state the church also must be independent, such is an honored Eastern Orthodox tradition. Therefore, it became imperative to sever ties with the Moscow Patriarchate. Interestingly enough, and in contrast to the creation of the first autocephaly in 1920–21, this meant not the creation of a new church but secession from the old church of a sizable segment of the flock with its hierarchical structure.

Understandably, the majority did not secede from the ROC. A large number of bishops, clergy, parishes, and the faithful remained loyal to the Moscow Patriarchate. As a reward, the latter consented to grant autonomy, but not independence, to the Ukrainian Orthodox Church. Thus a split into two church bodies has occurred among the ranks of Ukrainian Orthodoxy. One remained integrated with an overly centralized ROC, headed in Ukraine by Metropolitan Volodymyr Sabodan, and the other, led by Metropolitan Filaret Denysenko of Kiev, reunited with the UAOC of a newly elected patriarch from exile, Mstyslav Skrypnyk. The merger between two hitherto hostile church organizations has been achieved with the considerable support of Leonid Kravchuk's government.

If for a while this looked from the Ukrainian political point of view as a success, the spiritual head of autocephaly, the late Patriarch Mstyslav Skrypnyk (who died in June 1993), later repudiated the union with Metropolitan Filaret's church. He did so against the wishes of the majority of his following in Ukraine, while ignoring the governmental church policy of support for the union. Thus a conflict began within Ukrainian Orthodoxy that resulted in some clearly adverse effects: for one, Skrypnyk himself inspired in Ukraine the creation of a separate "authentic" Ukrainian Autocephalous Orthodox Church with a minuscule following and with a nonrepresentative leadership in western Ukraine. Its influence has been reduced to a minimum after the death of Patriarch Mstyslav.

Nevertheless, the protagonists of "true" autocephaly convened a Council in August 1993 and proceeded to elect a new patriarch in the person of Fr. Volodymyr Iarema, who took the name of Dmytro. Father Iarema was a Greek

Catholic priest prior to 1946, and in 1989–90 he became a leading organizer of the "third" autocephaly in Ukraine,[4] thus gaining praise from the late Patriarch Mstyslav. The bulk of the UOC—Kiev Patriarchate convened a separate Council in October 1993 and elected Metropolitan Volodymyr Romaniuk as their patriarch. Thus, there are now two independent Ukrainian Orthodox Churches and two patriarchs.

There also stands apart a third Ukrainian Orthodox Church, the largest in terms of bishops, priests, parishes, and monasteries. It is an autonomous part of the Moscow Patriarchate under the leadership of Metropolitan Sabodan, who also resides in Kiev.

A spokesman from the Ukrainian Orthodox Church in Canada appropriately calls the present situation the "time of church troubles" (*chas tserkovnoi smuty*) within Ukrainian Orthodoxy.[5] As in many similar historical cases, both church and government politics entered into play in affecting that church's present situation in Ukraine. This subject will be explored later.

Another important dimension of Ukraine's religious landscape must be presented. It has already been stated that present-day Ukraine demonstrates religious pluralism. This means that along with two Ukrainian traditional confessions, that is, Orthodox and Catholic of Eastern rite (Uniates), both deeply rooted in native soil, there are other more or less domesticated religious groups in Ukraine.

Roman Catholics

Since the fourteenth century, western and portions of central Ukraine have been open to gradual political and economic colonization by Poles, Germans, Hungarians, Czechs, and others. They were predominantly Roman Catholics, and they established their religious presence as well as a regular ecclesiastic organization. The Roman Catholic diocese of Halych (later in L'viv) was founded in 1412. In the eighteenth and nineteenth centuries other Latin rite bishoprics in Right-Bank Ukraine were created. Thus Ukrainian lands became not only a space for Polish and Hungarian political expansion but also for Roman Catholic inroads in the realm of Eastern Christianity. We do not consider here the Uniate Church as being strictly a Roman Catholic outgrowth, although some may dispute this formulation. Hierarchically, Polish and some German Catholics possessed the following dioceses in Ukraine: L'viv archdiocese, Luts'k Kamianets-Podils'k, and Zhytomyr.[6] There never existed a separate Roman Catholic Church province (metropolitanate) in Ukraine. All dioceses remained part of the Church of Poland or of the Roman Catholic community in the Russian Empire.

Under the Soviet regime, Roman Catholics in Ukraine shared their faith as well as certain organizational ties with other Roman Catholics in the USSR. It is only within an independent Ukraine after 1991 that Roman Catholics began trying to set up a full ecclesiastic organization of their own. Both the Vatican and the Church of Poland are anxious to advance this process. In the last three years, these efforts have had the following results: (1) réstoration of three Catholic dioceses of the Latin rite (five bishops) and the creation of a new *administratura* in Transcarpathia as an intermediary solution to the canonical creation of a full-fledged diocese, mostly for Hungarian faithful; (2) the extension of Roman Catholic bishops' jurisdiction over the entire territory of Ukraine; and (3) preparation for the establishment of a Roman Catholic ecclesiastic province in Ukraine with its own primate in Kiev. The temporary head of Roman Catholics in Ukraine, without that canonical status, is in fact the apostolic nuncio in Kiev, Archbishop Antonio Franco.

Although in reality the Church of Poland is very active in supporting Roman Catholics in Ukraine, it tends to disengage itself canonically from jurisdiction over Ukraine. That means the policy of the Holy See is very much in line with a conventional diplomatic-political approach in that it recognizes the state sovereignty of Ukraine. Yet there are certain minor modifications applicable to Ukraine and partly to Belarus. The Vatican tries to slightly deemphasize the Polish ethnic character of Latin-rite Catholics in Ukraine. For example, the Ukrainian and Russian languages, along with Polish, were admitted for liturgical use, thereby taking into account the fact that many Roman Catholics have been linguistically, even ethnically, assimilated.

There are also some new Roman Catholic converts among Ukrainians, Russians, and others, as evidenced by a tremendous increase in parishes, from 114 in 1989 to 580 in 1993. There are now three periodicals being published, including a Ukrainian-language monthly, *Khrystians'kyi visnyk* (Christian messenger), published in Zhytomyr. A Catholic college in Kiev, a seminary in Kamianets-Podils'k, missionary institutions, and several monastic orders all have become active in the last four to five years.[7]

In order to raise the status of Roman Catholicism in Ukraine as a viable local phenomenon, the Holy See has created the Catholic Bishops' Conference of Ukraine, consisting of Ukrainian Eastern- and Latin-rite bishops and one Armenian Catholic prelate, with the papal nuncio as a temporary presiding hierarch. This Conference does not yet have canonical status but rather functions experimentally. One can question whether this newly established Conference intends to substitute the desired status of the Ukrainian-rite Catholic Patriarchate, but certainly it is meant to institutionalize the equality of the two rites in Ukraine. Some claim that this move pursues the objectives of proselytization in Orthodox-dominated Ukraine, and thus jeopardizes ecumenical dialogue with the Orthodox, especially with the Moscow Patriarchate, which still claims Ukraine as being within its sphere of influence.

There is an additional international dimension to this situation. Two other historically "mother churches" on Ukrainian territory, those of Poland and Hungary, are attempting to influence Roman Catholics in Ukraine, albeit indirectly, as part of their ethnic policy.

Other Christian Communities

The variety of Protestant churches and congregations in Ukraine today are presented in the official statistics recorded by the Ukrainian Council for Religious Affairs in Kiev (see Table 1).[8] Among the Protestant denominations, one of the oldest in Ukraine is the Hungarian Reformed Church, which is of Calvinist persuasion, in Transcarpathia. This church has also acquired a juridical structure as a separate diocese with strong spiritual, cultural, and human links to Hungary. It has over ninety congregations and 60,000 faithful.

There is also a revival of a once-flourishing German Lutheran Church, which now numbers more than ten congregations. With the promotion of repatriation of Ukrainian Germans from Asian republics, this religious group will tend to grow.

Another mostly non-Ukrainian church group is composed of Russian Old Believers, consisting of two branches: (1) the Concord of Bila Krynytsia (administrative seat) and (2) the Priestless Concord (*bezpopovtsy*), which together represent some sixty communities.

Among Protestant religious groups the most influential in Ukraine are Evangelical Baptists, numerically the third largest religious denomination after the Orthodox and Greek Catholics. However, they are presently divided into the three separate organizations discussed below.

The All-Ukrainian Alliance of Evangelical-Christian Baptist Associations, formerly part of the All-Union Council of Evangelical Baptists, is currently a separate Ukrainian church body (with the name changed in February 1994), headed by pastor Hryhorii Komendant. He also presides over a loose Euro-Asian Federation of Baptist Unions, successor to the All-Union Council, which was established in November 1992 with the aim of preserving some ties to, and engaging in practical cooperation between, the Baptists of the former USSR. The Baptists of Ukraine now have six pastoral schools (seminaries) and a Bible Institute. They also publish two periodicals: in Kiev, the Ukrainian-language *Khrystians'ke zhyttia* (Christian life); and in Donets'k, the Russian-language *Slovo very* (Word of faith). In all, there are over 1,280 congregations, evenly spread throughout Ukraine, with the Chernivtsi Oblast (the smallest in Ukraine) having the largest number (approximately 100), with 106,600 baptized members as of February 1994. This church body has, over the last four years, recorded an increase of approximately 300 congregations and 16,650 baptized adult members.[9]

The Autonomous Baptists, formerly called the Council of Evangelical Christian-Baptist Churches, is an underground splinter group that separated from the All-Union Council in the 1960s and 1970s (also known as *Initsiativniky*). This group now has fewer than forty local churches, many churches having recently been reconciled with the main Evangelical Church body of Ukraine. The group is presided over by Pastor Mykola Velychko.

The third and smallest Baptist community is composed of a few Baptist congregations in Ukraine that remained loyal to the Russian splinter group, also

Table 1

Principal Confessions in Ukraine in 1994

Church (Religious Confessions)	Parishes (chapters)	Eparchies (regional administrations)	Priests (pastors)	Convents/ Monastics	Brother-hoods	Sunday Schools	Seminaries/ Students	Periodicals
Ukrainian Orthodox Church—Moscow Patriarchate	5,764	27	1,854	48/1,507	7	1,129	8/1,870	12
Ukrainian Greek Catholic Church	2,897	8	1,691	39/1,217	0	1,014	6/1,670	8
Ukrainian Orthodox Church—Kiev Patriarchate	1,892	20	1,080	14/37	9	593	7/774	6
All-Ukrainian Alliance of Evangelical-Christian Baptist Associations	1,268	23	1,970	0	2	542	11/440	2
Union of Christians of Evangelical Faith (Pentecostalists)	626	18	1,000	0	0	380	3/130	3
Roman Catholic Church	581	5	256	16/86	1	173	3/199	3
Seventh-Day Adventist Church	369	7	157	0	0	157	0	16
Ukrainian Autocephalous Orthodox Church	281	1(5)*	571	0	1	116	0	0
Jehovah's Witnesses	142	2	485	0	13	0	0	0
Hungarian Reformed Church of Transcarpathia	91	1	32	0	0	55	0	0
Islam	77	2	72	0	0	15	2/15	0
Judaism	57	2	29	0	0	15	0	9

*Since authorities refused for some time to duly register UAOC, only one entity (patriarch) was de facto recognized; but as of 1994 this church has five bishops (eparchies).

opposed to the former All-Union Council. These are individual congregations without a common organization in Ukraine. Numbering some thirty congregations, they are also known as the Independent Baptist Church.

There are also three branches of Pentecostalists, who during the Soviet period were forcibly united with the All-Union Council of Churches. They have now emancipated themselves from the common Baptist Council. The largest among them is the Union of Christians of Evangelical Faith (Pentecostalists) of Ukraine, with some 630 communities. Its spiritual leader is the Reverend Mykola Mel'nyk. There is also a minuscule Union of Free Churches of Christians of Evangelical Faith (about twenty local communities). About eighty Pentecostal congregations that do not belong to any organized union exist on their own, relying on voluntary cooperation with other groups.

The Jehovah's Witnesses of Ukraine have their own communities of believers in about 145 localities, with their largest presence in western Ukraine. The Church of Seventh-Day Adventists has various branches. The main body comprises some 370 local communities, and the reformist group comprises some 20 communities. Mostly in Transcarpathia, there are over forty churches (prayer houses) of Adventists or Evangelical Christians who keep Saturday as their holy day.

The Ukrainian Charismatic Church today numbers some forty local groups. Moreover, there are over twenty other registered Christian sects in Ukraine. Some of these groups are more or less aggressive in their missionary zeal. To them, Ukraine is certainly fertile soil for gaining new converts.

Many Protestant and other Christian sectarian groups display certain common characteristics. They mostly trace their origin to the nineteenth and twentieth centuries, and practically all are of foreign import. Being, as a rule, small, close-knit communities composed of individual converts easily identifiable by their fraternal cohesion, they are known for their strict religious practices and moral behavior. These groups are mostly fundamentalists, who are quite rigid in their doctrinal interpretation of Scripture. With the exception of the Jehovah's Witnesses and possibly the dissident branches in the Orthodox Church, that is, the Old Believers, they are not extremist or radical.

All these denominations fully enjoy the new religious freedoms of the post-glasnost period and, in principle, are involved in honest proselytizing. The majority of them maintain connections with their international centers, thus benefiting from their generous support for missionary and charitable activities. This aspect might constitute the weak side of contemporary Ukrainian Protestantism: many new converts are motivated not so much by purely religious convictions but by practical considerations (humanitarian assistance, opportunities to travel abroad or even emigrate, and so on).

The government of Ukraine tends to be neutral in its treatment of these and other religious groups. More traditional churches, however, demonstrate a somewhat reserved attitude toward the Protestant denominations, and particularly to small aggressive groups because of their missionary activism, which is being conducted at the expense of the established traditional churches. Yet, Ukraine does not provide us with the kind of legislation and religious policies vis-à-vis certain minority sects that have been attempted in the Russian Federation, such as introducing legislative measures to restrain foreign-inspired missionary activities strongly resented by the Russian Orthodox Church.

It appears that the government of Ukraine does not face particular challenges from these Christian groups and is not succumbing to pressures from the Orthodox or Catholic churches. On the whole, one can assume that the Ukrainian government views rather favorably their presence and activity in Ukrainian society. For their part, these groups do not question the legitimacy of the state and accept the principle of church-state separation, which is a cornerstone of Ukrainian religious policy. In contrast, that principle is viewed with some suspicion by the traditional churches, at least on their "historical" territory. In that sense, one may assess the new Ukrainian law concerning religious organizations and their activities as being a progressive and constructive legal foundation for religious life.

Non-Christian Denominations

The oldest organized religion, along with the Orthodox/Catholic churches, is Judaism, which dates back to the princely period of Rus´-Ukraine. However, the phenomenal growth of Jewish communities in Ukraine began in the sixteenth century. It was also in Ukraine where the Judaic sect Hasidism originated in the eighteenth century. By the middle of the nineteenth century, one-third of world Jewry lived on Ukrainian territory. A mass Jewish emigration overseas prior to World War I and the Nazi Holocaust during World War II resulted in a drastic reduction of Ukraine's Jewish population. As a consequence of recent waves of emigration to Israel and the United States and the assimilation of many Jews, the process of secularization made strong inroads into Jewish life in Ukraine. Despite liberalization of Ukraine's religious policy, only about sixty Jewish congregations were reestablished, mostly in Kiev and in the western oblasts of Transcarpathia and Chernivtsi. Ukrainian Jewish communities have one chief rabbi in Kiev, plus a few cultural and charitable institutions, such as Solomon University. The university, along with a rabbinical school, was opened with the help of Israel and Jewish organizations in the West.

Islam in Ukraine, a traditional religion in the Crimea, has also been revived. Out of some eighty Muslim communities, three-fourths are in the Crimea. In terms of religious organization there is a chief mufti in Ukraine residing in Bakhchisarai, Crimea. With the increase in repatriation of Crimean Tatars, a policy favored by the Ukrainian government, one can expect the continued growth of Muslim communities in Ukraine.

There are also seventeen Buddhist communities in Ukraine, mostly in eastern

Ukrainian cities. The believers are Asian ethnics residing in Ukraine, primarily the Kalmyks. Other Asian religious groups are the Society for Krishna Consciousness (with some twenty local branches) and the Baha'i religious community, which has six branches. The latter two religions recruit their adherents from among the local Ukrainian and Russian population.

A strictly non-Christian group is the Native Ukrainian National Faith (RUNvira), imported to Ukraine from the diaspora during the last three to four years. It claims some fifteen local groups, half of them in Kiev itself. RUNvira is a blend of pagan Slavic beliefs and mythology, with a strong nationalist ideological underpinning. Its leader, Lev Sylenko (Master), started the movement in the 1960s in the United States and Canada.

In October–November 1993, world opinion was struck by the appearance in Kiev of a vocal religious group, the White Brotherhood. They (about 2,000 adherents) congregated there preaching the message of the end of the world, practicing civil disobedience, and engaging in fanatical destructive behavior against the establishment and nonbelievers. Some Ukrainians suspected the appearance of the White Brotherhood (whose members are mainly from Russia) as an attempt to destabilize the Ukrainian political situation.[10]

Religious Statistics and Geography

The late 1980s marked the beginning of religious revival in Ukraine and in the USSR in general. Some 3,500 religious communities (parishes, congregations, local groups) of over a dozen confessions (churches) were registered with the Council for Religious Affairs of the Ukrainian SSR. A few more existed illegally (without registration). The situation has dramatically changed in the 1990s. Subsequent data recorded by the same Council show some 14,000 communities (13,936 to be exact) of 60 diverse denominations (as of 1 January 1993). A year later that figure had increased by 1,000 to 14,973 communities and 67 denominations. The present situation indicates continued growth momentum.

It is interesting to consider regional differences both in terms of numbers of local units (which is the only viable indicator of religious dynamics, since the figures on registered believers or practitioners are simply not available) and territorial extension of certain religious groups or churches.

Table 2 illustrates the present status of all religious groups by indicating the number of registered communities of all denominations along with the population in a given oblast and the resulting number of Ukraine's inhabitants served by one community (church). Ternopil' Oblast has the largest number of religious communities per capita: one church group for fewer than 1,000 people. Six other western Ukrainian oblasts and one neighboring oblast in Right-Bank Ukraine indicate one church for every 1,000 to 2,000 inhabitants. Three Right-Bank oblasts and one northern (mostly rural) oblast have one religious community per 2,000 to 5,000 people. The city and oblast of Kiev, plus three southern oblasts, one central oblast, and one northeastern oblast hold one church religious community for every 5,000 to 10,000 people. In the Republic of Crimea and in one central and two eastern oblasts, there is one church group per 10,000 to 15,000 people. In the three eastern (and largest) oblasts of Ukraine, there is one religious community per 15,000 to 20,000 inhabitants (see map and Table 2).

The most intensive religious life and organization exist in western Ukraine. Right-Bank Ukraine is moderately intense in its religious life, while southern Ukraine and the eastern oblasts, where one church community services between 15,000 and 20,000 inhabitants, are least religiously intensive. The wide range of intensities can be explained by the fact that the seven western oblasts were incorporated by the USSR only in 1944. Demographic changes in Ukraine's industrialized south brought in eastern cosmopolitan elements there, which had also weakened eastern ethnic Ukrainian rural areas.

Table 2 presents the status of twelve major religious groups, including two non-Christian denominations, along with their religion-related institutions. The table also indicates the number of regional church administrations (eparchies), monasteries with their religious members (nuns and monks), and institutions of priestly/pastoral formation and their students. One has to note the significant numbers of religious orders, which as a rule in the old established Orthodox and Catholic churches assist clergy in their pastoral work, and the relatively large number of students in seminaries. The orders and students in seminaries promise a continued future influx of clergy and pastors. The Sunday schools are also promising institutions, particularly if one considers that five years ago they were not even permitted to function. Equally important is the increase in religious periodicals, although the new secular press has also become in recent times more open to religious writings.

The religious geography of Ukraine provides interesting data on areas where certain religions dominate and areas where some denominations are almost totally absent. The map on page 176 presents five major religious groups in each oblast in order of their numerical strength based on the number of local registered groups (churches).

From the map one can conclude that, with the exception of three western Ukrainian oblasts (populated before 1946 primarily by Ukrainian Catholics), the Ukrainian Orthodox Church of the Moscow Patriarchate predominates in all regions. In the western Ukrainian oblasts, there is found the strongest following of the Ukrainian Orthodox Church—Kiev Patriarchate. This denomination still holds second or third place in three other western Ukrainian oblasts. In the eastern Ukrainian oblasts (Kiev, Poltava, Kherson, Chernihiv), the UOC—Kiev Patriarchate occupies a distant third place. The Ukrainian Autocephalous Orthodox Church (UAOC) has some following in three western Ukrainian oblasts but is comparatively very low in numbers and is almost absent in the eastern Ukrainian oblasts.

Roman Catholics occupy fourth place in L'viv, Ternopil', and Vinnytsia

Table 2

Religious Communities (Parishes, Congregations) by Oblast, 1 January 1993

Oblast	Number of units	Population of oblast	Unit per population
Cherkasy	322	1,531,800	4,757
Chernihiv	326	1,398,000	4,288
Chernivtsi	666	940,000	1,411
Dnipropetrovs'k	201	3,918,600	19,495
Donets'k	363	5,352,600	14,745
Ivano-Frankivs'k	1,110	1,451,500	1,308
Kharkiv	192	3,188,600	16,503
Kherson	169	1,270,000	7,515
Khmel'nyts'kyi	766	1,521,500	1,986
Kiev	562 (130+432)	4,588,890	8,165
Kirovohrad	189	1,247,500	6,600
Krym (Crimea)	254	2,596,000	10,223
Luhans'k	187	2,877,400	15,387
L'viv	2,281	2,771,300	1,215
Mykolaiv	158	1,350,800	8,549
Odessa	448	2,634,500	5,881
Poltava	167	1,762,800	10,556
Rivne	763	1,181,600	1,549
Sumy	234	1,430,700	6,114
Ternopil'	1,326	1,177,100	888
Transcarpathia	1,116	1,271,600	1,140
Vinnytsia	807	1,908,400	2,365
Volhynia	684	1,072,700	1,568
Zaporizhia	163	2,108,500	12,935
Zhytomyr	482	1,503,700	3,120
Total = 25 oblasts	13,936	52,056,600	3,735*

* According to the most recent report (1 January 1994), the average of religious units per population is 1 per 3,574.

oblasts and second place in the Zhytomyr and Khmel'nyts'kyi oblasts. As a non-Ukrainian denomination in Transcarpathia, Roman Catholics occupy fifth place, while the Hungarian Reformed Church is fourth.

Protestant churches (denominations) present an interesting picture. In a number of eastern Ukrainian oblasts (Vinnytsia, Dnipropetrovs'k, Donets'k, Kiev, Luhans'k, Odessa, Poltava, Sumy, Kharkiv, Kherson, Cherkasy, and Chernihiv) and in the western oblast of Chernivtsi, the All-Ukrainian Alliance of Baptists occupies a distant second place after the UOC—Moscow Patriarchate. In the Crimea and the Khmel'nyts'kyi Oblast, they rank third. Other Protestant groups also present a substantial showing: Pentecostalists in the Volhynian and Rivne oblasts are second in predominance. In Dnipropetrovs'k, Donets'k, Kirovohrad,

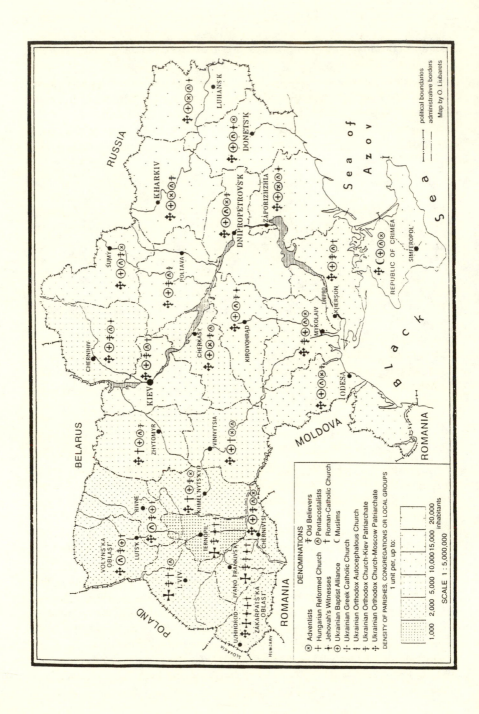

DENOMINATIONS

⊗ Adventists ⊹ Old Believers
✝ Hungarian Reformed Church Ⓐ Pentacostalists
✝ Jehovah's Witnesses ✝ Roman-Catholic Church
⊕ Ukrainian Baptist Alliance ℂ Muslims
✝ Ukrainian Greek Catholic Church
✝ Ukrainian Orthodox Autocephalous Church
✝ Ukrainian Orthodox Church-Kiev Patriarchate
✝ Ukrainian Orthodox Church-Moscow Patriarchate

DENSITY OF PARISHES, CONGREGATIONS OR LOCAL GROUPS
1 unit per, up to:

1,000 2,000 5,000 10,000 15,000 20,000
inhabitants

SCALE 1 : 5,000,000

political boundaries
administrative borders
Map by O. Liubarets

Odessa, and Sumy they rank third. The Pentecostalists are a typical eastern Ukrainian and Volhynian phenomenon. Kharkiv and Cherkasy oblasts demonstrate some support to the Adventists (third place), while Transcarpathia along with the Ternopil' Oblast are the strongholds of Jehovah's Witnesses (third place). Seventh-Day Adventists rank fourth in Vinnytsia, Dnipropetrovs'k, Odessa, Kharkiv, and Kherson oblasts. Old Believers show their presence in Zhytomyr, Kirovohrad, Odessa, and Chernivtsi oblasts (fourth and fifth place).

Muslims are the second strongest religion in the Crimea; most of the Judaic communities exist in Kiev and in the Chernivtsi and Transcarpathian oblasts.

Current Issues

There are a number of pending issues common to some, if not most, religious groups in Ukraine that are being resolved or are still awaiting resolution. As such, they provoke interconfessional conflicts and generate serious problems in church-state relations, some of which are discussed in the following sections.

The Question of Houses of Worship and Disputes Over Church Property

Since in the last four to five years many believers changed their allegiance and a large number of new churches emerged as legal entities, questions arose as to which community (church) possessed legal title to the various church structures and houses of prayer, what to do about formerly closed churches, and how to proceed with the construction of new ones.

The previously existing church buildings continue to be in the possession of the communities to which they were registered in the past. New congregations of any religion can request the use of churches that were closed but which after repair may be deemed usable. Local authorities on the oblast level can resolve such issues on a case-by-case basis. Problems arise when there is more than one claimant to a vacant building. Usually, the former title of a church group would be considered, or in a case where there is not a claimant to the previous title, another religious group might be awarded the use of (but not property title to) the building. When there are several claimants, the disputes are resolved by the local administration in cooperation with the oblast representatives of the Council for Religious Affairs. The relative strengths of the religious groups, previous title, available alternative buildings, and other factors are taken into consideration. Often the solution is imposed arbitrarily, depending on the pressure from below and above. Thus serious conflicts emerge, often lasting several months, or even years. In some instances the branch of the former community that was barred from using the church building engages in protest worship outdoors near the contested structure. In some places, physical confrontations and violence have taken place, especially in western Ukraine between Orthodox and Greek Catholic communities fighting for the same church building. A similar situation arose when two Orthodox communities (of different allegiance) disputed the use of the same building.

Not uncommonly, the minority or community that had been prevented from using a disputed church has elected to erect a new church building. As a result, in many localities of Ukraine, the construction of new churches is a widespread activity. New construction is being accomplished by the community itself, sometimes with the assistance of diocesan or national church authorities, while the civil authorities normally offer space for such buildings.

An interesting solution has been suggested and condoned by the government in order to resolve ownership/usage disputes: joint use of the same building by two communities on a prearranged timetable. Usually, the minority favors it; however, the majority group seeks every excuse to prevent such compromises. As a result, the minority group usually resorts to construction of a separate building. Still, there are a few cases in which joint use is practiced as a temporary device. Obviously, civil authorities also favor it, yet emotional outbursts hinder this reasonable method of conflict resolution.

Problems of the Reestablished Ukrainian Greek Catholic Church

The vibrant community of Greek Catholics in western Ukraine has lost some following, yet it remains the strongest church organization in their traditional territory. They are the best organized, are relatively disciplined, and display typical western Ukrainian dynamics. Some assistance has been granted for the restoration of church structures by the Vatican, by the diaspora (which maintains a viable church structure in the West), and by Western Roman Catholic churches. The primate of the UGCC, Cardinal Myroslav Liubachivs'kyi, along with his entourage, has returned from Rome to his metropolitan see in L'viv. This created some tension between the émigré leadership and some local hierarchs, yet this tension is gradually subsiding.

More serious is the tense relationship between the Greek Catholic Church and the Roman Curia concerning issues such as local autonomy of the church, the establishment of a Ukrainian Catholic patriarchate (which the Vatican opposes), and ideological orientation of the Greek Catholic Church along the lines of Westernization or Easternization. Some concessions were made recently by Rome, yet the papal administration still refuses to acknowledge the jurisdiction of the L'viv archbishop major over all Ukraine. Also, until recently Rome supported claims of a Transcarpathian eparchy to its own separate status and refused to recognize it as an integral part of the autonomous Ukrainian Greek Catholic Church.[11]

The Ukrainian government in Kiev seems to take a neutral stand in the dispute, although a more active role might strengthen the cause of Ukrainian Catholics. Ukraine has not sent an ambassador to the Vatican and does not express an intention to conclude a concordat with the Holy See, which might normalize relations and resolve many questions concerning the status of the Catholic Church of both rites in Ukraine.

Consolidation of the Orthodox Jurisdictions

Presently, one Ukrainian Orthodox community consists of three different church structures, each with its own hierarchies, distinct ideologies, and policies vis-à-vis the other Orthodox bodies. Furthermore, personal animosities exist among ecclesiastic leaderships. From the beginning, former President Kravchuk and the Ukrainian government offered their full support to the unified Ukrainian Orthodox Church—Kiev Patriarchate. The patriarchate has been opposed by the branch of the UOC under the Moscow Patriarchate. Such a religious policy of the Ukrainian political leadership has been criticized by the majority (Metropolitan Sabodan's UOC—Moscow Patriarchate).[12]

When an original version of the Autochephalous Orthodox Church in Ukraine came into existence in June 1992 at the council of unification (which elected Mstyslav Skrypnyk as patriarch of the UOC), the government viewed the event favorably but did not move to fully endorse the new church. Ukrainian politicians gradually embraced the cause of the Kiev Patriarchate, especially after the referendum on Ukrainian independence. The action might have been understandable from the point of view of state interest; however, the position alienated the bulk of Orthodox believers together with the leadership of the largest church body in Ukraine. This led directly to a split in the ranks of the UOC. After Filaret's mission in Constantinople to acquire recognition of the Ukrainian patriarchate failed (even with the endorsement of President Kravchuk to the ecumenical patriarch), the government in Kiev tended to pursue a more cautious and evenhanded policy vis-à-vis all three Orthodox branches. After the establishment in Ukraine of three Ukrainian Orthodox Church structures and two competing patriarchates, the need for an honest and authoritative arbitrator remains urgent. The Ukrainian government cannot be an arbitrator, and certainly the patriarch of Moscow will not perform such a mission. Only the ecumenical patriarch of Constantinople could be a mediator, provided he does this without antagonizing Moscow. Constantinople may be in a position to persuade Moscow Patriarch Aleksii II to grant autochephaly to the Ukrainian Orthodox Church. Presidents Yeltsin and Kuchma (although the latter is less anxious to be involved in church politics) could only perform "good office" services in this politically and canonically delicate task. Former President Kravchuk's letter to Patriarch Bartholomew I of 19 October 1993 could serve as a modest initiative in this direction.[13]

A possible solution would require the resignation of the two present patriarchs and the election of a third one, who may be a mutually agreed on churchman. A canonically recognized single Ukrainian Orthodox Patriarchate in Kiev continues to be a still distant prospect.

Ecumenism

A true modern post-Vatican II ecumenism does not exist in Ukraine. This is understandable, though not excusable, because churches and other denominations are now busy in establishing their own identity, status, and image. They are working hard to recover from their miserable state of affairs prior to the 1990s. They have not reached as yet the stage when they would be in a position to realize their potentiality. They have not achieved any degree of understanding, compassion, and sense of community of Christian faith that would be needed in order to initiate ecumenical dialogue. In addition, there is much resentment and many counterclaims, leading sometimes to confrontation. No previous ecumenical experience and basic education in ecumenism, which Western churches have been experiencing for at least three decades and now take for granted, are avaliable.

The exiled segments of the major Ukrainian churches have not developed sufficiently the ecumenical spirit, because only a few theologians and laypeople succeeded in embracing ecumenical values. They are having difficulties in popularizing them. Yet ecumenical ideas are not totally unknown among Ukrainians. With the spread of Western writings, a few individuals from among the clergy and laity have already become better informed, and they are trying to articulate ecumenical concepts. There was even an attempt to formulate an ideology of Ukrainian ecumenism.[14] Internal practical problems to be resolved take priority in the Ukrainian Christian agenda. One can single out a few Orthodox intellectuals who could participate and are willing to engage in a Catholic-Orthodox dialogue. There might be more intelligent people on the Ukrainian Catholic side capable of indulging in such an endeavor; however, their voice could be silenced by interconfessional polemics on unresolved issues and interdenominational grievances. The closest position to the ecumenical agenda was recently expressed in an official way by Cardinal M.I. Liubachivs'kyi in his pastoral letter in April 1994 concerning the relationship between the Greek Catholic Church and other confessions in Ukraine.[15] As yet, there has been no appropriate response from other churches.

Quite a courageous position regarding the Ukrainian Catholic-Orthodox dialogue was taken by the Orthodox bishop in exile, Vsevolod Kolomyitsev (under the Constantinople Patriarchate), who also favors Ukrainian Catholic-Orthodox dialogue. Consultations among representatives of different religious communities were initiated by the Kiev Council for Religious Affairs; however, this was a forum to resolve practical interdenominational issues and not to indulge in theoretical intercourse over spiritual problems of churches. Moreover, this experiment has been halted, hopefully only temporarily. Yet it could have become a useful forum to instill peace, cooperation, and a modus vivendi among diverse religious communities in Ukraine. A true Ukrainian ecumenism has still to wait until a reasonable coexistence and consensus among the churches in Ukraine is established.

Notes

This article should be viewed as tandem to Dr. B.R. Bociurkiw's contribution, since both chapters address similar issues of the Orthodox and Uniate churches. The author focuses specifically on issues of church politics of the main religious bodies, while simultaneously attempting to analyze religious polices of independent Ukraine and its government.

1. See V. Markus, "Religion and Nationality: The Uniates of the Ukraine" in *Religion and Atheism in the USSR,* ed. B.R. Bociurkiw and J.W. Strong (London: Macmillan, 1975), pp. 101–22.

2. On the Ukrainian Autocephalous Orthodox Church (UAPTs) in western Ukraine (restored in 1990–91), see "Aktual'ni relihiini problemy v Ukraini," *Patriarkhat* (New York), 1990, no. 10 (October).

3. Such allegations were rumored even by some local politicians in western Ukraine during this author's first visit to Ukraine in April–May 1990.

4. The first Ukrainian autocephaly was achieved in 1919–21 in Kiev, the second in 1942 in Volhynia–Kiev, and the third in 1989–90 in L'viv–Kiev. Western Ukraine and the diaspora played a significant role in the autocephalist movement.

5. T. Minenko, "Do pytannia tserkovnoi smuty v suchasnii Ukraini," *Visnyk—The Herald* (Winnipeg), 1993, nos. 4, 5.

6. See *Annuario Pontificio* (Rome), 1993.

7. N. Kochan, "Ryms'ka katolyts'ka tserkva na Ukraini," *Uriadovyi kur'ier* (Kiev), 1994, no. 9.

8. The table of twelve leading denominations in Ukraine is prepared on the basis of internal (unpublished) reports of the Council for Religious Affairs, a department in the Ukrainian government, courtesy of A. Zinchenko, head of the council. The report of 1 January 1993 lists 60 registered churches and religious sects, and that of 1 January 1994 lists 67 groups. In all, Ukraine had in 1994 approximately 16,000 local religious groups (parishes, congregations, branches), 41 seminaries or pastoral schools with 5,150 students, 13,250 priests and pastors, and over 4,250 Sunday schools. The actual number of believers cannot be given or assessed with more precision.

9. "22 z'izd ievanhel's'kykh khrystyan baptystiv Ukrainy," *Khrystians'ke zhyttia* [Christian life] (Kiev), 1994, no. 2–3.

10. "Ukraine Seizes Chiefs of End-of-World Cult," *New York Times,* 12 November 1993.

11. Cf. unpublished resolutions of the UGCC Synod in L'viv in February 1994, and the published address of the Vatican's envoy, Archbishop Antonio Franco, in *Patriarkhat* (New York), 1994, no. 6.

12. J. Martyniuk, "The State of the Orthodox Church in Ukraine," *RFE/RL Research Report,* vol. 3 (18 February 1994).

13. *Ukrinform Report* (Kiev), 19 October 1993.

14. See writings by clergy and laity in the so-called patriarchal press (Ukrainian Catholic movement for a patriarchate), and the published works of Ie. Sverstiuk, M. Marynovych, and others in Ukraine.

15. Ukrainian Church Head Letter on Unity of the Holy Churches, *Sower* (Stamford, CT), 22 May 1994.

9

The Kiev Patriarchate and the State

Serhiy Bilokin

The present-day stage of the history of Ukrainian Orthodoxy shows all the signs of something temporary and transitional. We have just seen the end of the Bolshevik period, during which the church completely subordinated itself to the atheist government. In a certain sense, it was a product and an extension of that government, no matter how terrible that may sound to some people. On the other hand, a wholly new period has just begun in which the church now operates in an independent Ukrainian state, where it faces very different conditions deriving from its new status.

At this major turning point in world history Orthodoxy has found itself exposed to divergent powerful forces, external and internal, centripetal and centrifugal, constructive and destructive, and has failed to preserve its unity, which was already seriously undermined by the Bolsheviks. Formerly confined within the rigid structure of the Russian Orthodox Church, Orthodoxy had just begun to assume national forms by the time Ukraine proclaimed its independence. The church did not have any influence on the internal politics of the USSR. Quite the contrary, it was an instrument of these internal policies. Under these conditions, no analyst has yet succeeded in being wholly impartial and unbiased, and the monumental problem of the present-day condition of Ukrainian Orthodoxy still awaits objective assessment.[1]

Also, a truly comprehensive analysis of specific aspects, such as the relations of Ukrainian Orthodoxy with the state, still lies ahead. The most important documents concerning this subject, including those dating back to comparatively recent times and retaining much of their relevance to what is now going on, remain inaccessible. But we must start moving in that direction. For this we must consider the context, that is, the underlying circumstances, of these processes and also examine various points of view.

Subversion of the Church by the Bolsheviks

Since some archives that had previously been out of reach and closely guarded—primarily those of the Communist Party and the KGB—first began to open up in the years of so-called perestroika, we have obtained documentary evidence confirming many things that we had suspected all along. Publication has begun of party documents demonstrating that ever since the very first days of Soviet government the Communist Party had been engaged in systematic subversive activities against the church. Having espoused the old Roman principle *divide et impera*, the Bolsheviks spared no effort to provoke disunity and schisms in the church.[2] And whereas the so-called Renovationist Church, also called the Living Church, was nothing but a bunch of GPU stooges,[3] this institution was also actively involved in setting up the "Active Christian Church" and provoking the "Lubny Schism" and other dissident movements. Suffice it to say that party officials sanctioned the allocation, in July 1923, of 128 million rubles from the state treasury for the holding of the Synod of the Living Church.[4] On 4 July 1922, the Politburo of the Communist Party of Ukraine set up its commission for antireligious propaganda. Ten days later commission members made a report at a Politburo session, whereupon that body passed a resolution committing the party to "bringing about a dismemberment of the church along class, national, and territorial lines."

The Politburo commission was named the main coordinating center of all antireligious propaganda and was instructed to work out a "plan of concrete actions."[5] On 7 October 1922, a secretary of the Central Committee of the Communist Party of Ukraine (CPU), D. Lebid, reported, in a letter to Stalin, Molotov, and Kuibyshev, that the Ukrainian Central Committee had issued a "forceful directive" to foster disunity and division in the church. In accordance with the theses of the Politburo, which were not to be published, already then (July 1923) the party had about thirty informers and secret agents in the capital and in the provinces. Without them, the document said, "we would not be able to control church organizations."[6]

On 8 March 1928, Panas Liubchenko approved an estimate of budgeted expenditures for "GPU work with religious groups in the first half of 1928." The allocations were itemized as follows:

I. Maintenance of Secret Collaborators in Religious Groups and Sects
1. For the *Synodal movement*:[7] 2 secret collaborators per each district diocesan council for a total of 41 districts: 10 rubles per secret collaborator per month = 820 rubles, 6 months = 4,920 rubles;
2. For the *Tikhonite movement*:[8] 2 secret collaborators per district: 10 rubles per secret collaborator per month = 820 rubles, 6 months = 4,920 rubles;
3. For the *autocephalists*:[9] 3 secret collaborators per district in 22 districts: 15 rubles per secret collaborator per month, 6 months = 5,940 rubles;

4. For the *Council of Bishops Church*:[10] 2 secret collaborators per district in 18 districts: 15 rubles per secret collaborator per month, 6 months = 3,240 rubles.

II. Maintenance of Informers in Governing Bodies of Religious Groups and Sects
  1. For the Ukrainian Synod: 150 rubles per month, 6 months = 900 rubles;
  2. For the SOCC [Supreme Orthodox Church Council][11] (autocephalists): 200 rubles per month, 6 months = 1,200 rubles;
  3. Council of Bishops Church: 150 rubles per month, 6 months = 900 rubles.

An explanatory note attached to the budget said:

I. Maintenance of Secret Collaborators in Religious Groups and Sects
  Synodal and Tikhonite movements. These groups have extended their influence to all the districts of Ukraine. The Synodal Movement is being used by us for undermining the Tikhonites, since the latter constitute an extremely reactionary group that has great authority with the masses of believers. Control of the Synodists' activities for the purpose of combating the Tikhonites will only be possible if we have secret collaborators in both these groups and use them for imposing a line desirable for us. It is for this purpose that we have provided for a minimum of two informers per each group per every district in the estimate attached hereto. In each district the actual number of informers certainly exceeds our figure of two, but we have proceeded from the assumption that the district departments will pay for the most valuable reports essential to the pursuit of our church policy.

  Autocephalists. These are active in 22 districts of Ukraine and represent the second most important religious group. Although after the Intercession-Day Synod the autocephalists were given the opportunity to exist as a legal denomination and have since been loyal to us, we must not lose sight of their activities. This is because in its composition the Autocephalous Church remains the same nationalistic group that it was before the Intercession-Day Synod. For covering all aspects of their activities we need to have not fewer than three paid informers in every district where this group has a following.

  Council of Bishops Church. In our struggle against the Tikhonites we have been making wide use of the Council of Bishops Church group (pro-Tikhon autocephalists). The material condition of this group is weak. To support its activities and to maintain constant control over it we need to have two paid informers in every district.

II. Maintenance of Informers in Governing Bodies of Church Groups and Sects

All the church groups, with the exception of the Tikhonites, have their supreme governing bodies:

1. the Renewal Church—a synod;
2. the autocephalists—a Supreme Orthodox Church Council (SOCC);
3. the Council of Bishops Church.

To ensure our constant control of these bodies we must keep under our influence simple majorities of their members. Through them we impose necessary policies and obtain information on the conduct of individual members.[12]

The Destruction of Orthodoxy

Manipulating their puppets in all religious organizations and bodies, the GPU provoked conflict situations and mutual struggle. This provocation was accompanied by fierce attacks by the atheistic regime on all forms of worship of Jesus Christ. Step by step the state waged its offensive on religion in general. In the end, it implemented all of its plans drafted during the so-called godless five-year period (1932–37), and by the outbreak of the war there were almost no active churches left in Ukraine. All church hierarchies were suppressed and disbanded,[13] first of all the Ukrainian Autocephalous Orthodox Church[14] and the "Tikhonite" (Old Slavic) church, which were smashed by the Bolsheviks with particular ruthlessness and ferocity. Practically no clerics of either church survived.[15]

Yet the process of destruction of Orthodoxy by the Bolsheviks must not be simplified. Archpriest M. Pol'skii divided it into two stages, as far as the Russian Orthodox Church was concerned. According to him, the first stage, the canonical period, lasted until 1927, when Metropolitan Sergii made his collaborationist declaration,[16] the like of which the NKVD had been unable to extort from either Patriarch Tikhon or Metropolitan Petr (Krutitskii), or any other hierarch. The original bishops who held their sees under Patriarch Tikhon protested against the state's policies and openly defied the authorities. Some were liquidated outright, like Bishops Iosif of Leningrad (Petrovykh), Dmitrii of Gdov (Liubimov), and Filipp of Zvenigorod (Gumileovskii). Others were kept in confinement or in exile until they died of old age or other natural causes.

Archpriest M. Pol'skii treated their successors in the following, noncanonical period as a separate group. Having traced their social migrations, he established that those of the bishops who were released after the end of their terms or who were treated with suspicion by the authorities for any reason either had to retire or would obtain sees in remote provincial dioceses. On the other hand, sees in the central part of the country were given to priests who publicly declared their readiness to adhere to Metropolitan Sergii's declaration. As a result, the finest and firmest bishops were succeeded by people of low moral caliber and questionable reputations. Nevertheless, both the former and the latter were eventually liquidated. Some of them, like Metropolitan Anatolii of Odessa (Hrisiuk), died in prisons or in camps. Others, such as Metropolitan Serafim of Stavropol (Meshcheriakov), Archbishop Iuvenalii of Briansk (Mashkovskii), and Bishop Pitirim of Velikii Ustiug (Krylov), were summarily shot.[17]

The method applied by this outstanding historian, who was an expert in the history of the Russian Orthodox Church under Bolshevik totalitarianism, should probably be extended to the Ukrainian Autocephalous Orthodox Church (UAOC). Here is meant not so much the division of the UAOC history into chronological periods (e.g., before and after 1930), since there are still no sufficiently clear criteria for that, but rather the study of the activities of those clerics who yielded to the state's terror and intimidation. Until now the Ukrainian historical tradition, restrained as it is by a mistaken notion of patriotism, has identified national honor with practically every single UAOC cleric, as though they had all stood united. Thus, soon after the arrival of Archbishop Mstyslav to Canada (1947), church historian S. Savchuk suggested that he publish the outline of UAOC history of 1921–30 by Metropolitan Vasyl' (Lypkivs'kyi) in full as an appendix to I. Vlasovs'kyi's brief history of the 1939–45 period. But Mstyslav declined the proposal, explaining that Metropolitan Vasyl' revealed certain "terrible things," which, if published, could harm both certain individuals and "the common cause of the church."[18]

From his own point of view, Greek Catholic Archbishop Ivan Buchko tends to identify even weaker figures of the past with the same notions of national virtue. In his opinion, Metropolitan Vasyl' left "for the generations to come an important document of our religious and church history, which after all, was made by Ukrainians with their own hands."[19] Finally, Archpresbyter S. Savchuk, the publisher of Metropolitan Vasil''s *History,* which is the most authoritative text on this subject, observes that

> It is not easy to speak with some ardent followers of the UAOC of 1921, primarily those who witnessed its revival, growth, and liquidations, especially if they were persecuted by the Soviet government for their loyalty to the UAOC. They find it difficult, and sometimes impossible, to understand that in the course of the UAOC history some of its clerics could be guilty of certain shortcomings, and maybe even deliberate wrong actions, and here the slightest allusion to such things causes such a vehement reaction from them that all attempts at calm discussion and objective analysis are condemned from the start.[20]

Both Patriarch Mstyslav (who was still an archbishop in 1947) and Archbishop Ivan Buchko, as well as "ardent followers of the UAOC" approached even the most common human weaknesses as though there had been no pressure of the cruel totalitarian state exerted upon the clerics of the 1920s and 1930s and as if those clerics enjoyed genuine freedom of choice and had no human vulnerabilities. Actually, they were caught amid a war waged against both God and the people. And this dual objective was pursued by the Bolsheviks at the same time. Aleksandr Solzhenitsyn was absolutely right when he said:

> Yet complete destruction of religion in this country, which was one of the most important goals of the GPU and the NKVD throughout the twenties and the thirties, could be achieved only by large-scale incarceration of Orthodox believers.[21]

Life showed, however, that even from the point of view of the Bolsheviks the policy of genocide proved insufficient.

The Establishment of the Soviet Church

In 1943 Stalin created a new, Soviet church that had little in common with the martyred churches.[22] It is not accidental that after the old, "true" church had been destroyed it was none other than Metropolitan Sergii who was elected patriarch in September 1943.[23] Evidence of his collaboration with the authorities speaks for itself. As early as 15 February 1930, for example, he gave this answer to journalists' questions as to whether there was any persecution of religion in the USSR and in what forms it was resorted to:

> There has never been any persecution of religion in the USSR. Under the Decree on the Separation of Church and State, confession of any faith is free and is not persecuted by any state bodies. Moreover, the latest resolution of the All-Union Central Executive Council and the RSFSR Council of People's Commissars of 8 April 1929 completely rules out even the slightest semblance of any persecution of religion. It is true that some churches are closed down. But they are closed not on the initiative of the authorities but in accordance with the population's wishes and in some cases even by the decision of believers themselves. The repressions of the Soviet government against believers and priests are applied to them not for their religious convictions but on common grounds.[24]

In 1943 the government decided to use the church in the interests of state administration and created for it a special niche that was ostensibly free from Marxist ideology. There the church was allowed to exist as long as it served the interests of the authorities. Such a status was even useful for the Stalinists, especially the KGB, since the existence under the Soviet regime of an organization with a non-Marxist system of values demonstrated that the class struggle was still far from over and that opposition in the USSR was still very much alive. The very fact of the existence of the church added credibility to any accusations and disloyalty charges brought against the intelligentsia, including for antigovernment activities. Thus, this concordat of Stalin with the Russian church hierarchies turned into a provocation of enormous proportions.

Toward the end of his life, Stalin intended to make the church a part of his propaganda machine in order to influence Orthodox believers throughout the world and religious people in general, regardless of their confessions. Preparations started for an Ecumenical Orthodox Council (it was to be held in the fall of 1947), but the Eastern patriarchs refused to attend it.[25]

The aggressive church policy of the Kremlin was a farce, because the only cult it was intended to promote was that of Stalin himself. In an address sent to Stalin on the occasion of his seventieth birthday, seventy-four Soviet hierarchs headed by Patriarch Aleksii made this statement:

> Owing to your statesman's wisdom and the full scope and freedom of their church activities, the Russian Orthodox people guard the interests of their great motherland more firmly than ever before, thus deserving even greater attention from you for the needs of the Orthodox Church.[26]

And in a speech made in the patriarchal cathedral, Patriarch Aleksii said of Stalin:

> May the Lord let him stand for many years, in good health and well-being, at the helm of our beloved country, and may our country prosper under his wise leadership for many, many years to the joy and happiness of its people.[27]

The atmosphere of the patriarchal service held in the Epiphany Cathedral of the Moscow Kremlin was thus described in the journal of the Moscow Patriarchate:

> An especially festive mood reigned in the crowded patriarchal Epiphany Cathedral, where the priests of all the Moscow churches assembled to assist the most holy patriarch in the public prayer after the liturgy. When the dean of the cathedral, Archpresbyter N.F. Kolchitskii, had given the final blessing, the most holy patriarch, accompanied by Metropolitan Nikolai of Kolomna, Archbishop Vitalii of Dmitrovsk, Bishop Makarii of Mozhaiak, and a congregation of Moscow clergy, came out to the ambo and, addressing the heedful people, spoke about the believers' feelings of gratitude to the great Leader of our country, I.V. Stalin, his attention to the needs of the church, and prayers offered by the clergymen to celebrate the Leader's birthday.[28]

Thus the official church in the USSR reached the very bottom of political servility. In the postwar years a priest could be ordained or obtain an episcopal chair only with the sanction of the regime. In Ukraine such sanctions were given by the CPU Central Committee, the Kiev KGB, and the so-called Council for Religious Affairs (a specialized section of the KGB), and in the regions by regional party committees, local KGB departments, and regional soviets. Ecclesiastical superintendents were appointed by local authorities after receiving approval at all levels. A former chairman of the Council for Religious Affairs attached to the USSR Council of Ministers, K.M. Kharchev, admitted, "No one was appointed bishop, let alone an important hierarch or a member of the Holy Synod, without confirmation by the CPSU Central Committee and the KGB."[29] Knowing this situation, a group of priests wrote an open letter, dated 18 February 1993, accusing Father Volodymyr Iarema of collaboration with the KGB. That priest had been a superintendent in L'viv, which would have been impossible without the backing of that agency. Also, for a transfer to a rich parish or an earlier-than-expected conferment of a title or a bishopric, the beneficiary had to pay a certain sum to his superior. For prompt registration of a monk at a monastery, a drinking party was given at the diocesan council to entertain the policy official who had arranged it. Fr. Georgii Edel'shtein relates:

> I had a priest friend. When he went to the Council for Religious Affairs he took along a bag with the finest liquors. And after his visits it was no use going to those departments of the council where he had just been, because everybody there was roaring drunk.[30]

It is curious to read a reference issued to a Ukrainian Orthodox metropolitan by a certain commissioner of a certain region's Council for Religious Affairs as late as 10 March 1989. I deliberately name no names, for this document was rather standard, but instead I draw your attention to the date, for this was rather late in the perestroika period:

> As a ruling bishop he proved to be a good organizer. Although he is a religious man, he shows no signs of fanaticism and is not without pride and human dignity. He systematically reads periodical press and subscribes to many newspapers and magazines.
> He has a sensible attitude toward religion and the church, correctly understands his civic duty, shows loyalty, and constantly demonstrates his patriotism.
> He has considerable experience working with foreign delegations, has gone abroad several times as a member of delegations of the Soviet Peace Committee, visited the USA (in 1984 and twice in 1988), Canada (1983), France (1987), the FRG (1985 and 1987), and Greece (1985), where he masterfully defended, from ecclesiastical positions, the interests of our state and the cause of world peace.
> He coordinates all matters connected with the activities of the diocese with the commissioner's staff. His reaction to criticism is prompt and proper.
> He spends his free time mostly at home and, as a rule, informs the commissioner's staff whenever he leaves the region.

True faith was driven so deeply underground for many decades that uncorrupted clerics could probably be found only in some distant, godforsaken places where they were out of reach of both the state and the state-owned church.

Numerous publications telling the story of the involvement of the old-guard

Russian Orthodox bishops in the operation of the KGB create a corresponding moral and psychological atmosphere around the Russian Orthodox Church and serve as evidence of the profound crisis in which the church has found itself.

Aspects of Relations Between the Kiev Patriarchate and the State

Viewed as a social institution, a church always has enough stimuli for its self-development. But its evolution largely depends on the influence of its social environment, particularly in the relationship between the church and the state. The Bolshevik decree of 1918 on the separation of church and state, the underlying concept of which was confirmed by the Stalinist constitution of 1936, had both a practical significance and a propaganda value. As to the practical aspect, ecclesiastical and religious associations were forbidden to own property and to act as legal entities.[31] Thus, the state "separated" the church itself by depriving it of its rights and expropriating its property. As to propaganda, which relies on people's disposition to understand words in their literal sense, the state kept making much noise about that separation, as if dissociating itself from the harsh practices applied to the church by its own agency, that is, the Cheka-GPU-NKVD. In fact, as was once pointed out by one theologian whose name has since been forgotten, separation of church and state "is something quite impossible. History knows of no examples of such separation. States have always either taken care of the church or persecuted it."[32]

In January 1990 the editorial board of the newspaper *Nasha vira* (Our faith) published four main principles of the UAOC. The fourth principle was formulated in this way:

> The church must be neither a state establishment nor a state-influenced institution. It is above material earthly matters. But the church must not be entirely divorced from life on earth and must operate in a domain that cannot be occupied by any other organization.
>
> In performing its mission, the church assists the secular government if the latter directs its activities along the path of Christian ideals and shows a positive attitude to the activities of the church by establishing harmonious relations with it. And the church exists only as long as it is independent of the secular government. This independence, however, must not make the church an isolated institution, for it would then lose its authority, being unable to exercise a general organizing influence on social life. The church also loses its authority when it becomes a tool in the hands of secular rulers, because then it appears to sanction abuse of power whenever it occurs.
>
> The church can maintain and preserve its authority, an authority "not of this world," only if, maintaining its complete independence of secular power, it exercises an organizing influence on society in the spheres of religious, national, and spiritual life.[33]

Such a position reflected the character of the relations between the then unrecognized UAOC and the empire on the eve of the latter's disintegration. After the rise of the Ukrainian state, Metropolitan Filaret's rebellion, and the creation of the Kiev Patriarchate, the attitude of the church toward the state changed drastically, with the UAOC evolving toward the status of a state establishment. This is how M. Voskobiinyk characterizes this new relationship:

> The importance to the Ukrainian state of consolidation of the Ukrainian Ortho-
> dox churches is underscored by the fact that President of Ukraine Leonid
> Kravchuk has been pursuing, tactfully but consistently, a course of action
> aimed at unification of all the Orthodox churches of Ukraine in order to have
> one strong and well-controlled Ukrainian Orthodox Church that would serve as
> a firm and reliable pillar of the Ukrainian state.
>
> The church hierarchs have found a good pro-state formula for Orthodoxy in
> Ukraine—"Kiev Patriarchate." This provides an acceptable framework both
> for those who have traditionally favored the autocephalous movement and for
> those who, because of Ukraine's colonial status, belonged, or continue to
> belong, to the Russian Orthodox Church in Ukraine. It is difficult to overesti-
> mate the importance of the Ukrainian president's actions and the efforts of a
> group of deputies of the Verkhovna Rada aimed at gaining recognition for the
> formula of "Kiev Patriarchate."[34]

At present, the relations between the Ukrainian churches and the state consist of a wide range of component elements. Different factors may predominate in this relationship at different moments, which are sometimes only a day apart. As far as the direct church-state relations are concerned, seven component elements can be identified:

- the Ukrainian Orthodox Church, under Filaret (USSR, until indepen-
  dence);
- UAOC (USSR);
- UOC (independent Ukraine);
- UAOC (Ukraine);
- UOC, under Volodymyr Sabodan (Ukraine);
- UOC—Kiev Patriarchate (Ukraine); and
- UAOC, under Volodymyr Iarema and Petro Petrus' (Ukraine).

From the theoretical point of view, all these relationships would have to be maintained primarily through the Council for Religious Affairs attached to the Cabinet of Ministers. And it is only natural that these relationships have been influenced to a considerable extent by the replacement of the chairman of the council, Mykola Kolesnyk, who represented the old guard of communist offi-cials, by Arsen Zinchenko, a national democratic deputy to the Verkhovna Rada who was an original member of the anticommunist faction in parliament (ap-pointed in August 1992). The former acted in accordance with the precepts of the old state policy and, therefore, did all he could to curtail the church's activities and impose new restrictions on it, whereas the latter has been supporting the church in keeping with both his personal views and the general changes in the sociopolitical climate.

But while the Council for Religious Affairs mostly confined its role to registering and formalizing new aspects in the relations between church and state, the actual course of events has often been shaped by the policies of the secret police services. Thus, to the list of factors may be added relations between the UOC and the KGB; the UAOC and the KGB; the UOC and the Security Service of Ukraine, or SSU; the UAOC and the SSU; the UOC under Volodymyr Sabodan and the SSU; the UOC—Kiev Patriarchate and the SSU; and the UAOC under Volodymyr Iarema and Petro Petrus' and the SSU.

The usual historical sources that could be used in studying these relations are still out of reach, which is why we can only guess about the role played by the KGB in the formation of the UAOC, the extent to which the SSU is penetrated by the KGB, and so forth. We can only express some general observations on this subject, making it clear, however, that any conclusions we may draw will necessarily be approximate and temporary.

Here we can cite three examples illustrating situations in which forces previously hidden from view suddenly revealed themselves.

Example 1

On 1–9 July 1992, Patriarch Mstyslav, who had his permanent residence in Bound Brook, New Jersey, visited his congregation in Kiev. His visit came only a couple of weeks after the unification of the two churches proclaimed in his absence and without his consent.

The newspaper *Nasha vira,* whose editor in chief, Ievhen Sverstiuk, can hardly be suspected of any affectionate feelings for Metropolitan Filaret and the newly unified church, covered the visit in these terms:

> The most holy patriarch Mstyslav of Kiev and all Ukraine has now concluded his visit to Ukraine. Last week the most holy patriarch presided over a Council of Bishops, which discussed some important matters of the life of our Church.
> The most holy patriarch blessed the unification of the two largest Ukrainian churches, the Ukrainian Autocephalous Orthodox Church and the Ukrainian Orthodox Church, into one Ukrainian Orthodox Church—Kiev Patriarchate, which will be headed by the patriarch of Kiev, and also blessed the new church as the legal successor to the rights and properties of the two former churches. The patriarch signed an edict appointing Metropolitan Filaret his deputy in Ukraine. Metropolitan Antonii was appointed administrative superintendent of the church. The most holy patriarch granted an audience to Metropolitan Filaret and deputies of the Verkhovna Rada of Ukraine and was received by President of Ukraine Leonid Kravchuk.

On Friday, 10 July the most holy Patriarch Mstyslav of Kiev and all Ukraine departed for his residence in Bound Brook.[35]

Meanwhile, somewhat different reports were sent from the patriarch's entourage in Kiev to the émigré press. A press communiqué of the Kiev-based office of the UAOC patriarch was published by at least two newspapers of the diaspora, *Svoboda* (14 July 1992) and the *Natsional'na Trybuna* (19 July 1992). The two texts are essentially identical, but in the latter case it was dated 19 July and attributed to a Iu. Kryvolap, who, the paper said, had phoned it in from Kiev. The full text of the communiqué ran as follows:

The Most Holy Patriarch Mstyslav of Kiev and All Ukraine visited Kiev, the capital of Ukraine, from 1 to 9 July. His Holiness called on President of Ukraine, Leonid Makarovych Kravchuk, at the latter's invitation. In a conversation, which lasted for more than an hour, they exchanged opinions on the affairs of the church and the state on the path of strengthening the independence of Ukraine.

During his sojourn in Kiev His Holiness had meetings with representatives of ecclesiastical, political, and social groups, the scientific community, and mass media. Among other things, the Most Holy Patriarch Mstyslav of Kiev and All Ukraine devoted his special attention to the cause of Orthodox unity in Ukraine. For this His Holiness met with metropolitans Volodymyr, Filaret, Antonii, and Andrii.

On Wednesday, 8 July 1992, the bishops of the Ukrainian Autocephalous Orthodox Church in Ukraine held a conference at which they expressed their views on the unification of the UAOC and the Ukrainian Orthodox Church in Ukraine into one Ukrainian Orthodox Church—Kiev Patriarchate under the omophorion of His Holiness Mstyslav the First. These conversations and discussions show that the cause of unity of Ukrainian Orthodoxy meets with understanding both in the ecclesiastical circles and in the government. The recommendations of the UAOC bishops will soon be studied by His Holiness Patriarch Mstyslav and, thus, will probably bring about an all-Ukrainian unification of Ukrainian Orthodox churches both in Ukraine and in the diaspora.[36]

Thus, while the first information speaks of the approval of the unification as a fait accompli, the second one, which originated from the American entourage of the patriarch, mentions only some preliminary "conversations and discussions." In other words, certain forces were interested in preventing the Orthodox union at any cost. Back in the fall of 1991, when the idea of unification was already under consideration, the Information Office of RUKH (People's Movement of Ukraine) sent a sensational report from Kiev. In it was claimed that "today, on 9 September Metropolitan Filaret has started negotiations with the UAOC on unification for the good of the Ukrainian people."[37] The patriarch's reaction to this information was immediate and sharply negative. Apparently, the patriarch, now back in the United States, yielded to the pressure of those who opposed immediate unification. Returning to Ukraine in October, he gave anti-unification interviews to two newspapers sponsored by the Communist Party, *Kievskie vedomosti* (Kiev gazette) and *Nezavisimost'*, and *Vechirnyi Kyiv* carried a facsimile of his address to the believers, in which, on the one hand, the patriarch stated that "the process of unification is irreversible" but, on the other hand, nullified all real chances of unification by saying that "in the interests of the Ukrainian Orthodox Church and for their own good as Christians Metropolitan Filaret and Metropolitan Antonii must withdraw from the leadership of the church."[38]

Example 2

The statements made by Patriarch Mstyslav against the Kiev Patriarchate were like a signal that caused a fierce campaign in the media. A wave of corresponding articles swept across the Kiev periodicals, particularly those with pro-communist leanings. If we bother to analyze those texts, we shall find out the real arguments were not too numerous and that they somehow found their way from one newspaper to another. These were: (1) the Unification Council held in June was called without the patriarch's blessing; and (2) the patriarch had no residence in Kiev and had to stay in hotels and other such places. This second argument merits our special attention. It was to demonstrate that the prelates of the Kiev Patriarchate failed to take proper care of their superior. But we know from Metropolitan Antonii that the patriarch was offered apartments on Tereshchenkivs'ka Street (in the building where poets P. Tychyna and M. Bazhan had lived) and Liuterans'ka Street and a suite in the headquarters of the former exarchate in Pushkins'ka Street. But he turned down all these offers. What is really interesting here is the fact that the very same argument had already been used in a wholly different set of circumstances, only then it had been used against the Soviet regime. Several months before the attempted coup of August 1991, the Ternopil'-based newspaper *Ukraina pravoslavna* (Orthodox Ukraine) published this rejoinder, titled "Who Needs Lies?":

> Recently Radio Liberty and the newspapers *Molod' Ukrainy* and *Ternopol' Vechirnyi* reported that UAOC Patriarch Mstyslav was again homeless and that he was not allowed to travel to the Kharkiv region.
> These reports are not true, because UAOC Patriarch Mstyslav is still quite comfortable in the Ukraina Hotel, where he has been staying. The patriarch recently visited L'viv, Vinnytsia, Khmel'nyts'kyi, Poltava, and the Kharkiv regions.[39]

As we can see, before the August coup and independence this accusation, which could be brought against the UAOC, was justly brought against the communist regime. In independent Ukraine it was used not against the authorities but against the Kiev Patriarchate. This creates an impression that this accusation appeared after yet another careful study of the patriarch's dossier, because it is clear that the church could offer only those apartments that it owned or could rent, and the Kiev Patriarchate has not received the official residence of Kiev metropolitans at St. Sofia Cathedral to this day.

Example 3

In October 1992 the newspaper of the Ukrainian Republican Party, *Samostiina Ukraina*, published a circular of a previously unknown Russian Union for the Defense of the Motherland (UDM) addressed to "Representatives of the UDM in legal organizations and organs of power" and dated July 1992:

> According to our information our actions aimed at the neutralization of the nationalist faction in the UOC and the subversion of the authorities have failed because of the so-called forecasting and analysis group, whose legal members, deputies Pavlychko, Horyn, Skoryk, Porovs'kyi, Chervonyi, Ternopils'kyi, and others (thirty-seven persons in all), exert influence on Kravchuk, Pliushch, Fokin, and other top officials.
>
> In view of the above, we suggest that our work be intensified along the following lines:
> —neutralization of the forecasting and analysis group
> —further steps aimed at fostering division and discord among political and social organizations of separatist orientation
> —recovery of lost positions in the UOC leadership.
> We recommend that you focus your attention on the following:
> 1. prevention of unity of separatists within one organization.
> 2. maximum use of Mstyslav in the "celebrations" for the purpose of re-covering lost positions in the UOC leadership
> —use of the old name "Ukrainian Autocephalous Orthodox Church"
> —recommending Metropolitan Volodymyr to propose a joint liturgy in St. Sofiia Cathedral to be conducted by Mstyslav
> —insisting that this liturgy be broadcast over television and radio in the hope that the age of Mstyslav and his frail health, which it will be impossible to conceal in a live broadcast, will operate in Volody-myr's favor, and the very fact of a liturgy jointly conducted by Mstyslav and the hierarch of the Moscow Patriarchate . . . will cause a quarrel between Mstyslav and the bishops of the so-called Kiev Patriarchate and Filaret.[40]

It is interesting that almost until the end of 1992, events developed more or less according to this scenario. Contacts were established between seemingly uncompromising and irreconcilable adversaries: Patriarch Mstyslav and Metropolitan Volodymyr (Sabodan) of the Moscow Patriarchate. There were press reports about their meeting in room 201 of the Zhovtnevyi Hotel on 6 July 1992.[41] Further, a wedge was driven between the patriarch and Metropolitan Filaret. Actually, the patriarch grew cool toward all the bishops of the Kiev Patriarchate and refused to attend their Council on 15 December. Finally, the appeal of the popular name of the Ukrainian Autocephalous Orthodox Church,

which had been destroyed in the thirties, was also exploited: it was misappropri-
ated by a small fraction of the Kiev Patriarchate headed by Archbishop Petro
(Petrus') (a Local Council of this church, held in Kiev on 7 September 1993,
elected Father Volodymyr Iarema patriarch under the name of Dmytro).

The examples above illustrate the importance of influences exerted by secret
services. There can be no true history of the church without due consideration of
these factors.

The list of the external relationships of the Kiev Patriarchate would be incomplete without a mention of its relations with the Ukrainian Orthodox Church of
the Moscow Patriarchate, relations that are basically the same as those with the
Russian state. In fact, they represent rudimentary leftovers of the Ukrainian
Orthodoxy–USSR system of relations.

A complete reconstruction of all the stages and aspects of the relations between the Kiev Patriarchate and the state will be possible only when historical
evidence is available and accessible.

Relations with the State Today

As has been described, after the Bolsheviks had established their rule, the
church, despite all false declarations about separation, became more dependent
on the state than ever before. The forms of its existence as a social institution
were simply shaped by current state policies.

It would be a mistake to think that the present political institutions in the
territory of the former Soviet Union already have nothing in common with the
Leninist-Stalinist traditions. It is clear that, despite certain cosmetic changes,
such as denouncing and debunking Stalin's personality cult, the Soviet
nomenklatura has never abandoned its authoritarian practices, not even after the
great leader's death and not even after the Twentieth Party Congress. It is
equally clear that the new independent states that have emerged on the ruins of
the Soviet Union are largely products of the same nomenklatura.

The religious movement in Ukraine came into being in the wake of the
national liberation movement. Generated by aspirations for an independent
Ukrainian state, it has been trying to create or, rather, restore national forms of
Orthodoxy and, in the long run, attain autocephaly.

As early as 1955 Metropolitan Ilarion (Ohiienko) in Canada called for restoration
of the autocephaly of the Ukrainian church.[42] Father Vasyl' Romaniuk (now patriarch), imprisoned in a labor camp in Mordovia (since 1972), wrote to UOC Metropolitan Mstyslav, who lived in the United States and called himself a cleric of the
UAOC.[43] Then Father Romaniuk identified the UAOC with the UOC in the United
States. Toward the end of the 1980s the autocephalists formed a mass movement.

There can be no doubt that freedom from ideological *diktat*, the return to
traditional norms of social life, and, finally, everyday material hardships caused

many people, especially in the lower social strata, to turn to God. Outer manifestations of religious feelings ceased to be regarded as a brand of social inferiority. Traditions of the ritualized rural life made President Kravchuk baptize his grandson, and appeals to God sometimes escape from the lips of "people's deputies" taking the floor in parliament. Yet few people would dare to claim that a sizable portion of professional politicians have become genuine believers. Nor can we speak of any church influence on state policies. On the other hand, there can be no doubt that the state, or, to be more precise, secular institutions, exert an increasingly powerful influence on the church.

We have every reason to believe that during the formation of the UAOC in the last years of the USSR, the KGB made every effort to plant its men among the top UAOC leaders. On 7 September 1993, the leading hierarchs of the Kiev Patriarchate accused Archpriest Volodymyr Iarema, Archbishop Petro Petrus', and B. Rozhak, chairman of the L'viv Regional Brotherhood, of collaboration with the KGB and disclosed their KGB aliases.[44] The zeal with which pro-communist journalists got busy writing compromising stories about Metropolitan Filaret can be explained by the latter's decision to break with the KGB.[45] It is revealing that there have been no similar disclosures concerning any of the old-guard Russian bishops still serving in Ukraine. It appears that the church is still very much a hostage of state policy.

The complexity of the situation is compounded by the ecclesiastical schism, due to which Ukraine now has not one but as many as three Orthodox churches. Their political orientations are quite different, but they more or less follow the corresponding political preferences of various factions of the government.

At the very beginning, when the basic political concepts of the newly proclaimed state were still taking shape, the policy of UOC head Metropolitan Filaret was quite in harmony with the policies of the secular authorities. This was vividly demonstrated by his participation, on 30 November 1991, on the eve of the referendum, in an important television program designed to urge the population to vote for independence. President Kravchuk even sent a message to the Council of the Russian Orthodox Church that was to consider the matter of granting autocephaly to the Ukrainian Orthodox Church. But subsequent events, full of fine nuances and major complications, made the president take a more cautious approach. He was especially disappointed and discouraged by the conduct of Patriarch Mstyslav, who was apparently unwilling to play an active part in building up the church in Ukraine. He visited Ukraine six times but never stayed long, and having made a brief visit to some city, he immediately returned to the United States. It was widely reported that President Kravchuk had met with the patriarch several times, and this is why the latter's unwillingness to burden himself with everyday administrative matters, as well as his controversial speeches and statements, drove the president, who is a very cautious person by nature, to the conclusion that he had better avoid being identified too closely with any particular church.

But Mstyslav was recognized by the Kiev Patriarchate as its head to the very last days of his life. No wonder, then, that the relations of the secular administration with the Kiev Patriarchate, whose beginnings were quite unpromising, worsened sharply. In fact, they became so bad that an appeal of the Bishops' Council to the president urging him "to receive, as soon as possible, the members of the Holy Synod of the Ukrainian Orthodox Church—Kiev Patriarchate to discuss a wide range of issues relating to the development of the church in Ukraine and maintenance of interconfessional and interethnic peace" has remained unanswered to this day.[46]

Moreover, it has actually strengthened the positions of those members of the administration inclined to favor Metropolitan Volodymyr (Sabodan) of the Russian Orthodox Church. Arguments in favor of this orientation were the formal organizational integrity of the Russian Orthodox Church, the absence of conflicts in its midst, its canonical status, and its mass following. According to the press center of the Ukrainian Greek Catholic Church, in the summer of 1993 there were 5,590 parishes of the Ukrainian Orthodox Church that recognized the supremacy of the Moscow Patriarchate, whereas the Kiev Patriarchate had the loyalty of only 1,091 communities.[47]

Analyzing the present church situation, Canadian Archpriest Tymofii Minenko states that "whether we are willing to recognize it or not, the revival of the church and the building up of an independent state in Ukraine are inseparable."[48] This is corroborated by the fact that the Ukrainian Orthodox Church of the Moscow Patriarchate is supported by those members of the administration who either do not have firm pro-independence convictions (Mikhalchenko, Sereda, et al.) or who belong to the Ukrainian Greek Catholic Church (Z. Duma). On the other hand, the Supreme Church Council of the Kiev Patriarchate includes such active members of the democratic faction in parliament as M. Provs'kyi, V. Chervonyi, and Ie. Shevchenko.

The future of the Kiev Patriarchate is inseparably linked with the future of Ukraine as an independent state. If the state survives and becomes stronger, the Kiev Patriarchate will become stronger too. Conversely, the Ukrainian Orthodox Church of the Moscow Patriarchate will decline. If we proceed from the assumption that Ukraine will continue to exist as an independent state, we will have to conclude that the future belongs to the Kiev Patriarchate. As to the UOC of the Moscow Patriarchate, it will inevitably be reduced to the status of a foreign diocese, unless it is artificially maintained with subsidies from abroad.

This interrelationship must be obvious both to us and to those church and lay politicians who are not interested in the strengthening of the Ukrainian state. Plain logic tells us that such politicians benefit from the present schism and thus helps to understand what has really been behind the activities of Archbishop Petro Petrus' and Archpriest Volodymyr Iarema, who was elected UAOC patriarch on 7 September 1993.

There are no visible signs of any influence exerted by the Kiev Patriarchate on the internal policies of the Ukrainian state. In other words, there is no steady flow of information from the church to the state institutions. Since the dominant faction in the Ukrainian parliament is represented by the Communist partycrats who do not care for Ukrainian statehood, this communication has never been established. The only real influence that we can observe is the influence of the state institutions on the church. Such a situation is quite dangerous.

To be sure, the priests of the Kiev Patriarchate do influence their parishioners. The strengthening of the national religious awareness among the masses will sooner or later make the administration face an unpleasant surprise: the discrepancy between the ideals of the ruling nomenklatura and those of national-minded Christians.

Notes

1. The first attempt at such analysis was made by Canadian Tymofii Minenko in his article "Do pytannia tserkovnoi smuty v suchasnii Ukraini," *Visnyk* (Winnipeg), 1993, March, pt. 3 (2579), pp. 7–8; April, pt. 4 (2580), pp. 7–8; May, pt. 5 (2581), p. 7.

2. I. Sukhopluev, "Tserkovnyi raskol v Rossii i na Ukraine," *Put' kommunizma*, 1922, nos. 8–9; Archimandrite Ioann (Snychev), *Tserkovnye raskoly v Russkoi tserkvi 20-kh i 30-kh godov XX stoletiia—Grigorianskii, Iaroslavskii, Iosiflianskii, Viktorianskii i drugie, Ikh osobennosti i istoriia* (Kuibyshev, 1965). [1], 2, 423 pp. [typescript]. I. Ia. Trifonov, "Raskol v Russkoi pravoslavnoi tserkvi, 1922–1925 gg." *Voprosy istorii*, 1972, no. 5, pp. 64–77.

3. See V.M. Andreev, "Nekotorye aspekty formirovaniia ideologii obnovlenchestva v russkom pravoslavii," *Uchenye zapiski* (Leningrad State Pedagogical Institute [Hertzen]), vol. 462 (1970), pp. 118–28; N.S. Gordienko and P.K. Kurochkin, "Liberal'no-obnovlencheskoe dvizhenie v russkom pravoslavii nachala XX v," *Voprosy nauchnogo ateizma*, 1969, no. 7, pp. 313–40; A.K. Kozyreva, "Khristianskii sotsializm obnovlencheskoi tserkvi," *Uchenye zapiski*, vol. 284 (1967), pp. 223–39; M.M. Skachkov, "Dinamika otnosheniia Moskovskoi patriarkhii k obnovlenchestvu," *Aktual'nye problemy izucheniia istorii religii i ateizma*, 1977, pp. 69–77; A.A. Shishkin,, *Sushchnost' i kriticheskaia otsenka "obnovlencheskogo" raskola Russkoi pravoslavnoi tserkvi* (Kazan: Izd. Kazanskogo universiteta, 1970).

4. H. Kas'ianov, *Ukrains'ka intelihentsiia 1920-kh–1930-kh rokiv: Sotsial'nyi portret ta istorychna dolia* (Edmonton: University of Alberta, 1992), p. 36.

5. F. 1, op. 6, spr. 30, ark. 9, Partarkhiv Instytutu istorii partii pry TsK Kompartii Ukrainy. See V.M. Danylenko, H.B. Kas'ianov, S.B. Kul'chyts'kyi, *Stalinizm na Ukraini: 20–30-ti roki* (Kiev: Lybid', 1991), p. 274.

6. H. Kas'ianov, *Ukrains'ka intelihentsiia*, pp. 35–36.

7. Obnovlens'ka tserkva (Renovationist Church).

8. Rosiis'ka pravoslavna (staroslov'ians'ka) tserkva (Russian Orthodox [Old Slavic] Church).

9. Ukrains'ka avtokefal'na pravoslavna tserkva (Ukrainian Autocephalous Orthodox Church).

10. Brats'ke ob'ednannia Ukrains'kikh Avtokefal'nikh Tserkov (Brotherly Union of Ukrainian Autocephalous Churches). Other names: Buldovshchina, Lubens'kyi rozkol.

11. Vseukrains'ka pravoslavna tserkovna rada (All-Ukrainian Orthodox Church Council).

12. "Osobaia papka," ark. 92–95, f. 1, op. 16, spr. 34, Tsentral'nyi derzhavnyi arkhiv

hromads'kykh ob'ednan'. Price list was made by chief of secret department of the GPU USSR Gorozhanin.

13. For a review of the administrative system of the Orthodox eparchies with a list of bishops, see S. Bilokin, "Pravoslavni eparkhii Ukrainy 1917–1941 rr.," *Istoryko-heohrafichni doslidzhennia na Ukraini: Zbirnyk naukovykh prats'* (Kiev: Naukova dumka, 1992), pp. 100–120.

14. Mytrofan Iavdas', *Ukrains'ka avtokefal'na pravoslavna tserkva: Dokumenty dlia istorii* (Munich: Ingolstadt, 1956); Ivan Vlasovs'kyi, *Narys istorii Ukrains'koi pravoslavnoi tserkvy,* vol. 4, pt. 1 (New York, Bound Brook Ukrainian Orthodox Church of USA, 1961); Vasyl' Lypkivs'kyi, *Istoriia Ukrains'koi pravoslavnoi tserkvy* (Winnipeg: I. Gryshuk, 1961); Nataliia Polons'ka-Vasylenko, *Istorychni pidvalyny UAPTs* (Munich, 1964); Vasyl' Potiienko, *Vidnovlennia iierarkhii Ukrains'koi pravoslavnoi avtokefal'noi tserkvy* (Novyi Ul'm: UAOC, 1971); Demyd Burko, "Ukrains'ka tserkva pid suchasnym rezhymom, 1920–1930-ti roky," *Naukovy zapyski Ukrains'koho Vil'noho universytetu,* vols. 11–12 (Munich: Ukrains'kyi Vil'nyi universytet, 1984), pp. 28–64; Semen Savchuk and Iuryi i Mulyk-Lutsyk, *Istoriia Ukrains'koi koi hreko-pravoslavnoi tserkvy v Kanadi,* vol. 1, *Kyivs'ka tserkovna tradytsiia ukraintsiv Kanady* (Winnipeg, Ekkleziia, 1984); Bohdan Bociurkiw, *The Politics of Religion in the Ukraine: The Orthodox Church and the Ukrainian Revolution, 1917–1919* (Washington, D.C.: Kennan Institute, 1985); *Martyrolohiia Ukrains'kykh tserkov u chotyr'okh tomakh.* vol. 1, *Ukrains'ka pravoslavna tserkva: Dokumenty, materiialy, khristiians'kyi samvydav Ukrainy* (Toronto and Baltimore: Smoloskyp, 1987); Demyd Burko, *Ukrains'ka avtokefal'na pravoslavna tserkva: Vichne dzherelo zhyttia* (South Bound Brook: Ukrainian Orthodox Church in the USA, 1988).

15. Using materials from the history of the Russian Orthodox Church in Ukraine, we need to mention the resolution of the All-Ukrainian Brotherhood on the conception of Ukrainian theology in *Pravoslavnyi visnyk,* 13 December 1992 (Kyivs'kyi Patriiarkhat: Press Release, Kiev, 1992), no. 2, p. 7.

16. We can find the same periodization in Alexander Kischkowsky, *Die Sowjetische Religionspolitik und die Russische Orthodoxe Kirche* (Munich: Institute for the Study of the USSR, 1960), and others.

17. M. Pol'skii, *Kanonicheskoe polozhenie vysshei tserkovnoi vlasti v SSSR i zagranitsei* (Jordanville, Tipografiia Iova Pochaevskago v sv. Troitskom monastyrie, 1948), pp. 39–41. For biographies of the following clergy, Metropolitan Manuil (Lemesevskij), *Die russischen Orthodoxen Bischofe von 1893 bis 1965.* Teil I–VI (Erlangen: Lehrstuhl für Geschichte und Theologie des Christlichen Ostens, 1979–1989): Iosif, Dimitrii, Filipp, Anatolii, Serafim, Iuvenalii, and Pitirim.

18. Lypkivs'kyi, *Istoriia Ukrains'koi pravoslavnoi tserkvy,* p. xv.

19. Ibid., p. xxxiv.

20. Ibid., p. xiv.

21. A. Solzhenitsyn, *Arkhipelag GULag, 1918–1956: Opyt khudozhestvennogo issledovaniia* (Paris: YMCA-PRESS, 1973), p. 49.

22. For a detailed account of Stalin's 1943 deal with representatives of the Russian Orthodox Church with regard to its new status, see Ivan Bilas, "Kremlivs'ka zmova derzhavnykh i dukhovnykh vladyk," *Ukrains'ke pravoslavne slovo* (South Bound Brook), no. 5–6 (April–May 1992), pp. 22–27.

23. See Manuil, *Die russischen orthodoxen Bischofe,* pt. 6 (1989), pp. 168–91.

24. *Izvestiia,* 16 February 1930, p. 2. For commentary on this interview, see A.A. Bogolepov, *Tserkov' pod vlast'iu kommunizma* (Munich, 1958), p. 32.

25. See "Nevdacha moskovs'koi pravoslavnoi tserkvy," *Vezhi* (Munich, 1948), ch. 2, pp. 47–49.

26. "Molitvennyi kul't Stalina," *Pravoslavnaia Rus'* (Jordanville), 1963, no. 21, p. 6.

27. Ibid.

28. Ibid., pp. 6–7.

29. "Chekisty . . . v riasakh," *Argumenty i fakty*, September 1991, no. 36, p. 7.

30. Ibid.

31. *Dekrety Sovetskoi vlasti,* vol. 2 (Moscow, 1959), p. 561.

32. "Otnoshenie tserkvi k gosudarstvu v istoricheskom svete," *Svobodnoe slovo khristianina* (Kiev), 1918, nos. 5–7, p. 21.

33. *Nasha vira* (Kiev), January 1990.

34. M. Voskobiinyk, "Konsolidatsiia Pravoslavnoi tserkvy—Tverda osnova dlia derzhavnoi nezalezhnosti Ukrainy," *Ukrains'ki visti* (Detroit), no. 26 (27 June 1993), p. 2.

35. "Khronika," *Nasha vira,* 1992, ch. 13/28, p. 3.

36. "Presovyi komunikat Patriiarshoi kantseliarii UAPTs v Kyivi," *Natsional'na trybuna,* 19 July 1992, p. 1; "Obmirkovuiut' ob'ednannia UPTserkov," *Svoboda,* 14 July 1992, p. 1.

37. "Do preosviashchennykh arkhyiereiv, pochesnykh iereiv ta pobozhnykh brativ i sester UAPTserkvy," *Ukrains'ki visti* (Detroit), no. 34 (8 September 1991), p. 1. Negotiations on the unification of the churches did not take place at this point.

38. "Mstyslav proty Filareta i Antoniia," *Vechirnyi Kyiv,* 2 November 1992.

39. "Bozhe, nam ednist' podai . . ." *Ukraina pravoslavna* (Ternopil'), 1991, no. 3, p. 6.

40. "P'iata kolona die," *Samostiina Ukraina* (Kiev), 1992, no. 36/57, p. 2. See also "V Ukraini dye taemna vlada," *Svoboda,* 4 June 1991, p. 1.

41. *Mova ie natsiia* (Kiev), 1992, no. 12, p. 1.

42. Metropolitan Ilarion, "Vernit' avtokefaliiu Ukrains'kii tserkvi," *Vira i kul'tura* (Winnipeg), 1955, no. 3 (15), pp. 3–4.

43. Metropolitan Mstyslav spoke out in defense of Father Romaniuk on 21 January 1976. The letter addressed to him by the imprisoned priest, written not earlier than December 1976, was published on 31 March 1978, in the Jersey City, NJ, daily *Svoboda* (*Martyrolohiia Ukrains'kykh tserkov,* vol. 1, pp. 867–68, 1063).

44. Maksym Strikha, "Fars v budynku uchytelia," *Khreshchatyk,* 14 September 1993, p. 6.

45. For example, V. Anisimov, "Predstavitel' prezidenta v pravoslavii," *Nezavisimost',* 27 June 1992, pp. 1–2; "Moskovs'kyi vladyka v Ukraini—agent KGB 'Antonov,'" *Svoboda,* 6 March 1992, p. 2; Metropolitan Filaret, "Boh proshchav i nam veliv," *Kul'tura i zhyttia,* 31 October 1992, p. 3.

46. Kyivs'kyi Patriiarkhat: press release, December 1992, no. 3, p. 8.

47. "Konfesii v Ukraini," *Shliakh peremohy,* 10 July 1993, p. 8. The imprecision of the figures cited is explained by the fact that the article has not included those parishes of the Kiev Patriarchate that have not yet re-registered—they were counted as belonging to the UAOC of Archbishop Petro (Petrus'). It is interesting that within weeks the Research Institute of Radio Free Europe/Radio Liberty made public the results of an opinion survey that listed completely different figures: 49 percent of the people interviewed identified themselves as faithful of the Kiev Patriarchate, 6.1 percent as belonging to the Moscow Patriarchate, while UAOC faithful were included in the category "Others"—1.1 percent.

48. Tymofii Minenko, "Smuty v suchasnii Ukraini," *Visnyk* (Winnipeg), 1993, ch. 3 (2579), p. 7.

10

The Baltic Churches and the
Democratization Process

Robert F. Goeckel

The Baltic states have varying cultural traditions, but they share a fundamental Western orientation that includes a religious tradition based on Christianity acquired from Rome.[1] However, in the cases of Estonia and Latvia this tradition was altered by the Reformation and affected by the historical domination of the Baltic Germans, leaving the predominant Lutheran Church with the image of a *Herrenkirche* and hence a weaker link to the nation. The Lithuanian Catholic Church, on the other hand, did not suffer from this onus of foreign domination, although the tie between nation and religion is weaker than in Poland due to the relatively late Christianization of Lithuania and the extensive Polonization of the church prior to the communist period. Orthodoxy was not indigenous to these areas, although conversion to Orthodoxy under the influence of tsarist policies of Russification did create a national Orthodox population. This chapter will concentrate primarily on these national churches (Catholic in Lithuania, Lutheran and Catholic in Latvia, and Lutheran in Estonia), addressing three issues: the effect of the communist period on the churches, the role of the churches in the liberalization process under Gorbachev, and the role of the churches in the postindependence period of democratization.

The Legacy of the Communist Period for the Churches

The role of the Baltic churches in the postcommunist period owes much to the legacy of the communist period.[2] The Soviets' ideological and political campaign against religion and the churches left the latter greatly weakened when compared with their prewar condition. This sad fate, shared with all the churches in the former Soviet Union, dictated a defensive attitude during the communist period and explains the current priority on institutional rebuilding. Although the

Baltics (like other areas of the western USSR) experienced only fifty, rather than seventy, years of communism, the churches were left only marginally more intact than others in the USSR.

After initially registering most churches in the Baltics after World War II, the Soviets began a policy of harsh Stalinization, including arrest, deportation, and intimidation of numerous church leaders and clergy.[3] Churches that were not closed were nationalized.[4] The churches' social presence was eliminated totally, including charitable institutions, religious instruction in the schools, and auxiliary organizations (especially important in the Catholic Church). Access to the media was restricted to propagandistic appearances or limited amounts of narrowly religious materials.[5] Theological education for clergy became practically impossible, compounding the shortages due to deportations and wartime emigration of clergy.[6] International ties of the churches were ruptured.[7] Naturally, this repression resulted in drastic declines in church adherence, particularly among Protestants, after an initial increase after World War II. De-Stalinization brought a brief respite from the state's antireligion campaign. Church openings and reconstruction were permitted on a limited basis. The churches were allowed to resume international contacts on a bilateral basis and under the aegis of the Russian Orthodox Church. Lutherans were permitted to train a limited number of clergy in so-called theological seminaries. Church adherence increased considerably in the population.

As is well known, the Khrushchev period brought new repression to the churches and believers in the USSR. Although relatively fewer churches were closed in the Baltics than in Russia, many parishes were closed, including some symbolically important churches.[8] The regime used parishes' increasing inability to maintain a minimum membership, as well as financial pressure, to deregister them. An intense pro-atheism campaign was undertaken to wean believers from the church, including "new Soviet traditions," which were secular rites of passage designed to replace the traditional religious rites. The regime tightened its control by marginalizing the clergy in matters of parish governance.

The fall of Khrushchev relieved the worst repression of the churches and religion but did not bring a true liberalization. Formal bilateral and multilateral relations were established; even limited contacts with the exile churches were permitted in the hopes that these would soften the criticism by émigré Balts of conditions in the Soviet-occupied Baltics. Yet the de-Christianization process continued inexorably throughout the 1960s and 1970s. The clergy shortage reached crisis proportions, particularly in the Lutheran churches. The Lutheran leadership became increasingly resigned and compromised in the eyes of many believers and clergy. Efforts of the "scientific atheist" cadres focused increasingly on the residual psychological motivation for religion and the success of the "new Soviet traditions."[9] The Latvian statistics in Table 1 indicate that the repression of believers and the administrative strictures affected all churches.

Table 1

Number of Parishes by Denomination
Latvia, 1939–93

Denomination	1939	1989	1993
Lutheran	319	202	290
Catholic	194	182	191
Orthodox	166	86	100
Old Believers	88	64	56
Baptists	108	60	69
Adventists	28	23	33
Pentecostals	na	2	44
Methodists	27	0	3
Reformed	2	0	2
Jewish	221	4	5
Other	12	0	18

Source: Information on the Status of Churches in Latvia, provided to the author by the Department for Religious Affairs, Ministry of Justice, Latvian Republic, 20 October 1993.

To be sure, religion survived the communist assault more intact in the popular consciousness. Cultural traditions with religious dimensions, such as Christmas or cemetery services commemorating the dead, retained their resonance. In the 1980s, youth evinced a new interest in religion and the church, in part out of curiosity.

The communist period thus left the churches—particularly the Lutheran churches—dramatically weakened as institutions. Their relationship with the regime was influenced by this institutional weakness, as well as by their theological tradition. After initially opposing or attempting to delay the measures of Stalinization, the Lutheran churches pursued a policy of accommodation toward the regime, calling for an end to armed resistance in the 1940s, supporting Stalin's peace campaign in the 1950s, and issuing obsequious declarations supportive of Soviet foreign policy thereafter. Only recently freed from German Lutheran influence, the Baltic Lutherans' response to communism was dictated by Luther's deference to authority. The task of mere survival sapped them of the strength to develop an alternative social doctrine that might have guided their relationship with the regime.[10]

As a result, the Lutheran Church played a minor role in the limited political dissent that did arise in the early 1980s, particularly in Estonia.[11] This nonreligious dissent criticized the regime for environmental degradation, the arms race and militarization, the invasion of Afghanistan, and youth alienation, but it ultimately focused on the national question, calling for an end to Russification, or "decolonization" of the Baltics.[12] Until the late 1980s the regime met such protests with repression and administrative measures. There is no evidence that the Lutheran Church leadership in either Latvia or Estonia lent support to such dissent. Isolated pastors in Estonia, such as Harri Motsnik in the early 1980s, did in fact criticize the regime for its foreign policy as well as its antireligious policy and Russification policy.[13] But the church sought to control dissent in its own ranks and was unable to protect its own clergy, let alone nonreligious dissenters, from repression, as the arrest and exile of Motsnik in 1984 demonstrated.[14]

In the 1980s some younger pastors sought to reinvigorate church life. For example, Vello Jurjo sought to attract youth to the church by organizing youth retreats, defying a state ban on them.[15] In Latvia young pastors, such as Modris Plate and Juris Rubenis, pressed for increased enrollments of younger students in the theological seminary and developed links with dissenting secular intellectuals. In both cases they met resistance from the church leaders backed by state officials.

The Catholic Church was more closely associated with dissent, both religious and nonreligious. In the early postwar period the Lithuanian church gave assistance to the armed opposition, and both the Latvian and Lithuanian churches were reluctant to participate in the official peace campaigns.[16] Religious instruction of youth continued throughout the Soviet period, and church adherence remained higher among Catholics.

Yet the pattern of dissent in the Lithuanian and Latvian Catholic churches diverged in the later period of communist rule. The Lithuanian church continued steadfastly to resist the regime.[17] Priests were trained and ordained on an underground basis. Massive petition drives supported the reopening of churches or completion of church construction. A robust samizdat industry developed in the form of the *Chronicle of the Lithuanian Catholic Church,* the most consistent and comprehensive samizdat publication in the USSR. The *Chronicle* not only extensively documented religious dissent and repression but served as the unofficial organ of the nationalist opposition.

By contrast, the Latvian Catholic Church made greater accommodation to the regime after 1960. The naming of Julian Vaivods as bishop and successor to Metropolitan Antonii Springovich was to a great extent engineered by the regime and accepted by the Vatican.[18] Vaivods advocated a low profile for the church, focusing on maintenance of the organization and abstinence from politics. Unlike Lithuanian bishops, he was permitted relatively unhindered access to the Vatican. The Catholic seminary in Riga was permitted to train limited numbers of priests for other republics, especially Belorussia. No counterpart to the *Chronicle* was developed in the Latvian case.

The divergence between the Lithuanian and Latvian Catholic churches can be attributed to several factors. The tie between Catholicism and nationality is looser in the case of the confessionally plural nation of Latvia, leaving the Catholic Church on the defensive. This also left it less autonomy with respect to the Vatican, which likely saw the accommodation of the Latvian Catholics as useful in pursuing its interests in the wider Soviet Union, particularly in terms of training priests for non-Baltic service.

The communist period also left a legacy of tension between the dominant national churches and the smaller denominations. The communist authorities sometimes attempted to use the small churches, such as Baptists, against the more powerful national churches.[19] Over time, however, the authorities realized that their proselytizing and lay orientation made the Baptists (and Estonian Methodists) a greater threat than the tradition-bound Lutheran Church.[20] Likewise, the Lutheran and Reformed churches in Lithuania, although small, were given a profile by the state in an obviously futile effort to offset the power of the Catholic Church.

More importantly, the communist period left a legacy of increasing tension between national churches and "immigrant churches." The primary focus of this problem was the Russian Orthodox Church, which symbolized the Russification process. The indigenous Orthodox churches had maintained autocephalous status during the period of independence but were forced by Stalin in 1940 to recognize the Moscow Patriarchate. The Orthodox Church assumed a leading role among the churches, reinforced by official policy in Moscow and the bureaucratic structure of the authorities dealing with the churches.[21] All international ties of the national churches were overseen by the Russian Orthodox Church. Local Orthodox hierarchs assumed intelligence roles, reporting routinely on the activities of non-Orthodox church leaders.

The Russian challenge took on heightened importance as a result of massive immigration of non-Balts after the 1950s. Although most of these immigrants could be described as highly secularized "Soviets," many identified with the Orthodox faith, swelling its size. Under the tutelage of the patriarchate, ethnically Balt Orthodox church life was gradually marginalized: in Latvia, for example, the number of Latvian Orthodox parishes declined from seventy-two in 1939 to twelve by 1993.[22] The non-Balts were also more likely to be attracted to the Protestant sects, such as Baptist, Methodist, and Pentecostal, due to their greater emotionalism and evangelization across ethnic lines. Like the Lithuanian Catholics, these groups were more likely to engage in underground activity. These developments disturbed the stable status quo in the church-state relationship and alarmed the leadership of the national churches as well as state officials.[23]

Even greater ambivalence characterized the Lutherans' relations with another immigrant group, the Soviet Germans. On the one hand, they had an image problem based on memories of German domination of the Baltics; on the other hand, they shared a common Lutheran heritage with the Balts.[24] Thus when Soviet Germans were given amnesty by the regime in 1964 and began to migrate to the Baltic republics in the hope of emigrating eventually to West Germany, the local churches were confronted with a dilemma—help meet the religious needs of their fellow Lutherans or keep a distance from the politically charged issue of Soviet Germans. The Latvian church authorized Pastor Harald Kalnins to undertake religious work with the Germans in Latvia, but both the church hierarchy and the republican leadership opposed extending this mandate to include the Germans in Siberia and Central Asia.[25]

Thus, the communist period damaged all Baltic churches, but some suffered more than others. The traditional influence of the Lutheran churches in Estonia and Latvia was eroded as both the institution and church adherence atrophied. On the other hand, the Catholic Church remained popular and vital as an institution, although this conclusion must be qualified in the case of Latvia. The quality of church leadership declined as the churches fell prey to state penetration. The relative absence of democratic structures, even in Lutheran churches with a synodal tradition, handicapped these organizations: they were not particularly good training grounds for democracy, unlike the East German Lutheran churches or the Polish Catholic Church.[26] Yet, as Stanley Vardys noted, even in the more de-Christianized republics of Latvia and Estonia, the churches are "deeply rooted in national tradition and provide rallying points for the maintenance and furthering of these traditions."[27]

For their part, the republican authorities in Estonia and Latvia became increasingly indifferent to religion as a result of the atrophy in the Lutheran churches. On the other hand, Moscow was forced to take seriously the convergence of national and religious dissent in Lithuania.

The Role of the Churches During Perestroika

Religious policy and church-state relations were hardly the main priority of perestroika; Gorbachev saw changes in the economy and political process as primary. However, these issues could no more be isolated from the process of liberalization than any other. By 1988 Gorbachev had widened the agenda of perestroika to include an opening up to the Russian Orthodox Church and the prospect of revision of the repressive legislation on religion.[28] But this process suffered a setback when conservative opposition in the CPSU apparatus and the KGB (and, some argue, in the Orthodox hierarchy) succeeded in ousting the relatively liberal Konstantin Kharchev as chair of the Council for Religious Affairs, replacing him with the hardliner Iurii Khristoradnov in 1989. Promulgation of the new legislation was thus delayed until 1990.[29]

The different responses of the churches to communist rule helps one understand their different roles under conditions of liberalization. The Lithuanian opposition in the Catholic Church nurtured the active opposition of the Sajudis movement, although Sajudis was largely a movement of the laity.[30] On the basis of the *Chronicle*'s network and experience, Sajudis was able to gear up quickly a republicwide organizational capacity. The more co-opted Latvian Catholic Church, on the other hand, was affected by the general demoralization of the Latvian populace in the face of intense Russification and played little active role in promoting liberalization.[31]

The Lutheran churches, on the other hand, were too weak to give birth to the opposition movement. But liberalization removed the veneer of unity and brought demands for internal church perestroika, calling into question the prior relationship of the church leadership to the communist regime. In Latvia, for example, a faction of clergy who opposed the co-opted church leadership and supported the Popular Front eventually brought about a microrevolution in the church. Alarmed at the inertia of the church leadership in the face of declining religiosity, a group of young pastors formed around Modris Plate and Juris Rubenis, providing testimony to the ferment below the surface in Latvia in the early 1980s. With the advent of perestroika, they became more vocal, organizing as the Rebirth and Renewal Movement and supporting the Popular Front. They opposed the candidacy of Eriks Mesters, who was narrowly elected archbishop in 1985, because of his close relations with the regime.[32] Mesters sought to undercut support for the movement by criticizing the unorthodox liturgical style of Plate. Latvian authorities viewed the movement in procrustean fashion as "an attempt to counteract the crisis situation in the church" and unsuccessfully pressured the church to oust Plate in 1987.[33] Eventually, an extraordinary synod in 1989 altered the church constitution and replaced Mesters with Karlis Gailitis, a strong supporter of Latvian independence. Thus, although weak, the Latvian Lutheran Church did serve as the vehicle for the expression of rising societal disaffection and the renaissance of national identity.[34]

Internal divisions also developed in the Estonian Lutheran Church, although with less dramatic results in terms of the church leadership. Although Kuno Pajula was elected archbishop in 1986 in a relatively open election, he was clearly the state's favored candidate.[35] His opponent was Jaan Kiivit, Jr., son of the popular late Archbishop Jaan Kiivit. Pajula offered the prospect of a stable relationship with the communist regime, but younger pastors favored the more dynamic Kiivit. Unlike his counterpart in Latvia, Pajula managed to retain his position. But a majority of the consistory was removed in 1990, including the compromised general secretary, August Liepins.[36] Political differences continued to divide Kiivit and Pajula, with Kiivit supporting the Popular Front movement and Pajula compensating for his past by aligning with the more nationalistic Estonian Congress.

The Estonian Popular Front was driven largely by secularized intellectuals; church leaders played a minor role. The church leadership assumed a neutral stance toward it, as Pajula argued that the church could not assume a political position.[37] Individual pastors supported the autonomy-oriented Popular Front, but most preferred to support the more independence-minded Estonian Congress movement.

Perestroika also brought division to the small Lithuanian Lutheran Church. It has been headed since the 1970s by Bishop Kalvanas, in fact a native Latvian who was closely identified with the regime during the communist period. Even during the communist period, groups in the former German territories of the

Memelland had rejected his authority, although many later emigrated to West Germany. Since perestroika, however, splinter parishes that had been refused registration by the communists have formed, challenging his authority anew.[38]

Under increasing pressure to reform, the communist governments in the Baltic republics moved to defuse areas of conflict with the churches. The motives differed somewhat: the Lithuanian party had little choice, given the level of religious dissent and Sajudis's demands for religious liberty; in Latvia, the internal unrest in the church demonstrated the bankruptcy of previous state policy; in heavily de-Christianized Estonia, relative indifference to the atheism campaign led to concessions by the regime. But in all cases republican authorities made significant concessions to the institutional churches and to believers. Demands by the nascent popular front movements for religious liberty and an end to restrictions on the churches certainly contributed to the forthcomingness of the communists. But the renaissance of religion and the churches should also be attributed to the relaxation of restrictions by communist governments seeking to deal with more pressing political and economic issues and to forestall greater erosion of their leading role.[39] The fact that the religious issue—after all, one of the key tenets of the ideology—was not heatedly contested in these parties suggests that the campaign against religion had long since become a greater policy priority for Moscow than for these republican parties.

The communists' new course entailed various symbolic gestures. For example, they returned important buildings, such as the cathedrals in Vilnius and Riga. Lithuanian bishops Julijonas Steponavičius and Vincentas Sladkevičius were permitted to return from internal exile, and most religious prisoners of conscience were released. Jews were allowed to open a cultural center in Vilnius. The republican authorities also replaced hardline officials charged with overseeing the churches.[40] The new plenipotentiary in Latvia, Alfreds Kublinskis, even apologized to the 1989 Lutheran synod for past abuses by the state. Official status was restored to religious holidays, such as Christmas and Easter.

Glasnost also brought new media possibilities for the churches. Church journals and weekly newspapers were permitted in Lithuania and Latvia beginning in early 1989. The translation of the New Testament into Estonian—the first since World War II—testified to the greater toleration of the Bible. More important perhaps, the churches were granted access to the electronic media: the first regular religious program was broadcast by Lithuanian television in July 1989, although this had been preceded by full coverage of the reconsecration by Bishop Steponavičius of Vilnius Cathedral in February 1989; Latvian authorities followed in November 1989. Later this was extended to encompass Christmas services and classes in the Bible and the fundamentals of Christian faith. These new media opportunities represented a quantum leap in access to society for churches whose media work had been limited to an annual calendar used in an ad hoc propaganda volume designed for foreign consumption.

Theological education was permitted on a wider basis. Initially this entailed an end to state interference in the admissions processes of existing seminaries. Eventually the churches were permitted to open new seminaries, for example the Catholic seminary in Telšiai, Lithuania. In 1990 the theological faculties at the universities of Riga and Tartu were restored.

Restrictions on clergy and parishes were lifted. Confiscatory levels of taxation on clergy were eliminated unilaterally by the Estonian Republic in 1989.[41] The committees that monitored sermons of clergy were quietly disbanded.[42] Impediments to international travel by church leaders and clergy were removed. Flooded by applications to reopen parishes, the authorities became increasingly liberal, even permitting construction of new churches. Religious orders were permitted to organize anew.

The disagreement between the Baltic communist authorities and Moscow was most evident in the debate regarding revision of religious legislation. The Baltic authorities solicited the input of the various churches. Proposals from the churches included recognition of conscientious objection to military service, anathema to Moscow at this time. With the ouster of Kharchev in 1989, the republican authorities abandoned any pretense of collaboration with Moscow on legal changes and religious policy in general.[43]

Although conditions were eased for all churches, political liberalization particularly benefited the national churches, as Table 1 indicates in the case of Latvian parishes. Individual church adherence correspondingly experienced a dramatic upsurge, as Table 2 illustrates in the case of Estonia. The Lutheran clergy, spread thin in the lean Brezhnev years, now were completely overwhelmed by the pent-up demand for their services. Even in Lithuania priests could hardly manage the increase.

The early support for religious liberty by the popular fronts did not translate into uniform church support for the popular front movements or warm relations with the popular front governments that eventually took power in 1990. Some feared a reversal of perestroika or were comfortable with the old ways; others were hopeful of incremental change under the new communists. Still others found the tempo of change too slow and advocated immediate independence.

In Estonia, the Lutheran Church assumed a standoffish attitude toward the Popular Front government of Edgar Savisaar. Numerous issues of contention arose between them. Pursuing autonomy from Moscow, the government abolished the plenipotentiary position and replaced it with an Office for Religious Affairs in the Ministry of Culture.[44] The church leadership saw this as deemphasizing religious issues by equating them with other aspects of culture and lobbied for an office directly subordinate to the prime minister's office. The other denominations were less upset with this outcome, fearing any attempt to link the Lutheran Church with the Estonian state. Another issue of contention was that of church property. In a case of strange bedfellows, the Lutheran Church hired Rein Ristlaan, former plenipotentiary of the last communist government in Tallinn, as a consultant in its claims for restitution for state expropria-

Table 2

Increase in Church Adherence During Liberalization
Estonian Evangelical Lutheran Church

	Baptisms	Confirmations	Contributors	Contributions (rubles)
1970	885	494	na	na
1980	712	654	na	na
1987	1,832	1,179	49,354	652,128
1988	4,534	2,711	50,510	853,061
1989	12,585	8,814	57,127	1,508,187
1990	18,608	11,691	63,891	2,069,773

Source: Burchard Lieberg, "Aus dem Leben der Ev.-Lutherischen Kirche Estlands," *Kirche im Osten,* vol. 33 (1990), p. 127, and vol. 35 (1992), p. 131.

tion of four hundred churches. The church was hardly in a financial position to maintain these churches, nor was the Savisaar government in a financial position to pay the compensation sought by the church. Finally, the Savisaar government sought to reintroduce religious instruction in the schools along the lines of a history of religions; the church, on the other hand, sought confessional instruction.

As indicated above, the Latvian Popular Front was more closely linked to church leaders, especially the "young turks" in Rebirth and Renewal. The opening congress of the Latvian Popular Front in 1988 included the first service in the Riga Cathedral since its expropriation in 1959. Former Prime Minister Ivars Godmanis attended the parish in which Juris Rubenis was pastor, permitting direct contact on an informal basis. The government formed a multireligious council that revised the draft liberal legislation, thereby weakening the role of the Department of Religious Affairs and removing reference to the "secular character" of the educational system.[45]

Yet even with this closer cooperation, differences arose between church and state. The government sought to avoid siding too closely with the Lutheran consistory in its disputes with splinter-group Lutherans. Led by Pastor Sigurds Sprogis of Liepaja, this group had supported Mesters earlier and rejected the authority of Gailitis, seeking to create an autonomous Lutheran Church. The consistory asked that the law be changed to preclude conferring juridical status on groups of fewer than ten parishes, rather than three as the original law had stipulated. The government refused to change the legislation, seeing this as an attempt to manipulate the government on behalf of the interests of one church. In the final analysis, the Sprogis faction did not obtain the requisite number of parishes and hence was not registered as a religious center.

Sajudis in Lithuania had the closest relations with the national church of any in the Baltics. Sajudis allocated representation to the Catholic Church at its congresses and sought to recruit priests as candidates. Although the church refused to permit priests to enter electoral competition, it actively supported Sajudis. Non-Catholics also gave strong support to the Sajudis movement: Sajudis's leader, Vytautas Landsbergis, is Reformed by background, and Emmanuelis Zingeris, former chair of the Foreign Relations Committee of the parliament, is Jewish. Polish Catholics, on the other hand, were less supportive of Sajudis. The historical tension between Poles and Lithuanians, manifested also in the Catholic Church, reduced the Poles' support for Lithuanian independence.[46]

Despite this broad-based national support, the Sajudis government clearly favored the Catholic Church. It signed an agreement with the church in 1990, approving church cultural and charitable work and obligating the state to subsidize its charitable organization, Caritas. Intervention by the Catholic hierarchy over the issue of religious instruction in schools resulted in a temporary delay in liberal legislation on the legal status of the churches.[47]

The churches played a key role in the drive for independence as well. As bearers of national culture, the churches not only facilitated the revival of national culture under perestroika but raised questions about the dangers of Russification. The 1989 synod that ousted Mesters also endorsed publication of the Molotov-Ribbentrop pact and supported the Popular Front. Lutheran Archbishops Pajula and Gailitis became identified with groups demanding rapid independence (the Estonian Congress and Latvian National Independence Movement, respectively). Their lobbying at the Lutheran World Federation (LWF) Assembly in Curitiba, Brazil, resulted in a strongly worded resolution favoring Baltic independence in 1990. They regularly appeared at rallies and on the public media in the context of the showdown with the Kremlin during 1990–91.[48]

The churches also promoted national independence by spinning off their pastoral efforts toward co-confessionals in other republics. The Estonian Lutheran Church turned over its responsibility for the Finnish parishes near Leningrad to the newly formed Finnish Lutheran Church.[49] More calculatingly, the Latvian Lutheran Church challenged the role of Harald Kalnins, the Latvian pastor entrusted with serving the Soviet Germans since 1968.[50] In spring 1991 Jonas Baronas, previously Kalnins's assistant, was ordained as dean in Leningrad by former Archbishop Mesters, oddly enough with Gailitis's blessing. Given Baronas's intention of forming an Evangelical Lutheran Church in Russia, Gailitis evidently hoped to bring an end to Kalnins's Riga-based, all-union organization constituted with Moscow's approval. Even the Catholic Church was affected: the Riga Seminary lost its role as the primary unionwide center for training non-Lithuanian priests when most non-Latvians transferred to the new seminary opened in 1990 in Grodno, Belorussia, thus permitting the reintroduction of Latvian instead of Russian as the language of instruction in the Riga Seminary.[51] Thus the Baltic national churches pursued policies designed to promote national independence and curtail church ties to the union.

In summary, the churches' roles in the period of liberalization differed considerably. To be sure, in all three republics the churches reinforced Western cultural traditions that supported alternative values, such as an emphasis on individual rights and toleration, and provided a basis for a restrained, democratic challenge to Soviet control. In all three republics the lifting of the totalitarian system also opened fissures that had been hidden earlier. But the Lithuanian Catholic Church represented an integral part of the Sajudis movement due to its status as a national church that retained great influence during the communist period. The Estonian Lutheran Church, on the other hand, had been greatly weakened as a national institution by Soviet rule. Because Russification had been less extensive than in Latvia, secularized intellectuals led the reform movement in Estonia, and the Estonian church became largely a beneficiary of the changes more than a driving force behind them. The Latvian Lutheran Church too had been weakened greatly, but the greater extensiveness of Russification of society and institutions left the church as one of the few distinctly Latvian institutions. It played a correspondingly greater role in promoting change than the Estonian church.

The Churches and Democratization Since Independence

Since independence in 1991 the Baltic churches have largely been preoccupied with overcoming the oppression of fifty years of communist rule: rebuilding the institutional church and accommodating the increase in church adherence. In the case of the Lutherans, they have also been preoccupied with internal factionalization. Moreover, as political parties have formed in the wake of the popular front movements, the churches' role as opposition has naturally diminished. The weakness of the new governments, on the other hand, has left them vulnerable to church claims for protection from foreign religions.

Their conservative character relative to Western churches—in both internal church affairs and issues of public policy—has become more obvious in the Baltic churches since independence. For example, the ordination of women, begun in the communist period in order to alleviate the severe shortage of pastors, has recently become an issue dividing the Latvian Lutheran Church, despite the fact that world Lutheranism has largely resolved the issue in favor of ordination. In all Baltic Lutheran churches there is a "Catholic" movement that opposes the liberal trends in Western Protestantism. Vatican II reforms have yet to be fully implemented in the Lithuanian Catholic Church. Ecumenical relations among the churches remain limited, in part due to ethnic differences.[52] This conservatism surely derives from their relative isolation in the Soviet period. But increased contact with Western churches since perestroika has convinced many of the decadence and sterility of Western Protestantism. They prefer to retain clear lines of authority, and they fear secularization.

As a result of this conservatism, as well as political differences, the churches' relations with the exile churches have remained lukewarm. A rapid process of merger between the exile churches and the home churches had been anticipated following the removal of communist barriers. This appeared particularly feasible in the case of Latvia following the microrevolution against Mesters in 1989. However, a merger has proved more problematic than anticipated: church leaders on both sides express disappointment over the differences in doctrine and style. The tension was played out in the January 1993 election to succeed the recently deceased Gailitis. Janis Vanags, a young pastor native to Latvia and strongly opposed to the ordination of women, narrowly defeated Elmars Rozitis, a more liberal leader from the exile church, in a controversial election that has divided the Latvian church and complicated a merger with the exile church.[53] In Estonia, where the continuation of Pajula as head of the Lutheran Church gave pause to exile Estonians, prospects were dimmer. Despite negotiations between the two churches, there has been no resolution. Pajula has recently named a bishop, Einars Soone, who aspires to become archbishop when Pajula retires, thus derailing the hopes of the young exile bishop of Toronto, Udo Peterson, to succeed Pajula as head of a unified Estonian church.

This cautious conservatism in church affairs extends as well to issues of public policy. The Catholic and Orthodox churches have, of course, opposed abortion; the Protestant churches are basically indifferent to the issue. Among Lutherans there has been some discussion regarding a rejection of capital punishment, but no official stance has been taken. Unlike its Western counterpart, the Estonian Methodist Church rejects the discussion of political issues, preferring a pietist orientation similar to the Baptist Church. The Estonian Lutheran Church does not even have a committee dealing with social-political questions, a standard feature of Lutheran synods elsewhere.

Regarding relations with the Russian minority and with Russia itself, the churches have assumed an ambivalent posture. On the one hand, the Lutheran churches have sought to moderate anti-Russian attitudes in the population. Shortly after the failed coup, Pajula called for "mutual understanding among the residents of various nationalities," and the Latvian church supported protection of the human rights of Russians. But the Latvian church opposed citizenship for retired Soviet military personnel, and both churches have avoided applying the general commitment to human rights to the controversial proposals regarding citizenship. Moreover, the national churches have laid claim to a special role in the national renaissance. A prominent Estonian pastor/politician claimed, for example, that "historically seen, we Estonians were tied culturally to the Lutheran Church. Even the communists understood that."[54]

Like other sectors of society, the churches have been greatly affected by the economic upheaval. Despite increases in membership, high inflation has left many pastors below the official poverty line and forced the churches to appeal for aid from Western churches. Western aid has been both multilateral, in particular from the Lutheran World Federation and various German Lutheran organizations, as well as bilateral from sister churches.[55] Ad hoc aid to individual parishes by foreign partners has expanded greatly, increasing their autonomy from the church headquarters and a concomitant inequality across Lutheran parishes. Despite the foreign assistance, the churches still rely on subsidies from the state. Efforts by the Estonian Supreme Council to curtail them met with opposition from the church, forcing at least temporary restoration. In Estonia 70 percent of the state funds go to the Lutheran Church, naturally a source of discontent to other denominations despite the Lutheran preeminence among believers.[56] Support for the theological faculties at the state universities in Tartu and Riga constitutes an indirect state subsidy for the churches. This financial dependence of the churches leaves them more closely tied to the state and, to a certain extent, impedes their ability to develop as autonomous organizations in civil society.

Another potential impediment to the democratization process is the loss of credibility due to previous ties to the Soviet regime and, more particularly, the security forces. Thus far this has not been the case in the national churches. The KGB files have been destroyed, returned to Russia, or remain closed to the public by the new governments. In some cases personnel decisions have been affected by suspicions of those close to the communist regime. For example, the fact that neither of the assistants to Cardinal Vaivods was selected by the Vatican as his successor suggests that it considered them suspect politically.[57] In any case the fact that both Lutheran churches were largely compromised by the communists and that neither one was instrumental in making the revolution suggests that these churches do not risk the plummet in prestige experienced by the East German church.[58]

The churches have contributed to democratization by providing party leadership in some cases. In part because of the apolitical stance of Pajula and the church leadership in Estonia, several pastors became personally involved in politics. In particular, activist pastors Illar Hallaste and Vello Jurjo formed the Christian Democratic Union and were elected to parliament in 1990. The prime minister of the conservative coalition government, Mart Laar, was also a Christian Democrat. Their emphasis on rapid independence and radical market reforms, as well as their ties to the CDU in Germany, suggest that it would be a mistake to view the Estonian Christian Democrats as a narrowly confessional party. In Latvia, on the other hand, no pastors have been elected to parliament until recently, suggesting that the main focus of their political activity has been within the church itself. The Christian Democrats in Latvia are weak, winning only six seats in the recent elections. Similarly, the Lithuanian Christian Democrats are weakly represented. Unlike its counterpart in East Germany, the church proved a limited source for the recruitment of political leadership.

Relations between the national churches and nonnational churches pose a potential minefield for the democratization process. As indicated above, the Orthodox Church was viewed as the extension of Moscow's influence in these republics. As the church of the immigrant population, it could be expected to defend their interests in the face of pressures to forcibly repatriate or deny citizenship to the nonindigenous ethnic groups, producing tension with the national churches. In the case of Lithuania, the tension has been limited. The Sajudis government registered the Society of Russian Orthodox Religious Education and accepted the continued subordination of the Orthodox Church to Moscow. In part this outcome may be attributed to the vocal support for Sajudis and Lithuanian independence by Archbishop Khrizostom. Of course, it also reflects the relatively minimal threat posed by the small Russian minority. Nonetheless, recent Orthodox protests against religious instruction in the schools indicate that sources of tension do exist.[59] The Poles in Lithuania have expressed greater concern about their minority rights and greater preference for the former communists. Theoretically, the Catholic Church should transcend these ethnic divisions, but resentment of the historical Polish influence in the church hampers its role as a mediator. The caution of Pope John Paul II on his recent trip to Lithuania confirms the tenuousness of relations.[60] Finally, the government of Vytautas Landsbergis showed itself insensitive to the Jewish minority and Holocaust victims with its initially blanket reversal of Soviet wartime convictions.[61]

In Estonia, Orthodox-Lutheran relations were initially good during the early phase of perestroika but have soured since independence. Many ethnic Estonians profess Orthodoxy, including some leaders in the independence struggle.[62] Although subject to Moscow, the Estonian Orthodox Church was long led by Metropolitan Aleksii, an Estonian of German origin (on his father's side; Russian origin on his mother's side). When Aleksii was chosen patriarch in 1988 it was expected that he would be supportive of the striving for greater freedom in the Baltics. But even under the Savisaar government, problems developed. Aleksii urged participation in the union referendum called by Gorbachev in March 1991, rather than the earlier Estonian referendum, provoking protest from Estonia.[63] Since the failed coup, Aleksii has sought to prevent separation of the Estonian Orthodox Church from the Moscow Patriarchate and subordination to Constantinople. In an effort to relieve political pressure for this shift—manifested in continued lack of clarity regarding property rights—the Moscow Patriarchate moved in 1992 to grant autonomy in nontheological matters to the Estonian and Latvian Orthodox churches.[64]

Similarly problematic for the development of freedom of religion seems to be the "tendency by nationalist leadership to use legislation to promote the spiritual hegemony of 'traditional faiths.' "[65] In Lithuania, the Catholic Church vetoed the creation of a Christian college proposed by Western Protestants and rejected even the offer of the Polish Catholic Church to supply priests for the Polish minority. In Latvia, Archbishop Gailitis declared that "we do not need such prophets from America," maintaining that foreign missionaries "import spiritual chaos to Latvia."[66] The Estonian government ousted an Indian cult leader on charges of sexual abuse of followers. The International Society for Krishna Consciousness, long rejected for registration by former communist authorities, is active but does not appear to qualify as a "traditional Lithuanian church" protected by the new constitution.[67] Under a narrow interpretation of its legislation,

Latvia has delayed the registration of nontraditional religions for three years "for the purpose of becoming acquainted with them" and signed an agreement with the Lutheran Church creating military chaplains in order to "create defense forces with faith in God and unite the people in love of the fatherland."[68] Under the new Estonian law religions must have their centers in Estonia in order to enjoy legal status. Thus, although freedom of religion remains strong, the national churches appear to be demonstrating their political influence regarding the nonnational and nontraditional religions. The relative fragility of the newly elected governing coalitions certainly leaves them vulnerable to such influence.

Recent electoral shifts in the Baltic states have not affected the church-state relationship uniformly.[69] The 1992 victory of the former communists in Lithuania sent a shock to the Catholic Church. In a pastoral letter prior to the election, the church's opposition to Algirdas Brazauskas and his Democratic Labor Party was clear. But the hierarchy quickly shifted to emphasize support for the outcome. For his part, Brazauskas embraced the church, meeting quickly with Archbishop Sigitas Tamkevicius and greeting the impending visit of the pope.[70] Unlike the situation in Poland, where a similar reversal occurred in 1993, the defeat of Sajudis can be attributed to the economic crisis and the popular perception that Brazauskas could better maintain economic ties with Russia. The power and conservative social agenda of the Catholic Church—a major factor in the Polish outcome—was of secondary importance in Lithuania.[71]

In Latvia and Estonia, on the other hand, the popular front governments that won independence were turned out of office not by former communists but by center-right coalitions. The Estonian victory of Mart Laar's Fatherland coalition has ushered in a government more congenial to the interests of the Lutheran Church.[72] Responding to Lutheran criticism of the Savisaar government, Laar upgraded the status of the church by moving the state Office for Religious Affairs from the jurisdiction of the Ministry of Culture to the Ministry of Interior and naming a lay leader in the church to head it. A relatively liberal Law on Churches and Congregations was passed by parliament in 1993. It focuses on the rights of citizens and church organizations, makes no mention of religious instruction in the schools, and guarantees no subsidies for the churches.

Tension with the Orthodox Church has increased since the election, however. The new law proscribes property ownership by churches whose administrative headquarters are not in Estonia. This was apparently targeted at continued subordination of the Estonian Orthodox Church to the Moscow Patriarchate and encouraged the Estonian Apostolic Orthodox Church in Exile, headquartered in Sweden, to seek registration and challenge the Estonian Orthodox Church for ownership of Orthodox Church property in Estonia. The Tallinn court has recognized Aleksii's Estonian Orthodox Church as legal successor to the precommunist Orthodox Church, but a key government official has rejected this claim.[73] Despite Aleksii's efforts to stop it, a schism in the Orthodox Church along ethnic lines is likely, with the Estonian Apostolic Orthodox Church representing the dwindling number of Orthodox Estonians and the Estonian Orthodox Church retaining the larger Russian minority.[74] Thus, the political disputes between the Russian minority and the government, for example, over the new citizenship law and voting rights, have spilled over into the religious sphere.

The effect of the June 1993 elections in Latvia is more difficult to ascertain. One early casualty of the elections was the head of the Department for Religious Affairs, Alfreds Kublinskis, a former communist who retained his post under the Godmanis government. A schism similar to that in Estonian Orthodoxy has developed, although current government policy seems more neutral than in Estonia. It is likely that the government will now be somewhat less secular in orientation, but two factors militate against a neo-Constantinian outcome in Latvia: the plural religious context in which Lutherans, Catholics, and Orthodox are roughly equal in strength; and the low profile of clergy in the parliament, unlike the situation in Estonia.[75]

The national churches in the Baltics have thus been on the defensive, despite the increase in religiosity among the population and the lifting of the communist straitjacket on their activities. They have been preoccupied with rebuilding the institutional church, relying heavily on Western assistance, particularly in the cases of Estonia and Latvia. But their fundamental conservatism and national orientation clashes with their co-confessionals in the West, with sects from the West and the East and, to a lesser extent, with the Russian Orthodox Church. Working in favor of the Lutheran churches is their secondary role in the downfall of communism, making a collapse of credibility in public opinion unlikely.

Conclusions

It would be wrong to expect the churches to spearhead the democratization process in the Baltics. Only in the case of Lithuania was the Catholic Church crucial in the overthrow of communism; in Latvia the Lutheran Church helped catalyze segments of the national movement; in Estonia the church was largely on the sidelines. Moreover, most churches are too preoccupied with overcoming the legacy of communist oppression of religion and the church and coping with economic turmoil to pursue the longer-term interests of society. Some are confronted with nascent schisms and internal divisions as well, which impede the development of a unified position.

Nor did the churches function particularly well as training grounds for democracy. They were rather hierarchical in structure; even the Lutheran and Baptist churches tended to be centralized and elitist. The Lithuanian Catholic Church was hierarchical but developed a vibrant grassroots movement of dissent that was more conducive to democratic skills and attitudes. Certainly the general political abstinence under the communist regime helps one understand the apolitical tendency and social conservatism of the Protestant churches today. The centralization in the churches may have been an advantage in dealing with a totalitarian state, but it may not be conducive to democratization in the postcommunist setting.

Religion can only partially fill the moral vacuum left by the collapse of the communist belief system in Baltic society. The fact is that even before the communist period, Latvians and Estonians were not particularly religious. Since the advent of communism even Lithuania had begun to be highly secularized. The conditions of liberalization tend to favor the national churches, as the marginal members return to the fold, attracted on the basis of tradition rather than conviction. Yet this does not necessarily translate into greater influence for the church in society, much less in the political system.

A situation of relative confessional homogeneity, such as in Lithuania and Estonia, raises the possibility of an alliance of throne and altar, of neo-Constantinian relations between the dominant confession and the state. Yet the movement for independence from Moscow seemed to militate against this: in the face of outside threats from the hardliners in Moscow there was a premium on unity. Since independence, the external threat has diminished, permitting the assertion of church interests. And yet the splintering of the popular fronts into political parties of various hues since independence has certainly complicated any such alliance. In Latvia the plural religious situation even among ethnic Latvians makes such an alliance unlikely, although it does raise the prospect of confessionally based political parties.

Though the institutional churches were not the crucial factors in the demise of communism in the Baltics, they do represent components of the broader culture and did support the strengthening of national consciousness. As Walter Clemens has argued, the "national awakening throughout the Baltic in the 1980s was not a substitute for religion or some other ideology, for it occurred in tandem with a resurgence of traditional culture and religion."[76] Western Christianity in no small measure created a political culture in the Baltics very different from that obtaining in other parts of the former Soviet Union. It fostered values of individual responsibility and freedom and promoted high levels of literacy and cultural expression, dimensions quite manifest in the restrained yet persistent drive for independence. One may hope that these dimensions of the political culture will continue to inform the political discourse in these newly independent democracies.

Notes

I wish to thank Karen Dawisha and Bruce Parrott for their helpful comments on the draft of this chapter. Also I gratefully acknowledge the information and assistance provided by John Finerty of the Commission on Security and Cooperation in Europe, Hilja Kukk of the Hoover Institution, Rebecca Ritke of Westview Press, Gerd Stricker of the institute Glaube in der 2. Welt in Zurich, and the Department of Religious Affairs, Latvian Republic.

1. V. Stanley Vardys, "The Role of the Churches in the Maintenance of Regional and National Identity in the Baltic Republics," in *Regional Identity Under Soviet Rule: The*

Case of the Baltic States, ed. Dietrich Andre Loeber et al. (Hackettstown, NJ: Institute for the Study of Law, Politics and Society of Socialist States, University of Kiel, 1990), pp. 151–64.

2. The following discussion of Soviet policy draws upon Robert F. Goeckel, "Soviet Policy Toward the Baltic Lutheran Churches and Their Role in the Liberalization Process," *Kirchliche Zeitgeschichte,* vol. 6, no. 1 (1993), pp. 120–38.

3. On the pre-Gorbachev era, see V. Stanley Vardys, *The Catholic Church, Dissent, and Nationality in Lithuania* (Boulder, CO: Westview Press, 1978); and Edgar C. Duin, *Lutheranism Under the Tsars and the Soviets,* vols. 1 and 2 (Ann Arbor, MI: University Microfilms, 1975).

4. Most church buildings had been unaffected by the law on nationalization of large buildings in 1941. As a result a new drive to nationalize property was undertaken in the Baltics in 1947–48. In Estonia and Latvia the state relied only on the implicit extension of the RSFSR Lenin decree to persuade the churches; by contrast, in Lithuania resistance by the Catholic Church necessitated the promulgation of special republican legislation to accomplish nationalization. Kivi to Pusepp and Karotamm, "Predstoiashchie zadachi, 1947," memorandum, f. R–1989, o. 2, d. 5, l. 79–85, Estonian State Archives.

5. The Lutheran churches were permitted after Stalin's death to publish an annual calendar that highlighted major developments in church life but also noted the propagandistic holidays of the state.

6. The theological faculties at the universities in Tartu and Riga were closed in 1940. This affected in particular the Lutheran churches, which lost approximately half of their clergy due to emigration and deportation. Lithuanian Catholic priests, on the other hand, showed less propensity to emigrate than Lutheran pastors. The Catholic seminary in Vilnius was closed, but the one in Kaunas remained open.

7. Prewar Lutheran churches had active ties to ecumenical organizations. Karpov and Polianski to Kivi and Korsakov, memorandum no. 616s, 24 July 1948, (f. R–1989, o. 2, d. 8, l. 129–129r, Estonian State Archive) reports on the Russian Orthodox meeting condemning the World Council of Churches and pressuring the Baltic Lutherans to reject participation.

8. For example, the Riga Cathedral was converted into a concert hall in 1959, the Vilnius Cathedral into an art gallery. Exorbitant revaluation of church property for insurance purposes forced the closing of many churches; arbitrary tax assessments on clergy hurt clergy replacement.

9. The visit of Hungarian officials to Estonia was used to publicize the success of the secular rites, as discussed in Kuroedov to Central Committee, CPSU, memorandum no. 3002, 26 December 1968, f. 5, o. 60, d. 24, 1. 178–80, Central Depository for Contemporary Documentation (former Central Committee archive). The final scholarship by Baltic researchers of "scientific atheism" is found in Otdel propagandi i agitatsii TsK KP Estonii et al., *Ideologiia i praktika sovremennogo liuteranstva* (Tallinn, 1987, pamphlet).

10. Other Lutheran churches in the Soviet bloc reflected theologically on their situation and attempted to formulate a doctrinal justification of their stance: the East German church elaborated a doctrine of "church within socialism" or "church for others" in an effort to balance social criticism with general support for socialism; more dubiously, the Hungarian church leadership formulated a "theology of service," highlighting its greater subordination to the communist regime.

11. The exposure to Finnish tourists and television in part explains the greater levels of dissent in Estonia. Alexander R. Alexiev, *Dissent and Nationalism in the Soviet Baltic* (Santa Monica, CA: Rand, 1983), pp. 38–42; V. Stanley Vardys, "Polish Echoes in the Baltic," *Problems of Communism,* vol. 32, no. 4 (July–August 1983), pp. 21–34. On youth alienation, see *RFE Situation Reports* (Baltic), no. 1 (27 January 1986), pp. 5–15.

12. On environmentalism, see *RFE Situation Reports* (Baltic), no. 6 (26 July 1985), pp. 9–23. Regarding the issue of peace, see Rein Taagepera, "Citizens' Peace Movement in the Soviet Baltic Republics," *Journal of Peace Research,* vol. 23, no. 2 (1986), pp. 183–92.

13. For example, he defended human rights and criticized Soviet actions in Afghanistan and Poland, as well as the proscription of religious instruction of youth. Michael Bourdeaux, *The Gospel's Triumph Over Communism* (Minneapolis: Bethany Publishers, 1991), pp. 148–49. *RFE Situation Reports* (Baltic), no. 4 (23 April 1985), pp. 13–15. Speaking about the USSR, Motsnik blamed "the worldwide threat of war and our fear for the future . . . on the evil that abides in our laws." Another pastor who decried Russification and called for a national renaissance in Estonia, Vello Salum, was more fortunate: his sermons were published abroad, but he was not ousted from his post.

14. Under state pressure, the church hierarchy forced Motsnik to resign his position; shortly thereafter he was arrested and later "recanted" his ideas and was exiled to Sweden.

15. Jurjo was briefly arrested in 1983 but was allowed to return to church service, albeit in a different parish. A Society for Protection of Historical Monuments, with latent nationalist goals, was also founded in Estonia.

16. Romuald Misiunas and Rein Taagepera, *The Baltic States: Years of Dependence, 1940–1990,* 2d ed. (Berkeley: University of California Press, 1993), pp. 84–85.

17. Bourdeaux, *Gospel's Triumph,* pp. 134–138.

18. Liepa to Puzin, "Otchetno-informatsionyi doklad 1962," no. 4, 19 February 1963, (f. 1448, o. 1, d. 262, l. 15–17, Latvian State Archive) discusses the manipulation involved in promoting Vaivods.

19. Initially, for example, the regime favored the Baptists in Estonia and Latvia by giving them church buildings that had previously belonged to the Lutherans.

20. The Lutheran Church certainly encouraged this shift in policy, arguing that attacks on Lutheranism would only lead to an increase in these more dangerous sects. Archbishop Jaan Kiivit, quoted in "Informatsionyi otchet . . . 1. iulia 1949," no. 38/0527, 6 July 1949, f. 1, o. 14, d. 37, l. 122–24, Estonian State Archive (Party Filial).

21. The creation under Stalin of two separate organizations—the Council for the Affairs of the Russian Orthodox Church and the Council for the Affairs of Religious Cults—for dealing with religious organizations reinforced the preeminence of the Orthodox Church in official policy.

22. "Informatsiia o polozhenii tserkvi v Latvii," communication to the author by the Department for Religious Affairs, Republic of Latvia, 20 October 1993.

23. Republican officials nominally supported immigration but feared a concomitant "enlivening of religion." Goeckel, "Soviet Policy Toward the Baltic Lutheran Churches," pp. 8–9.

24. The Teutonic Knights had conquered and Christianized the areas of modern-day Latvia and Estonia. Under Russian occupation the Baltic German landlords retained their political and economic control over the local population. In the Lutheran churches, German influence extended even into the period of independence. German occupation during World War II did little to rectify the image problem of the Germans in the Baltic region.

25. A decision at the highest level in Moscow was necessary in order to approve Kalnins's pastoral work with these Germans after 1968, eventually leading to registration of parishes and the establishment of an ecclesiastical framework in the 1980s. Republican opposition is indicated in Liepa to Titov, memorandum no. 2/169, 1 March 1977, f. 1448, o. 3, d. 17, l. 142–44, Latvian State Archive.

26. See Robert F. Goeckel, *The Lutheran Church and the East German State: Political Conflict and Change Under Ulbricht and Honecker* (Ithaca, NY: Cornell University Press, 1990), especially the concluding chapter, pp. 274–98.

27. Vardys, "The Role of the Churches," pp. 151–52. Making a similar argument of civil religion is Andrew Hart, "The Role of the Lutheran Church in Estonian Nationalism," *Religion in Eastern Europe,* vol. 13, no. 3 (1993), pp. 6–12.

28. Sabrina Petra Ramet, "Religious Policy in the Era of Gorbachev," in *Religious Policy in the Soviet Union,* ed. Sabrina Petra Ramet (Cambridge: Cambridge University Press, 1993), pp. 31–52.

29. Kharchev had favored rapid legal changes and sought to purge the CRA of KGB agents, engendering opposition. For detailed discussion of the "Kharchev affair," see John Dunlop, " 'Kharchev Affair' Sheds New Light on Severe Controls on Religion in USSR," *Report on the USSR,* vol. 2, no. 8 (23 February 1990), pp. 6–9; and Jane Ellis, "Some Reflections About Religious Policy Under Kharchev," in Ramet, ed., *Religious Policy in the Soviet Union,* pp. 84–104, especially pp. 91–103.

30. Sajudis was formed on 3 June 1988 as an umbrella movement of various groups, including Christians, environmentalists, and intellectuals, among others. Like the other Baltic popular fronts, its initial goals were to support the process of perestroika, including religious freedom, but it focused increasingly on national autonomy and eventually complete independence. See Bourdeaux, *Gospel's Triumph,* pp. 138–48. Senn emphasizes the initial distance between Sajudis and the church hierarchy. Alfred Erich Senn, *Lithuania Awakening* (Berkeley: University of California Press, 1990), pp. 66–70.

31. Livija Johnson, untitled paper presented at the Southwest Political Science Association, Austin, TX, spring 1992, p. 16.

32. Mesters had served in the Red Army in World War II and received awards for this service. The state also proposed Mesters as pastor at the 1980 Olympics in Moscow, an indication of his favored status, according to Sakharov to Fitsev, memorandum no. 618, 23 August 1979, f. 1419, o. 3, d. 198, l. 123, Latvian State Archive.

33. Kokars-Trops to Kharchev, letter no. 282, 12 August 1987, l. 40–50, Correspondence of the Plenipotentiary of the CRA, LSSR. The church leadership succumbed to the state pressure to oust Plate, but his parish in Kuldiga refused to accept the decision.

34. Walter Sawatsky, "Protestantism in the USSR," in Ramet, ed., *Religious Policy in the Soviet Union,* pp. 335–37; Bourdeaux, *Gospel's Triumph,* pp. 152–57.

35. Unlike earlier elections, an opposing candidate was permitted by the regime. Pajula had been favored by the regime with a study tour to West Germany in 1957 and was closely identified with the pro-regime course of his predecessor, Edgar Hark.

36. *Glaube in der 2. Welt,* vol. 18, no. 7/8 (July–August 1990), pp. 4–5.

37. A consistory spokesman was quoted as saying that participation in the Popular Front was not "a matter of the church," since pastors cannot afford the time to participate. *Informationsdienst für Lutherischen Minderheitskirchen in Europa,* no. 5/1989 (12 May 1989), pp. 14–16.

38. Kalvanas's close association with the Latvian Lutheran Church, in particular the late Janis Matulis (archbishop from 1968 to 1985), hurt his image among nationalistic Lithuanians, who in any case identified the Lutheran Church with German domination.

39. For an insightful review of the liberalization of religious policy in the Baltics under perestroika, see Bourdeaux, *Gospel's Triumph,* pp. 141–58.

40. Sawatsky, "Protestantism in the USSR," p. 337. For example, the plenipotentiary for religious affairs in Estonia, Oya, was replaced by Rein Ristlaan in 1988. Although Ristlaan had a reputation as a hardliner while ideological secretary of the Estonian CP under Karl Vaino, he pursued a very liberal policy toward the churches during his brief tenure as plenipotentiary until spring 1990, causing some to view him as opportunistic.

41. Ramet, ed. *Religious Policy in the Soviet Union,* p. 37.

42. These local committees, formed in the 1960s to oversee legality at the local level, primarily monitored sermons for antistate or ideological deviations by the clergy. It is not

clear how effectively they functioned, even in the 1960s, but they doubtless had a chilling effect on sermons.

43. In 1988 Estonia awaited "with great hopes" the new union legislation, but by mid-1989 it unilaterally drafted its own new legislation, as reported in Ristlaan to Khristoradnov, "Informatsionnyi otchet za 1990 god," no. 3497, 13 February 1990, l. 18, working archives, Office for Religious Affairs, Estonian Republic. Lithuania liberalized its constitution already in November 1989, a full year before the union. *Glaube in der 2. Welt,* vol. 18, no. 1 (January 1990), p. 4. Latvia passed liberal legislation in September 1990.

44. *Glaube in der 2. Welt,* vol. 18, no. 12 (December 1990), p. 4.

45. The Law of the Latvian Republic, "On Religious Organizations of 11 September 1990," found in Paul Roth, *Die Religionsgesetze der Sowjetunion* (Munich: Kirche im Not, 1992), pp.151–56, analyzed on pp. 50–52.

46. For example, Sajudis's first congress was composed of 96 percent Lithuanians and only 0.9 percent Poles, according to Stanley Vardys, *Lithuania: The Rebel Nation* (Boulder: Westview Press, forthcoming), p. 195.

47. Ernst Benz, "Neue Freiheit nach langer Unterdrückung: Die Kirchen in den baltischen Staaten," *Herder Korrespondenz,* vol. 46, no. 1 (January 1992), p. 37. According to members of the consultative committee, the Catholic Church initially cooperated with other denominations in drafting the legislation but then pressed for confessional instruction instead.

48. *Glaube in der 2. Welt,* vol. 19, no. 3 (March 1991), pp. 5–6. The Riga Cathedral served as a first aid station for those wounded in the OMON attacks in January 1991.

49. The regime had approved Estonian jurisdiction over these previously unregistered parishes in the 1970s, in the context of the special confessional and linguistic relationship between the Estonian and Finnish churches. The parishes provided tinder for disputes between the state officials in Leningrad Oblast and Estonia.

50. Kalnins had been permitted by Soviet authorities to assume the title of bishop in 1988 and formed a German Evangelical Lutheran Church of the Soviet Union with its chancellory in Riga. Ironically, this new organization immediately became increasingly anomalous in the context of the Baltic drive for independence in 1990–91. *Glaube in der 2. Welt,* vol. 19, no. 5 (May 1991), p. 9.

51. The LWF and the German Lutheran churches, as well as the Vatican, had promoted this extrarepublican role for Latvia during the communist period. But under liberalizing conditions, the Lutheran actions reflected *Latvian* national assertion; the Catholic changes, however, were due to a shift in *Vatican* strategy and detente with the Kremlin, facilitating the extension of Polish Catholic influence in Belarus and other areas of the former Soviet Union. *Glaube in der 2. Welt,* vol. 19, no. 3 (March 1991), p. 6.

52. Archbishop Janis Vanags, elected in 1993 to succeed Gailitis, who died in November 1992 in an auto accident, opposes the ordination of women. Plate has always exhibited "Catholic" tendencies in his celebration of the liturgy. In Estonia this has become increasingly fashionable as well. For a broad discussion of the internal problems facing the Latvian church, see Klaus Friedrich, "Lettlands Kirche und die Freiheit," *Glaube in der 2. Welt,* vol. 20, no. 11 (November 1992), pp. 19–24; Gerd Stricker, "Umstrittene Frauenordination," *Glaube in der 2. Welt,* vol. 21, no. 6 (June 1993), pp. 20–24.

53. Criticism of the election has focused on the failure of Vanags to obtain an absolute majority of voting representatives and the necessity of amending the church constitution in order to permit his candidacy, since he was ordained only seven years ago. In an overture to the exile church, Vanags has foregone the title "archbishop" for that of "bishop," permitting a potential election of a single archbishop for both exile and native churches in the future. *Herder Korrespondenz,* vol. 47, no. 9 (September 1993), p. 452.

54. *Glaube in der 2. Welt,* vol. 20, no. 1 (January 1992), pp. 4, 8; *Informationsdienst für Lutherischen Minderheitskirchen,* no. 6/1992 (1 July 1992), pp. 9–10.

55. In 1992 the Latvian church appealed to its parishes to maintain their pastors' salaries above the poverty level, according to *Glaube in der 2. Welt,* vol. 20, no. 3 (March 1992), p. 6. The Finnish Lutheran Church has continued its special relationship with the Estonian church, funding church construction, training religion instructors for the schools, and providing theological faculty through Finnchurchaid. Latvia lacks such a "natural" partner but has received aid from Germany and Sweden.

56. Interview with Jaan Kiivit Jr., 3 August 1993; *Glaube in der 2. Welt,* vol. 21, no. 4 (April 1993), p. 4.

57. *Glaube in der 2. Welt,* vol. 19, no. 6 (June 1991), p. 9; Benz, "Neue Freiheit nach langer Unterdrückung," p. 35.

58. The East German and Polish churches enjoyed great prestige on the basis of their apparent challenge to the communist regime. In East Germany and Russia revelations of complicity with the secret police have damaged the churches' credibility. Archbishop Khrizostom, head of the Lithuanian Orthodox Church, has admitted ties to the KGB in a recent interview but defended his actions as engagement for church interests. Michael Pozdnyaev, "Ich war kein Spitzel," *Glaube in der 2. Welt,* vol. 20, no. 5, (May 1992), pp. 15–17.

59. Letter to *Ekho Litvy,* 2 February 1993, reflecting Khrizostom's opposition to the teaching of theology in the schools.

60. *New York Times,* 7 and 11 September 1993. The pope avoided the extemporaneous use of Polish during his visit to Lithuania. Charges of discrimination have been made both by Poles in Lithuania and Lithuanians in Poland, according to *Glaube in der 2. Welt,* vol. 20, no. 1 (January 1992), pp. 25–26.

61. For a discussion of the historical role of Jews in the Baltics and their relationship with the independence movements, see Anatol Lieven, *The Baltic Revolution: Estonia, Latvia, Lithuania and the Path to Independence* (New Haven: Yale University Press, 1993), pp. 139–58.

62. For example, Rein Helme, historian and now chair of the Defense Committee of the parliament, is Orthodox. Konstantin Pats, last president in interwar Estonia, was reburied in an Orthodox ceremony with national symbolism.

63. Aleksii's role is analyzed in Gerd Stricker, "Patriarch Aleksy im Gleichklang mit Gorbachev," *Glaube in der 2. Welt,* vol. 19, no. 2 (February 1991), pp. 26–32.

64. *Herder Korrespondenz,* vol. 47, no. 9 (September 1993), pp. 453–54; *Glaube in der 2. Welt,* vol. 20, no. 10 (October 1992), p. 4. The Holy Synod invoked the 1920–21 decisions of Patriarch Tikhon as justification and named Bishop Kornilii and Bishop Aleksandr as heads of the autonomous churches of Estonia and Latvia, respectively.

65. "Human Rights and Democratization in Estonia," Report of the Commission on Security and Cooperation in Europe, Washington, D.C., September 1993, p. 4.

66. *Baltic Independent,* 25–31 October 1991, p. 6; *Glaube in der 2. Welt,* vol. 21, no. 5 (May 1993), p. 5. During his recent visit, the pope admonished Lithuanians to forswear sects, fearing defections to evangelical Protestantism. *New York Times,* 7 September 1993.

67. On the International Society for Krishna Consciousness, see Oxana Antic, "The Spread of Modern Cults in the USSR," in Ramet, ed., *Religious Policy in the Soviet Union,* pp. 252–72. Article 43 of the Constitution of the Republic of Lithuania, printed in *Lituanus,* vol. 39, no. 1 (1993), p. 15.

68. "Informatsiia o polozhenii tserkvi v Latvii." The Latvian authorities also seem more concerned with the loyalty of Baptists and Pentecostals in Latvia, who often came from other republics and now use Latvia as a base for proselytizing and aiding other

former republics. Regarding the military chaplaincy, see *Sweetdeenas Rihts* (Riga), 9 May 1993, pp. 3–5, and 21 February 1993, p. 3.

69. On the political developments since independence, see Anatol Lieven, *The Baltic Revolution,* pp. 255–373.

70. The pastoral letter expressed doubt that former communists had undergone a change of heart until they made "a public condemnation of all crimes" and a "restitution for all suffering." See *Glaube in der 2. Welt,* vol. 20, no. 11 (November 1992), p. 4; *Herder Korrespondenz,* vol. 47, no. 9 (September 1993), pp. 450–51.

71. Indeed, Cardinal Sladkevičius sought to distance the Lithuanian church from the "Polish model" by saying that "in Poland the church identifies too closely with the state. We certainly do not want that." See *Glaube in der 2. Welt,* vol. 20, no. 4 (April 1992), p. 4.

72. *Glaube in der 2. Welt,* vol. 20, no. 12 (December 1992), p. 4.

73. Ernst Benz, "Probleme der estnischen Orthodoxen Kirche nach der Unabhängigkeit," *Information und Berichte: Digest des Ostens,* March 1993, pp. 10–16.

74. The Law of Churches and Congregations, passed by the State Assembly on 20 May 1993 and promulgated by President Lennart Meri on 8 June 1993, published in *Riigi Teataja,* I, no. 30 (15 June 1993), item 510, pp. 721–26, especially art. 21, para. 2. Regarding the schism, *WPS* (What the Press Is Saying), 27 September 1993, quoting *Estoniia,* 10 September 1993; *Herder Korrespondenz,* vol. 47, no. 9 (September 1993), pp. 453–54; and *Glaube in der 2. Welt,* vol. 21, no. 6 (June 1993), p. 5.

75. In the previous parliament, only one clergyman was represented. The election of Aida Predele, editor of the Lutheran church newspaper, and Visvaldis Klive, an American-Latvian instructor at the Theological Faculty, assures that church interests will be represented in the new parliament. Lieven, *The Baltic Revolution,* p. 290.

76. Walter C. Clemens Jr., *Baltic Independence and Russian Empire* (New York: St. Martin's, 1991), p. 7. See also Ernest Gellner, "Ethnicity and Faith in Eastern Europe," *Daedalus,* vol. 19, no. 1 (winter 1990), pp. 287–90.

III

The Southern
Newly Independent States

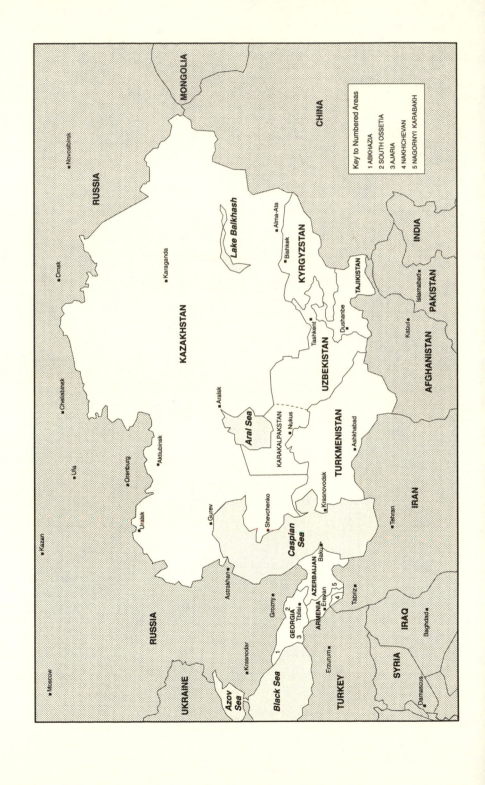

Key to Numbered Areas

1 ABKHAZIA
2 SOUTH OSSETIA
3 AJARIA
4 NAKHICHEVAN
5 NAGORNYI KARABAKH

11

Religion and Politics in the Caucasus

Rafik Osman-Ogly Kurbanov and
Erjan Rafik-Ogly Kurbanov

With the collapse of the Soviet Union, the relationship between religion and politics in the Caucasus, and their combined effect on civil strife, assumed greater significance. Governments, political parties, and movements of the Caucasus, as well as neighboring countries, have begun to take elements of religion into consideration in their search for internal and external support.

The emergence of new alliances and unions on a religious basis can lead to completely new political divisions in this and neighboring regions. However, the current political developments demonstrate that after many years of suppression of religion in the region, which previously had been under Moscow's control for a century and a half, the weight of religion in politics is not very heavy. The possibility of realizing political unions based on religion is weak.

At the same time, a revival of religion is indeed taking place, leading some observers to argue that at the present time such regional superpowers as Beijing and Moscow feel the necessity to unify their efforts in preventing the creation of regional "axes" of unions on a Turkic or Islamic basis in order to keep the current balance of power.[1]

The Armenian-Azerbaijani War

It is worth noting, especially in connection with the current Armenian-Azerbaijani war, that the ancient history of Christianity and Islam in the Caucasus has acquired some political importance.

One of the oldest Christian states of the Caucasus, Caucasian Albania, came into existence in the sixth century B.C. and existed for ten centuries as a unitary state. After the second century A.D., the official religion of this state became

Christianity. Many scholars confirm the existence of an independent Albanian church. The Caucasian Albans, some of the ancient ancestors of ethnic Azerbaijanis, were in fact Christians. Their religion differed from the Armenian-Gregorian branch of Christianity, and they had an independent catholicos in Karabakh at Gandzasar.

After the Arab Khalifat took control over Azerbaijan in the seventh century, he supported the Armenian church and increased its influence in the region. Eventually the independent Alban catholicos was dismissed, and later the Alban catholicoses were elected only with the approval of the Armenian catholicos. Since then, the Armenian-Gregorian branch of Christianity came to dominate the Albano-Chalcedon branch, and after the Islamization of Caucasian Albania, what was left of the Albanian church merged with the Armenian church. Eventually, the Christian Albans were "Armenianized."[2]

Noticeably, in Soviet times, official Azerbaijani historians declared the beginning of Azerbaijani statehood after the seventh century, with the Islamization of Azerbaijan. Therefore the previous period was somehow "left" to the Armenian side, which claimed that the Christianity of Caucasian Albans proves that they were in reality Armenians. After the liberalization of the Soviet Union, many scholars in Azerbaijan began to challenge this approach.[3] Since the territory of Nagorno-Karabakh, a source of conflict between Azerbaijan and Armenia, is a part of historic Caucasian Albania, the history of religion in this area has acquired specific political importance.

Azerbaijan is the only former Soviet republic with a predominantly Shi'ite Muslim population. As Audrey Altstadt argues, the adoption of the Shi'ism branch of Islam by the Azerbaijani Turks (or Azerbaijanis) in the early sixteenth century led to a "twofold result: (1) a strengthening of the bonds with the Iranian state and what was by the 16th century its Turco-Persian culture . . . and (2) a sectarian division from other Turks. Realignment along ethnic lines would become a serious issue for Azerbaijani Turkish intellectuals in the 19th and 20th centuries."[4]

The acceptance of Christianity by the Armenian king Tiridates in 301 or 303 A.D. made Armenia the first country in history that had Christianity as a state religion. Traditionally strong connections between church and state led to a situation whereby during the absence of statehood the Armenian church played the role of "hidden state": when Armenians had no state of their own and were subjects of foreign invaders, the church was an active defender of the Armenian nation against forcible assimilation; it inspired the people to carry on the struggle against persecution and contributed to the development of Armenian culture. "The history of the Armenian church reflects the history of the nation."[5] The Armenian nation and Armenian church are related very closely.

As Ronald Suny argues, "Russian policy toward the Armenians fluctuated in the imperial period from declarations of protection for fellow Christians to persecution of a newly conscious national minority. The shifts in Russian perceptions of the Armenians were contingent on both the changes in Russia's interests in Caucasia and the developments taking place among the Armenians themselves."[6] While this can easily refer to any other ethnic group in the Caucasus, Armenians and the Armenian church always enjoyed more favored status than any other religious confession of the Caucasus. In 1779 the Russian empress granted Armenians living in Russia "rights and advantages equal to the Russians," and in 1836 the Russian tsar granted the Armenian church the special statute by which Armenians received full freedom of worship, control over their schools, and official recognition of their institutional autonomy.[7] In spite of periods of cold relations between the Russian government and the Armenian church, these relations were always on a much higher level than Russia's relations with the Muslim clergy.

The inclusion of Armenia into the Soviet Union in 1920 became a way for that country to avoid the danger of Turkish dominance. After that, the Armenian church was under as heavy pressure as any other religious confession in the communist state. However, the Moscow government and the Armenian church ultimately struck a compromise based partly on the church's willingness to support Moscow's policy toward foreign countries—particularly Turkey—and its ability to serve as a link between the USSR and the large Armenian diaspora.[8]

Consequently, the Armenian church had the opportunity to provide the most important basis for unity and cooperation of dispersed Armenians all over the world, and in this sense determined political support for Armenian policy in countries with a strong Armenian diaspora. The influence of the Armenian church became even stronger after the earthquake of 1988, when the efforts of the church to save people were much more successful than the "efforts" of the corrupt communist state officials at union and local levels.

The Armenian church was not suspected by any Armenian sources of possible collaboration with the communist authorities or the KGB during the Soviet era, a well-known predicament for other religious bodies in the former Soviet Union. The Armenian church's influence and status among political movements and ordinary Armenians was always very high. The leader of the church, Catholicos Vazgen I, was regarded by many as the true head of the nation.[9]

The Armenian-Azerbaijani conflict currently determines virtually all aspects of political life in both countries. This confrontation began in 1988 with Armenian demands for the incorporation of the territory of the Nagorno-Karabakh Autonomous Oblast within the Azerbaijani SSR into Armenia and eventually led to a full-scale war between the now independent states of Armenia and Azerbaijan. In its usual way, the mass media have described this conflict since its beginning as a conflict between Muslim Azerbaijanis and Christian Armenians. It can be considered an accurate description only in the sense that historically Armenians are Christians and Azerbaijanis are Muslims. However, this description implicitly attributes a simple explanation for these hostilities.

In the very beginning of the conflict, on 8 November 1988, several Armenian nationalists died in an accidental explosion while trying to blow up the famous monument Friendship of Peoples of the Transcaucasian Republics, which was situated at the intersection of the Armenian-Azerbaijani-Georgian borders. One of the persons who died was Stepan Davtian, abbot of the Makaravan Monastery of Armenia.[10] However, this event was an exception, and after that incident, priests from neither side participated in acts of violence.

This territorial dispute has little to do with religious animosities. In addition to radical nationalism and demographic trends, the borders established by Moscow in regions with heterogeneous populations, as well as manipulations by the central authorities, became sources of tension. The widespread tendency to explain this conflict as a result of confessional animosities is similar to understanding the Iran-Iraq war "in terms of Shi'i-Sunni differences and the threat of Shi'i revolt in Iraq, though the cause of fighting had much more to do with a straightforward dispute over territory."[11] Shireen Hunter argues that the main problem for this conflict "has never been religion but the lack of democracy. Thus, religious abuses that the Armenian community in NKAO [Nagorno-Karabakh Autonomous Oblast] suffered . . . were the consequence of the anti-religious dimension of Communism and not the anti-Christianism of Islam."[12] Other observers argue that while Islamic-Christian differences did contribute to tensions in the Caucasus, it would be an oversimplification to equate the sometimes negative impact of religious affiliation with the effect of religious institutions per se.[13]

The Karabakh conflict to some extent can be compared with the events in the former Yugoslavia, where territorial and ethnic disputes are painted in religious colors by participants and outside powers.

Each of the religious leaders of Armenia and Azerbaijan (Armenian Catholicos Vazgen I and Azerbaijani Sheikh ul-Islam Allakhshukur Pasha Zade) repeatedly rejected the idea of a religious element in this war and had several meetings attempting to reach a peaceful resolution. However, the lack of success of these attempts indicates that in spite of the high level of prestige of the religious leaders among their peoples, their influence on political decisions in the Caucasus is not great.

The North Caucasus

While the Azerbaijani and Armenian sides reject the religious element in their conflict, political movements among the mountain peoples of the North Caucasus often try to emphasize it. Among other reasons, history as well as the ethnic and social environment in this linguistically heterogeneous region play an important role.

Many observers on the subject of religion in politics in the region cite as an example the Iranian Islamic revolution, perhaps forgetting the role of Islam in the political history of the mountain peoples of the North Caucasus. According to historians, the Islamic religion played an integrative role in unifying the different peoples of the Caucasus under the green banner of Islam against Russian colonial policy in this region.[14]

The mountain peoples who belonged to the various linguistic groups (Turkish, Iranian, Ibero-Caucasian) were at different stages of their social development, ranging from the prefeudal clan to feudalism, and they had never been organized into a formal state. During the anticolonial war against the Russian Empire, the theocratic state came into existence, headed by Shamil, the legendary hero of the mountain peoples of the Caucasus. As he had been the imam (spiritual and political leader), the state came to be called Imamat. Under Shamil's leadership (1834–59) the mountain peoples of the Caucasus quite successfully fended off attacks from the much more powerful Russian military forces.

In the first years of communist rule, Marxist historians did not deny that the North Caucasian peoples viewed the Russian invaders as people of another faith and language and that Russia's Caucasian policy was in essence anti-Muslim and constituted outright colonial conquest (the so-called Pokrovskii line).

In the early 1930s, however, Soviet historians began to rewrite the history of the country, proceeding from a new conception of history ("the least evil" conception). Actually, this conception had been put forward by the first secretary of the Azerbaijan Communist Party, Mir Chafar Bagirov (a close friend of security police boss Lavrentii Beria), who condemned the scientific work of Azerbaijani Academician Heydar Huseynov (vice president of the Azerbaijan Academy of Sciences).[15] Huseynov was blamed just for mentioning in his monograph that Shamil was a national hero of the mountain peoples of the North Caucasus, thus justifying their struggle against Russian colonialism. After unbearable persecution Huseynov committed suicide.[16]

Official Soviet history after that began to regard Islam as the most reactionary of religious ideologies, and Muridism (a Muslim sect that carried out *gazzavat*— holy war against infidels under the leadership of Shamil) was severely condemned. The leaders of Muridism were declared to be "reactionary, nationalistic, and in the service of British capitalism and the Turkish Sultan."

According to the rewritten history, the annexation of new territories by the Russian Empire supposedly enabled the peoples of the Caucasus to subsequently gain national independence, the right for future self-determination in a federal socialist state, and the means to enjoy the fruits of socialism. The annexation was unconditionally considered an absolutely progressive phenomenon. Official Soviet historians proclaimed that the annexation of the North Caucasus was carried out voluntarily, even though in some cases it proceeded forcibly and the Russian colonial army often faced fierce resistance, especially from Caucasian Muslims. It followed then that national liberation movements of these peoples were reactionary. After the Twentieth Congress of the Communist Party of the Soviet Union in February 1956, however, the line laid down in history by Bagirov was changed, and Shamil was to some extent rehabilitated.

"Islamic Fundamentalism"

Under Russian and Soviet rule the Muslim peoples of the Caucasus were still under much stronger pressure than Christians. In the North Caucasus, Russian expansion met tenacious resistance from mountain tribespeople led by Shamil, whereas other Caucasian groups, particularly the Armenians but also the Georgians, viewed Russian expansion as a welcome counterweight against Turkish domination.[17] Historically, Christian nations of the Caucasus were considered by the Russian authorities as more trusted groups, and this tendency prevailed later on as well. For example, former KGB General Viktor Belozerov, who had served more than eleven years in Chechnia, witnessed severe coercion of Muslims there, while the Russian Orthodox Church enjoyed a more privileged status in this historically Muslim land.[18] In 1988 there were only twenty-seven mosques in Dagestan; at the beginning of the century there were more than eight hundred.

After Gorbachev's liberalization began, Muslims had the opportunity to exercise their religious rights. The revival of national culture and long-suppressed traditions necessarily led to the revival of Islam as a part of national culture. Interest in Islam grew quickly. The KGB and the nomenklatura reacted slowly and at the same time tried to avoid unification of the liberation movements of the people of the North Caucasus under a religious banner. At the same time, ethnic and territorial differences came to prevail. As a result, the Islamic movement in this region, which in the beginning seemed to be developing into a single political force, did not emerge as such. Ideological differences in the Islamic movement coincided with ethnic differentiation, which apparently was caused by political and economic competition among ethnic groups, not by ideological factors.[19]

The Kremlin's policy of painting the anti-Moscow forces in historically Muslim regions in colors of radical Islam and the term "Islamic fundamentalism" were often used by communist rulers in Moscow in their justification of the war in Afghanistan as a fight for the "progressive future of the Afghan working people" against "religious fanatics fed by the imperialist West." Later, the same manipulation was used as an excuse for suppressing different movements of historically Muslim people.

The first application of this label to the internal political force in the Soviet Union probably took place in 1990, when Gorbachev ordered the crushing of an anticommunist rebellion in Baku, Azerbaijan. He blamed the Azerbaijani Popular Front for attempts to overthrow Soviet power and to create an "Islamic republic."

During this upheaval the Soviet mass media repeatedly claimed that there were appeals by the "extremist forces" "for unification of northern and southern Azerbaijan under the banner of a united Islamic state."[20]

This argument was clearly groundless. The Soviet government knew that the prime orientation of the Popular Front of Azerbaijan, the major opposition force in the republic, was pro-Turkish: the religious element had never been significant in its policy. Shireen Hunter argues that there is "certainly no valid evidence which would support the accusation made by the Soviet authorities that the Azerbaijan national movement was a religious fundamentalist movement. . . . Islamically oriented groups . . . exist but mostly in clandestine form."[21] The Soviet government justified the invasion also as an attempt to save the lives of ethnic Armenians in Baku. The invasion, which independent reporters called an "organized shooting of peaceful people,"[22] was eventually supported by Western governments, including the Bush administration in the United States.

However, as many observers argue, neither radical Islam nor anti-Armenian pogroms were the main reasons for the Soviet military invasion; rather, the real reason was a genuine threat to the local communist boss Vezirov and to Moscow's control over Azerbaijan in general. "Gorbachev sent troops to Baku to shore up Communist power there, justifying that act with the barrage of excuses, playing on internal Soviet and Western misinformation and fears of a resurgent Islam."[23] It is likely that the anti-Armenian pogroms, as well as the portrayal of the Popular Front in "Islamic" colors, were initiated by the Soviet KGB with the goal of discreditation and arrest of the Front's leaders, who protested the corrupt regime that could not effectively deal with the political crisis in Azerbaijan. Hunter agrees that "there seems to be enough circumstantial evidence to support the thesis that some degree of manipulation by local and central authorities was indeed involved, both in Sumgait and Baku events."[24] The major initiator of such plans was probably Viktor Polianichko, then the second secretary of the Azerbaijani Communist Party, who openly encouraged Popular Front activists to use religious elements in their movement.[25]

Azerbaijan's Sheikh ul-Islam Allakhshukur Pasha Zade, together with Popular Front leaders, participated in negotiations with the communist authorities immediately before the Soviet military attack in an attempt to prevent bloodshed. Later, he rejected the claim that the Soviet invasion had anything to do with Islam. When Iranian spiritual leader Ayatollah Ali Khamenei declared that "anyone who thinks or pretends that the motives behind these movements are ethnic or nationalistic is making a big mistake,"[26] the Azerbaijani Muslim leader rejected this initial claim about religion as the source of the conflict.[27] Allakhshukur Pasha Zade openly opposed Moscow's brutal policy toward Azerbaijan, and his popularity in all spheres of Azerbaijani society grew quickly thereafter. Many of the democratic forces in Russia opposed Gorbachev's appeals to the "Islamic threat" as an excuse for the use of force.

Previously, the "anti-Soviet" label gave a sufficient rationale for suppression of the opposition, but Gorbachev greatly needed sympathy from the West for this action in the period of perestroika. The emphasis of the "Islamic threat" was clearly pointed at the West. Undoubtedly, the thesis of "Islamic fundamentalism" played an important role in the West's indifference to or even approval of this bloody invasion. The alleged threat of spreading radical Islam beyond Iranian borders was considered the most frightening scenario for many in the West, much more dangerous than Soviet or Russian expansion.

Currently, comparable events are going on in Tajikistan: the Russian mass media continue to call the Tajik opposition "Islamic fundamentalists" and argue that this in fact justifies Moscow's support of the authoritarian regime in Dushanbe. Thus, the labeling of opponent forces as "Islamic fundamentalists" in traditionally Muslim republics has been proven to work, and some political groups will definitely continue to use it in the future.

Georgia

The history of Christianity in Georgia began in 337 A.D., when shortly after Byzantium accepted Christianity, King Mirian of Karthli introduced Christianity as the state religion of Georgia. The Georgian Orthodox Church, one of the oldest branches of the Christian Orthodox Church, became self-governing in the fifth century and remained so until Georgia became part of Russia. The church was headed by the Georgian patriarch, the catholicos. The Russian tsarist government put an end to the independence of the Georgian church by placing it under the rule of the Holy Synod, the highest body in the administrative system of the Russian Orthodox Church. It was only after the 1917 October Revolution in Russia that the Georgian Orthodox Church regained its independence.

There are some cultural differences between eastern and western Georgia as a result of separate and influential historical events. When Arabs captured Tbilisi in 637, western Georgia remained under the control of the Byzantine Empire. In the sixteenth and seventeenth centuries, while eastern Georgia remained a vassal state of the Persian Empire, western Georgia came under the influence of the Turks. The two parts of Georgia were reunited in 1801 when annexed by Russia. As attested to in the current strife, former president Zviad Gamsakhurdia, who came from western Georgia (Mingrelia), continued his struggle against his successor Eduard Shevardnadze by exploiting the political and cultural rivalry between western and eastern Georgia.

After the revolution in Russia in 1917, Georgia became an independent state in 1918. The period of independence was very short. After the withdrawal of British forces from the Caucasus and Red Army advances, Georgia became a part of the communist Soviet Union.

As Stephen Jones argues, the first Georgian president, Zviad Gamsakhurdia, whose radical nationalism is well known, "considered the Georgian church the embodiment of Georgian nationhood. Despite a constitutional provision separating Church and State, Gamsakhurdia openly promoted the Christianization of the republic."[28] Ironically, after Gamsakhurdia lost power, he found shelter in Muslim Chechnia, started to promote the idea of a "Caucasian Home," and repeatedly appealed to the unity of Caucasian peoples. After his tragic death while fighting the Shevardnadze forces in Georgia, Gamsakhurdia was buried in Chechnia.[29]

The main political slogan of Gamsakhurdia's nationalistic policy of uniting all Georgians against non-Georgians, whom he called "temporary guests," was "Georgia for Georgians." The Meskhetian Turks deported from Georgia to Central Asia during World War II (in 1944) were not permitted by the Georgian government of Gamsakhurdia to return to their homeland. Moreover, six hundred thousand ethnic Azerbaijanis living in the Georgian Republic received no representation in the parliament. South Ossetia was officially renamed "Shida Karthli"—Georgian land. Academician Andrei Sakharov called Georgia then a "little empire."

Georgia's ethnic policies did little to ease the political situation. Many Azerbaijanis in Georgia, who reside in the regions bordering Azerbaijan, in consequence of Gamsakhurdia's policy were forced to leave the land where they had lived for many centuries.[30] The Georgian policy, which can be easily considered anti-Azerbaijani, according to Elizabeth Fuller, could well lead to interethnic bloodshed.[31] Moreover, as a result of anti-Islamic propaganda in the Georgian media, in which the Meskhetian Turks have been associated in the Georgian mass consciousness with Turkish Muslims—"aggressors" and "historical enemies" of Georgian and Christian culture—the evicted Turks are now facing greater obstacles in their return to and settlement of Meskhetia.[32] The Gamsakhurdia government based much of its ethnic policy on the distinction between "indigenous" and "settlers." Ethnic minorities living in Georgia (Russians, Azerbaijanis, Armenians, Greeks—in total more than 1.5 million people) were considered the major threat to the future national destiny of the Georgian people. In one of his speeches Gamsakhurdia even called for the removal of all non-Georgians who took shelter in Georgia.[33] Such ethnic policies in multiethnic Georgia naturally reinforced the minorities' alienation from the new Georgian state and resulted in the decision of the South Ossetian parliament to unite with North Ossetia, and thus become a part of the Russian Federation. Also the South Ossetian parliament decided to establish friendly relations with the republics of the North Caucasus and Abkhazia.[34] The chairman of the Supreme Soviet of Abkhazia, Vladislav Ardzinba, responded with "Abkhazia is for Abkhazians" in answer to Gamsakhurdia's "Georgia is for Georgians." It provoked the ethnic cleavages in Abkhazia, where ethnic cleansing is forcing almost all ethnic Georgians to leave this autonomous republic and become refugees. Some analysts consider Abkhazia and Ossetia the lost territories of Georgia.[35] This status is preserved de facto by the Russian military peacekeeping forces.

The Abkhazians are one of the Circassian peoples (like the Kabardians, Adyges, and Abazians) who live in the North Caucasus in the territory of the Russian Federation. The majority of these peoples left their homeland during the Russian-Caucasian wars and at present live in Turkey, Jordan, and other Eastern countries.[36]

238 RAFIK KURBANOV AND ERJAN KURBANOV

As Ramazan Traho argues:

> In the course of many years the Circassian people, like other peoples living in the USSR, were subjected to unheard of political and national oppression, unparalleled in the history of Colonialism and Great Power politics. . . . Thus Circassians saw clearly that they with all the peoples of the Caucasus, could be free politically and prosperous economically only if Bolshevism and its entire system was totally destroyed."[37]

There are several possible explanations of the roots of the Georgian-Abkhazian conflict. One includes the demographic situation in Abkhazia. The mass migration of Georgians, Armenians, and Russians has been under way in Abkhazia since the end of the nineteenth century. In 1897 ethnic Abkhazians made up 55 percent of the total population, followed by Georgians, 24 percent; Armenians, 6 percent; and Russians, 5 percent. The situation in 1979 was completely different, with 47 percent of the population Georgians, 18 percent Armenians, and only 17 percent ethnic Abkhazians. The intentional Georgianization of Abkhazia resulted in Abkhazians becoming a minority in their own republic. Even at the present time, after the ethnic cleansing and migration of the majority of Georgians from Abkhazia, the Abkhazians are only in third place after Russians and Armenians in the list of ethnic groups.

The other possible source of conflict in Abkhazia, according to some observers, is the "hidden Russian hand" in the internal affairs of the newly independent states of the former USSR, which tries to ensure Russian "zones of influence" and "strategic interests."[38] Presumably, Russia implicitly supports rival minorities in those newly independent states that do not pursue a pro-Russian policy (Azerbaijan, Georgia, Moldova). Russian defense minister General Pavel Grachev recently announced that his country desired to keep at least five Russian military bases in Georgian territory. Grachev mentioned such cities as Batumi, Poti, Akhalkalaki, Tbilisi, and Gudauta for the bases' location.

Gamsakhurdia, who came to power as a result of the October 1989 elections with 87 percent of the electorate vote, was militarily overthrown by the opposition in January 1992. Russia clearly supported the opposition and provided it with ammunition and 65 million rubles, while more than 200,000 Russian soldiers were stationed in Georgia at that time.[39] Shevardnadze faces the fact that Georgia's security depends above all on relations with the bordering states and mainly with Russia, which was irritated by the anti-Russian policy of the previous Georgian administration.

Another possible contributing factor in the Georgian-Abkhazian conflict is the creation of the Confederation of Peoples of the North Caucasus (CPNC). Although not formally a political union, this organization united sixteen ethnic groups in the region. Its leaders hope that in the near future, the CPNC will be transformed into the Mountain Republic, a nonreligious, secular state based on the Western model, with some elements of Caucasian culture and traditions. The president of the CPNC, Musa Shanibov, when speaking of the history of the Caucasus, noted that "all our ancestors were closely connected with each other, but the empire separated us. Therefore our main goal is to build a united state [in the Caucasus]."[40]

Shanibov's comments have led to the belief that the military assistance provided by the CPNC to Abkhazian forces could be explained by the desire of the future leaders of the Mountain Republic to have access to Black Sea ports.

During the fighting in Tbilisi between Gamsakhurdia's forces and the opposition, Catholicos Ilia II expressed his readiness to become a mediator in the conflict.[41] However, the Georgian church in fact later supported the overthrow of the legally elected leader of the country. The Catholicos of Georgia, Ilia II, personally blessed and baptized Shevardnadze in spite of the fact that the former prominent communist previously was the first secretary of the Georgian Communist Party and later served as a member of the Politburo of the CPSU. As a result of the baptism, Shevardnadze was given a new Christian name, Georgii.

Ilia II (Irakli Georgievich Shchiolashvili) was born in Ordzhonikidze in 1933 and received a religious education. He, as well as the Georgian church in general, was frequently blamed for alleged connections with the KGB. For example, some Gamsakhurdia supporters argue that on 10 January 1962, Ilia II was recruited as a KGB agent by Colonel Imiashvili, the director of the Fifth Department of the KGB of the Georgian SSR, and received the code name "Iverieli." At that time, Shevardnadze was chairman of the Georgian KGB and, as his opponents believe, had working contacts with him. As Shevardnadze opponents argue, this was the reason for the catholicos's quick recognition of him after he became a leader of Georgia for the second time.

However, embracing of religion by the older generation of Caucasian political leaders is a common event in almost all the former Soviet republics, including Azerbaijan. Iranian newspapers "credited [Azerbaijani President] Aliev with erecting some two hundred mosques in the Nakhichevan region, and described his pilgrimage to the tomb of Imam Reza in Mashad."[42] Nevertheless, this change in images of the former communist leaders indicates their turn to nationalism—where religion is a part of ethnic identity—not a deep religious feeling. It also signifies an open demonstration of the rejection of the communist past.

The pro-Russian orientation of the current Georgian authorities is in part legitimized by underlining the common faith of Russians and Georgians. During the last visit of Russian President Yeltsin to Georgia, he and Shevardnadze visited Sion Cathedral in Tbilisi. They met Georgian Catholicos Ilia II and members of the Holy Synod of the Georgian Orthodox Church. During this gathering it was emphasized that this was a meeting with the leaders of Christian, and therefore friendly, nations.

It is not an easy task to determine specific political and social factors in overall political developments in Abkhazia, which can serve as an example for the conflicts in this region and the religious element in them. The Abkhazians, who are famous as a people with great longevity, of course try to survive as a distinct ethnic group. Their determination is one of the reasons for the conflict. Powerful external forces, however, are using this conflict for their own ends. Religion probably does not play an important role in political developments in Abkhazia, although it is claimed as an ideological justification for outside interference.

The new Georgian president, Eduard Shevardnazde, declared that "Georgia's disintegration can be halted by force alone."[43] In his statement regarding the defeat of the Georgian army in Abkhazia, President Shevardnadze stressed that "Georgia suffered a defeat in this war, which was unleashed to ensure the strategic interests of this country. Namely by imperial forces is the conflict in Abkhazia inspired, as a result of which more than half of the territory of Abkhazia is occupied."[44] He is prepared to launch military action to recover the secessionist provinces unless a political solution is achieved quickly.[45] The desire of Georgian officials to reunite Georgia and restore its territorial integrity is quite understandable, particularly since three subunits named after Georgian nationalities—Abkhazians, Adjarians, and Ossetians—are decidedly unfriendly toward Georgians. They occupied a significant portion (16,000 out of a total 90,000 square kilometers) of the Georgian Republic's territory.[46] But this goal can hardly be realized with the help of military force alone.

The hope of improving the internal situation in Georgia under the leadership of Shevardnadze is manifestly expressed in the "Appeal to the World Public" by representatives of the religious centers of Georgia—the Christian churches of Georgians, Armenians, and Greeks, and the Muslim and Jewish communities.[47] The appeal stressed that Georgia for many centuries was famous for ethnic and religious tolerance. In Tbilisi, the capital, mosques, synagogues, and Armenian and Orthodox churches have been situated on the same street, side by side since the Middle Ages. In those distant times, when the world did not yet know the legal mechanisms for the protection of minority rights, representatives of the different nationalities coexisted peacefully. Though some observers consider this peaceful coexistence "an image of harmony and friendship that existed more in the hopes of international socialists and liberal journalists than in the streets of Tiflis and Baku,"[48] few arguments can dispute the facts of the protracted peaceful times, significant levels of intermarriages, and mutual cultural interaction and affinity in the Caucasus.

Over the centuries tolerance of the Georgian nation toward minorities became the guarantee of observance of national and religious rights. In this appeal the hope was expressed that Shevardnadze would also help to defend the rights of minorities. However, the level of mutual trust of the sides in the conflicts is already extremely low, and it will be difficult to reach peace quickly.

Currently, only one region of Georgia—Ajaria—is relatively stable. Some religious tolerance can be found there: Orthodox churches have been returned to Russians, Gregorian Apostolic churches to Armenians, synagogues to Jews, and, formerly prohibited by the Bolsheviks, mosques to Muslims. Ajarian leader Aslan Abashidze, the chairman of the Ajarian Supreme Soviet, is a unique political figure in the Caucasus: his ancestors ruled Ajaria from 1462 to the end of the nineteenth century. His grandfather, Memed Abashidze, was the first chairman of the Ajarian Mejlis (parliament) from 1918 to 1921. In 1937, during Stalin's repressions, he was executed. Of course, Aslan Abashidze could not have held a high position in Soviet times with such predecessors.[49]

Currently, Abashidze is considered by the majority of local analysts the only political figure who could probably bring real peace to Georgia. He is an ideal candidate for that, except for his religious roots: "in spite of the increasingly high rating of the Ajarian leader, it is very difficult to imagine modern Georgia headed by an Ajarian—a man raised in the traditions of the Muslim culture. The national pride of Georgians, which is very strongly mixed with their Christian-Orthodox belonging, cannot tolerate him."[50] It is significant that, in spite of the fact that Abashidze is a proclaimed atheist (although contradictory information is available), he was baptized in childhood by relatives and also went through all the necessary Muslim rituals.[51] Probably Abashidze, who was born in a Muslim family, was later baptized by his relatives during the anti-Muslim campaigns of the Soviet authorities.

The current political developments in Georgia include an active participation of the people from the North Caucasus in what they consider the liberation movement of the Abkhazian people. Half of all fighters of the Abkhazian units came from the North Caucasian region. Remarkably, the name of the deputy minister of defense of Abkhazia is Shamil Basaev, who at age twenty-eight has been proclaimed "a hero of the Abkhazian war." In the Caucasus he is nicknamed the "Second Shamil." He is from the city of Vedeno (Chechen Republic), the former capital of the mountain state founded by Shamil. Basaev was recently asked by a correspondent of an independent newspaper whether the religious factor was important in the continuing war in Abkhazia. The correspondent mentioned that the majority of Abkhazians were Muslims, whereas Georgians were Christians. Basaev answered that the war was not a religious one, and he was sorry to learn that the majority of Abkhazians were atheists.[52]

At the same time, when Russian vice president Aleksandr Rutskoi accused the CPNC of "unlawful acts of sending armed volunteers to Abkhazia," the chairman of the Muslim organization Religious Communities of the Caucasus, Magomet Magomaev, publicly responded that the CPNC in this case was following Muslim laws, not the laws of the Russian Federation. He also said, "Abkhazians are our brothers. We have to help them because this pleases Allah."[53]

The theme of *gazzavat* had been repeatedly used in the North Caucasus as a motive for unification against outside interference. For example, in December 1993, numbers of representatives of various military formations of Chechnia were making oaths on the Koran, swearing that they would start *gazzavat* against anyone who would allow Russian soldiers to go to Chechnia.[54]

Ossetian-Ingush Conflict

The bloody interethnic conflict that took place in November 1992 in North Ossetia between the Muslim Ingush and the Christian Ossetians has been interpreted by some analysts as a religious confrontation.[55] More likely, this conflict was a result of the decision by the Russian government to rehabilitate the Ingush people, who were deported in Stalin's time, without any consideration to their dispute with neighbors over territorial claims. In particular, the Ingush desired the return of their lost territories near the North Ossetian capital of Vladikavkaz ("Prigorodnyi raion"), which they lost after their deportation by Stalin to Central Asia in 1944. The disputed land was eventually settled by Ossetians from Georgia, purportedly only with the aim of cleansing Georgia of Ossetians. The Law on Rehabilitation of Deported Nations was understood by the Ingush as a statement securing their lawful right to take possession of the Prigorodnyi raion. Boris Yeltsin introduced Russian military units to the zone of the Ossetian-Ingush conflict as a peacekeeping force. "However, the 'Russian peacemakers' came not as an instrument of peace, but rather an instrument of exile of the Ingush from Prigorodnyi raion."[56]

Indeed, it seems as if the Russians were allies of the Ossetians, their Christian brothers. One observer argues that "with regard to the bloody conflict between North Ossetia and Ingushetia, the Northern Caucasian peoples were under the strong impression that Russian involvement was an important factor in the escalation of the conflict and in the disproportionately high number of casualties suffered, particularly among civilians."[57] Another observer maintains that "in early November 1992 . . . 30,000 Russian troops using tanks and other powerful forces, backed by Ossetian paramilitaries, ethnically cleansed the disputed territory of all Ingush. These Russian peacekeeping forces . . . failed to remain strictly neutral between the North Ossetian and Ingush government. They appear to have colluded with the Ossetians before, during and after this very tragic event."[58] All Ingush houses in the region were destroyed, and the Ingush living in North Ossetia were deported to the Ingush Republic. The Ingush considered these actions of the Russian military and Ossetian forces in the Prigorodnyi raion as genocide.

Noticeably, Ossetians from South Ossetia (Georgia) took an active part in the fighting on the side of their northern brothers. It seems this conflict was a continuation of the tragic events that took place in North Ossetia in October 1981.[59]

The Ingush president, Ruslan Aushev, argues that the "Russian government nevertheless was constantly informed about the serious conflict situation in the region and the level of tensions. However, very little was done to prevent bloodshed. The Russian government did not take a clear stand, and when the fighting began it acted hastily and unwisely. Now it is repeating the same mistakes that were made during Gorbachev's years in Karabakh, where the conflict has been going on for five years in spite of the number of decisions and agreements."[60]

Russia's apparent indifference is borne out by the fact that, in discussing the conflict in North Ossetia, President Boris Yeltsin met with the chairman of the Supreme Soviet of North Ossetia but did not invite the leaders of Ingushetia, who were deeply insulted. The Ingush were saying that "Yeltsin openly demonstrated that Russia has sons and stepsons."

After the restoration of their statehood, the Ingush, unlike the Chechens, did not intend to secede from the Russian Federation and hoped that Russia would help them get back what they consider their lost territory. But they were disappointed when Yeltsin met representatives of only the Ossetian side. Only recently did he meet with leaders from both Ossetia and Ingushetia.[61]

In the "Appeal of the Heads of Religious Confessions and Public Organizations of North Ossetia to the President, Government, and Supreme Soviet of the Russian Federation," the Ossetian side proposed that "in order to avoid a new turn of the tension in the conflict zone and in the Caucasus on the whole, taking into consideration the ethnopsychological peculiarities of mountaineers, we consider that temporarily it is impossible for the peoples of North Ossetia and Ingushetia to live together."[62] In their appeal the heads of the religious confessions also asked not to give religious colors to this conflict.

This appeal reflected the official, political position of the Ossetian leadership, which proceeded from the incompatibility and impossibility of Ossetians and Ingush living together. Such a position was deemed by the Ingush as a demonstration of racism. Said the Ingush: "This statement by the leadership of some ruling circles of North Ossetia on the incompatibility and impossibility of Ossetians and Ingush living together is utter cynicism and overt racism."[63]

President Yeltsin and the leaders of North Ossetia and Ingushetia eventually worked out a mutual agreement over the conflict, according to which the Republic of North Ossetia was to renounce its previous thesis "on the incompatibility and impossibility of Ossetians and Ingush living together," and the Republic of Ingushetia was to forsake its territorial claims to Ossetia, namely to the Prigorodnyi raion. North Ossetia returned to Ingushetia four villages formerly belonging to the Ingush. It is supposed that in the course of time all refugees of Ingush nationality will return to their homes in Ossetia.[64]

However, for this to succeed all the necessary conditions for the peaceful coexistence of the two ethnic groups must be met. The head of the temporary administration of the emergency zone, V. Lozovoi, hopes that the religious representatives of the various North Caucasian communities will help to establish lasting peace in the region.[65]

Incidentally, the assassination of Russian vice premier Viktor Polianichko, who served as the fifth head of the temporary administration of the emergency zone, caused yet another delay in the return of Ingush refugees to the disputed Prigorodnyi raion and therefore has also aggravated the Ossetian-Ingush conflict.[66]

Like the conflict in Abkhazia, the interethnic conflict in North Ossetia hardly can be determined as having a religious element. Despite their religious differences, Ossetians and Ingush have in common many traditional North Caucasian cultural practices. The Ossetians, for one, "do not appear to see Islam as a threat to national identity."[67] Muslim Chechens and Ingush, and Christian Ossetians as well, who have their own particular ethnic consciousness, also have a North Caucasian national consciousness that helped them restore peaceful relations in the past and, it is hoped, will help them in the future.

Conclusion

Political movements based on religion still play an insignificant role in Transcaucasia. In the North Caucasus the influence of religion is stronger, but not decisive. After seventy years of antireligious propaganda, the strength of religious unity is much weaker than the feeling of ethnic identity. The appeals to religious solidarity as a source for possible alliances became a notable phenomenon in the Caucasus soon after the center started to lose its ideological control, and it is possibly the only way, except labeling opponents "Islamic fundamentalists," that religion can be found in politics. Religious leaders, in spite of the level of their popularity and prestige, do not have significant influence on political decisions, and their negotiating efforts are often unsuccessful.

The pleas to Russia and the West, which are, supposedly, "natural allies" of the Christian nationalities, have not brought the expected results so far: Christian solidarity did not prevent crucial Russian support to Abkhazian separatists in their fighting against Georgians. The same picture is to be found for the Muslims in the region: the last example of the weakness of Muslim solidarity are the revenge attacks by Chechen nationalists on trains going to Azerbaijan through Chechnia. It started after the Aliev administration of Azerbaijan had stopped the support for rival Chechnia that had been given by the previous Azerbaijani government.[68] Key political players in the region, such as Russia, Turkey, Iran, and the West, more or less often indicate sympathetic views to their religious brothers. Nevertheless, they have more important criteria for determining their political priorities and actual decisions, such as national security and the economy. The same criteria are used by the local political actors in the Caucasus, while religion plays only a marginal role in this process.

Notes

1. A. Muradian, "Workshop on Central Asia in Modern International Relations System (in Russian)," *Vostok-Oriens* (Moscow), 1993, no. 5, p. 168.

2. Audrey Altstadt, *The Azerbaijani Turks: Power and Identity Under Russian Rule* (Stanford: Hoover Institution Press, 1992), p. 7.

3. Farida Mamedova, "Politicheskaia istoriia i istoricheskaia geografiia Kavkazskoi Albanii," *Vyshka,* 1 July 1989.

4. Altstadt, *Azerbaijani Turks,* p. 5.

5. *Encyclopedia Britannica,* 1958, vol. 2, p. 382.

6. Ronald Suny, *Looking Toward Ararat: Armenia in Modern History* (Bloomington: Indiana University Press, 1993), p. 31.

7. Ibid., pp. 39–40.

8. Karen Dawisha and Bruce Parrott, *Russia and the New States of Eurasia: The Politics of Upheaval* (New York: Cambridge University Press, 1994), p. 119.

9. Suny, *Looking Toward Ararat*, p. 186.

10. *Neob'iavlennaia voina* (Baku: Kommunist, 1991), p. 42.

11. D. Pipes, "Understanding Islam in Politics," *Middle East Review*, winter 1983/4, p. 7.

12. Shireen Hunter, "Azerbaijan: Search for Identity," in *Nations and Politics in the Soviet Successor States*, ed. Ian Bremmer and Ray Taras (Cambridge: Cambrige University Press, 1993).

13. Dawisha and Parrott, *Russia and the New States*, p. 120.

14. Alexandre Bennigsen and Chantal Lemercier-Quelquejay, *Islam in the Soviet Union* (London: Pall Mall, 1967), p. 8; Loweel Tillet, *The Great Friendship: Soviet Historians on the Non-Russian Nationalities* (Chapel Hill: University of North Carolina Press, 1969), chap. 7.

15. Geidar Guseinov, *Iz istorii obshchestvennoi i filosofskoi mysli v Azerbaidzhane v XIX veke* (Baku: Akademii nauk Azerbaidzhanskoi sse, 1949).

16. *Bakinets*, 23–30 September 1993.

17. Dawisha and Parrott, *Russia and the New States*, p. 47.

18. R. Batyrshin, *Nezavisimaia gazeta*, 12 March 1992, p. 3.

19. D. Khalidov, *Islamskie novosti*, 25 September 1992, p. 3.

20. See, for example, *Pravda*, 20 January 1990.

21. Hunter, "Azerbaijan."

22. A. Krainy, *The Times*, 22 January 1990.

23. Altstadt, *Azerbaijani Turks*, p. 217.

24. Hunter, "Azerbaijan," p. 250.

25. Bill Keller, "Did Moscow Incite Azerbaijanis? Some See a Plot," *New York Times*, 19 February 1990, p. A8.

26. *Newsweek*, 29 January 1990, p. 44.

27. Altstadt, *Azerbaijani Turks*, p. 217.

28. Stephen F. Jones, "Georgia: A Failed Democratic Transition," in Bremmer and Taras, eds., *Nations and Politics in the Soviet Successor States*, p. 304.

29. "Georgians to Bury President," *Moscow Times*, 18 February 1994, p. 5.

30. Elizabeth Fuller, "The Azeris in Georgia and Indigenous in Azerbaijan," *Central Asian Survey*, vol. 3, no. 2 (1984), pp. 75–86.

31. Elizabeth Fuller, "Marneuli: Georgia's Potential Nagorno-Karabakh?" *Radio Free Europe/Radio Liberty Research Bulletin*, no. 477 (1988), pp. 1–5.

32. Anatolii Khazanov, "Meskhetian Turks in Search of Self-Identity," *Central Asian Survey*, vol. 11, no. 4 (1992), p. 13.

33. *Molodezh Gruzii*, 7 September 1990.

34. *Krasnaia zvezda*, 27 October 1993.

35. *Moskovskie novosti*, 31 October 1993, p. 4.

36. Ramazan Traho, "Circassians," *Central Asian Survey*, Special North Caucasus Issue, vol. 10, nos. 1–2 (1991), pp. 1–63.

37. Ibid., p. 63.

38. Thomas Goltz, "Letter From Eurasia: The Hidden Russian Hand," *Political Science* (fall 1993), pp. 92–116.

39. Mikhail Podoliak, *Respublika Armeniia*, 3 February 1994.

40. *Nezavisimaia gazeta*, 2 September 1992.

41. Nodar Broladze, "Patriarkh Il'ia II vnov' prizval k dialogu," *Nezavisimaia gazeta,* 24 September 1991, p. 3.
42. Tadeusz Swietochovsky, "The Spirit of Baku, Summer 1993," *Azerbaijan International* (winter 1994), no. 1, p. 44.
43. *Moscow News,* 29 October 1993.
44. *Svobodnaia Gruziia,* 28 September 1993.
45. Raymond Bonner, "Georgian Talks of New War with Separatists," *New York Times,* 19 November 1993.
46. Edward Allworth, "The Precarious Existence of Small Nationalities in Russia and Georgia," *Central Asian Review,* vol. 12, no. 1 (1993), pp. 15–32.
47. *Svobodnaia Gruziia,* 25 September 1993.
48. Suny, *Looking Toward Ararat,* p. 50.
49. "Mir sredi voiny," *Izvestiia,* 21 December 1993.
50. *Novoe vremia,* 1993, no. 42 (October).
51. *Trud,* 28 May 1993.
52. *Nezavisimaia gazeta,* 16 October 1993.
53. *Kommersant,* 24–31 August 1992.
54. *Moscow News,* 21 December 1993.
55. Z. Leont'eva and V. Emel'ianchenko, "Gazavat kak otvet na genotsid," *Moskovskie novosti,* 15 November 1992.
56. *Moskovskie novosti,* 15 November 1993.
57. Gueorgui Otyrba, "War in Abkhazia: The Regional Significance of the Georgian-Abkhazian Conflict," in *National Identity and Ethnicity in Russia and the New States of Eurasia,* ed. Roman Szporluk (Armonk, NY: M.E. Sharpe, 1994).
58. Peter Jarman, "Ethnic Cleansing in the Northern Caucasus," *Moscow News,* 11–17 February 1994.
59. Iu. Sharaeev, "O tragicheskikh sobitiiakh v Ordzhonikidze v oktiabre 1981," *Materialy samizdata,* 7 September 1990, pp. 1–25.
60. Kazbek Karsanov and Ruslan Aushev, "Zemli khvatit vsem," *Chelovek i pravo,* vol. 19, no. 1 (1993), p. 4.
61. Sergei Snopkov, "Prezident prizyvaet k kompromisu," *Moskovskie novosti,* 8 December 1993.
62. *Severnaia Ossetiia,* 15 September 1993.
63. "Doroga, kotoroi nuzhno poiti," *Federatsiia,* no. 71 (1993), p. 3.
64. *Moskovskie novosti,* 8 December 1993.
65. *Izvestiia,* 13 October 1993.
66. *Moskovskie novosti,* 6 August 1993.
67. Jane Ornod, "Northern Caucasus: Fragmentation or Federation," in Bremmer and Taras, eds., *Nations and Politics in the Soviet Successor States,* p. 462.
68. *Current Digest of the Post-Soviet Press,* vol. 45, no. 49 (1993), p. 15.

12

Islam as Faith, Politics, and Bogeyman in Tajikistan

Muriel Atkin

Islamic "fundamentalism" has become the bugbear of choice of the New World Order. In the successor states of the Soviet Union, this was illustrated by interpretations of the political power struggle in Tajikistan between those who wanted to perpetuate as much as possible of the old Soviet order and the diverse coalition of advocates of change. Defenders of the old order largely succeeded in portraying themselves to their Central Asian neighbors, Moscow, and Washington as the sole hope for secularism and stability confronting the onslaught of Islamic extremists. For example, the speaker of Tajikistan's Supreme Soviet, Imomali Rahmonov, in an interview on Russian television, described the power struggle from which the communist hardliners emerged victorious as a clash between medieval "obscurantism, represented by Islamic fundamentalism, and the idea of progress and the democratic development of society."[1] This exaggerated notion of an Islamic menace led the Russian government to support in Tajikistan the same kind of old-guard forces President Yeltsin sought to crush within Russia. Some in the West accepted that interpretation and the Russian response. For hundreds of thousands of inhabitants of Tajikistan, the politics of Islamophobia brought persecution and the hardships of exile.

In a certain sense, Islam was stronger during the Soviet era and weaker in the post-Soviet era than has generally been recognized. Despite episodes of intense persecution of Muslims and long periods during which Soviet authorities attempted to curtail, manipulate, and penalize Islamic instruction and observance, Islam remained important to more people in Tajikistan (and elsewhere) than Soviet officialdom acknowledged. Once the degree of underestimation became clear and international events belied the social science axiom that modernization inevitably leads to the waning influence of religion, estimates of Islam's strength swung to the other extreme. The new platitude was that Islam was the sole, overriding concern of most Central Asians outside the ruling elite. It became commonplace in the Soviet Union, the successor states, and abroad to assume that to be a Muslim was to be an advocate of radical Islamicizing politics.

The term "Islamic revival" should be used with caution, given the long-term efforts of many ordinary Muslims to maintain their faith and also the way Soviet sources misrepresented the status of Islam to conform to the official dictum that the evolution of Soviet society brought with it the decline of religion. Aspects of what appeared to be new by the late Soviet era were in reality part of a continuous process newly perceived by outsiders when political conditions permitted a greater range of discourse. That in turn affected assumptions about both the internal dynamics of Muslim society within the former Soviet Union and the extent to which Muslims there were responding to developments abroad when they asserted their Islamic identity. For example, the Islamic Rebirth Party, which held its unionwide founding conference in 1990, had already existed as a well-concealed underground organization since sometime in the late 1970s. One of the United States' leading Central Asia experts dates the start of the Islamic revival even earlier. In Martha Brill Olcott's judgment, the 1960s saw the ripple effect of Nikita Khrushchev's political reforms reach Soviet Muslims (after Khrushchev's ouster). The decreased repression in the countryside permitted the more open observance of traditional Islamic rites, while Central Asian intellectuals could—judiciously—include the role of Islam in discussions of their heritage.[2] Yet there is an indication that in Tajikistan the "revival" was underway even earlier. In 1960, while Khrushchev's harsh antireligion campaign was underway in the Soviet Union as a whole, officials considered popular adherence to Islam to be so strong in Tajikistan's southern province of Qurghonteppa that they permitted the construction of a mosque in the provincial capital. The apparent reason for this decision was that it was safer to have people practice their religion in association with an institution that Soviet authorities could control (through the officially sanctioned Muslim Spiritual Administration of Central Asia and Kazakhstan).[3] A leading Uzbek expert on the social context of Islam, Talib Saidbaev, pushed the start of the Islamic revival back another twenty years, to the World War II era.[4] Roughly twenty years before that, Islam in Central Asia underwent another "revival" during the relatively tolerant era of the New Economic Policy, as it recovered from the impact of the postrevolutionary civil war and the radical policies of War Communism. None of this means that some seventy years passed without change or that Tajikistan's indigenous peoples saw the world in the early 1990s in exactly the same way that they or their ancestors did in the 1920s or earlier. However, it does appear that elements of Islam remained important to many Tajiks even when outside observers thought the religion was in eclipse.

The overwhelming majority of Tajikistan's population belongs to nationalities that are historically Muslim. (In the absence of reliable, large-scale opinion polls or census data on religion, there are no credible statistics on the number of practicing Muslims, cultural Muslims, or nonbelievers among these nationalities.) Roughly 90 percent of the population belongs either to the Tajik majority, the large Uzbek minority, or the small minorities of Kyrgyz, Turkmens, Volga Tatars, and Crimean Tatars.[5] They are all by tradition Sunni Muslims of the same school of religious law, except for several tens of thousands of Pamir peoples, whose homeland is the southeastern province of Badakhshan and who follow the Isma'ili form of Shi'ism (in contrast to the Imami form of Shi'ism, which predominates in Iran.)

One important factor in the preservation of Islamic identity in Tajikistan despite Soviet antireligion policy was the continued use of pre-Soviet ways of disseminating religious information. Rather than invent a new, covert religious network in reaction to the pressures of the Soviet system, something that would necessarily be anti-Soviet, Tajikistan's Muslims perpetuated long-established practices. These had existed in urban as well as rural areas before the Soviet era, but Soviet rule brought a changed intellectual climate to the cities as well as tighter control over people's activities there. Thus, grassroots forms of devotion survived primarily, though not exclusively, in the countryside.

For example, despite Soviet legal constraints, the religious instruction of children continued, although with more difficulty and in smaller numbers, using methods that long predated the Soviet era. In the emirate of Bukhara, the eastern part of which eventually formed the core of Tajikistan, numerous rural as well as urban primary schools (*maktab*) had provided primarily religious instruction. Although emirs founded some schools, groups of neighbors founded others on their own accord.[6] In that sense, there was a precedent for grassroots initiative in establishing maktabs, albeit with the significant difference that the government of the emirs of Bukhara wanted to be seen as an upholder of Islam, while the Soviet regime made maktabs illegal. Further north, in the densely populated Fergana Valley, part of which lies within contemporary Tajikistan, there was a similar proliferation of small, local maktabs operating in simple facilities with one teacher and a few students. Instructional materials, then as now, included books in Persian and a Central Asian Turkish lingua franca, Turki, that were collections of various texts on religious themes.[7] The number of students at a local maktab, in the recent past as in pre-Soviet times, remained small. For example, one former policeman incurred the wrath of authorities in Tajikistan's southern province of Kulob for teaching twelve students about Islam.[8]

The family was and remains an important setting for religious instruction in the Islamic world; it assumed particular importance in Soviet-era Tajikistan, given the impediments to religious instruction outside the home.[9]

Another source of encouragement for interest in Islam that is unique to recent years was made possible by the technology of consumer electronics: radio broadcasts and audio- and videocassettes from abroad. These come from several countries with differing attitudes toward the role of Islam in contemporary society.[10] It is easier to say that there is communication by these means than to be certain how Muslims in Tajikistan interpret such messages; as in communications anywhere, the intended audience may assimilate information selectively and in ways that seem reasonable to the audience, even though their understanding is not what was intended by the people who made the broadcasts or tapes. For example, one Tajik intellectual interpreted rhetoric about the importance of supranational Islam to mean primarily that newly independent Tajikistan, which faced enormous economic problems, would be able to obtain loans through "Islamic banks" at interest rates far below prevailing world levels.[11]

One aspect of religious life that was particularly disrupted by Soviet policy was the maintenance of a corps of religious functionaries. Those who became the learned of the faith usually received further religious education than that obtained by ordinary male believers in maktabs or at home. Traditionally, youths went on to study in seminaries (*madrasah*), which, historically, were numerous in Central Asia's cities. The sharply restricted access to advanced religious education in the Soviet era effectively limited the number of men who could acquire the expertise to become Islamic functionaries. The Soviets closed all the madrasahs for years but then allowed one to operate in Bukhara (since 1945) and, for more advanced study, opened an Islamic Institute in Tashkent (in 1971). Enrollment at both schools was kept low. Late in the Soviet era, enrollment at the madrasah was raised to two hundred and at the institute to one hundred.[12] The course of study at the madrasah lasted seven years, and at the institute, four years. Even smaller numbers of students were sent abroad to complete their education in Egypt, Libya, Syria, Jordan, Saudi Arabia, or Turkey.[13] The head of Islamic institutions in Tajikistan from 1988 until he was forced to flee late in 1992, the chief *qadi* (judge), Akbar Turajonzoda, was the product of this educational system, having attended the madrasah in Bukhara, the Islamic Institute in Tashkent, and the Department of Islamic Law of the University of Jordan.[14]

In the early 1990s, as the old controls were dismantled, opportunities for further Islamic education in Tajikistan increased significantly. Tajikistan acquired its own schools: five madrasahs and one Islamic university, with a total enrollment exceeding eight hundred by mid-1992.[15]

Another important limitation on Islamic functionaries was the Soviet regime's creation of an "official clergy,"[16] registered by the state and subject to one of the four regional Muslim Spiritual Administrations—in the case of Tajikistan, the muftiate of Tashkent. The number of official clergy was kept low. No one outside its ranks had legal standing to serve as an Islamic functionary.

Soviet policy also restricted the public venues for religious observance. Although Muslims do not have to attend mosques in order to practice their religion, gathering in mosques can be important for encouraging a sense of membership in the community of believers, for conveying ideas or information, and as a social center. For decades, Soviet authorities closed mosques, converted them to secular use, or allowed them to become dilapidated. By the late 1980s, Tajikistan was left with only seventeen of the large mosques used for the gatherings for Friday noon prayers. To compensate, people built covert mosques that appeared to serve some secular function, such as a clubhouse or teahouse, and used them in off hours for prayers and to accommodate maktabs. There were over one thousand such mosques in late-Soviet Tajikistan.[17] In the more tolerant atmosphere that prevailed after 1989, the republic's Muslims began to establish mosques at a rapid rate. By the second half of 1991, according to Qadi Turajonzoda, there were nearly 130 Friday mosques and more than 2,800 smaller mosques.[18] (Given the destructiveness of the combat in parts of Tajikistan during the 1992 civil war, it is uncertain how many mosques survived in serviceable condition.)

In addition to mosques, many people also prayed and met with religious figures at the numerous holy places throughout Tajikistan. These included saints' tombs, springs, groves, rock formations, and various other natural settings. Such sites had a tradition of veneration that predated the Soviet era. Soviet authorities tried to end the use of these sites for religious purposes through a combination of physical neglect, conversion to secular use, and propaganda campaigns intended to discredit their veneration. However, those efforts had only limited success because of the sheer number of holy places, the difficulty of controlling access to many of them, and the widespread public belief in their sanctity.[19]

In the 1970s and 1980s, some observers dubbed the ways in which Muslims continued to practice their religion outside Soviet constraints "parallel Islam" and were inclined to see in this an anti-Soviet underground. This interpretation treated those aspects of Islamic practice not controlled by the Soviet regime as an innovation in reaction to Soviet constraints. It did not give due credit to the historic strength of folk Islam among ordinary believers. It also made the assumption that Islamic observance was motivated at least as much by politics as by religion, reflecting, even if inadvertently, the widespread but questionable assumption of the mid-twentieth century that the significance of religious activity could not be primarily religious but had to be the expression of secular concerns through other means. By the standards of Soviet anti-Islamic policy, which remained in effect in Tajikistan into 1989, merely being a practitioner of folk Islam constituted anti-Soviet activity, even when the people involved did not address political issues directly. Thus, one unofficial mullah was denounced by the authorities for such activities as telling people stories about death and resurrection, urging people to be good, establishing a maktab, and lamenting the decline of Islam in the Soviet Union; he received a three-year sentence for polygamy.[20]

For years, the discussion of the politically destabilizing role attributed to parallel Islam focused on Sufism, seeing in it a ready-made underground network that was militantly anti-Soviet and awaiting the opportunity to take up arms.[21] Yet Sufi organizations did not play a dominant political role in Tajikistan in the late-Soviet and early independence periods; the Sufi-led "holy war" did not happen. Sufis there, though not indifferent to politics, turned out to have been far more interested in spiritual matters than some outside observers had assumed.

By the close of the Soviet era, speculation about a Sufi uprising fell out of fashion, but a new alleged menace from parallel Islam received attention: Wahhabism. Foreign observers' discussion of this subject must have been encouraged by the sudden spurt of warnings about the Wahhabi threat that appeared in Soviet sources in the Gorbachev era. These alarms were raised in the context of the Soviet regime's ongoing hostility toward Islam in general.[22] (In the first half of the Gorbachev era, the climate of reform brought a call for more effective anti-Islamic activity, not tolerance.) Thus, the Gorbachev-era head of the Communist Party of Tajikistan, Qahhor Mahkamov, in the context of a diatribe against Islam, stated that Wahhabis were active in parts of Tajikistan. He characterized Wahhabism as a synthesis of religion and politics that was "extremely reactionary and nationalist."[23] A similar theme was sounded by Igor' Beliaev, of *Literaturnaia gazeta,* who in the 1980s issued a number of dire warnings against the Islamic menace to Soviet power. In a statement that illustrated how much old Cold War rhetoric about foreign-sponsored subversion blended with Soviet Islamophobia, Beliaev implied that there was a link between the Afghanistani government-in-exile, which he characterized as Wahhabi dominated and backed by the United States and Saudi Arabia, and the spread of Wahhabism to Central Asia. This was, in that much-used Soviet expression, "not accidental. It appears that it is linked to the attempt to create an 'Islamic barrier' on our southern border."[24] Some Western observers noticed the Soviet comments about Wahhabism and accepted polemic as fact. For example, one commentary, echoing Mahkamov, asserted that Islam was becoming an increasingly serious political threat in Central Asia and especially in southern Tajikistan, where "the most prominent of the militant Islamic movements in the Soviet Union is that of the so-called Wahhabis."[25]

Yet it is not clear that the Wahhabis were the extremists they were alleged to be, or even that they were Wahhabis. A Western reporter interviewed some people in Uzbekistan who had been labeled Wahhabis; they claimed that they did not consider themselves to be members of that sect but had been given the designation by the mufti of Tashkent, whom they had criticized as an agent of the Soviet authorities.[26] (They were not alone in mistrusting the mufti.) Even an official of the muftiate described the people alleged to be Wahhabis simply as critics of the Islamic "official clergy" for being preoccupied with material gain rather than spiritual matters.[27] Similarly, a group of young Tajikistanis alleged to be Wahhabis who staged a demonstration in the provincial capital of Kulob were reported (by the authorities) to have criticized the member of the "official clergy" who was the preacher (*imam khatib*) at the Kulob city mosque and to have faulted older people for not being sufficiently observant Muslims.[28] Some members of the "official clergy" in Kulob later showed themselves to be staunch supporters of the hard-line faction of the Communist Party during the post-Soviet political upheaval. Thus, it is possible that the people who were called Wahhabis after criticizing the imam khatib were not militant sectarians but rather exponents of the view that the dignitary in question was more a servant of the regime than of the faith.

The whole concept of "parallel Islam" as opposed to "official Islam" became largely irrelevant in the late-Soviet and post-Soviet eras. The virtual elimination of restrictions on religious activity after 1989 and the consequent rapid increase in the number of mosques and expansion of religious education left the Soviet-founded religious administration little choice but to meet its increased personnel needs by drawing on the religious figures who had operated without state recognition. Qadi Turajonzoda employed, by his estimate, 95 percent of the "non-state clergy" in the new mosques.[29] As the Soviet order crumbled, the "official clergy" itself was divided between those who opposed any change in religious views and those, especially younger ones, who advocated change, particularly in the form of social concerns and opposition to lavish rituals. Contrary to the old assertions that parallel Islam was the avenue by which the "spillover" of Islamic "fundamentalism" from abroad had penetrated the Soviet Union, many of the younger dissidents in the "official clergy" were the ones who were politicized by the example of Islamic activism abroad. Indeed, they were much more radical than members of Tajikistan's Islamic Renaissance Party (IRP, also known as the Islamic Movement Party).[30] In the political confrontations in Tajikistan in 1991 and 1992, some members of the "official clergy" sided with communist hard-liners. The most prominent of those who did so was Haidar Sharifov, who became head of a separate, pro-hardline qadiate in Kulob. Others sided with the opposition coalition; the most prominent member of that group was Qadi Turajonzoda. The leadership of the Islamic Rebirth Party of Tajikistan drew people from a variety of backgrounds, not just the "unofficial clergy": some obtained religious education through Soviet-endorsed institutions; others came from the ranks of folk Islam; some were not religious functionaries at all but had secular careers. For example, Davlat Usmon, one of the founders of the IRP in Tajikistan who became deputy prime minister of the country in the short-lived coalition government of 1992, is a lawyer.[31]

The number of Islamic functionaries who remained active in post–civil war Tajikistan probably diminished considerably, since those who supported the vanquished opposition coalition either were punished by the victors or went into exile. The anti-Islamic climate was so intense by the end of 1992 that, in the words of an official of Tajikistan's KNB (successor to the KGB), "Men are even afraid to grow beards" lest they be taken for Islamic functionaries and punished.[32]

By the close of the Soviet era, there could be no doubt that a large proportion of Tajikistanis who were Muslim by ancestry still thought of themselves as Muslims, regardless of how strictly observant they were. After years of depicting Islam as a fading remnant that survived primarily among housewives and the elderly, the Soviets acknowledged that Islam was important to those social groups that were supposed to embody the modern, Sovietized society: the young, skilled workers, and the educated.[33]

Although the long-standing Soviet practice was to describe Islam's continued importance as a rural phenomenon (and therefore, by implication, backward), many city residents in Tajikistan, including Communist Party members, wanted Islamic rituals for the major life-cycle events, even if they also appeared to conform to party expectations by having secular Soviet rituals performed as well. Some communist officials turned a blind eye to Islamic activity occurring within their jurisdiction even before the party's shift to a more tolerant approach at the end of the Soviet era.[34] One inkling of the continued importance of Islam to Communist Party veterans was evident in a political maneuver used by Qadi Turajonzoda to obtain a more favorable state policy toward Islam. As a member of Tajikistan's Supreme Soviet, Turajonzoda sought such things as the establishment of state holidays on Islamic holidays and an exemption from the land tax for buildings used by Muslims for religious purposes. Despite his willingness to settle for the partial fulfillment of his objectives, a majority of the legislators rebuffed him completely. At that point, Turajonzoda announced that Islamic functionaries would no longer say the prayers for the dead for any communist. The speaker of the legislature, Qadriddin Aslonov, sought out Turajonzoda and urged him to end this prohibition, which Aslonov termed cruel. Turajonzoda responded by asking why communists cared about the prayers for the dead, since communism rejects Islam. In the end, the legislature resolved the dispute by giving in to Turajonzoda on one point, making Islamic holidays state holidays.[35]

For all that Tajikistan's Muslims succeeded in preserving elements of their faith in an environment not conducive to their doing so, by the end of the Soviet era, most of them were poorly informed about Islam and were not strictly observant. This was a result not only of the explicitly antireligious measures implemented by the Soviet regime but also of the kinds of changes in outlook taking place among people of various religions in many countries over the course of this century. Within the former Soviet Union, Korans were in chronically short supply. Saudi Arabia began sending Korans to Central Asia in the early 1990s, but that effort, though large in absolute terms, was small in proportion to the millions of people in the region who probably considered themselves Muslims. In any event, few people in Tajikistan knew Arabic at that time and therefore could not read the Koran in the original.[36] Although rural families tried to preserve the traditional books that were used to teach children about Islam, the authorities had ferreted out and destroyed many volumes over the years.[37] Even those that survived were useless to anyone who could not read the Arabic alphabet. Qadi Turajonzoda, speaking to a domestic audience by radio in mid-1992, asserted that most of the republic's Muslims knew hardly anything about Islam.[38] On another occasion, he stated that only 3 percent of the country's inhabitants knew the prayers correctly.[39] One of the new opposition newspapers that sprang up in independent Tajikistan must have agreed with Turajonzoda's estimate of believers' ignorance, because it tried to explain the fundamentals of Islam, the five pillars of the faith, to its readers in the most basic terms.[40] A witness to opposition demonstrations in Tajikistan saw members of the urban intelligentsia teaching villagers who had joined the demonstrations how to pray.[41] In light of the low level of religious knowledge, assertions that independent Tajikistan was rocked by a broad-based, radical Islamicizing movement should not be accepted automatically but should be subjected to the same skeptical questioning as any other interpretation of a complex subject.

As people in many parts of the former Soviet Union began to call for the transformation, even the dismantling, of the old order, some people in Tajikistan also criticized the status quo, although they did not advocate complete independence from the central government before the Soviet Union dissolved.[42] From 1991, a coalition of diverse groups and individuals openly criticized elements within the Communist Party of Tajikistan for their determination to preserve a monopoly of political and economic power and repress any critics.[43] For some members of the opposition, association with Islam was a prominent element of their public image; Qadi Turajonzoda and the members of the Islamic Renaissance Party belonged to this group. For others, notably the members of the Democratic Party of Tajikistan, the Rastokhez popular front, the La''li Badakhshan Party, and presidential candidate Davlat Khudonazarov, that was not the case. However, all agreed that Muslims ought to have complete religious freedom. There was a widespread tendency to describe the opposition coalition as simply "Islamic." That blurred the distinctions among the constituents of the opposition coalition and facilitated the stigmatization of the opposition's members as dangerous Islamic extremists.

Tajikistan's communist hardliners repeatedly depicted the opposition coalition as dominated by Islamic "fundamentalists" (a term widely used in the former Soviet Union as well as the West, despite its inaccuracy). The veracity of the hardliners' allegations of a fundamentalist threat was rendered suspect by the contradictions in the message. If they used the charge as something that could be made or ignored to suit the circumstances, ought it be taken as anything more than a calculated attack on an adversary? Tajikistan's president (November 1991–September 1992), Rahmon Nabiev, and his allies routinely claimed that opposition "Islamic fundamentalists" schemed to take power and linked the alleged fundamentalists to Iran and Afghanistan.[44] Yet Tajikistan's Supreme Soviet, composed primarily of communists and former communists, sent a message to President Yeltsin, urging him not to believe Nabiev's alarmist view of the opposition. According to the legislators, the opposition was not radical but sought change through legal means; the legislators contended that the real problem was that Nabiev lacked the public's confidence.[45]

Foreign Minister Lakim Qayumov (in office from 1989 to 1992, subsequently Tajikistan's emissary to the United Nations) sent contrasting signals in quick succession to Turkey and Saudi Arabia as he sought their help for newly independent Tajikistan. In both cases he played on their rivalry with Iran but implied opposite meanings in his messages to the two countries. He told a Turkish publication that there were youths in Tajikistan who adhered to the principle of neither East nor West (a slogan associated with revolutionary Iran) and who actively disseminated an Islamic fundamentalist message in contemporary Central Asia. Qayumov highlighted the threat to women's rights in Tajikistan if those youths should have their way. He held forth Turkey as the country that ought to serve as an example for young Tajikistanis.[46] Thus, by implication, he endorsed a separation of religion and government. In an interview with a Saudi newspaper he painted a different picture. He said that there was an Islamic revival on which the rhetoric of "certain other countries" exerted influence but denied that there were radical Islamicizing groups in his country. To prevent conflict over the place of Islam in Tajikistani society, he said the country's leaders ought to "avail ourselves of the experience of other Islamic states that have combined Islam and progress. . . . We must have good relations with such countries."[47] He did not discuss how Islamization would affect the status of Tajikistan's women, as he did in his interview with the Turkish press, even though traditional Islamic attitudes towards women prevail in Saudi Arabia, nor did he employ his government's rhetoric about the evils of Islamic fundamentalism, a term that applies in Saudi Arabia if it applies anywhere.

In fact, the communist hardliners claimed Islamic legitimacy for themselves when it suited their purposes. For example, as Nabiev faced intensifying demonstrations against him in the spring of 1992, he claimed that he had been elected president with God's help (he did not mention that the election was not fully free and fair) and refused to resign unless God wanted him to do so.[48] During the political power struggle of 1992, the self-styled independent *qadi* of Kulob Province, Haidar Sharifov, was a vocal supporter of the communist hardliners. His activities on their behalf included holding what was termed an Islamic conference that endorsed the hard-liners' stance.[49]

Another aspect of the stereotyped depiction of Islam's role in Tajikistan's politics was the argument that militant Islamicizers were far more powerful than other members of the opposition coalition. This assertion was widely accepted as fact without corroboration. The head of the hard-line communist government that was installed toward the end of the civil war, Imomali Rahmonov, dismissed the notion that there was a genuine diversity of opinion within the opposition coalition. As he stated in an interview on Russian television, "those forces in Tajikistan that acted under the cover of democracy were just a screen for the Islamic Renaissance Party. It is a fact that in its composition there are professional murderers, cut-throats, aggressors, and thieves who plunder their own people and can hardly be called democrats."[50] This presumption of IRP predominance was widespread among outside observers as well. For example, a Council on Foreign Relations associate expressed the opinion that the IRP had "strong support in rural areas where the majority of the Tajiks live."[51] *Izvestiia*, which sometimes carried articles that contradicted the Islamophobic stereotypes about Tajikistan's opposition, nonetheless depicted the IRP as having a highly organized and far-reaching organizational network with an extremely large following.[52]

It is more accurate to say that there is no irrefutable evidence to support any assertion about the extent of support for the IRP or others who combine Islam with politics. Members of the opposition who did not belong to the IRP have stated that IRP supporters were not nearly as numerous as alleged.[53] Of course one may wonder whether people who were not IRP members might underestimate its strength. The IRP won an unimpressive share of the vote in the November 1991 presidential election, 10 percent or less.[54] Yet that figure might be artificially low because of the irregularities in that election. Estimates of the number of IRP members are contradictory. During 1991, the head of the IRP's Moscow branch claimed the party had twenty thousand members throughout the USSR. However, a few months later, a high-ranking member of the IRP in Tajikistan put the figure at fifty thousand for the USSR as a whole. Shortly after that, estimates of the number of members in Tajikistan alone ranged from ten thousand to seventy thousand.[55] The number of IRP members within Tajikistan must have dropped precipitously in the wake of the civil war because of deaths in combat and the wave of repression directed against the opposition in general as well as the flight of many citizens into exile.

Exactly what role the IRP or Qadi Turajonzoda wanted Islam to play in Tajikistan's political future is no more certain than any other aspect of the interaction between Islam and politics there. It is even possible that some of the advocates of Islamic politics were themselves uncertain about what the alternative to the old order ought to be. That would not be surprising, since Islamic politics means many different things throughout the Muslim world. It is not like communist politics at the height of Moscow's ascendancy, with its centralized determination of doctrine and tactics. For example, Islamic law prohibits usury, which it defines broadly, although Muslims have used various devices over the centuries to bypass the prohibition. In the world's most populous Muslim country, Indonesia, the 1992 elections were preceded by the opening of the country's first Islamic bank, with the president's endorsement; the bank planned to obey Islamic law by not paying interest but instead would pay "profits" obtained from deposits.[56]

In the heady days following the apparent collapse of the Communist old order in the aftermath of the August 1991 coup, Turajonzoda remarked that he wanted Tajikistan to become an "Islamic democracy" but had no "prepared formula" for what that entailed. He noted that democracy in the West had evolved over a period of two centuries and recommended a synthesis of Islam and Western democratic principles for Tajikistan. "Tajikistan," he said "must be a secular, democratic state, but Islam's role must be sufficiently great, and any government must deal with the Islamic clergy."[57] He subsequently decried the tendency to view the increased standing of Islam in Tajikistan as ominous. The West was mistaken, he contended, when it equated Islam with "aggression and fanaticism," which he deemed antithetical to the teachings of the faith.[58] He continued to espouse democracy and civil liberties during the civil war.[59] Muhammad

Himmatzoda, head of the IRP in Tajikistan, disavowed the kind of radical, anti-Western politics that the West commonly associates with "Islamic fundamentalism." As he said,

> I don't know why this [Islamic revival] is frightening for the West. They understand the word "fundamentalism" as meaning extremist groups or tendencies. It's not like that. . . . Fundamentalism is a return to the Islam that our prophet Mohammad preached. So if we are called fundamentalists, not in the Western sense but in the sense of a return to pure Islam . . . that for us is honour and glory.[60]

He did not mention that Muslims disagree among themselves about the specifics of what the restoration of the pure Islam of Muhammad's time entails.

Although the IRP called for the establishment of an Islamic state in Tajikistan as an *ultimate* objective, it was vague about what that would mean. To the extent that IRP leaders identified more specific objectives, these embodied the concerns with popular sovereignty, civil liberties, and economic reforms that were typical of the opposition as a whole, whether secular or Islamic. Two of the founders of the IRP in the republic repudiated extremism, advocated religious freedom for Muslims and non-Muslims alike, and called for unspecified economic policies that respected both the environment and Islamic principles. They also asserted that only the electorate should determine whatever form of government Tajikistan would have.[61] Before it became clear that the Soviet Union would not survive, IRP activist Davlat Usmon even proposed that Tajikistan could adopt an Islamic government while remaining part of the union, a condition that would necessarily have limited the extent of change possible in the name of Islam.[62]

On one characteristic of the future Islamic state both the *qadi* and the IRP were clear—it would not copy the Islamic Republic of Iran. As Turajonzoda stated many times, the large Sunni majority in Tajikistan would not want to emulate the political system in predominantly Shi'i Iran and would hardly be able to do so, given the decentralized character of the Sunni religious leadership in contrast to the centralized hierarchy in Iran. He said this not only to Western reporters and the Moscow press, whom he might theoretically have wished to deceive, but also to opposition demonstrators in Dushanbe.[63]

The Islamic opposition cooperated with others who agreed with them that the continuation of Soviet-style politics was unacceptable but did not share their views on the political role of Islam.[64] This alliance may have been a consequence of the fact that the advocates of Islamic politics did not have the support of a large proportion of Tajikistan's inhabitants.[65] It may also reflect a recognition that it was not desirable to seek a monopoly of power for practitioners of Islamic politics, as in the archetypal image of an Islamic republic. Whatever the reason, the IRP entered into a coalition with parties that explicitly called for the creation of a secular, democratic state in Tajikistan, the Democratic Party of Tajikistan, Rastokhez, and La''li Badakhshon. In 1992, this coalition became known as the United Democratic Opposition. Qadi Turajonzoda also supported this coalition. In addition, he gave repeated and strong public support to a secular reformer, Davlat Khudonazarov, in the presidential election of November 1991 and in Khudonazarov's attempt to reconcile the opposing parties during the 1992 civil war.[66] The IRP endorsed Khudonazarov's candidacy as well.[67] During the spring 1992 demonstrations by the opposition, which eventually forced some short-lived concessions from the government, the opposition coalition did not press for the establishment of an Islamic state in Tajikistan. Instead, it criticized the regime's adherence to the old Soviet economic policies and political repression. Working with members of the secular opposition and communists who were willing to accept reforms, they called for civil liberties and efforts to raise the country's low standard of living.[68]

The opposition coalition and Turajonzoda as an individual strove to reassure the Russian inhabitants of Tajikistan that the opposition was not hostile to Russians but, on the contrary, sought common ground with them.[69] In addition to the conciliatory statements of leading opposition figures, one opposition newspaper printed a letter from a group of villagers who depicted the Christian minority in a positive light and as fitting in well in Tajikistani society; the article made the point that there were Russians and Ukrainians in Tajikistan who, although Christian, were respectful of Islam and their Muslim neighbors and who were in turn respected by the Muslims among whom they lived.[70] The head of an armed group in Dushanbe that supported the coalition government presented the political conflict as not inherently ethnic and religious, claiming that Russians (and Uzbeks) joined with Tajiks in defending Dushanbe when hardliners tried to seize it in October 1992.[71]

Nonetheless, many Russian and other nonindigenous inhabitants of Tajikistan appear to have feared the changes an opposition victory would bring, not because the Russian speakers wanted to assert a different, non-Islamic religiosity, but because they perceived the opposition as representing "alien" attitudes in comparison with those that prevailed in the late Soviet era; once the civil war began, they were concerned primarily with their personal security and the provision of basic material necessities.[72]

Whatever he hoped Tajikistan might eventually become, Qadi Turajonzoda stated many times to many different audiences that Tajiks were so poorly informed about Islam that the establishment of an Islamic form of government was impossible in the near term. He thought it would take thirty to forty years before Tajiks learned enough about Islam to make this goal attainable. Even then, he thought it ought not to be attempted unless there were public support for the idea. In the meantime, Tajikistan would continue to need people with the expertise to run a modern state—they were not, he contended, the same people as the small minority who were well versed in Islam.[73] The IRP also deemed the creation of an Islamic state impracticable for the time being and insisted that there would be no attempt to create one without the endorsement of a referendum. Davlat

Usmon, like the *qadi*, spoke of an interval of about forty years before an Islamic state might become feasible.[74]

There is always the possibility that some or all of the prominent Islamic political figures would have attempted radical Islamization without regard for the wishes of others if only they had the power to do so. There is no way to judge this with certainty, since the opportunity did not arise. Islamic political forces and other members of the opposition never had more than a share of power in a coalition government that held office for a few months during 1992 amidst the growing chaos of an expanding civil war. Given the widespread acceptance on face value of so many negative statements about the Islamic political opposition made by its enemies, a balanced inquiry requires at least consideration of other perspectives, including the group's own words and deeds while its members still had hopes of bringing about change through peaceful means. The fact that the political confrontation escalated into civil war in 1992 does not prove extremism on the part of any of the components of the opposition, since it was the communist hardliners who began the fighting, though they blamed the opposition. The fact that some opposition fighters committed brutal acts during the civil war also does not prove inherent fanaticism on the part of the opposition leadership. No atrocity should be excused, no matter who committed it. Yet the worst some people did in the worst of times, amidst the total breakdown of order, including horrendous violence meted out by the hardline fighters, ought not to be taken as proof of the goals of a much larger number of people in times of peace. The same reasoning applies as the international community watches what the Islamic opposition will become, since it has been embittered by its defeat in the civil war, the massive repression meted out by the victorious hardliners, and the feeling of abandonment by reformers in Russia and by the West.

Islamic religious and political assertiveness in Tajikistan had major repercussions for the country's international relations. That large and complex subject cannot be done justice here, but a few observations are warranted on the evolution of Tajikistan's relations with Russia, Uzbekistan, Iran, Afghanistan, and the United States. Of all Tajikistan's neighbors, Uzbekistan was the one that exerted the most influence on Tajikistan's affairs, while Afghanistan's influence, at least through the end of the civil war, was much less than often thought to be the case. Russia, too, intervened in independent Tajikistan's affairs, with major consequences. Iran, often suspected of supporting Islamic revolution in Tajikistan, in fact took a far more prudent and pragmatic stance. The United States, toward which the opposition expressed goodwill, believed the worst of the opposition during the civil war.

The escalating political conflict within Tajikistan was viewed with open concern in other newly independent Central Asian states, but above all in Uzbekistan. The intensity of the alarms raised by Uzbekistan's government reflects some general problems in the relations between that state and Tajikistan, but also the particular interests of the regime of President Islam Karimov. Relations between Tajiks and Uzbeks have deteriorated over many years because of the growth of nationalism among the intelligentsias of both peoples, the presence of large minorities of each nationality in the eponymous republic of the other, and the conflict of interests between the two states over regional problems, such as environmental degradation and access to water. The emergence of a strong opposition in Tajikistan was especially significant to President Karimov, since his approach to politics closely resembled that of the communist hardliners in Tajikistan, and he, too, faced the growth of an opposition that combined secular and Islamicizing elements. By raising the alarm about an alleged Islamic fundamentalist menace in Tajikistan, Karimov could justify the suppression of both Uzbekistan's opposition and the Tajik minority, which pressed for greater cultural freedom. He could also use the fear of Islam to deflect foreign criticism of his own deplorable human rights record and enlist the backing of the Russian government. The Karimov propaganda machine kept up a steady stream of warnings about the disastrous international consequences of an opposition victory in Tajikistan. He accused Qadi Turajonzoda of leading a group of "fanatics and extremists" who sought political power and who allegedly smuggled drugs and weapons from Afghanistan into Tajikistan and from there to other Central Asia states, with Europe the ultimate objective.[75] All of Central Asia and Russia, too, were threatened, according to Karimov, by a chain reaction sparked by Tajikistan's Islamists, for "an explosion of Islamic fundamentalism and thousands of hapless people could lead to an explosive situation throughout this vast region" that could touch "Russia itself."[76] The relentless barrage of propaganda in Uzbekistan's mass media about the Tajikistani threat enabled the Karimov regime to stigmatize all Uzbek and Tajik advocates of change as Islamic fundamentalists and laud himself as Uzbekistan's savior from that peril. That in turn provided a rationale for the suppression of the domestic opposition.[77] Uzbekistan and Russia jointly intervened in Tajikistan to ensure the hardliners' victory in the civil war (see below).

Moscow heard the same kinds of scare stories from Tajikistan's hardliners as it did from Karimov. One example of this is the tirade against the opposition by the hardline forces from Kulob Province, which *Literaturnaia gazeta* accepted uncritically. The article presented the only options in Tajikistan's politics as the red or the green (Islamic.) The reporter whitewashed the particularly brutal assault by Kulobis on the neighboring province of Qurghonteppa, on the grounds that the targeted province had been controlled by vovchiks, KGB derogatory slang for anti-Soviet Muslims; the article depicted these vovchiks as tyrants who alienated the province's peasants. The article quoted Kulob's vice-governor, Mahmadsaid Ubaidulloev, as he played on Christian-Muslim antipathy by claiming that the opposition called the Russians and the Kulobis infidels. Ubaidulloev warned, "I think that Islam, which today they try to foist upon us, is frightening not only for us but also for you. . . . Islamization is dangerous for you Russians, too!"[78] (Ubaidulloev became first deputy prime minister in the hardline government installed in Dushanbe late in the civil war.) President Nabiev's allies routinely characterized the opposition as "Islamic fundamentalists."[79] In the short-lived coalition government, the first deputy chairman of Tajikistan's KNB (successor to the KGB), Jurabek Aminov, dismissed such warnings as a politically motivated attempt to discredit the opposition and gain support for the hardliners in Russia and the West. The Islamic fundamentalist threat was, in his opinion, no more than a "myth."[80] (Aminov was assassinated in November 1992.)

The reasons some Russians so readily believed exaggerated stories of an Islamic threat lie beyond the scope of this chapter. However, the extent of such fears is worth noting. A late-Soviet-era publication attributed worries about an Islamic threat to more than half the inhabitants of the Russian Republic.[81] The political turmoil in various successor states of the Soviet Union would most probably have intensified the Islamophobia of those susceptible to it. The political assertiveness of Muslim peoples in the early 1990s, regardless of whether it was actually couched in terms of religious ideology, threatened the territorial integrity of the Russian state, as Tatars of the Volga River valley, the neighboring Bashkirs, and the Chechens of the North Caucasus all pressed their claims for independence from Moscow.

Yet there were others in Russian public life who rejected hostile oversimplifications of the power struggle in Tajikistan. Several Moscow-based newspapers, especially *Nezavisimaia gazeta* and also *Moskovskie novosti* as well as *Izvestiia* and occasionally others, presented quite a different picture of events in Tajikistan and often reported the views of members of the opposition themselves rather than what hardliners attributed to the opposition. Some reformers spoke out against the general stigmatization of Tajikistan's opposition. Elena Bonner and St. Petersburg mayor Anatolii Sobchak were among those who challenged the prevailing assumptions.

However, cries of alarm over the alleged Islamic menace fell on generally sympathetic ears in Moscow, where members of the Yeltsin administration and people who were reformers except when dealing with Muslims became the strange bedfellows of hardliners in their Islamophobia.[82] The rhetoric of those who accepted the Islamic fundamentalist interpretation also reflected lingering bitterness over the war in Afghanistan and the implied intent to refight it, this time successfully, in Tajikistan. Some in Moscow appeared to think that, although the Soviet Union no longer existed, the sovereignty of a former constituent republic like Tajikistan ought to be subordinated to Russia's interests. For example, Russia's Ministry of Foreign Affairs declared that Tajikistan was in Russia's vital interest zone; therefore, no interference in Tajikistan's internal affairs would be tolerated, from any quarter, for any reason. This was a reference to the allegedly subversive role played by Afghanistan, and especially the Islamic extremist Hizb-i Islami, in Tajikistan during 1992; Iran and Pakistan were supposedly behind this subversion.[83] Some, especially people associated with the military, expressed themselves in a tone of aggrieved belligerence reminiscent of the Soviet war in Afghanistan, as in references to those who plunder and kill along the Tajikistan-Afghanistan border using Allah as a justification and who have Stinger missiles from "across the ocean."[84]

Russia had an armed presence in Tajikistan during the civil war and after in the form of border guards, who were under Russia's control (though not composed entirely of Russians), and the 201st Motorized Rifle Division of the Russian army. Russian troops were supposed to be neutral, but they tilted increasingly toward the hardliners as the civil war intensified. Late in 1992, Russian and Uzbekistani troops aided the hardliners' final drive on Dushanbe. Military, KGB, and police personnel from both states remained in Tajikistan after that to shore up the new hardline government and crush the opposition.[85] The new head of state, Imomali Rahmonov, acknowledged his government's heavy dependence on the support of these two countries to remain in power.[86]

Russia's role in the civil war and since has left some members of Tajikistan's opposition embittered.[87] The tone of the Russian government and some in the mass media became even more Islamophobic after the civil war than it had been during it. Having committed itself to defend the hardline regime it helped install in Tajikistan, Russia found its own troops being killed by opponents of that regime. That led to more Russian anger and the determination to fight on. By the fall of 1993, Russia had more than fifteen thousand soldiers in Tajikistan.[88]

The Russian government justified its stance in various ways, including the need to protect Tajikistan and Russians living outside Russia, enmity toward the opposition fighters, the alleged participation of Afghanistanis as well as Tajikistanis in the attacks on Russian troops,[89] and above all Russia's strategic interest in combatting Islamic fundamentalism. Russia's minister of defense, Pavel Grachev, depicted Russian troops in Tajikistan as preventing an Islamic fundamentalist domino effect.[90] On one particular occasion, after an incursion from Afghanistani territory in mid-July 1993 that left more than a score of border guards killed or wounded, Grachev described the cross-border fighting there as the start of an undeclared war on Russia, but declared that he, with Yeltsin's backing, would make plans to defend the Russian people.[91] Even before that incident, Moscow told the Kabul government that Russia was "determined to defend the Tajik border with all the combat means available," for, if the cross-border fighting continued, there was "a very great risk" that more Central Asian states would be destabilized. That could quickly lead to "a full-fledged armed conflict blazing on a vast territory from central Asia to southwest Asia."[92]

Russia's concern with the continued, though small-scale, fighting on the Tajikistan-Afghanistan border and the determination to obtain international support for its policy in that quarter was such that Foreign Minister Andrei Kozyrev raised the issue as a discordant note amidst the otherwise conciliatory rhetoric of the Israeli-Palestinian recognition ceremony in Washington in September 1993. Kozyrev devoted a considerable portion of his brief remarks to a digression from the step toward peace between Palestinians and Israelis to warn of the danger of what he described as subversion, terrorism, and extremism of both religious and nonreligious kinds on the border between Tajikistan and Afghanistan.[93]

In a remarkable symbolic gesture, the first person to receive a medal at a ceremony honoring members of the Russian armed forces for their efforts during the fighting in Moscow between President Yeltsin and his opponents in October 1993 was not a participant in those events but a sergeant of the Russian border guard in Tajikistan; he received the medal of Hero of the Russian Federation for fighting "Tajik and Afghan bandits."[94] The use of the term "bandits" is reminiscent of Soviet rhetoric about the Afghanistani mujahideen and the Basmachi opposition to the establishment of Soviet rule in Central Asia.

The fear of Islamic radicalism in Tajikistan was linked to the fear that Iran and Afghanistan were plotting Islamic revolution there. Examples of the mistrust of Afghanistan have been noted above. One Moscow commentary on Iranian designs in Central Asia was predicated on the unstated assumption that the inhabitants of newly independent Central Asian states could not possibly have political objectives of their own and therefore would pass from Moscow's dominance to Tehran's. The editorial claimed that Tehran hoped that "fundamentalism can fill the political vacuum created in those countries after the collapse of communism and the weakening of Moscow's influence."[95] However, actual relations between Iran and Tajikistan did not substantiate allegations of a revolutionary conspiracy.

That Tajikistani Islamicizers did not belong to an "Islamintern" directed by Tehran has been discussed above. Many Tajikistani intellectuals were interested in Iran, but for cultural, not religious, reasons, as they sought to reclaim their Persian heritage after decades of Soviet distortions.[96] Secular political figures, both among the opposition and the hardliners, expressed goodwill toward Iran to advance their own political objectives. While the hardline regime in Dushanbe depicted itself as the sole alternative to an Islamic revolution in Tajikistan, it also encouraged relations with Iran, praised Iran's Islamic revolution and Ayatollah Khomeini, and sent Tajiks to study at the school of the Ministry of Foreign Affairs in Tehran. President Nabiev visited Iran in mid-1992 and after his return spoke to a Tajikistani newspaper about the "common religion" and other ties that bind the two countries.[97] This approach was continued by the new hardline regime installed late in the civil war.[98]

Iran certainly tried to expand its influence in Tajikistan, but this was largely in the sphere of state-to-state relations, communications, culture, and economics. During the political power struggle of 1992, Tehran encouraged the opposition to reach a modus vivendi with the Nabiev regime rather than press for a complete transfer of power.[99] Iran criticized the violence directed against the opposition during the civil war, but that did not stop the Tehran government from inviting the head of state in the post–civil war government to visit Tehran, an invitation that was accepted.[100] Iran also continued to pursue its own advantages by cultivating good relations with Russia and Uzbekistan, despite the role both played in defeating the Tajikistani opposition. Iran's President Rafsanjani gave symbolic expression to this in his visit to Uzbekistan in October 1993. Tehran also cultivated good relations with the regime of Turkmenistan's Communist Party leader turned president, Saparmurad Niyazov, who has not permitted any Islamicizing politics.

Contact between Tajikistan and Afghanistan occurred before and during the civil war, but its extent was wildly exaggerated both by those who had a political motive to link the opposition to Islamic fundamentalism in Afghanistan and those who believed the politically motivated claims. The majority of arms used by combatants in the civil war came from within Tajikistan, including from armed forces there. Only a minority of weapons was obtained from Afghanistan by people who bought or bartered for them at a time when the spread of violence made more people want to arm themselves; such arms traffic as existed was not part of a concerted mujahideen effort to fuel an Islamic revolution in Tajikistan.[101] Even Nabiev protégé Akbarsho Iskandarov, at the time speaker of Tajikistan's legislature, rejected claims that rival mujahideen leaders Gulbeddin Hekmatyar and Ahmad Shah Mas'ud were arming fighters in Tajikistan. Much of such cross-border contact that occurred before late 1992 took the form of apolitical smuggling.[102]

The situation changed by late 1992, as large numbers of Tajiks fled to Afghanistan to escape the violence at home, often encountering horrific conditions along their way. (In the absence of a definitive count, the prevailing estimate of the number of refugees was 50,000–60,000, of whom a minority returned within a few months.) Most of the refugees were neither combatants nor political activists, although there were members of the opposition, including the Islamic Renaissance Party, among them. Once in Afghanistan, a minority of the refugees came under the influence of Islamic radicalism, expressed in the form of hostility toward international relief workers and raids into Tajikistan, including attacks on the Russian-controlled border guards. The size of this radicalized faction was unclear. One of the largest cross-border incursions it staged in 1993 involved, according to a Russian source, 250 men.[103] It is too soon to assess the strength of any political orientation among the refugees in the longer term, or even whether a large number of Tajikistanis will remain in Afghanistan for a prolonged period.

The United States government looked at the transition to independence of Tajikistan and the other Central Asian states with apprehension over the possibility that they would be destabilized by Iran or Afghanistan. Secretary of State James Baker told the Senate Foreign Relations Committee that the United States decided to establish embassies in all the newly independent Central Asian states, not just Qazaqistan and Kyrgyzstan, as originally planned, because of a perceived need to compete with Iran for influence there. As an unnamed "senior official" told the press, the Central Asian states "are up for grabs, and we need to make sure that they look north and west and not south and east."[104] Given the embittered state of U.S.-Iranian relations, perhaps some U.S. officials shared the assumption of a high-ranking official of the Commission on Security and Cooperation in Europe that Tajiks, as Persian speakers, were especially susceptible to radical Islamic political influence from Iran and Afghanistan.[105]

The hardline leadership in Tajikistan perceived the United States as seeing that country primarily in terms of fears of the spread of radical Islamization from Iran and Afghanistan.[106] Secretary Baker lent credence to that perception during his meeting with President Nabiev early in 1992. Baker told Nabiev that Tajikistan ought not to adopt an Islamic fundamentalist government. Nabiev exploited the Secretary's concern by describing himself as having no interest in Islamic fundamentalism, while implying that the country's rural majority might be drawn to such an ideology.[107] Baker reinforced the impression that invoking the Islamic menace was the way to obtain U.S. support when he chose not to meet with any opposition leaders while in Tajikistan. Yet the Islamic opposition did not share Iran's anti-American rhetoric any more than it shared the Iranian approach to politics. The IRP's Davlat Usmon, while deputy prime minister in the coalition government, voiced good wishes toward the United States and the desire for good relations between Dushanbe and Washington.[108] The U.S. government remained cool to the opposition, both secular and Islamic, throughout 1992 and into the early months of the Clinton administration.

By the end of the Soviet era, the dissatisfaction with the old order that was widespread in the union as a whole affected many Tajikistanis. Tajiks, like other members of minority nationalities and religions within the union, had additional reasons to resent a status quo that put the interests of the center over those of the periphery and disparaged the heritage of non-Russians and especially the Muslim nationalities. The climate of change at the end of the 1980s and beginning of the 1990s enabled Tajiks to voice long-standing concerns for more equitable treatment and the right to reclaim their own identity, instead of being forced to assent to Moscow's disparaging version. In that context, Tajiks became increasingly open about the significance of Islam to them. Their motives were mixed. For some, their ancestral faith linked them to a rich civilization that disproved the old Soviet rhetoric that the Tajiks were a "formerly backward people" who owed everything to Russian and Soviet mentors. For many, the waning of Soviet anti-Islamic measures brought the opportunity to learn more about a body of religious teachings that had been largely inaccessible even to people who considered themselves believers. Some Tajiks hoped that Islamic values would play a greater role in public life so that they, after decades of control by others, could draw on their own heritage to shape their future. Just how Islam would play this role was something the Islamicizers did not make clear; given the disparity of views on the subject in the Muslim world in general, they may themselves have been uncertain. The leading Islamicizers also supported the establishment of a parliamentary democracy and a market economy, as did the secularist reformers who were their allies.

The effects of Islamization and the Islamicizers' abilities to govern were not tested in Tajikistan because the opposition to the old order achieved only limited power for a few months. The coalition government established in May 1992 included members of the secular and Islamic opposition as well as elements of the Communist Party who opposed change. Almost as soon as the coalition government was established, the communist hardliners set about overthrowing it and reestablishing their own monopoly of power. Their methods included armed violence that soon escalated into civil war and the demonization of the opposition as religious extremists. These techniques succeeded, culminating in December 1992 with the hardliners' victory, aided by Russia and Uzbekistan. In the short term, the hardliners' tactic of demonizing the opposition on religious grounds appeared shrewd, since that helped provide the pretext for outside intervention in aid of the hardliners and made many in the West leery of the opposition. However, this was a dangerous way to win. The battering inflicted on the opposition and on civilians caught up in indiscriminate attacks is what so often undermines moderates and strengthens the appeal of extremists' messages of anger and simple solutions to complex problems. If the opposition finds outside support only from those who endorse radical Islamic politics, those who choose to continue the struggle for power may have no choice but to be drawn into that camp. The very victory of those who claimed to be fighting Islamic fundamentalism may prove to be the most powerful cause of radicalization among the Islamic opposition.

Notes

1. Ostankino Television (Moscow), 30 May 1993, as translated in *FBIS Daily Report: Central Eurasia,* 2 June 1993, p. 72.
2. M.B. Olcott, "Soviet Central Asia: Does Moscow Fear Iranian Influence?" in *The Iranian Revolution: Its Global Impact,* ed. J.L. Esposito (Miami: Florida International University Press, 1990), p. 212.
3. "What Imam-Khatyb Muradjah Sabit Recounts," *Muslims of the Soviet East* (Tashkent), 1989, no. 1, p. 14.
4. T. Saidbaev, *Islam i obshchestvo,* 2d ed. (Moscow: Nauka, Glavnaia redaktsiia Vostochnoi literatury, 1984), p. 191.
5. According to the last census, taken in 1989, Tajiks accounted for 62.3 percent of the population, Uzbeks for 23.5 percent, and Volga Tatars, Kyrgyz, Turkmens, and Crimean Tatars each accounted for less than 1.5 percent. See *The First Book of Demographics for the Republics of the Former Soviet Union: 1951–1990* (Shady Side, MD: New World Demographics, L.C., 1992), p. D–8; T.W. Karasik, ed., *USSR: Facts and Figures Annual,* vol. 17 (Gulf Breeze, FL: Academic International Press, 1992), pp. 449–50.
6. N.V. Khanykov, *Opisanie Bukharskogo khanstva* (St. Petersburg: Tipografiia Imperatorskoi akademii nauk, 1843), p. 210.
7. V.P. Nalivkin and M. Nalivkina, *Ocherk byta zhenshchiny osedlago tuzemnago naseleniia Fergany* (Kazan: Tipografiia Imperatorskago universiteta, 1886), pp. 57–59; M.N. Shahrani, "Local Knowledge of Islam and Social Discourse in Afghanistan and Turkistan in the Modern Period," in *Turko-Persia in Historical Perspective,* ed. R.L.

Canfield (Cambridge: Cambridge University Press, 1991), pp. 166–68; M. Atkin, "The Survival of Islam in Soviet Tajikistan," *Middle East Journal,* vol. 43, no. 4 (autumn 1989), p. 611.

8. G. Krivonogov, "Oboshlis' bez apolodismentov . . ." [*sic*], *Agitator Tadzhikistana,* 1989, no. 3 (February), p. 13.

9. Atkin, "Survival of Islam," pp. 611–12.

10. Ibid., p. 613.

11. A. Istad, "Davlati milli chi guna boyad?" *Adabiyot va san''at* (Dushanbe), 4 June 1992, p. 6.

12. G. Utorbaev, "Podgotovka musul'manskikh bogosluzhitelei," *Komsomolets Uzbekistana,* 12 October 1990, p. 2.

13. Ibid.

14. *Moskovskie novosti,* 30 August 1992, p. 11.

15. Dushanbe radio, in Tajik, 16 July 1992, as translated in *FBIS Daily Report: Central Eurasia,* 20 July 1992, p. 61; Reuter Library Report, 1 December 1991; M. Olimi, "Oghozi id az namozgoh," *Adabiyot va san''at,* 4 June 1992, p. 12.

16. "Clergy" is not a term used traditionally in Islam to describe all those who are learned in the faith and perform a variety of religious functions. However, that is the term used in the Soviet Union for a group of people who had legal recognition as "servitors of the cult" of Islam.

17. I. Rotar', "My khotim islamskoi demokratii," *Nezavisimaia gazeta,* 11 September 1992, p. 3.

18. Ibid.; Reuter Library Report, 1 December 1991.

19. M. Usolkina, "Ba naslihoi oyanda chi boqi meguzorem?" *Adabiyot va san''at,* 11 June 1987, p. 13; F. Rajabova, "Kori doimi," *Tojikistoni soveti,* 23 September 1986, p. 2; Atkin, "Survival of Islam," pp. 614–15; Muriel Atkin, *The Subtlest Battle: Islam in Soviet Tadjikistan* (Philadelphia: Foreign Policy Research Institute, 1989), pp. 25–26.

20. N. Yodgori, "Badargha," *Tojikistoni soveti,* 12 September 1989, p. 3.

21. Representative of the large body of literature on the subject is A. Bennigsen and M. Broxup, *The Islamic Threat to the Soviet State* (New York: St. Martin's Press, 1983), pp. 77, 147, 148.

22. M. Atkin, "Islamic Assertiveness and the Waning of the Old Soviet Order," *Nationalities Papers,* vol. 20, no. 1 (spring 1992), pp. 56–57.

23. TadzhikTA, "Vospityvat' ubezhdennykh bortsov za delo partii," *Kommunist Tadzhikistana,* 3 September 1986, p. 3.

24. Igor' Beliaev, "Konsolidatsiia, a ne raskol," *Literaturnaia gazeta,* 13 September 1989, p. 11.

25. A. Hetmanek, "The Mullahs vs. Moscow," *Washington Post,* 25 September 1988, p. C1.

26. D. Sneider, "Soviets Face Muslim Activists," *Christian Science Monitor,* 5 February 1991, p. 5.

27. O. Brushlinskaia, "Prishlo vremia . . ." [*sic*], *Nauka i religiia,* 1989, no. 11 (November), p. 20.

28. N. Yodgori, "Kulob: ruzi jum''a," *Tojikistoni soveti,* 13 October 1989, p. 2.

29. Rotar', "My khotim islamskoi demokratii."

30. Ibid.

31. S. Tadjbakhsh, "The Bloody Path of Change: The Case of Post-Soviet Tajikistan," *Harriman Institute Forum,* vol. 6, no. 11 (July 1993), p. 6; G. Tett, "Soviet Mullahs Who Threaten Gorbachev," *Financial Times,* 17 August 1991, p. 1.

32. Reuters, 21 December 1992.

33. L. Bashirov, "Islam v nashi dni," *Slovo lektora,* 1989, no. 1, p. 33. The article did

not provide information on the number of people surveyed, the date of the survey, or the wording of the survey questions; Atkin, *The Subtlest Battle,* pp. 9–10.

34. E. Subhon, "Oinhoro ki vairon mekunad?" *Adabiyot va san''at,* 6 July 1989, p. 12; V. Vorob'ev, "Za kritiku . . . no s ogliadkoi," *Kommunist Tadzhikistana,* 28 February 1987, p. 2; Atkin, "Survival of Islam," p. 617.

35. A. Lukin and A. Ganelin, "Podpol'nyi obkom deistvuet," *Komsomol'skaia pravda,* 23 March 1991, p. 2.

36. Helsinki Watch, *Conflict in the Soviet Union: Tadzhikistan* (New York and Washington, D.C.: Human Rights Watch, 1991), p. 14; Atkin, "Survival of Islam," p. 607.

37. A. Ma''ruf, "Sabriston yo Savriston?" *Adabiyot va san''at,* 4 June 1992, p. 11.

38. Radio Dushanbe, in Tajik, 16 July 1992, as translated in *FBIS Daily Report: Central Eurasia,* 20 July 1992, p. 61.

39. *Moscow News,* 6–13 September 1992, as reprinted in *FBIS Daily Report: Central Eurasia,* 7 October 1992, p. 117.

40. "Binoi musulmoni," *Shahodat* (Dushanbe), 1370/1992, no. 4 (Bahman/February), p. 2.

41. S. Tadjbakhsh, "Causes and Consequences of the Civil War," *Central Asia Monitor,* 1993, no. 1, p. 12.

42. M. Atkin, "Tajikistan: Ancient Heritage, New Politics," in *Nations and Politics in the Soviet Successor States,* ed. I. Bremmer and R. Taras (Cambridge: Cambridge University Press, 1993), pp. 361–62, 365.

43. No opposition parties had legal permission to exist in Tajikistan before 1991. That changed during the course of that year, as different parties obtained legal standing at various times. The last major party to be recognized officially was the IRP, in October 1991.

44. See, for example, ITAR-TASS, 2 September 1992, in Russian; O. Panfilov, "Sangak Safarov: 'Est' mnogo liudei, zhelaiushchikh prodolzhit' bratoubiistvennuiu voiny'," *Nezavisimaia gazeta,* 4 August 1992, p. 3; see also "President of Tajikistan Is Removed From Power," *Washington Post,* 3 September 1992, p. A36.

45. A. Karpov, "Ot prezidenta Tadzhikistana trebuiut tol'ko odnogo—zaiavlenie ob otstavke," *Izvestiia,* 3 September 1992, p. 2.

46. *Anatolia* (Ankara), in Turkish, 4 February 1992, as translated in *FBIS Daily Report: Central Eurasia,* 5 February 1992, pp. 89–90.

47. Middle East News Network, 6 January 1992, citing *ash-Sharq al-Awsat.*

48. Interfax, 16 April 1992, as reprinted in *FBIS Daily Report: Central Eurasia,* 16 April 1992, p. 63.

49. O. Panfilov, "Spaset li Shaposhnikov Nabieva?" *Nezavisimaia gazeta,* 1 September 1992, p. 3.

50. Ostankino Television, 30 May 1993, as translated in *FBIS Daily Report: Central Eurasia,* 2 June 1993, p. 72.

51. T.F. Weber, "Tajikistan's Troubles Could Embroil Others," *Christian Science Monitor,* 9 October 1992, p. 19.

52. A. Lugovskaia, "Politicheskii krizis v Tadzhikistane byl neizbezhen," *Izvestiia,* 4 September 1992, p. 3.

53. Statements made in the author's presence.

54. Tadjbakhsh, "Bloody Path of Change," p. 6; statements made by opposition members in the author's presence.

55. V. Kazakov, "Gotovy k dialogu," *Literaturnaia Rossiia,* 8 March 1991, p. 6; Tett, "Soviet Mullahs"; Rotar', "My khotim islamskoi demokratii"; "Soviet Central Asia: The Next Islamic Revolution," *Economist,* 21 September 1991, p. 58.

56. "Islamic Bank Opens in Jakarta," *Financial Times,* 15 May 1992, p. 6.

57. Rotar´, "My khotim islamskoi demokratii."

58. "Khodzhiakbar Turadzhonzoda," *Moskovskie novosti,* 30 August 1992, p. 11.

59. Ibid. Also see Radio Dushanbe, in Tajik, 16 July 1992, as translated in *FBIS Daily Report: Central Eurasia,* 20 July 1992, p. 61.

60. Reuter Library Report, 1 December 1991.

61. Lukin and Ganelin, "Podpol´nyi obkom deistvuet."

62. "Partiia, kotoroi ofitsial´no u nas net," *Komsomolets Tadzhikistana,* 21 November 1990, p. 2.

63. Istad, "Davlati milli chi guna boyad?" p. 6; U. Babakhanov and A. Mursaliev, "Pust´ govoriat ob islamskom Tadzhikistane: A kazi protiv," *Komsomol´skaia pravda,* 4 October 1991, p. 1; R. Wright, "Report from Turkestan," *New Yorker,* 6 April 1992, p. 75; "Khodzhiakbar Turadzhonzoda."

64. Lukin and Ganelin, "Podpol´nyi obkom deistvuet."

65. Tadjbakhsh, "Bloody Path of Change," p. 6.

66. See, for example, Radio Dushanbe, in Tajik, 16 July 1992, as translated in *FBIS Daily Report: Central Eurasia,* 20 July 1992, p. 61; *Moscow News,* 6–13 September 1992, as reprinted in *FBIS Daily Report: Central Eurasia,* 7 October 1992, p. 117; "Khodzhiakbar Turadzhonzoda"; Reuter Library Report, 23 November 1991.

67. Russian Press Digest, 1 November 1991, summary of article in *Soglasie.*

68. Voqif, "!Qavme hunkhor?" [sic], *Shahodat,* 1371/1992, no. 9 (Farvardin/April), p. 3; "Posukhta ba labi ob meravad," ibid., p. 2; Domullo Davlatshoh, "Girdihamoniro himoya mekunem," ibid., p. 1; "Murojiatnomai muslamononi nohiya," ibid., p. 1; "Ba mardumi sharifi Khatlonzamin," *Jomi jam* (Dushanbe), 1992, no. 6 (April), p. 3.

69. ITAR-TASS, in English, 14 April 1992, in *FBIS Daily Report: Central Eurasia,* 15 April 1992, pp. 55–56; Radio Rossii, 12 May 1992, as translated in ibid., 13 May 1992, p. 68; ITAR-TASS, 12 May 1992, as translated in ibid., 13 May 1992, p. 69; *Izvestiia,* 8 May 1992, as translated in ibid., 19 May 1992, p. 43.

70. "Sipos az Klius," *Shahodat,* 1371/1992, no. 9 (Farvardin/April), p. 4.

71. O. Panfilov, "Polevye komandiry dogovorilis´ o mire," *Nezavisimaia gazeta,* 27 November 1992, p. 3.

72. A. Azamova, "Dekolonizatsiia? . . . ili tsivilizovannyi iskhod?" *Moskovskie novosti,* no. 41 (October 1992), p. 9; O. Gorshunova, "Bez oreola neprikosnovennosti," *Rossiiskie vesti,* 22 September 1992, p. 2.

73. Tadjbakhsh, "Bloody Path of Change," p. 6; V. Vyzhutovich, "Krasnoe znamia kommunizma ili zelenoe znamia islama?" *Izvestiia,* 5 October 1991, p. 2; "Khodzhiakbar Turadzhonzoda"; U. Babakhanov and A. Ganelin, "Budet li v Dushanbe ploshchad´ pobedivshei oppozitsii?" *Komsomol´skaia pravda,* 22 May 1992, p. 1; ITAR-TASS, in Russian, 11 September 1992, reprinted in *Russia and CIS Today,* 11 September 1992, p. 19; *Moscow News,* 6–13 September 1992, as reprinted in *FBIS Daily Report: Central Eurasia,* 7 October 1992, p. 117.

74. *Izvestiia,* 8 May 1992, as translated in *FBIS Daily Report: Central Eurasia,* 19 May 1992, p. 43; TASS, in English, 30 September 1991, as reprinted in *FBIS Daily Report: Soviet Union,* 1 October 1991; Tett, "Soviet Mullahs"; Reuter Library Report, 9 September 1992; *Report on the Helsinki Commission Visit to Armenia, Azerbaijan, Tajikistan, Uzbekistan, Kazakhstan, and Ukraine* (Washington, D.C., Commission on Security and Cooperation in Europe, 1992), p. 25; Wright, "Report from Turkestan," p. 74.

75. Interfax, in English, 28 September 1992, as reprinted in *FBIS Daily Report: Central Eurasia,* 28 September 1992, p. 47.

76. *Komsomol´skaia pravda,* 9 October 1992, as translated in *FBIS Daily Report: Central Eurasia,* 14 October 1992, p. 54.

77. A. Azamova, "Nuzhna li musul´manam demokratiia?" *Moskovskie novosti,* no. 39,

1992, as reprinted in *Russia and CIS Today,* 24 September 1992, p. 44; *Nezavisimaia gazeta,* 21 January 1993, as summarized in *Current Digest of the Post-Soviet Press,* vol. 45, no. 3 (17 February 1993), p. 9; *RFE/RL Daily Report,* 15 July 1992, p. 3.

78. O. Blotskii, "Tadzhikistan: Zelenoe—krasnoe," *Literaturnaia gazeta,* 4 November 1992, p. 11.

79. See, for example, ITAR-TASS, in Russian, 2 September 1992.

80. A. Azamova, "Tadzhikistan: 'Afganskii variant ne iskliuchen,'" *Moskovskie novosti,* 6 September 1992, p. 9.

81. Y. Ro'i, "The Islamic Influence on Nationalism in Soviet Central Asia," *Problems of Communism,* vol. 39, no. 4 (July–August 1990), p. 60, n. 68.

82. Atkin, "Islamic Assertiveness," pp. 56–57.

83. ITAR-TASS, in Russian, 8 September 1992; Interfax, in English, 26 October 1992, as reprinted in *FBIS Daily Report: Central Eurasia,* 27 October 1992, p. 9.

84. "Na Tadzhiksko-Afganskoi granitse," *Voennoe reviu,* 6 June 1993, as reprinted in *Russia and CIS Today,* 7 June 1993, p. 16.

85. O. Panfilov, "General-Polkovnik Nabiev ostaetsia Tadzhikskim prezidentom," *Nezavisimaia gazeta,* 22 August 1992, p. 3; Agence France Presse, 17 December 1992; Ostankino Television, 25 May 1993, as translated in *FBIS Daily Report: Central Eurasia,* 26 May 1993, p. 15; *Moskovskie novosti,* 23 May 1993 [*sic*], as translated in *FBIS Daily Report: Central Eurasia,* 21 May 1993, p. 5; Reuter Library Report, 12 November 1992 and 19 December 1992; S. LeVine, "Ex-Leaders Rebound in Central Asia," *Washington Post,* 26 December 1992, p. A25; Interfax, in English, 10 April 1993, as reprinted in *FBIS Daily Report: Central Eurasia,* 13 April 1993, p. 15.

86. ITAR-TASS, world service, in Russian, as translated in *FBIS Daily Report: Central Eurasia,* 26 May 1993, p. 15.

87. Agence France Presse, in English, 1 August 1993; *Human Rights and Democratization in the Newly Independent Sates of the Former Soviet Union* (Washington, D.C.: Commission on Security and Cooperation in Europe, 1993), p. 23; statements made in the author's presence.

88. Reuters, 6 October 1993.

89. For example, Boris Yeltsin voiced all these themes: Ostankino Television, 15 July 1993, as rebroadcast in English on C-SPAN2, 15 July 1993.

90. See, for example, *RFE/RL Daily Report,* 9 February 1993, p. 3.

91. Ostankino Television, 16 July 1993, as rebroadcast in English, on C-SPAN, 16 July 1993.

92. Radio Moscow, world service, in English, 1 June 1993, as reprinted in *FBIS Daily Report: Central Eurasia,* 3 June 1993, p. 18.

93. Remarks made on the White House lawn, 13 September 1993, as broadcast by the Public Broadcasting System.

94. ITAR-TASS, in English, 8 October 1993.

95. M. Iusin, "V Tegerane ob''iavili 'velikuiu bitvu' za vliianii v Srednei Azii," *Izvestiia,* 7 February 1992, p. 7.

96. Comments made in the author's presence by Dust Muhammad Dust, historian and deputy chairman of the Democratic Party of Tajikistan; see also M. Qurbon and S. Ayub, "Tehron, Kobul, Dushanbe," *Adabiyot va san''at,* 10 August 1989, p. 2; M. Atkin, "Religious, National, and Other Identities in Central Asia," in *Muslims in Central Asia,* ed. J.A. Gross (Durham, NC and London: Duke University Press, 1992) pp. 55–57.

97. "Novyi shag na puti k sotrudnichestvu," *Narodnaia gazeta,* 7 July 1992, p. 1; see also TIA Khovar, "Za ukreplenie mezhdunarodnykh pozitsii Tadzhikistana," *Narodnaia gazeta,* 18 July 1992, p. 1; Radio Dushanbe, in Tajik, 11 February 1992, as translated in *FBIS Daily Report: Central Eurasia,* 13 February 1992, p. 88; *Resalat* (Tehran), in

Persian, 3 May 1992, as translated in *FBIS Daily Report: Central Eurasia,* 19 May 1992, p. 44.

98. Radio Dushanbe, in Tajik, 16 June 1993, as translated in *FBIS Daily Report: Central Eurasia,* 18 June 1993, p. 50.

99. S. Erlanger, "Tajik Ex-Communists Prosecute Opposition," *New York Times,* 10 January 1993, p. 15.

100. Reuter Library Report, 30 September 1993.

101. A. Karpov, "I.O. Prezienta Tadzhikistana pytaetsia vlast' upotrebit'," *Izvestiia,* 24 September 1992, p. 2; idem, "Tadzhikistan: chislo zhertv izmeriaetsia tysiachami," *Izvestiia,* 29 September 1992, p. 2; I. Rotar', "Grazhdane Tadzhikistana v voennykh lageriakh Khekmatiiara?" *Nezavisimaia gazeta,* 23 September 1992, p. 1; S. LeVine, "Tajiks Turn to Moscow for Help," *Washington Post,* 3 November 1992, p. A14.

102. Postfactum (Moscow), in English, 13 May 1992, as reprinted in *FBIS Daily Report: Central Eurasia,* 14 May 1992, p. 56; Panfilov, "Sangak Safarov"; "Khodzhiakabar Turadzhonzoda"; ITAR-TASS, in Russian, 23 August 1992; I. Rotar' and A. Abrashitov, "Vnutri chuzhoi voiny," *Nezavisimaia gazeta,* 15 August 1992, p. 3; Agence France Presse, in English, 6 November 1992.

103. *Tajikistan: Recommendations and Report on Refugees International's Assessment Mission* (Washington, D.C.: Refugees International, 1993), pp. 6–7; Ostankino Television, 13 July 1993, as rebroadcast in English by C-SPAN2, 13 July 1993.

104. T.L. Friedman, "U.S. to Counter Iran in Central Asia," *New York Times,* 6 February 1992, p. A3.

105. Reuter Library Report, 27 January 1992.

106. "Khabarhoi nav," *Jumhuriyat* (Dushanbe), 4 April 1992, p. 1.

107. "Tajikistan Agrees to Curbs on Arms," *Jumhuriyat* (Dushanbe), 14 February 1992, p. A7.

108. "Priem v posol'stve," *Narodnaia gazeta,* 7 July 1992, p. 1.

13

Islam and the Political Culture of "Scientific Atheism" in Post-Soviet Central Asia

Future Predicaments

M. Nazif Shahrani

O David! We did indeed make thee a viceregent [khalifah] *on earth: so judge thou between men in truth (and justice).*
Koran 38:26

Throughout most of human history religion has been intimately involved in the whole life of man in society, and not least in his politics.
W. Montgomery Watt, *Islamic Political Thought*

Colonialism plays both a conservative and revolutionizing role in underdeveloped areas: similar to a man who feeds the fire under a boiling kettle with one hand while keeping the lid down with his other hand. When the man leaves, because the pressure of the steam has become too high or he has developed other interests, and stops feeding the fire, the fire may keep burning but the lid may blow off.
John M. Kautsky, *The Political Consequences of Modernization*

Do not be fooled by the swarms of locusts leaving your fields, because they leave their larvae behind.
Somali proverb

Introduction

The sudden and relatively peaceful demise of the once powerful Soviet empire is said (by politicians and global media pundits alike) to promise the dawn of a still undefined "New World Order."[1] It has also set the academic community abuzz with all forms of "intellectual" speculations. For example, Francis Fukuyama, a policy analyst and Soviet watcher, declared that the collapse of the Soviet system heralded "the end of history" through the triumph of capitalism and liberal democracy. And for Samuel P. Huntington, a political theorist, the same event signaled the "next pattern of conflict," that of the "clash of civilizations" in world politics.[2] The meanings and impact of these apparent changes for the Russian peoples, especially the discontented elite, who effected the demise of the Soviet system, and for other peoples of the former Soviet empire and beyond who are affected by its demise, are issues that have yet to be fully and systematically explored.

If the changes are indeed as vast and fundamental as they are proclaimed to be, both *in* the new post-Soviet states and *for* these societies, especially the new successor states of Central Asia, then a radical change in our approaches to research and analysis in the region is also in order. Continued reliance on Soviet and Russian accounts and on worn-out approaches of Western Sovietology will not do if we are to comprehend the full meaning and significance of these transformations from the perspectives of the Muslim peoples of Turkistan (that is, formerly Soviet Central Asia). This is particularly necessary in view of the fact that the track record of the studies of Islam and Muslims in Central Asia under the Soviet system by both Soviet scholars and Western Sovietologists has been seriously wanting, to say the least. We can all recall how some Soviet and Western scholars repeatedly asserted that Islam and Soviet Muslims posed the most serious threat to the integrity of the Moscow regimes. Now other voices, including some leaders of new "Muslim" successor states in Central Asia, are joining the Russian- and Western-orchestrated chorus saying that (largely nonexistent) "fundamentalist Islam" and radical Muslim political movements in the region threaten the post-Soviet "New World Order." With perfect hindsight, we now know that Islam and Muslims, at least within the borders of the former Soviet empire, played no role whatsoever in the collapse of the Soviet state.

The critical issue of the future role of religion in Central Asian politics, however, should not be simply assumed, and it certainly cannot be ascertained or predicted with any degree of certainty on the basis of information and analysis about Central Asian Islam from the Soviet period. Are Muslims attempting to reclaim Islamic knowledge and redefine Muslim identity, and if so, how? How, when, and under what circumstances do Central Asians (leaders and citizens, "believers" and "nonbelievers," clergy and laity) make use of Islamic knowledge, values, ideals, and symbols, and toward the realization of what specific goals (political, economic, ideological, and/or spiritual)? Who among the diverse elements of the Central Asian populations (urban or rural, men or women, elders or youths, elites or ordinary citizens, and all or none of them) self-consciously identify themselves as Muslims, and why? And how does self-identity as Muslim influence the public behavior and social discourse of the individuals and groups, so identified, toward the "others" (individuals, groups, and states)? These questions must be studied and analyzed within the broader spectrum of the hegemonic Soviet cultural legacies, especially the all-pervasive political culture of "scientific atheism" in the region. The existing attitudes toward politics and religion in general, and Muslim beliefs, practices, and conceptions of political legitimacy in particular, are products of a long and oppressive colonial history. The painful and traumatic experiences of colonization, for individuals and groups, are often marked by deep emotional scars. The immediate and long-term effects of these experiences must be examined critically, and their implications for the present and future dynamics of religion and politics in post-Soviet Central Asian societies must be explored. For the purposes of this chapter, the "post-Soviet" realities in Uzbekistan (entailing particular events, political processes, and structural dynamics), therefore, provide the context for an examination of the Turkistanis, especially the Uzbeks' discourses on leadership and the cultural and ideological crises facing them as a consequence of this historic event.

Such an undertaking, although extremely difficult under the current research environment in post-Soviet Central Asia, would require, at a minimum, a serious examination and explication of relations among the following closely linked historical and sociological realities: (1) the nature of the Soviet colonial system and its unique cultural and political legacies in Muslim Central Asia; (2) the unprecedented circumstances leading to the declarations of "independence" from Soviet colonial rule by Central Asian Muslims since the summer of 1991; (3) the scope and limitations of their newly found "freedoms"; (4) the post-Soviet manifestations of the Central Asian Muslims' "consciousness of their own colonization and the colonization of their consciousness"[3]; and ultimately (5) the effects of all these factors on the dynamic processes of redefinition of personal and collective identities, expression of interpersonal and communal relationships, reconstruction of local and national histories, relations with other states (Muslim and non-Muslim), and excavation of the roots of their "Muslim" and national political cultures. We now turn to a brief discussion of some of these important issues.

Soviet Colonial Legacies

A detailed discussion of the Soviet colonial legacies (positive and negative, constructive and harmful, "revolutionary" and "conservative") and the challenges they present to the peoples of the successor states of Central Asia is beyond the scope of this chapter. I have, however, addressed some aspects of this issue elsewhere[4] and will here attempt to outline a few critical features of this powerful phenomenon that bear directly on the theme of this presentation: Islam and the discourse about leadership and legitimacy within the hegemonic political culture of scientific atheism in post-Soviet Central Asia.

In spite of exhaustion and internal collapse, the Soviet Russian colonial hand that fed and stoked the fire under the boiling cauldron of Muslim Central Asia seems to have accomplished its tasks of manipulating both the fire and the lid with skill. Contrary to many Soviet watchers' expectations, the Russian colonial fire kept burning, but the lid did not blow off, and certainly may not in Central Asia for some time yet.[5] As we know very well, the fires are still on in most of the newly independent states, and the old political lid (albeit under new names and flags) is very much in place and keeping autocratic power tightly in place. How can we explain this remarkable achievement, especially in the face of the apparent failure of the Soviet system itself?

Two important points offer some clue to this paradox. First, the disastrous outcome of the command and control of economic policies by the USSR should not obscure important successes of the regime in other areas (e.g., popularization of literacy and education, improved health care, introduction of modern science and technology, and expansion of an extensive communications and irrigation infrastructure throughout the former Soviet Central Asia). Second, although the system failed to meet the rising expectations of its dominant Russian and Slavic/European citizens, it nevertheless effectively shaped and molded the lives and experiences of the non-Slavic peoples in the colonized regions, especially Central Asia.[6] For example, the importance of the successful infusion and permanent settlement of well over ten million Slavic and other Europeans in Central Asia under Soviet colonization policies cannot be ignored. As the Somali proverb (quoted above) so aptly suggests, "the swarm of locusts"[7] may have left the fields, but their "larvae" remain, helping to keep the lid firmly in place.

The true legacy of the Soviet colonial system in Central Asia, however, is evidenced not only by the numerous Russians and Europeans as well as many other nonindigenous displaced and relocated minorities (e.g., Tatars, Koreans, Meskhetians) left behind, but by the remarkable numbers of highly educated native peoples forming cadres well versed in the art of Soviet political culture of "fear and favor" and in the political culture of scientific atheism. It is they who are serving as the enthusiastic guardians of the Soviet political traditions. Based on the long history of postcolonial states in Africa, Asia, and Latin America, where by comparison a much smaller colonial cadre (native and otherwise) has managed to perpetuate colonial traditions for many decades, the post-Soviet political realities should not surprise us at all.

Considerable attention has been paid in the literature to Soviet economic policies aimed at extracting raw materials and fostering the region's long-term economic and technological dependency on Russia and Eastern Europe, and to the ecological and economic consequences of these colonial policies in Muslim Central Asia.[8] No one should or could underestimate the magnitude of the economic and environmental challenges facing the post-Soviet states in Central Asia. However, as President Islam Karimov of Uzbekistan pointed out in a 1991 interview, "the gravest crisis that has befallen us [in Central Asia] *is not economic but moral*"[9] (emphasis added). President Karimov further said that "the destruction of age-old moral principles for ideological reasons will be far more difficult to overcome than the chaos in the economy."[10]

Indeed, the most significant achievement of the Soviet colonial rule in Central Asia may be the extent of its success in "colonizing" the minds and consciousness of the peoples of Central Asia. The incorporation of Central Asian Muslims into the Soviet *colonial state* met with remarkable success, despite claims to the contrary by many Sovietologists.[11] A colonial "state," as John Comaroff and Jean Comaroff have asserted, is "in both senses of the term: an institutional order of political regulations *and* a condition of being, a structure *and* a predicament."[12] We know much about the Soviet institutional order and the alleged "classless" structure of its political relations. What we sorely lack is insight into the processes of transformation of colonized Muslim peoples' consciousness, the "conditions of their being," and the expressions of their predicaments, both under Soviet rule and in their post-Soviet realities. This is, indeed, what I hope to be able to attempt to discuss, albeit in a cursory manner, later in this chapter.

Before turning to that important issue, however, a few brief observations about the nature of the Soviet colonial project in Central Asia are in order. The Soviet conquest of the tsarist colonies in the region was justified, first and foremost, on Marxist-Leninist revolutionary ideological grounds, and unlike most Western colonial ventures, not in terms of economic exploitation and territorial control alone.[13] Through ruthless use of superior arms and military technology, the Russian Bolsheviks employed the power of the Soviet state to realize their "revolutionary," but colonial, objectives. In Central Asia these included systematic destruction of Islam and traditional Muslim Central Asian social institutions and political culture and the inculcation of the new Soviet (Russian) socialist ideology (theology?) and political culture of scientific atheism to replace the Muslim ones.[14]

Along with kinship and kingship,[15] Islam constituted one of the most fundamental bases for self-definition and for the organization of all forms of social and political relations in pre-Soviet Central Asia.[16] As the religion of power for over a millennium, Islam was targeted for complete destruction. The goal was nothing short of eradication of the traditional Central Asian way of life and its social, political, economic, and moral order. The plans for the realization of this project were vast, systematic, and comprehensive. They included Soviet ideological, legal, linguistic, institutional, and educational methods that were enhanced by politics of fear and favor.

Ideologically, Islam and Muslim beliefs and practices were and are depicted and labeled by the Soviets as traditional, irrational, reactionary, fanatical, antiprogressive, evil, oppressive, superstitious, antimodern, the epitome of backwardness, and ultimately the "opiate of the people"; therefore, they are presumed to be the legitimate object of vilification and destruction.

Legally, until the last year of World War II, all public forms of Muslim worship, prayers, education, and ritual performances were prohibited, and individuals were tried and punished for "crimes of custom." In 1991, President Islam Karimov of Uzbekistan described the predicament of Central Asians under Soviet role as follows:

> After all, it wasn't so long ago that a Communist, especially if he held an important post, could not go to the cemetery to bid his loved ones farewell. Participating in a burial ceremony was equated with committing a mortal sin, and a person was expelled from the Party and dismissed from his job. So that they could live with their conscience without losing what they had worked for years to gain, people would go into the hospital or leave on an "urgent" business trip, even when one of their parents died.[17]

President Karimov concluded, "after this we say that there are very few things people still consider sacred." Endowed properties belonging to Muslim religious institutions (*awqaaf*) were confiscated, Muslim shari'ah laws abrogated, and mosques, madrasahs, *maktabs* (mosque schools), and shrines were destroyed or desecrated.

Linguistically, through the so-called language and alphabet reforms, Central Asian youth were denied access to the very rich Islamic religious literary traditions written in the Arabic alphabet. The Soviets widened the isolation of the colonized peoples from their Islamic and historical literary heritage by closing borders and imposing an "Iron Curtain" to prevent contact with adjacent Muslim populations to the south. In addition, the popular language of daily discourse, which included various forms of greetings filled with Islamic referents, was completely purged of any Islamic content.

In the area of social institutions, the Central Asian Muslim family/household, the *oiyila,* traditionally the most basic unit of social, cultural, and economic production and reproduction, was a constant target of anti-Islamic agitation. The Soviets' own assumptions about the "oppressive" nature of Muslim law and gender bias made the anti-*oiyila* campaigns of paramount importance on the Soviet agenda.[18] The severity, scope, and success of the *hujum* (assault, all-out attack, or sweeping advance) campaign is well documented in an excellent book, *The Surrogate Proletariat: Moslem Women and Revolutionary Strategies in Soviet Central Asia, 1919–1929,* by Gregory Massell.[19] *Hujum* became another effective vehicle for undermining Islam and Muslim marriage and family relations and for promoting a "theology" of scientific atheism. The Soviets introduced numerous new organizations and institutions to supplant the traditional functions of the Muslim family/household and to propagate Soviet mores and values.

The Soviet educational system, probably the most successful Soviet enterprise in Central Asia, claims to have achieved almost 100 percent literacy in the region. It was the principal means for the implementation of Soviet linguistic policies and the inculcation of Soviet values of Marxism-Leninism, scientific atheism, and "international socialist brotherhood."[20] Through schools, generations of Soviet Central Asians were exposed to contradictory and often confusing interpretations (and misinterpretations) of their history and the deeds (or misdeeds) of their important political, religious, and historical personalities. Changes in the Kremlin's political climate dictated the various shifts in the interpretations of historic realities (e.g., Western colonialism and its evils compared with tsarist Russian colonial virtues and/or evils) and treatment of Central Asian historical and/or revolutionary figures (e.g., Khawjah Ahmad Yasawi, Emir Ali Sher Navai, Shah Mashrab, Emir Temur, Zahiruddin Babur, or Jadidist leaders Abdur Ra'uf Fitrat, Zakirjon Furqat, Faizullah Khojaev, Munawwar Qari, and many others). Yet, despite varying interpretations, the Soviet educational machine succeeded in developing an extensive Central Asian cadre (nomenklatura) that was trained, rewarded, and empowered over the decades. Through the educational institutions, the coherent alternative ideological system emphasizing belief in scientific atheism was constructed and transmitted, affirming the legitimacy of the Soviet political and social order. A vast majority of Central Asians today are the beneficiaries of this educational and political system. Their past, present, and, in their view, their own future, both individually and collectively, are vitally linked to the preservation of the Soviet traditions and political system. This fact, obvious as it may seem, is at the core of post-Soviet Central Asian predicaments about the future.

The consequences of these and other Soviet anti-Islamic and pro-atheist policies for Muslim Central Asians have been broad and pervasive. Some of the most significant legacies of this unique and prolonged colonial experience may be summarized for the purposes of this chapter, as follows: First, Central Asian societies and polities that were divided by the Soviet empire generally along ethnolinguistic cleavages have now become independent and separate nation-states. Second, these artificial political communities and emergent multiethnic nation-states are dominated by a persistent political culture of fear and favor and scientific atheism. Third, the vast majority of Central Asians, especially those below the age of sixty, often lack any acquaintance with even the most basic tenets of Muslim belief and practice.[21] Fourth, the new "independent" states are economically, militarily, and culturally weak and continue to remain largely dependent on Russia. And finally, post-Soviet Central Asian societies are facing serious spiritual crises and are desperately in search of meaning and a moral compass. All these conditions have been either induced or seriously aggravated by the circumstances that led to the disintegration of the Soviet empire, the "fall from grace" of its legitimizing ideology, and the declarations of independence of successor states in the region. We must now turn our attention to the issue of independence.

Independence and Its Limitations

Unlike most postcolonial nation-states in Asia and Africa, the emergent Central Asian Muslim states did not have to fight anticolonial wars of liberation to gain their freedom. Their colonial masters, the Russians, due entirely to social and economic malaise within the Soviet empire, suddenly decided to abandon their direct colonial interests in Muslim Central Asia and elsewhere. As a result, the Central Asians were denied the opportunity to *earn* their independence through a national struggle, formulate alternative national ideologies (nationalist and otherwise), and find or create new national heroes. Instead, independence was thrust on them unexpectedly in 1991 because of the internal collapse of the colonizing, Russian-dominated Soviet state. This abrupt loss of Soviet Russians' interest in the Central Asian republics left the "traditional" communist leaders in command, and these local leaders were left with no choice except to declare their national sovereignty and independence.

The August 1991 putsch in Moscow, which precipitated this peculiar circumstance, led to the renunciation of communist ideology in Russia, the decline of the Russian Communist Party's power, and efforts by the virulent opposition groups to chart a new national ideological course for Russia. In the Central Asian newly independent states, however, no renunciation of communist ideology or infringements on the power of the national communist parties were evident. Indeed, with the exception of a brief period in Tajikistan during 1992, leaders from the Soviet era have managed to maintain a firm grip on power by manipulating name changes (e.g., of party, party and state organizations, administrative units, titles, and place names) and effectively curtailing the growth and development of "democratic" opposition movements, as well as the activities of various amorphous Islamic groups and movements.

Since the fateful events of August 1991, Russia under President Boris Yeltsin has attempted to steadily dismantle the former Soviet political structure and introduce a multiparty political process. No comparable initiative has been taken in any of the Central Asian countries, and perhaps none should be expected in the foreseeable future.[22] The emphasis in these countries is on political "stability" and national calm, and not on "democratization" or other forms of social and political transformation. What is astonishing, at least to outsiders, is the domestic acceptance and tolerance of an old political order that appears to have lost its ideological legitimacy. More important, there seems to be a total absence of any alternative coherent national ideologies or credible leaders to pursue them, either among the rulers or their meek and ill-organized opponents. Why?

Several significant points may shed light on current political realities and prospects for any meaningful political change in Central Asia, as well as the role Muslim movements may play in the future. First, in spite of the apparent "fall from grace" of Marxist-Leninist ideology, there are many in Central Asia, especially among the ruling elite, who continue to adhere to it, and even defend it.[23] Second, Central Asian intellectuals are not familiar or conversant with any of the non-Marxist ideological alternatives, secular or religious, and their access to sources of information is extremely restricted. The general public is even more isolated from the world outside the former Soviet orbit.[24] Third, the "former" communist and now "nationalist" ruling elites remain positively hostile toward Islamist political ideals and movements and, for the most part, are unable to articulate a meaningful and coherent secular nationalist agenda of their own. Fourth, despite a long and illustrious history, contemporary Central Asian societies lack genuine "national" heroes whom they can emulate—that is, they are faced with a serious crisis of moral and political leadership. The most recent genuinely nationalist heroes of Central Asia, the leaders of the Jadidist movement of the early twentieth century, were thoroughly demonized and liquidated during the Stalin era. Although most of the Jadidists were initially Muslim reformers and modernists, they later collaborated with Russian Bolsheviks and became national communists. Eventually they were killed by the Soviet communists, but a credibility gap about their role in Central Asian history persists.[25] Most of the precolonial political and religious leaders have suffered from many episodes of vilification at the hands of both native and Russian revisionist intellectuals, and doubts about their credibility are likely to persist. Fifth, the sudden collapse of the Soviet Union has resulted in such serious economic hardship and uncertainties in the region that the great majority of people cherish the political stability and familiarity offered by the existing regimes. Indeed, day-to-day survival seems to take precedence over the more abstract but fundamental national ideological concerns, at least for now. Last but not least, the continuation of the old political order is assured by the helping hand of the old center, Moscow, and the Russian-dominated domestic military and police forces, which are consistently willing and able to apply the familiar tools of former Soviet political culture, fear and favor, without any restraint or hesitation against an opponent, real or imagined.

Given these legacies of the Soviet past, as well as the realities of post-Soviet Central Asia, how do Central Asians talk about their colonial past? What do they say about the nature of their emerging political order and their own predicaments within them? How are they talking about their political leaders, and what do they say about them? Who is concerned with Islam and its place in post-Soviet Central Asian society now? What are people doing about it and why? To address these questions, I would like to use ethnographic data from Uzbekistan that I was able to gather during a preliminary research trip during the summer of 1992.

Muffled Voices: Colonial Consciousness and Consciousness of Colonialism

It is critical at this juncture to note that Central Asians did not accept their colonial state without a struggle. Indeed, many perished over the long decades, leaving only bitter memories, perhaps remembered only by a few family members and friends. Only now, some public figures such as Dadakhan Hasanov[26] are trying to pay tribute during public performances by calling the names of some of those who died in countless battles fought by the *Qurboshi* (the,

Basmachi in the Soviet accounts), national Islamic resistance fighters against the Bolsheviks. What most Central Asians thought of their own colonization and how they expressed their ideas over the last seven decades may not ever be known, since most suffered silently and resisted secretly. Only now are some beginning to speak out, but in muffled voices. What they say, how they say it, and what they mean, is not easily conveyed in words. We must, however, live with the limitations of our most common ethnographic medium, the cold printed word.

Let me begin with a brief conversation on a hot afternoon in the office of a well-known Uzbek writer in Tashkent. I asked him what he thought of the Soviet system and its accomplishments in Uzbekistan. A man in his mid-fifties who looked much older than his age, he replied tersely, "it was *buzughchi*," a destructive system, consisting of four principal elements: "excessive consumption of alcoholic beverages, eating pork (*chochqa*), unbridled sexuality, and atheism." Indulgence in these four things, he asserted, "increases telling lies and cheating, promotes mistrust and results in nothing but *buzughchilig*," or destructiveness. He concluded that "the Soviet system is inclined to destroy whatever is good in society, and build nothing useful." Another well-known Uzbek writer expressed the same sentiment with an aphorism that he attributed to the famous Persian poet Ferdowsi: "if Russian feet touch a river, it will dry up." Thus, he said, "wherever they go, devastation follows." This theme was regularly visited by many others during casual conversations in both urban and rural settings. The most common assertion I heard, almost in the form of a litany, was "Soviet society operates on the force of fear and intimidation, which has paralyzed society by creating an atmosphere of total mistrust and unreliability among individuals and groups."

The pervasiveness of the attitudes of mistrust (*yeshenchisizleg*) toward each other, and especially among officials, is most prominent among Uzbeks. A young and ambitious entrepreneur in Samarkand,[27] who was building a modern factory with considerable outside credit and technology, told me in exasperation:

> The real problem in our country is lack of leadership—that is, leaders who are not afraid, who have courage to take initiative and do what they say. For a long time our thinkers, writers, poets, and leaders have been saying good things, but when it comes to actually doing things, they are unwilling or unable to carry through.

I asked him "Why so? What are they afraid of or who are they afraid of?" He replied:

> We are afraid of ourselves. It is a psychological condition produced by the [Soviet colonial] system. We are not able to think for ourselves and do things for ourselves. For a long time the state and the Party planners and officials (a small cadre) have done all the thinking and planning for the people. The

ordinary people have become unable to do things for themselves. We have to liberate our people from this condition through proper education. We have to give people land and capital and let them take responsibility for planning and doing things for themselves. If we don't give them the opportunity to do it now, they will never be able to do it.

A scientist and academician who had spent some time overseas explained the crisis of leadership in Uzbekistan by saying, "The experiences of the past depleted Uzbekistan's best and brightest either through repeated flights to other countries in the region or liquidation through many purges during the long occupation, especially the 1930s." Those who are left, he said, are "yes" men, generally "passive and lacking in initiative." The Samarkand entrepreneur echoed the same concern, stating, "our leadership cadre have reached where they are by means of *lagan bardorlik*[28] and saying 'yes' all the time to a master. They are unable to take initiative and are afraid of responsibility." In a similar vein, in the Jami' Machit (Congregational Mosque) in the city of Kokand, while I talked with a group of some ten individuals, one older man said:

> The problem of leadership in Uzbekistan is that we don't have men of courage [*ghairatlug* or *qurqmas*] in positions of power. Our current leaders are scared and timid, and as such they seek to preserve their own power and prestige, not the welfare of the people. Therefore, they make promises but they cannot keep them. So eventually they will discredit themselves. Because [of this] people don't believe in their leaders' truthfulness and capabilities.

In the present political climate, individuals are generally extremely cautious in voicing their views about political issues, except in a very broad and oblique manner. Their fears are real and extremely well founded. In private conversations, however, the extent of popular concern about leadership and legitimacy crises at all levels is quite noticeable. Unable to effect changes in the existing political power structure or to publicly criticize the conduct of particular leaders, some Uzbeks attempt to explain the current puzzling political dynamics in "independent" Muslim Uzbekistan in very broad and muffled terms in the media. I heard one of the best examples of such a discussion in a radio interview given by Nurutdin Akramovich Muhitdinov[29] on the Youth Program (*Yashler Programasi*) of Radio Tashkent in July 1992. In a very long interview touching on various aspects of leadership, he summarized his remarks by stating that "leaders emerge from within the society, you cannot import them from elsewhere. In our society, leadership (*rahbarlik*) is afflicted with three major blights or diseases (*ofat wa kasaleg*). They are: (1) *'amal parastlik* (worshiping positions of power); (2) *koz ochlik* (avarice and greed); and (3) *wijdonsizlik* (amorality, irresponsibility, lack of integrity, and shamelessness)." "Of these three characteristics," he said, "if even one were found in a leader, it would spell disaster for society." He bemoaned the fact that these attributes have nevertheless been common under the Soviet system. Therefore he admonished Uzbek youth with these words:

For moral leadership it is absolutely essential to keep one's distance from these afflictions. A conscientious leader performs his duties with integrity and deals with everyone respectfully. His performance on the job produces a sense of peace and security among the people and contributes to the happiness and well-being of the nation. He should show compassion to youth. If in all aspects of his life, material and spiritual, he abides by these principles, his good name will be remembered in his village and in his ward. People will be content with him, and when he passes away, they will say may God bless his soul, and may God grant him Paradise.

A deep sense of malaise about lack of moral leadership pervades Uzbek society, both urban and rural. One runs across some of the most graphic depictions of this overwhelming concern, such as the following by an Uzbek matriarch in a village kolkhoz in Namangan. In response to my inquiry about local leaders, she said, "Now people are basically self-absorbed and don't care about the poor or anyone else. They [the leaders] are like wolves (*bori*). When they have a carcass they don't want to share it with anyone. This is terrible; there is no one that people would like to turn to."

The problem of Uzbek society, and those of other post-Soviet Central Asian states at present, is not simply finding the right kinds of leaders or waging a struggle against the current leadership. Rather, Uzbeks and other Muslim Central Asians are facing a predicament much like the one Gramsci described concerning the Italian educational system:

It was right to struggle against the old school, but reforming it was not so simple as it seemed. The problem was not one of model curricula but of men, and not just of the men who are actually teachers themselves but of the entire social complex which they express."[30]

It is this fundamental realization, the need for the transformation of the "entire social complex"—the cultural, ideological, and institutional legacies of the Soviet system—that must be acknowledged first and foremost if Central Asians are to eventually earn their true freedom and independence. And it is this daunting task to which increasing numbers of Central Asian intellectuals, Muslim leaders (from the ranks of both former "official" Islam and the "parallel" Islam), and youth are turning their attention.

Post-Soviet Predicaments

The shock of the sudden demise of the system persists. However, debate about the evils and virtues of the former Soviet system is slowly gaining momentum, both in public and private forums. Many individuals and some movements are beginning to muster the lost courage to speak their minds about the ills of the past. Personal accounts of sufferings are being shared hesitantly but increasingly in print media. A whole body of literature on personal, familial, communal, and societal victimizations under the Soviet system is emerging, in spite of the continued restrictions on the freedom of press and tight control over electronic media.[31] The next step, assessing how to address and remedy the misfortunes of history, individually and collectively, will be in order, and small steps are being taken. A remarkable consensus is emerging, at least in Uzbekistan and perhaps in other countries also, about ways to address post-Soviet Central Asian predicaments. It is a call for a new kind of education. As to what specific type of education, there are two broad trends reflecting the exaggerated urban-rural and secular (atheistic)-Islamic cleavages produced by the Soviet colonial experience. The highly educated, secularized, substantially Russianized, and atheistic urban segments wish to rely on Western secular education (a la the Turkish Kemalist model), while the rural population and those with strong rural roots are intent on rediscovering Islam and Muslim knowledge and practices first, then combining these with modern scientific education. The Western secular option has considerable domestic and international support, and major student exchange programs abroad are in place, including those with Turkey. Western-style secular education is presented as the only compatible course for the development of a market-oriented economy, capitalism, and liberal democracy both by Western interests and the current power elites in the newly independent states (NIS) of Central Asia. As a result, Islam and Muslim traditions are denied relevance to the construction of a post-Soviet national ideological and sociopolitical future.

The phenomenon of "resurgent" Islam in Central Asia, which has attracted much attention in the West, has little to do, however, with Islamist political movements in other parts of the world. It is fundamentally a popular and, to a large measure, provincial or rural educational effort to reclaim Islamic knowledge and learning and to gain the right to practice Islam in public without fear and intimidation. The intensity and high visibility of efforts such as rebuilding the ruined and desecrated mosques, visiting shrines, attending Friday prayers at major mosques, and publishing, selling, and buying Islamic texts and other materials in the vernacular are a clear indication of renewed interest in Islam as a religion on a wide scale. The most enthusiastic seekers of Islamic knowledge, based on my limited observations during the summer of 1992, appear to be young children (about seven years and older) and youth (high school and some college students). Most of the children and youth appear to be boys, but I have also seen many young girls, dressed in *hijab* (modest Muslim dress), attending Friday prayers in the old city of Tashkent.

Regional and gender differences in attitude toward, and the extent of participation in, the production and dissemination of Islamic knowledge and practices also exist in different states and within a single country such as Uzbekistan. For example, the historic city of Namangan and its rural peripheries in the Fergana Valley of Uzbekistan and the city of Osh in southern Kyrgyzstan have come to be known as regions with much stronger Islamic religious fervor. Undoubtedly, equally strong feelings of religious devotion to traditional Muslim beliefs and practices are in evidence in other local communities within the larger urban areas, such as the old city of Tashkent, as well as communities near major *ziyarat* (shrines and pilgrimage sites of Muslim Sufi saints), such as the tomb of Khwajah Baha'uddin Naqshband (d. 1389) near Bukhara, or the monument to Khwajah Ahmad Yasawi (d. 1166) in Turkistan, a small town in southern Kazakhstan.

Gender differences in religiosity of Central Asian Muslims, both past and present, are rarely investigated by ethnographers in any systematic and detailed manner. My brief observations clearly indicate that young girls are active in the educational efforts and even mosque attendance. Some professional, formerly atheistic women (teachers and physicians) are adopting modest Muslim dress, and when faced with resistance at home and in the workplace, they turn to local religious scholars for advice. However, to assume that these activities are evidence of the rise of Islamic "fundamentalism" is to stray far from the truth. Nevertheless, this does not mean that very small extremist groups do not exist in Central Asia or that they might not arise, as they have in the past and could in the future, in response to intolerable conditions of perceived injustice, corruption, and an impending threat of societal chaos.[32]

At present, however, most efforts among Islamic-minded peoples in Central Asia are directed at educating interested individuals about the fundamentals of Muslim beliefs and ritual practices, which are widely unknown, primarily due to the hegemonic Soviet political culture of scientific atheism during the past seven decades. These Muslim educational goals are pursued entirely on an ad hoc basis by individuals or local mosque communities through organizing classes, attending sermons, and associating with like-minded Muslim individuals. The struggle against almost universal consumption of alcoholic drinks and, to a lesser extent, pork products constitutes another dimension of Islamic revivalism.[33] My discussions with many individuals, including Muslim scholars, my attendance at Friday prayers and listening to the *khutbah* (sermon), and my review of vernacular Islamic written materials sold in the bazaars indicate other major areas of concern for Islamic-minded individuals and Muslim leaders. First, there is the ever increasing fear of Western Christian missionaries, who are apparently very active in the region;[34] and second, there are lingering concerns over the persistence of atheistic education in the post-Soviet Central Asian school systems and opposition (subtle and not so subtle) to Islam and Muslim practices within the vast state-run school system.[35]

Even a cursory examination of Islamic literature circulating in the market reveals the totally apolitical nature of Islamic activities in Central Asia in general and Uzbekistan in particular. Presently, Islamic movements in Central Asia are exclusively concerned with matters of ritual knowledge and religious belief and practice, not political mobilization. This does not necessarily mean, however, that Muslims are totally uninterested in politics (see the first two epigraphs above). As the imam (prayer leader) of a major mosque told me, "we have to find the beginning of the *kalowa* (skein of yarn) first." And, he said, the beginning of the *kalowa* is the first article of Muslim belief or confession: "*La-illaha Ila-Allahu Muhammadur Rasululah*" (there is no God but Allah, and Muhammad is his blessed messenger). He concluded, "once we have found the beginning of the skein, the rest will follow." Perhaps the imam is correct.

However, the economic, sociopolitical, educational, leadership, environmental, ideological, and spiritual predicaments facing the peoples of Muslim Central Asia are immense and complex—for all segments of the population, including the power elites, their ill-organized opposition, and the ordinary folk (men and women, urban and rural, atheists and believers) alike. The question nevertheless remains: What are the prospects for the leadership of these societies rising to face the monumental challenges of their emergent nations? Any attempt to respond to such a question without a crystal ball—which anthropologists hardly ever claim to possess—would be sheer folly at best. What I would like to do instead, by way of a conclusion, is to draw attention to the additional regional and world systemic constraints affecting the potential role of Islam and Muslim identities in the future sociopolitical dynamics of post-Soviet Central Asian states.

Conclusions

Putting aside the significant assertion by President Islam Karimov of Uzbekistan about the primacy of the "spiritual crisis" in Central Asia, one sees economics as the most fundamental and critical factor, at least in the short run, hindering positive developments toward the transformation of post-Soviet Muslim Central Asian societies. Economic crises in the region are rooted in the prolonged history of Russian colonial exploitation of raw materials, the excessive specialization in cotton resulting in a monoculture, underdevelopment of industrial infrastructure, outdated technology, and the economic management chaos that followed the collapse of the Soviet empire. These problems are further aggravated during the post-Soviet era by the ongoing wars and armed conflicts on the southern borderlands of Muslim Central Asia—specifically, the fifteen years of war in Afghanistan, the more recent civil war in Tajikistan, and the protracted warfare between Azerbaijan and Armenia. These so-called low-intensity armed conflicts, which are fueled by many outside forces, have had at least two serious consequences on socioeconomic, cultural, and political developments in post-Soviet Central Asia.

First, the regional wars have effectively curtailed any possibility of direct economic and cultural ties between the newly independent countries of Muslim Central Asia and their neighbors of Southwest Asia (Iran, Afghanistan, and Pakistan) and the Arab Middle East. Therefore, the earlier optimistic expectations of cultural and economic reorientation of Central Asian Muslim nations away from colonial Russia and toward Muslim South Asia and the Middle East

have quickly evaporated. Central Asians still remain firmly tethered to and dependent on the volatile Russian economy and polity. Sadly, as long as the fires of
armed conflicts are kept burning in the southern tiers of former Soviet Central
Asia, and Islam and Muslim "fundamentalists" are implicated in these destructive wars, there will be no hope of any meaningful economic and/or cultural ties
between the peoples of Muslim Central Asia and their southern Muslim neighbors. Unfortunately, for both Central Asian and South and Southwest Asian
Muslim peoples, there seems to be no promise of an end to the current armed
conflicts, at least not soon.

Second, while these regional conflicts deny economic or political benefits to
the Islamic Republic of Iran, Pakistan, and Muslim countries of the Middle East
in the commercial and investment markets of post-Soviet Muslim Central Asia,
the real beneficiaries of this state of affairs are the Russians and their Western
capitalist patrons. That is, the Russians continue to enjoy almost complete access
to the raw industrial goods from Central Asia, and European and American
companies have nearly exclusive access to the new Central Asian commercial
markets and investment opportunities. The continuation of this condition is unlikely to prove advantageous to the economic health and independence of the
emergent Muslim states in post-Soviet Central Asia.

Ironically, although not surprisingly, the persistence of regional warfare has
served the interests of the post-Soviet power elites by enabling them to consoli-
date their hold on the state apparatus as guarantors of peace and security in their
own nations. Readily accepting Western assertions concerning Iran's possible
involvement as the principal supporter of Muslim extremism in the regional
conflicts, the post-Soviet Central Asian leaders have adopted a particularly harsh
attitude toward any organized form of Muslim activism. The association of Islam
and Muslim political movements, with violence and armed conflicts is popular-
ized in the state-controlled media and is pervasive in the region. This concerted
effort to undermine Muslim movements, combined with the sad realities of inter-
necine fighting among former mujahideen in neighboring Afghanistan over control of state power, clearly has had a chilling effect on the attitudes of Central
Asian Muslim scholars regarding religion and the politics of state governance.
Most religious leaders, official and nonofficial, are advocating noninvolvement
of Islam in political struggles, albeit for different reasons. Many argue that Islam
is above politics and should be concerned with the higher moral issues, and this
moral high ground can be assured only without the contamination of politics.
Others encourage separation of state and religion in accordance with the dictates
of the Western political traditions encouraged by the state power elites. Yet there
are other Muslim scholars who advocate noninvolvement in state politics, not out
of a conviction that Islam and Muslims should be kept out of politics forever but
rather that Central Asian peoples are not yet ready for effective participation in
Islamist political movements. Therefore, they sense a palpable threat of serious
damage to Islamic causes and the community if they become embroiled in politi-

cal struggles prematurely. For most Central Asian leaders, Muslim religious revival is a spiritual undertaking and an act of personal and collective piety. It is not seen as a "crusade" against infidels, atheists, or, for that matter, Russians living in their midst. It is, as indicated earlier, a search to rediscover the beginnings of the long-lost "skein [*kalowah*] of Muslim religious and cultural yarn." This search, whether successful or not under the current stifling political and economic environment, is considered by at least one remarkable Muslim scholar in Uzbekistan to be the work of a generation or more and not any single leader or movement. Recently, Aleksandr Solzhenitsyn implored the Russian nation upon his arrival at Vladivostok from twenty years of exile that, "Our life, spiritual and otherwise, must be reformed from our own tradition, our understanding, [and] our atmosphere."[36] Similar spiritual and other reforms in Muslim Central Asia, and by Muslim Central Asians, are also needed if they are to realize the promises of post-Soviet freedom and independence. As to the future of Central Asia's post-Soviet political order, it might be best to conclude this discussion by quoting an eleventh-century Central Asian political sage, Nizam al-Mulk,[37] who said, "a kingdom may last while there is irreligion, but it will not endure when there is oppression."

Notes

Ethnographic data for this paper were collected during a brief six-week research visit to Uzbekistan during the summer of 1992, supported by an IREX travel grant and a research grant from the President's Council on International Programs at Indiana University. I am grateful to both institutions for their support. I have also benefited from the constructive comments of participants at the Russian Littoral Project conference, especially insights shared by Ashraf Ghani and Karen Dawisha. Additionally, the editorial and research assistance of Hattie Clark and Elizabeth Constantine at Indiana University deserves a special thanks. All responsibility for any and all flaws rest with me alone.

1. Noam Chomsky recently presented his definition of the term "New World Order" during his Patten Foundation Lecture, "The Middle East in the New World Order," Indiana University, Bloomington, 28 February 1994. Referring to the speech of former President George Bush addressing the nation on the eve of the American Persian Gulf War (1991), Chomsky defined the term tersely to mean "whatever we (the U.S.) say goes," and as such he contended that "the new world order is the same as the old one!"

2. Francis Fukuyama, "The End of History?" *National Interest,* summer 1989, pp. 3–18; idem, *The End of History and the Last Man* (New York: Free Press, 1992). Samuel P. Huntington, "The Clash of Civilization?" *Foreign Affairs,* vol. 72, no. 3 (summer 1993).

3. John Comaroff and Jean Comaroff, *Ethnography and the Historical Imagination* (Boulder, CO: Westview, 1992).

4. M. Nazif Shahrani, "Central Asia and the Challenge of the Soviet Legacy," *Central Asian Survey,* vol. 12, no. 2, (1993), pp. 123–35.

5. John H. Kautsky, *The Political Consequence of Modernization* (New York and London: John Wiley and Sons, 1972), p. 76.

6. Shahrani, "Central Asia."

7. This is a particularly apt metaphor, especially in light of the fact that, as Helene Carrere d'Encausse has pointed out, "Locusts were a permanent nightmare for the peas-

ants of Bukhara [and Central Asia at large]." *Islam and the Russian Empire* (Berkeley: University of California Press, 1988).

8. See Murray Feschbach and Alfred Friendly Jr., *Ecocide in the USSR: Health and Nature Under Siege* (New York: Basic Books, 1992); James Critchlow, *Nationalism in Uzbekistan: A Soviet Republic's Road to Sovereignty* (Boulder, CO: Westview, 1991); Boris Z. Rumer, "Central Asia's Cotton Economy and Its Costs," in *Central Asia: The Failed Transformation,* ed. William Fierman (Boulder, CO: Westview, 1991).

9. M. Berger, "We Have to Make Our Own Way: A Conversation with Islam Karimov, President of Uzbekistan," *Current Digest of the Soviet Press,* vol. 43, no. 4, p. 30.

10. Ibid.

11. Fierman, ed., *Central Asia: The Failed Transformation;* Michael Rywkin, *Moscow's Muslim Challenge: Soviet Central Asia* (Armonk, NY: M.E. Sharpe, 1990); Edward Allworth, *Central Asia: 120 Years of Russian Rule* (Durham, NC and London: Duke University Press, 1989).

12. Comaroff and Comaroff, *Ethnography and the Historical Imagination,* p. 236.

13. A recent paper by a Tajik historian, however, finds clear evidence in a document of the Turkommissiia (founded in 1919 to formulate the Bolshevik government's policy toward Turkistan) that in part states, "The second task [of the Bolshevik regime] is to exploit Turkistan economically." Kamoludin N. Abdulaev, "Bukharan and Turkestani Émigrés in Khurasan" (paper presented at the "Conference on Central Asia and the Caucasus," Ohio State University, Columbus, OH, 18–20 March 1994), also in *Central Asia Monitor,* nos. 4, 5 (summer 1994).

14. Shahrani, "Central Asia," p. 125.

15. A strong association between religion, kingship (leadership), and social order in Muslim political theories is suggested by Nizam al-Mulk, *The Book of Government,* trans. Hubert Darke (London: Routledge and Kegan Paul, 1978). According to al-Mulk,

> The most important thing which a king needs is sound faith, because kingship and religion are like two brothers; whenever disturbance breaks out in the country religion suffers too; heretics and evil doers appear; and whenever religious affairs are in disorder, there is confusion in the country; evil doers gain power and render the king impotent and despondent; heresy grows rife and rebels make themselves felt (p. 60).

16. W. Montgomery Watt, *Islamic Political Thought* (Edinburgh: Edinburgh University Press, 1968), p. 26.

17. Berger, "We Have to Make Our Own Way," p. 30.

18. R. Kh. Aminova, *The October Revolution and Women's Liberation in Uzbekistan* (Moscow: Nauka, 1985).

19. Gregory Massell, *The Surrogate Proletariat* (Princeton: Princeton University Press, 1974).

20. William K. Medlin, William Cave, and Finley Carpenter, *Education and Development in Central Asia: A Case Study of Social Change in Uzbekistan* (Leiden: E.J. Brill, 1971).

21. For example, the extent of the lack of basic knowledge of Islam, especially about the fundamental practices of performing daily Muslim prayers, became evident to me during a brief visit to the town of Turkistan in southern Kazakhistan during the summer of 1992. The city of Turkistan is the site of the shrine of Khawjah Ahmad Yasawi (d. 1166), the preeminent Sufi saint of Turkistan (Central Asia). My host for the tour of the shrine was a recent haji (pilgrim to Mecca) and a former atheist. He had recently taken an active interest in spreading Islamic knowledge through dissemination of popular Islamic literature in the vernaculars. He had already transliterated and published some older Turki (literary Uzbek) texts from the Arabic alphabet into the Cyrillic Kazakh and Uzbek

alphabets to render them more widely accessible. During late afternoon prayers (*'asr*), which we performed together at his home, I asked him to lead the prayers; he did so, but inaccurately. The four *ruk'ah* prayers are normally performed silently. He, however, proceeded to perform them aloud and recited additional verses from the Koran with *Fatiha* in all four *ruk'ahs,* while it is required in the Hanafi Sunni tradition of Central Asia to do so only in the first two *ruk'ahs.* These are, indeed, very simple ritual rules for daily prayers that observant Muslims ought to know, and most in fact do.

22. In Uzbekistan the central government decided to remove the most visible reminders of Russian rule, such as statues of Lenin and other major revolutionary figures, by taking them from significant points in the capital city, Tashkent, and also by changing names of important places that commemorated them. Although explicit orders were given by the Uzbek central government to provincial and local officials to do the same, in most rural and provincial areas I visited in the summer of 1992, no such changes were carried out. Several low-ranking officials suggested that they were not certain if these shifts in policy were going to last and that their reluctance to take a chance was based on past experiences. Thus, Lenin's shadow continued to loom large over some provincial communities. In Tajikistan, the coalition government of national democratic and Islamic parties, following the elections of 1991, was overthrown with help from Russia and neighboring CIS states in favor of the Communist Party of Tajikistan, perpetuating the bloody civil war in that impoverished country.

23. During the summer of 1992, I had several fascinating conversations with directors of rural kolkhoz and sovkhoz collectives in rural Uzbekistan (Samarkand and Namangan provinces) who defended the old order and its virtues with conviction. There were also others who condemned aspects of the system and the evils it had caused.

24. In general the peoples of former Soviet Central Asia are very poorly informed, especially about the Muslim countries to the south and west. What the post-Soviet Central Asians say about these areas is often negative and demeaning and always accompanied by an exaggerated sense of their own progress and modernity. However, with the increasing number of people going on pilgrimages and on visits to Turkey, Pakistan, and India, attitudes are beginning to change. One haji from Namangan who had just returned from his pilgrimage to Saudi Arabia, in August 1992 told me how impressed he was with the honesty and sense of propriety of people in Saudi Arabia where, he said with astonishment, "shopkeepers leave their shops unattended when they go to pray at mosques without any fear or anxiety. This would be impossible in crime-ridden urban Uzbekistan."

25. Carrere d'Encausse, *Islam and the Russian Empire.*

26. Dadakhan Hasanov is a very well-known Uzbek singer and Muslim political activist from Namangan, a city in the Fergana Valley region of eastern Uzbekistan.

27. I have avoided mentioning real names of individuals (with some exceptions) and altered locations to insure anonymity.

28. This concept is very widely used in everyday conversation in Uzbek; it literally means "to carry another person's tray" (a form of butler's syndrome) or serving the master's every wish and whim.

29. He was an important and much admired Uzbek political leader who had served as the Communist Party secretary during the 1950s but was purged from power in the late 1950s.

30. Antonio Gramsci, *Selections from the Prison Notebooks,* ed. and trans. Quintin Hoare and Geoffrey Nowell Smith (New York: International Publishers, 1971), p. 25.

31. Eric Johnson, *The Media in Central Asia: Kazakhstan, Kyrgyzstan, Uzbekistan* (analysis conducted by Internews for USAID) (Arcata, CA: Internews, 1994).

32. Abdujabar Abduvakhitov, "Islamic Revivalism in Uzbekistan," in *Russia's Muslim Frontiers: New Directions in Cross-Cultural Analysis,* ed. Dale F. Eickelman (Bloomington: Indiana University Press, 1993).

33. The offer of an alcoholic drink to guests has become part of Central Asian "national traditions" to such an extent that refusal to take a drink is considered bad manners. Recently, to avoid embarrassment, recent pilgrims to Mecca, the hajis, are wearing special Arab-style white garments over their local attire to signal to their hosts that they no longer drink.

34. The scope and extent of Christian missionary efforts may be ascertained from an article entitled "International Bible Society Accepts Challenge of Central Asian Republics," written by a Larry Jerden (published as an advertisement in *Today's Christian Women,* October 1992), accompanied by a fund drive (with a toll-free phone number) to translate, publish, and make available "the Gospel of Luke and children's introduction to the Bible for the people of Uzbekistan and Kirghizia" in their own languages.

35. To illustrate the predicaments of those who are willing to return to Islam within the school system, let me recount the story of a female teacher in Tashkent as it was told to me by a religious figure. The schoolteacher apparently had recently decided to practice Islam and had adopted the wearing of a head scarf to cover her hair, but did not use a veil. The school administrators objected to her wearing the head scarf and ordered her to either abandon it in school or resign from her teaching post, her only means of livelihood. In desperation she visited the respected local Muslim leader, seeking his advice as to what course she should follow. The Muslim leader advised her not to resign because that was exactly what the administration wanted, so that they could claim that she took this course voluntarily. Instead, he told the teacher to keep wearing the scarf to school and let the school administrators fire her. The teacher could then ask them, "What kind of democracy is this?" The Muslim scholar also added that "under communism, we Muslims suffered all forms of indignities and tolerated it, now let's see how much tolerance democracy will show to Islam and Muslims."

36. Serge Schmemann, "Solzhenitsyn Attacks Gorbachev and New Reforms," *New York Times,* 29 May 1994, p. 3.

37. al-Mulk, *Book of Government,* p. 12.

14

Independent Uzbekistan

A Muslim Community in Development

Abdujabar Abduvakhitov

Central Asia, with its strategic importance, has always drawn the close attention of researchers. The formation of new geopolitical structures arising from the independence of the former Soviet republics, however, has heightened interest in this area. The newly independent republics of Uzbekistan, Turkmenistan, Kazakhstan, Tajikistan, and Kyrgyzstan, formed after the dissolution of the Soviet empire, have suddenly become ranking members of the world community, negotiating political and economic relations with other nations. Although it is a short time since they proclaimed their independence, the huge economic potential of the republics of Central Asia can effectively influence the distribution of forces both within and outside the region. Russia's position, which used to dominate the region and was beyond competition, has been weakened significantly, and the positions of the republics have been strengthened. The republics' established goals are to achieve equal relations with all countries and to develop a stable independence in political, economic, financial, and other spheres.

Some experts may attribute the change in the balance of forces between Russia and the Central Asian republics to factors other than the internal strengthening of the republics. They refer to the activities of Turkey, Iran, and other neighboring countries of the East.[1] The activities of Turkey, Iran, South Korea, and China, however, limited for certain reasons, have been overshadowed by political steps that have enhanced the meaning and strength of the local republics.

Other observers question whether the change in the balance of forces is weakening the position of the Russian state, even though Russia still possesses solid military potential, runs the powerful military-industrial potential of the former USSR, manipulates economic ties between republics (not always successfully), and handles the currency system as of mid-November 1993.[2] Although the plants of the military-industrial complex that are situated in the territory of the newly created independent republics formally belong to the republics, it is difficult to exclude them from the structure of the military-industrial complex.

The transformation of the military-industrial plants under republican control is indeed progressing, albeit slowly. Because the armies of the independent states of Central Asia are only now being established, it is difficult to consider them a fully formed link in the state structure. Also, it is difficult to consider the viability of local armies without the Russian army, for obvious reasons: potential, experience, personnel, equipment, and so on.

Nevertheless, the measures now taking place here, the many structures being formed—military, economic, and financial—are coming into view more clearly. Most important are the political structures of these newly formed countries, which both guarantee and bring new content to the declared independence.

Under these conditions the republics are bearing responsibility for the region and resolving regional problems, but there are several other countries considered to be decision makers in the region. Thus, one cannot argue with the fact that Central Asia is influenced by outside powers also.

Given the recent history of the disintegration of the USSR into separate states and the rapid course of similar events in other regions of the world, researchers have to acknowledge that the contemporary world, with its complicated relationships among states, will have less and less continuity with previous decades; they need to be prepared for the rapid political and economic evolutions occurring today.

The period of independence for the Central Asian states has been brief, but it gives a basis for drawing certain conclusions, the most important being that states more or less take their place in the world's political and economic structure, gain real independence, and in their own way try to guarantee stability in their countries, orienting themselves toward regional stability at the same time.[3]

Among the states of Central Asia, Uzbekistan stands out more and more as a leader in terms of solving national and regional problems. Some analysts, viewing the economic potential of the republic, its strategic location as a connecting link in the region, its historical conditions, and its people's resources, correctly foretold the possibility of Uzbekistan becoming just such a leader.[4] There is competition among the republics and their leaders in resolving problems that could to a certain extent be dangerous for the region as a whole.[5] The competition for leadership among the five republics might lead to unstable political and economic development. Delimitation of boundaries in Central Asia may play its own destructive role. And there is a danger of regional conflicts should any of the Central Asian leaders choose to impose contradictory social and political standards on other nations.

There are many internal and external factors affecting stability in the region, and hence the peace and problem-solving situations.

Among the factors considered important in resolving the many common problems arising in relationships among the five Central Asian republics is Islam.

Over the course of ten centuries Islam was the dominant religion in Central Asia. Traditionally, local people, especially settled ones, looked at everything, including their way of life, through the lens of Islam. In the Middle Ages secularism was displayed only episodically, without leaving any trace other than in some scientific works interpreted by modern scientists, both secular and religious.

The mentality of the local person, in connecting the environment with the name of God (Allah), could not develop without also being influenced to a considerable extent by religion. On the government level, the clergy (in the form of certain structures) were invariably a part of the "establishment" and of domestic and foreign policy.

Moreover, Central Asia was becoming the center of religious thought, recognized by the Muslim world's theologians. Followers of the Sufi trend in the Muslim religion in fact link the origin and development of "Naqshbandi-Yaseviya" with that region. Even nowadays the religion has not lost its importance, and any consideration of Central Asian affairs must take Islam into account.

For the past 120 years, since the moment of conquest of this territory by the Russian Empire and the migration of Russians and Russian-speaking peoples from the parent state, local ethnic groups have dominated the major part of the territory except for areas of modern-day Kazakhstan, where the balance was not in favor of Muslims. In the republics of Uzbekistan, Turkmenistan, Tajikistan, and Kyrgyzstan the general balance favored the local nations traditionally professing the Islamic religion. In Uzbekistan, for example, out of 22 million people, only about 10 percent regard Russian as their native language (of these, 8 percent are ethnic Russians).

Changes over the past few years due to the outflow of the Russian-speaking population have been rather minimal, however, because the Russian presence has never been disproportionately large. Of course, the domination of a local ethnic population cannot be defined merely in terms of its size.

As a matter of fact, in Uzbekistan, even with the considerable role of religion in the everyday life of people in public and political spheres, such domination was not manifest. The role of religion did not change much during the years of perestroika and the achievement of independence.

Uzbekistan's experience in the processes of change in a Muslim society is significant and is drawing the attention of researchers. Here it is important to analyze these processes and the policy of the country with respect to religious tendencies and groups during the period of transition.

It is necessary to consider some aspects of the position of Islam during the Soviet period of development that have had relatively little detailed coverage by scholars. Our attention will be paid primarily to the evolution of processes during the period of perestroika and independence. The conditions of militant atheism, the introduction of certain disparities in the religious community, and the creation of the Spiritual Administration and its strict control of the Muslim community altered the practice of people's Islam and politicized it.

Owing to this politicization, religious leaders were divided over Islam's direction, and trends toward political activism emerged. In 1989 the leadership of the Central Asian Spiritual Administration (headquartered in Tashkent) changed, with Mohammad Sadyk Mohammad Yusuf replacing the conformist Shamsuddin-Qari Babakhanov. These changes took place under the influence of forces that to a considerable extent paralleled Islam's politicization.

By then Muslim society was freely building mosques, establishing religious schools, and spreading religious literature—processes that were not always connected with the leadership of the Spiritual Administration but rather were general results of the liberalization of the Soviet state and the republics' policies toward religion. The consequences of the change in the administration's leadership were expressed not only in the election of new people but also in the domination of politicized forces that sought decentralization of the administration of the entire Central Asian community, separating republican Muslim societies that had achieved independence.

Previously, official and nonofficial Islam existed in parallel. Decentralization of the Spiritual Administration caused a split inside both officially recognized Islam and other, more moderate independent groups having structures similar to that of the administration.

As groups in the Muslim community of Uzbekistan became more active, they set for themselves the goal of creating an Islamic Renaissance Party similar to the one organized in Tajikistan; this party became a leading force in Tajikistan's events of 1991–92, when conflict between the government and the political Islamic opposition led to bloodshed.

At the outset the new leadership of the Spiritual Administration under Sadyk, enjoying the government's revised policy of liberalization toward Islam, displayed a certain loyalty with respect to government measures. Sadyk publicly criticized the activity of young Muslim members who had been trying to create an Islamic Renaissance Party. In speeches before believers he also criticized a group of active members known in the mass media as Wahhabis, only to be contradicted by the turn of events in Tajikistan as the Muslim opposition there gained the support of another party and an analogous group of Wahhabis. In reality, the Spiritual Administration gradually moved against government policy. However, by the end of 1990, the power of the Spiritual Administration had been limited to the territory of Uzbekistan.

As an advocate of Islamic polarization and the strengthening of the position of the Islamic government structure, Sadyk oriented the Spiritual Administration, especially in international affairs, toward Libya, where he received his education. This position, however, did not coincide with the orientation of Uzbekistan's official foreign policy. The conflicting interests evoked, to say the least, mutual hostility.

At the same time, owing to the increase in financial support of religious institutions (mainly through donations from foreign Muslims and organizations), the Spiritual Administration began manipulating large sums of money. Charges of financial corruption soon followed. That some of these funds were being funneled to Islamic fighters in Tajikistan seems probable, given the link between the leaders of religious opposition groups in Tajikistan and the official leadership of the Spiritual Administration in Tashkent.

Investigation into the origin and development of Fergana Muslim groups holding political ideas has shown the name of Mohammad Sadyk Mohammad Yusuf to be among the first active members of those groups in the early 1980s. When he was elected mufti he hurried to disassociate himself from them. But his views did not change much after taking the post, leading to dissension in the Spiritual Administration of the Muslim community. Moreover, small groups of youths were mobilizing in the Fergana Valley, particularly in Namangan and Andijan.[6]

The end of 1990 may be considered the beginning of the second stage of the mobilization of politicized groups of Muslim youth. In Namangan, in December 1991, members of the Tawba and Adolat groups took over the building of the former regional committee of the Communist Party of the Soviet Union and demanded that the future president of the Uzbek Republic listen to their requests, which were presented as appeals of the community. President Islam Karimov met with the members and listened to their requests, which included the constitutional recognition of Islam as the state religion, the priority of *Shari'ah* in the republic, and the introduction of separate education of boys and girls. All the pleas, which boiled down to total Islamization of the state, were reminiscent of appeals by analogous groups of Muslims abroad. Karimov accepted the petitions for further consideration and promised to discuss them in the Supreme Soviet of the republic. Having shown their aggressiveness, the representatives of the religious groups, which included several hundred young members, returned the building to the authorities voluntarily after the meeting.

One of the requests concerned turning over the former House of Political Education to religious groups. This house, built by party authorities in all the major cities of the former USSR, was used for the "ideological bringing-up of people" and the spreading of ideas of militant atheism. Months after the house was handed over, the groups had still not come to any agreement about its division. Gradually the house became the source of opposition among the various groups of believers. Under such conditions, local authorities canceled their decision to hand over the house to the religious community in order to avoid clashes within the community.

After the return of the house, which in the long run was not divided by the groups, members of the Tawba faction, which included some dozens of people alienated from the so-called Wahhabi, resorted to extreme measures. Following one of the Friday prayers in the spring of 1992, some Tawba members, having left the Djami mosque in Namangan, seized several hostages from among the representatives of local authorities and destroyed personal property.

Negotiations for the release of the hostages, conducted in the presence of official representatives of the religious community, were not successful. The authorities brought in special militia to deal with the crisis. The show of force was enough to compel the Tawba to back down and release the hostages. Those members of the Tawba who had participated in the action were arrested and later sentenced to various terms of imprisonment. The leader of the group, Tahir, however, avoided arrest and fled the republic. This irreconcilable group later called itself Tavba and emerged from the subordination of Abdul-Ahad as an extremist organization.

The scenario described is a familiar one, recognizable for the way some members of an association, in this case Muslim brotherhood, become disenchanted with policy and procedure, break off into smaller groups, and adopt extremism to further otherwise common ends. The split, the unification of irreconcilable forces, and the fact that a majority of the members left set the stage for the development of the revival movement are also familiar.

A story worth noting is the origin of a more conservative group that appeared as a result of the split among the Wahhabi in late 1991. The youth, concentrated around Wahhabi mosques that were subordinate at that time to the Spiritual Administration and led by Abdul-Ahad, the imam of the Gumbaz mosque in Namangan, stood up to reject active political fighting and showed their support for the government in its efforts to solve the problems of social, economic, and cultural development in independent Uzbekistan. Only a few members, headed by Tahir, declared their disagreement and opted to participate actively in politics.

As for the Adolat (Muslim people's militia), the organization operating in Namangan and its suburbs, everything ended in a prosaic way. The Adolat, whose activity originally was to maintain order and help the government bodies of the militia, was transformed into a new structure interested in the distribution of wealth for the benefit of its leaders. Having been corrupted within a short period of time and having discredited both itself and the idea of people's squads to maintain order in cities and villages, the organization was banned and its leaders were imprisoned for financial abuse.

Given the conditions of the Tawba activization and its support for some Adolat activists, the newly elected president of the Republic of Uzbekistan decided not to introduce the Namangan demands for discussion in the Uzbek parliament, thereby effectively localizing the uprising in Namangan. Later, in the spring, these groups finished the process of discrediting themselves.

In mid-1992 it became apparent that the religious community, both its leaders and followers, was interfering less and less in the political sphere. An exception was Mohammad Sadyk Mohammad Yusuf, who was losing control over the community.

The Tajik events, in which the Islamic opposition played a primary role, were developing during this period and prompted Uzbekistan to defend its territory from encroachment of similar circumstances and to support the moderate trend of its own Muslim community. In the interest of preserving relative stability from the inroads of political activity by separatists in the Muslim community, the use of force by the government as a response to extremism would have been appropriate. Such an action, however, was not yet warranted.

In October 1992, during an international seminar organized by Khafiz Malik of Villanova University, Graham Fuller, in his lecture dedicated to the American interests in Central Asia, stressed that one of the important interests of the United States in the region was "to help to avoid civil war and interethnic conflicts." As for Islam and its politicization in Central Asia, he noted that the United States should help to prevent anti-Western hysteria and extremism. At the time he expressed his apprehension regarding the fact that official Islam was still weak and his belief that to maintain stability there was an urgent necessity to strengthen Islam and involve all Islamic groups in the political process in a democratic, reasonable way. Fuller added that these interests would be acceptable for other states, including the newly formed countries of Central Asia. More recently, Boris Rumer emphasized the same points in one of his articles.[7]

The course of events has testified in favor of Fuller's assertions. Tajikistan, with its civil war, could provoke a chain reaction in neighboring states. Other republics could direct their domestic and regional policy to ensure stability in the area. Choosing the correct methods for maintaining political stability in Muslim communities, therefore, is of critical importance. The example of Uzbekistan, where the official policy of the authorities corresponds to the scheme elaborated by Fuller, is rather significant.

On 8 December 1992 the Supreme Soviet adopted the constitution of the Republic of Uzbekistan, wherein one can see the secular direction of the political structure of the state. According to Article 31 of the constitution, "Everybody is guaranteed the right to freedom of conscience. Every person has a right to believe in a religion chosen by him or not to believe in any. Religious views cannot be inculcated by force." Article 57 outlaws the creation of an organization based on the ideas of national, racial, and confessional discrimination. It also prohibits the creation and activity of military, nationalistic, and religious political and public organizations that aim to overthrow constitutional order. Article 61 states that "Religious organizations and associations are separated from the state and they are equal before the law. The state does not interfere in the activity of religious organizations." Thereby the constitution establishes that Uzbekistan is a secular republic and at the same time guarantees freedom of conscience. The possibility of using some religious slogans while carrying out the policy of the state, be it foreign or domestic, is excluded constitutionally.[8]

In February 1993, during the All-Muslim Kurultai (Congress) of Uzbekistan, the new wing of the Spiritual Administration prevailed over the group led by Mohammad Sadyk Mohammad Yusuf, who at that time actually had the least ability to control most of the mosques in the republic. These mosques, which had gradually boycotted the decisions of the administration, came out from under their subordination to Sadyk's group and concentrated around the new wing.

The former administration leader, with his excessive political activity and past association with Tajik events, did not fit in with the new frame of mind of both the republic and the community. By the decision of the Kurultai, Mukhtar Abdullaev was chosen to head the Spiritual Administration of Muslims of Uzbekistan. Sadyk was officially discharged from his position and left the administration residence with several members—his relatives, to be exact.

One cannot say that the government structures directly promoted these changes in the Spiritual Administration. Indeed, the changes in Muslim community leadership took place under conditions in which the government kept silent and did not interfere in the process, though nonetheless accepted them as most favorable.

Abdullaev, the present mufti, was elected in a period of perestroika in an extreme situation by the Congress of Muslims, represented by believers from not only Uzbekistan but also other republics of Central Asia, including neighboring Tajikistan. Since he became administration leader, many things have changed. Uzbekistan has become an independent republic and has set new goals in all spheres of life.

The Communist Party and its complicated structure of committees at various levels exited the political scene in Uzbekistan. The newly formed People's Democratic Party of Uzbekistan, in the course of time, began playing quite a different role in comparison, without involving itself in running the state. Although a thorough analysis of the party's new emphasis is beyond the scope of this chapter, a reevaluation of party views and values is known to have taken place.

According to new state policy, a certain de-ideologizing stance is now shown toward communist ideas. And throughout the current transitional period in the development of the republic, the main emphasis has been on national values, which is quite normal for an independent national state.

Religious values, at first chaotically used by both religious structures and some groups of intellectuals under the new conditions of national independence, have been relegated to the background, though they are still of great importance. The political activity of Muslim groups required a certain amount of delimitation, though along democratic lines, that has been accomplished in part through community conciliation and government support of local authorities, who could not interfere in the community's affairs but kept some control over them nevertheless, especially through the mass media and *mahalla* (an Asian form of self-governing where there are compact groups of the native population). The *mahalla* have traditionally had much influence on public life, and their role could have a significant impact on Uzbekistan's future.

Hereditary Sheikh Mukhtar Abdullaev, who was elected mufti of the Spiritual Administration of Muslims of Uzbekistan, has an interesting service record. He was a teacher in the Muslim school Mir-Arab in Bukhara and for a long time taught in the High Ecclesiastic Institute of Tashkent. In recent years he was imam in the mosque and keeper of the Sheikh Bakhautdin Nakshbandy Mausoleum in Bukhara. Very active, with moderate views, especially in the sphere of politics but not quite indifferent toward it, Sheikh Mukhtar has a certain authority with both orthodox groups and the Wahhabis. One might expect that longtime service in the Spiritual Administration during the Soviet period would have killed all initiative in Abdullaev. But his interview with American researchers when he was imam of the Nakshbandy mosque gave them reason to think highly of him as a person having great ability to mobilize his followers in solving problems. In fact, he has taught fifteen hundred followers across the former Soviet Union, many of whom today occupy positions in various religious bodies and believe they would support him if necessary.

The increase in power of Mukhtar Abdullaev and his followers strengthened the political orientation of the Spiritual Administration of Muslims of Uzbekistan and reduced to a minimum the threat of extremism on the part of official Islam in that country.

Furthermore, the victory of the moderates in official Islam presented an opportunity for unifying the various groups alienated by the Spiritual Administration and getting them to participate in the pursuit of common goals. Significantly, followers of the Sufi trend in Islam, formerly active in Central Asian state affairs, may once again get involved in political and social activities.

A matter of interest for researchers of Islam is whether there are any groups of Muslims not covered by the Spiritual Administration that were typically ignored during the Soviet period of these republics' development. The display of the people's organized Islam, basically directed toward the celebration of religious rites, has always taken place without dependence on the existence of officially recognized religious organizations. It would be naive, therefore, to undervalue its importance in healing rifts and strengthening religious ties. The change of status of the Spiritual Administration, the increasing number of mosques, the renewed emphasis on the role of the *mahalla* in Uzbekistan—all are promoting the liquidation of borders between officially organized Islam and the people's Islam.

Uzbek society, in general, may have come to favor official Islam, but not all Muslim groups are in agreement with the new position. Measures of the Uzbek government to localize the activity of groups from the Fergana Valley, as has been seen, were successful in curtailing political extremism. But to ensure continued social and economic stabilization would require the mobilization of large forces and resources by both the government and the Muslim community, which for the moment are not readily available. To say that the irreconcilable Muslim groups are removing themselves from the political scene of the country entirely, even when faced with government restrictions on their activity, is just not true. Some have gone underground.

Even where Muslims constitute the religious majority, some countries, using different measures to suppress militant political activity by religious organizations, have succeeded in staving off social agitation. With the passage of time, however, the authorities may once again have to face an outburst of their activity. The process, in fact, is so recurrent and naturally expected, that small militant political structures bent on destabilizing society will surely arise to take on new forms. The new governments of Central Asia would do well to heed the experience of these countries when making foreign and domestic policy.

In any event, there is an ongoing awareness of nationalism in the transitional development of independent Uzbekistan. Emphasized on all levels is the still new, recently recognized idea that "Uzbekistan has a great future based on national values." "Uzbekistan has great roots" is another slogan that also fills the vacuum formed after the rejection of alien, amorphous communist ideas, and it produces a certain effect in promoting the rise of the Uzbek national identity. This slogan is linked with the Islamic religion. The history of the liberated countries of the Muslim world shows them renewing, reorganizing, and proclaiming their determination in a more subtle way. Their nationalism, directed at gaining real independence, was a combination of national and religious ideas.

It is only natural that Uzbekistan's attempts to strengthen itself, to develop its first independent steps, especially in spheres where nothing had been experienced before, would be beyond the competence of a republic long dependent on another government, namely the former Soviet Union. The creation of an army, the defense of borders, the reaction to possible domestic struggles of subgroups working toward achieving more independence in political, economic, and financial terms—these require not only the mobilization of all forces and resources of the state but also the support of a certain stability, civil peace, and the suppression of militant expression of group and personal ambitions. Concerning the last point, the Muslim community must set the task in this term and try to direct its activity in that course. And the task is well within the present stage of strengthening the position of the Spiritual Administration and achieving its priority in the Muslim community.

The new constitution of Uzbekistan gives no hint of the possible rejection of the secular orientation of Uzbekistan, in spite of prognoses, especially by Russian experts, that key government posts will be filled on the basis of religion. In October 1992 such a suggestion was made by Iurii Gankovskii at the Villanova University conference on Central Asian issues.

Nevertheless, Islam holds an important place in the program of the government. It especially touches the social-spiritual sphere, where it carries out the task of the revival of high moral principles and qualities engrafted by Islam, which is, according to the words of President Karimov, the "faith of our fathers, conscience, the essence of being and the way of life of Muslims."

The limits of activity of the religious community within the social-spiritual sphere are characteristically conditional. The potential of the religious community is much greater and extends, of course, into political and economic spheres.

Notwithstanding the complete separation of religion from the state in the constitution, one must not forget that the state (that is, the government) is responsible for its citizens and for their organizing in communities, concentrating its efforts on the support of stability and directing political activity to a democratic course.

The machinery of control formed in the days of militant atheism in the former USSR could not be kept in the old form under the new system. The system of inspectors in religious affairs on all levels would not correspond to new circumstances requiring constant dialogue rather than giving of instructions—a testament to the fact that the machinery of control was nothing but part of the command-administrative structures of the former totalitarian Soviet Union. Moreover, ruling the Muslim community from Moscow would have negative consequences for the community itself and would keep the structure of the Spiritual Administration from interacting with believers.

The new system of advisors being formed in the independent Republic of Uzbekistan cannot be called the final structure as yet. It should be considered transitional, and it at least meets the requirements of the present time. It brings much flexibility in itself. The main part of the system's multistep structure are advisors on religious problems in the Muslim community who are working with the president with *khokims* (mayors) of regions, cities, and districts. In the last case, key advisors are often appointed from among influential people in the Muslim community and from among Orientalists. For example, one advisor to the president, Abdulgani Abdullaev, is a well-known religious scholar who is influential in the community. In his participation in policy making, he expresses the interests of both sides, religious and governmental. Also, he is a connecting link in the healthy dialogue that could be arranged between the president and the leadership of the Spiritual Administration, though one cannot exclude direct communication.

The absence of communication between the state and the Muslim community in the formation of both domestic and foreign policy could create a new disparity, or renovate the old disparity, that would explain the contradictions arising between the structure of power and the Muslim community. Of course, this structure does not rest with only one person, though taking into account the specific conditions of Uzbek society's development, the role of one person does sometimes become of decisive importance.

The principle of policy formation with the help of advisors from the ranks of religious people and professional Orientalists is widely implemented on all levels of power. As deputies of the Supreme Soviet and the soviets of other levels, they are correspondingly involved as leaders of the Spiritual Administration in law-making activity. Also, as deputies of the Supreme Soviet of the republic, persons from the clergy can submit bills for consideration by the parliament, take part in discussion of them, and defend them. In practice, however, there are few examples of the clergy's active participation in the Uzbek parliament, because of the ongoing internal transformation of the highest legislative body into a new, independent variant. There is a legal base for such actions in the future, though, and such examples are likely to come.

The whole picture of the state of Islamic affairs in Uzbekistan would not be complete without some consideration of the trends in that country's foreign policy.

The preservation of the economic, financial, and information ties in the former USSR, which function in reality, has its impact on the formation of the foreign policy of all these countries. Political, economic, and financial ties, though much changed, are still strong.

The orientation in the sphere of economic ties is still being formed. The five republics of Central Asia carry out constant consultations and coordination of their actions in working out joint steps on the regional or former Soviet level. In spite of the fact that little time has passed since their declaration of independence and cooperation in their new capacity, they stand together in some cases and on some points. This kind of relationship can be a very good basis for achieving some form of federation in the future.

These republics are developing relations with other countries as well. The experience that Uzbekistan has gained in carrying on its own independent foreign policy during the last couple of years is significant. Having set up the goal of achieving general recognition, the republic desired the establishment and support of close relations with both neighboring countries and countries of the far abroad.

From the outset a close relationship was established with Turkey, the country closest to the Central Asian republics in spirit. Comprehensive cooperation is being developed in the interests of both countries and their people. Cooperative relations with Iran, China, India, Pakistan, Israel, Malaysia, and the Arab countries are also being cultivated.

Relations with industrialized countries such as Germany, the Netherlands, and South Korea were rapidly developed as well. Initially, factors of ethnic or religious closeness were expected to influence foreign policy. Such has not been the case, however, as those factors are not primary to this process.[9]

If relations with foreign countries continue as planned and the country reorients its economy toward the world market, Uzbekistan can balance its position in the Commonwealth of Independent States, although advisedly, under some new arrangement. The main essence of Uzbekistan's foreign policy would be secular, as it applies to domestic policy.

In the evolution of independent Uzbekistan, the policy toward Islam and the Muslim community should be considered as a process in development. The state, implementing various methods, cut off the militant political activity of small groups of believers and followed a hard line in carrying out its course of support of political stability in the country by all means. As a result of the evolution of the new government posture, the foundation of the Spiritual Administration is being reinforced, and conditions are being created for the display of political expression by Muslims in a democratic way. A situation has been formed in the Muslim community that permits it to support stability and exclude internal opposition for ideological and political business. At the present stage it is possible to avoid ethnic and confessional tensions.

Uzbekistan began using the religious factor very flexibly, most notably by carrying out the jubilee of Att-Termrzi, sheikh of B. Nakshbandy, and preparing the jubilee of imam Bukhari. Such actions work in favor of support of the Uzbek leadership by a majority of Muslims and other communities.

American researchers Robert Freedman, Barnet Rubin, and Bruce Lawrence, who visited Uzbekistan between May and September of 1993 and acquainted themselves with the state of Islamic affairs, noted how stabilized the Muslim community appeared, highlighting as well the difficulties in maintaining such a situation during the transitional period. Uzbekistan's rapid transition to a market economy will probably be accompanied by increased social differentiation, with the emergence of youth groups dissatisfied with their lives. Some of them are likely to resort to religious forms of political expression and will at times openly display militancy. Conflicts may break out locally and, if not contained, escalate into a national crisis. The situation will require flexible local power structures that are able to react quickly to sudden changes in the stability of the republic that has been achieved up to this point.

Notes

1. Rajan Menon and Henri T. Barkey, "The Transformation of Central Asia: Implications for Regional and International Security," *Survival,* vol. 34, no. 4 (winter 1992–93), pp. 68–89.
2. Gabriele Liebig, "Tajikistan Civil War Shows Folly of Geopolitics," *EIR,* vol. 20, no. 39 (8 October 1993), p. 52.
3. Konstantin George, "Developing Central Asia Is Key to Implement 'Productive Triangle,' " *EIR,* vol. 20, no. 39 (8 October 1993), pp. 57–58.
4. "Uzbekistan: The Quest for Economic Independence," *Central Asia Monitor,* 1993, no. 2, pp. 12–15.
5. Edward A. Allworth, "The Precarious Existence of Small Nationalities in Russia and Georgia," *Central Asian Survey,* vol. 12, no. 1 (1993), p. 11.
6. Abdujabar Abduvakhitov, "Islamic Revivalism in Uzbekistan," in *Russia's Muslim Frontiers: New Directions in Cross-Cultural Analysis,* ed. Dale F. Eickelman, (Bloomington: Indiana University Press, 1993).
7. Boris Z. Rumer, "The Gathering Storm in Central Asia," *Orbis,* vol. 37, no. 1 (winter 1993), pp. 89–105.
8. Constitution of the Republic of Uzbekistan (Tashkent, Uzbekistan, 1993), pp. 11–18.
9. Robert O. Freedman, "Israel and Central Asia: A Preliminary Analysis," *Central Asia Monitor,* 1992, no. 2, pp. 16–20.

Appendix: Project Participants

List of Workshop Attendees, November 11, 1993
Religion and Politics in Russia

Abdujabar Abduvakthitov, Meros Academy, Tashkent
Irina Akimushkina, Russian People's Friendship University
Vasilii Aksionov, George Mason University
Kathleen Avvakumovits, The John Hopkins University, SAIS
Serhii Bilokin, Institute of History, Kiev
Britta Bjornlund, The John Hopkins University, SAIS
Bohdan Bociurkiw, Carleton University
Anita Chapman, Washington Baha'i Community
Phil Costopoulos, Journal for Democracy
Kenneth Cummings, University of Maryland
Catherine Dale, George Washington University
Reverend Stan De Boe, St. John De Matha Monastery
Robert Destro, Catholic University
Clifford Foust, University of Maryland
Robert Freedman, Baltimore Hebrew University
John Glad, University of Maryland
Robert Goeckel, SUNY Geneseo
Patrick Gray, Institute of Religion and Democracy
Fr. Dmitrii Grigorieff, Orthodox Church in America
Lubomyr Hajda, Harvard Ukrainian Research Center
Dadahan Hasanov, Islamic Democratic Party for Turkestan
Philip Johnston, The John Hopkins University, SAIS
Abram Kagan, University of Maryland
Edy Kaufman, University of Maryland
Erjan Kurbanov, Moscow State University
Rafik Kurbanov, Institute of Philosophy, Moscow
Michael LaCivita, Catholic Near East Magazine
Lee LaMora, Jamestown Foundation
Kim Lawton, News Network International
Laura Libanati, American Enterprise Foundation
Fr. Taras Lonchyna, Ukrainian Catholic Church
Jane Madden, The World Bank
Vasyl Markus, Loyola University and Encyclopedia of Ukraine
Walter Melnik, University of Maryland
Zoya Mendjuk, Congress of Russian-Americans

George Mirsky, The American University
Anatolii Naimin, Kennan Institute
Galina Naimin, St. John the Baptist, Russian Orthodox Church
Daniel Olsen, St. John the Baptist, Russian Orthodox Church
Marta Peryma, U.S. Information Agency
Maria Potapov, St. John the Baptist, Russian Orthodox Church
Mark Potapov, St. John the Baptist, Russian Orthodox Church
Jerry Powers, U.S. Catholic Conference
Ilya Prizel, The John Hopkins University, SAIS
George Quester, University of Maryland
Vladimir Rakhmanin, Embassy of Russia
Peter Reddaway, George Washington University
Fr. Ron Roberson, St. Paul's College
Alexandra Service, St. John the Baptist, Russian Orthodox Church
Gary Shenk, The John Hopkins University, SAIS
Natalia Shevchenko, St. John the Baptist, Russian Orthodox Church
Nikolai Sirotkin, Voice of America
Yurii Suhir, The World Bank
Marilyn Swezey, Holy Archangels Broadcasting Center
Steve Szabo, The John Hopkins University, SAIS
Andrew Torre, The John Hopkins University, SAIS
Michael Turner, University of Maryland
Anthony Ugolnik, Franklin & Marshall College
Joan Barth Urban, Catholic University
Jim Voorhees, Congressional Research Service
Fr. Alexander Webster, Romanian Episcopate, OCA
Alexander Yakunin
Thomas Zamostny, Department of State
Lena Zezulin, Slevin and Hart
Marc Zlotnik, National Intelligence Council

November 12, 1993
Religion and Politics in Ukraine and the Baltics

Abdujabar Abduvakthitov, Meros Academy, Tashkent
Mykola Basyluk
Hilary Brandt, George Washington University
Reverend Canon Michael Bourdeaux, Keston Research, Oxford
Wayne Bowman, U.S. Information Agency
Fr. Vsevolod Chaplin, Moscow Patriarchate
Martha Chomiak, National Endowment for the Humanities
John Danylyk, Department of State
Orest Diychak, Helsinki Commission
John Dunlop, Hoover Institute
John Finerty, Helsinki Commission

Mykola Fransuzhenko, Voice of America
Valerie Gartseff, Voice of America
David Goldfrank, Georgetown University
Patrick Gray, Institute for Religion and Democracy
Alec Guroff, Center for Strategic and International Studies
Yurij Holowinsky
Israel Kleiner, Voice of America
Fr. Ted Kravchuk, Ukrainian Catholic National Shrine
Valeri Kuchinsky, Embassy of Ukraine
Erjan Kurbanov, Moscow State University
Rafik Kurbanov, Institute of Philosophy, Moscow
Kim Lawton, News Network International
Valentina Limonchenko, U.S. Information Agency
Fr. Taras Lonchyna, Ukrainian Catholic Church
Jane Madden, The World Bank
George Majeska, University of Maryland
Melissa Meeker, Center for Strategic and International Studies
Walter Melnik, University of Maryland
Yuri Mylko, Department of State
Marta Peryma, U.S. Information Agency
Fr. Hryhory Podaurec, St. Andrew's Orthodox Church
Vasilii Pospelov, Embassy of Russia
Ilya Prizel, The John Hopkins University, SAIS
George Quester, University of Maryland
Fr. Ron Roberson, St. Paul's College
Eric Ruben
George Sajewych, Window on America
Mark Saroyan, Harvard University
Mikhail Sivertsev, Institute of USA and Canada Studies, Moscow
Sonya Sluzar, Department of State
Christopher Smith, Pew Charitable Trusts
Robert Snyder, Christian Science Organization
Elena Suhir, The World Bank
Jim Voorhees, Congressional Research Service
Fr. Alexander Webster, Romanian Episcopate, OCA
Fr. Gleb Yakunin, Russian Parliament
Volodymyr Zabaihailo, Embassy of Ukraine
Volodymyr Zviglyanich, George Washington University

November 13, 1993

Religion and Politics in Central Asia and the Caucasus

Ibrahim Arafat, University of Maryland
Serhii Bilokin, Institute of History, Kiev
Reverend Canon Michael Bourdeaux, Keston Research, Oxford

Laurie MacDonald Brumberg, American Bar Association
Patricia Carley, U.S. Institute of Peace
Cliff Chanin, The Rockefeller Foundation
Fr. Vsevolod Chaplin, Moscow Patriarchate
Richard Dobson, U.S. Information Agency
Massoud Eghbarieh, University of Maryland
Ulughbek Eshankhojayov, Embassy of Uzbekistan
Steven Grant, U.S. Information Agency
Patrick Gray, Institute for Religion and Democracy
Richard Grimes, Central Intelligence Agency
Anne Herr, Department of State
Abram Kagan, University of Maryland
Frederick Kagan
Mark Katz, George Mason University
Davlat Khudonazarev, Kennan Institute
Judith Kipper, The Brookings Institute
Erjan Kurbanov, Moscow State University
Kim Lawton, News Network International
Eve Lebo, Central Intelligence Agency
Jack Lebo
George Majeska, University of Maryland
Serif Mardin, The American University
Jim Martin, Department of State
Dan Matuszewski, IREX
Melissa Meeker, Center for Strategic and International Studies
Jayhun Molla-zade, Embassy of Azerbaijan
Seyyed Hossein Nasr, George Washington University
Michael Oakes, Helsinki Commission
Christine Quickenden, University of Maryland
Vladimir Rakhmanin, Embassy of Russia
Sayed Said, International Institute of Islamic Thought
Janice Sebring, Central Intelligence agency
Nasir Shansab, Democracy International
Yurii Sigov, University of Maryland
Mikhail Sivertsev, Institute of USA and Canada Studies, Moscow
Christopher Smith, Pew Charitable Trusts
Robert Snyder, Christian Science Organization
Evgen Sverstiuk, *Nasha Vera*, Kiev
Joan Barth Urban, Catholic University
Ruth Urell, Amnesty International

Index

Family, 249, 278
Fergana Valley (Tajikistan), 249, 297
The Fifth Wheel (TV program), 52
Filaret (Denysenko), Metropolitan
    (Kiev), 21, 22–25, 30, 51, 152, 166
  internal opposition to, 149
  and KGB, 141
  and Patriarch Mstyslav, 192–95
  rebellion by, 141–50
Filaret, Metropoltan (Minsk), 28, 30
Filatov, S.B., 34
Finland, 39*n.62*
Finnish Lutheran Church, 212, 224*n.55*
Florovskii, Georgii, 17
Franco, Archbishop Antonio, 168
"Freedom of Religion in a Modern
    World," 120–22
Free Russian Orthodox Church, 46,
    57–58
Fukuyama, Francis, 274
Fuller, Graham, 299
Fundamentalism, 171
  American Protestant, 55, 61,
    70–71*n.40*
  Islamic, 11, 234–36, 247, 258, 266
Furman, D.E., 34

Gailitis, Karlis, 208, 212
Galicia (Ukraine), 132
Gamsakhurdia, Zviad, 236–37, 238
Gankovskii, Iurii, 302
Gazzavat, 233, 241
Geopolitical continuity parties, 78–79
Georgia, 28, 236–41
  Abkhazian conflict, 238–39
  ethnic policies, 237
Georgian Orthodox Church, 236
German Lutheran Church, 169
Godmanis, Ivars, 211
Gorbachev, Mikhail Sergeevich, 6,
    7–9, 22, 54, 114, 138, 207, 234,
    235
  discrediting of, 11
  new religion law of, 115–17
  reforms of, 136–37
Gorbunovs, Anatolijs, 27
GPU, 183, 185
Grachev, Pavel, 238, 263

Greek Catholic Church. *See* Ukrainian
    Greek Catholic Church

Hajj, 88, 89
Hallaste, Illar, 215
Hasanov, Dadakhan, 281
Hasidism, 172
Hekmatyar, Gulbeddin, 265
Helsinki Accords, 7, 16
Himmatzoda, Muhammad, 257–58
House of Political Education, 297
Hujum, 278
Human rights, 6, 7
Hungarian Reformed Church, 169, 175
Hunter, Shireen, 232, 235
Huntington, Samuel, 274
Huseynov, Heydar, 233

Iakiv, Bishop, 24, 146
Iarema, Volodymyr, 140, 166–67, 189,
    197
Il'ai II, Catholicos, 28, 239
Ilarion, Bishop, 57
Ilarion (Ohiienko), Metropolitan, 196
Independent Baptist Church, 171
Industrial parties, 83–84
Ingush. *See* Ossetian-Ingush conflict
Innokenti (Pavlov), Father, 121
Intelligentsia, 88
International Academy for Freedom of
    Religion and Belief, 120–21
Ioann (Bodnarchuk), Bishop, 22, 140,
    148
Ioann (Snychev), Metropolitan, 32–36,
    58–59, 62, 72*n.47*
Iran, 232, 258, 260, 264–65, 288
Iran-Iraq War, 232
Iraq, 232
Iskandarov, Akbarsho, 265
Islam, 8, 11
  Caucasus history of, 229–30
  and Communist Party members, 254
  in Dagestan, 87–90
  and education, 87–88, 90
  fundamentalism, 11, 234–35, 247,
    258, 266, 286
  ignorance of, 254–55, 290–91*n.21*
  in North Caucasus, 232–33

Ukrainian Orthodox Church—Kiev
  Patriarchate, 25, 145–46, 147–50,
  150, 174, 179, 192
 and government, 182–99
Ukrainian Orthodox Church—Moscow
  Patriarchate, 145–46, 179
Unemployment, 80
Ungureanu, Ion, 26
Uniate Church. *See* Ukrainian Greek
  Catholic Church
Union for the Defense of the
  Motherland (UDM), 195
Union of Brest, 132, 133, 135
Union of Christian Rebirth (UCR), 98
Union of Christian Regeneration, 62
Union of Christians of Evangelical
  Faith (Pentecostalists of Ukraine),
  171
Union of Church Brotherhoods, 44
Union of Free Churches of Christians
  of Evangelical Faith, 171
Union of Orthodox Brotherhoods, 34,
  35, 36, 52, 58, 60, 61–62, 142
United Democratic Opposition, 258–59
United States, 33, 72*n.47*, 260, 265–66,
  299
Usmon, Davlat, 253, 258, 259–60, 266
Uzbekistan, 260–61, 275, 285–86,
  291*n.22*
  Communist Party in, 300
  constitution of, 299
  foreign policy, 304
  Islamic development in, 293–305
  leadership crisis in, 282–84
  nationalism in, 302
  religious advisors in, 303–04

Vaivods, Julian, 205
Valentin, Bishop, 58

Vanags, Janis, 214, 223*nn.52, 53*
Vardys, Stanley, 207
Varennikov, Valentin, 20
Varnava, Bishop, 58
Vasil'iev Pamyat, 57–58
Vasyl' (Lypkivs'kyi), Metropolitan, 186
Vazgen I, Catholicos, 231, 232
Velychko, Mykola, 169
Vilnius (Lithuania), 11
Vitalii, Metropolitan, 57–58
Vladimir, Metropolitan, 26
Volodymyr (Romaniuk), Metropolitan,
  25, 148–49, 161*n.121*, 167, 196
Volodymyr (Sabodan), Metropolitan,
  24–25, 145, 146, 147, 149, 166,
  195, 198
Vorob'ev, Vladimir, 70*n.30*
Voskobiinyk, M., 191

Wahhabism, 252–53, 296, 298
Warrant for Genocide (Cohn), 32
White Brotherhood, 60, 61, 152, 173
Women, 213
World Council of Churches, 46, 48, 51,
  96

Yakunin, Gleb, 29, 31, 50, 51, 97, 100,
  116, 122
Yeltsin, Boris, 16, 21, 32, 33, 35, 42,
  45, 48, 280
  dissolution of parliament, 123
  and Georgia, 239
  and Ossetia-Ingush conflict, 242, 243
Youth, 34–35

Zhirinovsky, Vladimir, 36
Zinchenko, Arsen, 25, 147, 191–92
Zingeris, Emmanuelis, 212
Zlobin, Aleksei, 100